English B
for the IB Diploma

Brad Philpot

Cambridge University Press's mission is to advance learning, knowledge and research worldwide.

Our IB Diploma resources aim to:

- encourage learners to explore concepts, ideas and topics that have local and global significance
- help students develop a positive attitude to learning in preparation for higher education
- assist students in approaching complex questions, applying critical-thinking skills and forming reasoned answers.

CAMBRIDGE
UNIVERSITY PRESS

CAMBRIDGE
UNIVERSITY PRESS

University Printing House, Cambridge CB2 8BS, United Kingdom

One Liberty Plaza, 20th Floor, New York, NY 10006, USA

477 Williamstown Road, Port Melbourne, VIC 3207, Australia

314-321, 3rd Floor, Plot 3, Splendor Forum, Jasola District Centre, New Delhi – 10025, India

79 Anson Road, #06–04/06, Singapore 079906

Cambridge University Press is part of the University of Cambridge.

It furthers the University's mission by disseminating knowledge in the pursuit of education, learning and research at the highest international levels of excellence.

www.cambridge.org
Information on this title: www.cambridge.org/9781108434812

© Cambridge University Press 2018

First published 2018

20 19 18 17 16 15 14 13 12 11 10 9 8 7 6 5 4 3 2 1

Printed in the United Kingdom by Latimer Trend

A catalogue record for this publication is available from the British Library

ISBN 978-1-108-43481-2 Paperback

Contents

How to use this book

This coursebook is structured around the 5 new prescribed themes of the Language B guide:

- Identities
- Experiences
- Human ingenuity
- Social organisation
- Sharing the planet

Each theme is explored across 5 dedicated chapters, providing in-depth coverage of the latest Language B guide. Chapter 6 is devoted to exploring different text types, whilst chapters 7, 8 and 9 cover each of the 3 modes of assessment and provide both standard and higher level exam-style practice.

The coursebook features

This coursebook contains several special features, which are designed to enhance the learning experience of your students:

Guiding questions	Learning objectives
• Guiding questions at the start of each unit introduce important world issues and ensure that your learning reflects the mission of the IB Diploma – 'to create a better world through education.'	• Learning objectives are clearly stated at the beginning of each unit to help you engage with the content and skills covered and actively take responsibility for your own learning.

Activities

A wide range of activities provide the opportunity for you to develop skills across core areas such as writing, discussion, literature, form and meaning and exploring texts. These have been carefully selected to map an engaging and effective route through content from the 'Getting Started' activities at the beginning of units right through to wrap up activities which promote reflection and consolidation of your learning.

LEARNER PROFILE

This feature has been included to remind you of some of the qualities you should aspire to demonstrate as a student of the IB programme.

TOK

The Theory of Knowledge (TOK) component at the core of the Diploma Programme asks you: 'How do you know what you know?' These feature boxes help you explore the knowledge questions behind the content of the coursebook.

CAS

The Creativity, Activity and Service (CAS) component of the Diploma Programme encourages you to have a range of experiences from which you can learn. These feature boxes offer examples of CAS, while making connections to the content of the coursebook.

ATL

Approaches to Learning (ATL) are a set of skills that you should aim to develop throughout the Diploma Programme. These include communication skills, research skills, self-management skills, social skills and thinking skills. This feature will help you to develop these while engaging in coursebook activities.

Extended Essay

Extended Essay is a core requirement for the Diploma Programme. If you should decide to write your EE on English B, you will find these feature boxes useful. They offer guidance on research and tips on formulating research questions.

Watch and listen

Audio activities are included throughout the coursebook in all units to provide essential listening comprehension practice in line with the IB Language B guide. Clearly signposted icons show where an audio track is required for an activity. The transcripts for these audio clips can be found in the Teacher's book. Sometimes you will be directed to a suggested video which may help to further your understanding of a particular topic.

Word bank

At the beginning of each unit you will find a word bank containing key words and vocabulary related to that topic. Definitions for all word bank terminology can be found in the glossary at the back of the book. Key words in the word bank are shown in bold type when they first appear in the text.

EXTRA

Extra features encourage you to explore more about a particular concept or topic. These may take the form of additional activities you could partake in, further research or a related article or video that you could watch to take your learning further.

Tips have been included intermittently throughout the coursebook which will provide additional support and guidance on your learning and in preparation for exams.

READING STRATEGY

This feature encourages you to think about particular text extracts, and the different strategies that could be employed to understand and interpret them.

CONCEPTS

The IB encourages you to explore certain key concepts in the process of learning: audience, context, purpose, meaning and variation. These concepts and their relevance to a particular topic is explored in regular features.

TEXT AND CONTEXT

These boxes offer additional information about a given text to help you understand more about the context in which it was written.

Introduction

Who is this coursebook for?

This coursebook is for students taking the English B course for the International Baccalaureate (IB) Diploma Programme. As English B meets the Language Acquisition (Group 2) requirement for the IB Diploma, students are non-native speakers of the English language. The aim of the course is to develop communication skills, to help you become more proficient in the English language.

The texts in this coursebook are relevant for 16–19-year-olds who study in international contexts or have a broad outlook on the world. The activities and assignments encourage you to engage with language, while developing your own opinions about a wide range of topics.

English B can be taken at both standard and higher levels. Before registering for one or the other, it is important to know the expectations of both teachers and examiners for each level.

Standard level

At standard level you will be able to:

- understand the main points of a variety of texts in English
- write different kinds of texts, although your writing might not be perfect and your sentence structures might be simple
- understand and handle situations where spoken English is used and required, although you may require preparation and help before interacting with others.

Higher level

At higher level you will be able to:

- understand the main ideas of more complex texts about topics that might be more abstract in nature,
- write a variety of texts, although your writing might contain some errors
- understand complex conversations and interact with native speakers with some degree of fluency and spontaneity
- produce clear and persuasive arguments.

How does this coursebook support your study of IB English B?

This diagram represents the different elements of the English B syllabus:

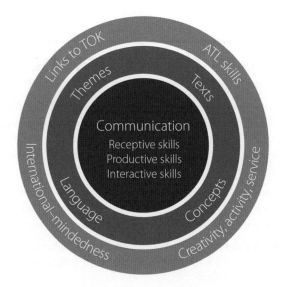

At the heart of the course is communication. This coursebook invites you to develop your communication skills through a range of activities. Each unit in the first five chapters uses the following structure to develop these skills:

*   The 'Getting started' section activates any knowledge you already have of a particular topic before it's explored in class.
*   The 'Watch and listen' section presents activities through video and audio recordings to help you develop your *receptive* skills.
*   Furthermore, productive and interactive skills are developed through text-handling activities in the 'Exploring texts' section of each unit.
*   Various phrases and sentences have been extracted from the texts presented in each unit to create a section on 'Form and meaning', which corresponds to the *language* aspect of the course.
*   Your *productive* skills are needed for the 'Writing, and, Discussion' sections in each unit.
*   Finally, *interactive* skills are required for the 'Discussion' section, which encourages you to engage with your teacher and classmates.

Themes and topics

The Language B syllabus outlines five required 'themes', which are addressed in the first five chapters of this coursebook. The themes are:

*   Identities
*   Experiences
*   Human ingenuity
*   Social organisation
*   Sharing the planet

Within each theme you are invited to explore various 'topics'. Each chapter contains three units, each of which explores a different topic. For example, the final theme, 'Sharing the planet', includes a unit on the topic of climate change. The contents list gives you an overview of the topics and themes that are explored in this book.

Texts

You will develop your language skills through the study of various topics. You will explore a wide range of 'text types', from brochures to speeches. Part of this course is about learning which forms of language are appropriate in certain contexts. How are news reports different from official reports? How are speeches different from blogs? These kinds of questions are explored in Chapter 6, where a unique text type is introduced and explored in depth in each unit, with examples and activities. The IB has categorised the following texts into 'personal', 'professional', and 'mass media' texts.

Personal texts	Professional texts	Mass media texts
blog	blog	advertisement
diary	email	article
personal letter	essay	blog
	formal letter	brochure
	proposal	editorial
	questionnaire	film
	report	instructions
	survey	interview
		leaflet
		literature
		news report
		pamphlet
		podcast
		poster
		proposal
		public commentary
		radio programme
		review
		speech
		travel guide
		web page

Concepts

This coursebook encourages you to explore the following five key concepts, which are fundamental to the English B course. The relevance of these concepts to the coursebook content is highlighted in regular features.

- **Audience**: To whom are you speaking? Use appropriate language for this target group.
- **Context**: For which setting or situation are you writing or speaking? This too will influence your use of language.
- **Purpose**: What is the goal of your communication? Use language that helps you achieve your aims.
- **Meaning**: What is the message that you are communicating? Select words and phrases that deliver this message effectively.
- **Variation**: How is your use of language different from other people's use of language? Differences in language use reflect differences in time, place and culture.

TOK, CAS and international mindedness

The outer ring of the syllabus diagram includes four further elements of the diploma programme:

- **International mindedness:** Most of the activities are designed around materials that encourage international mindedness. Unit 1.1 explores this notion in depth.
- **Theory of Knowledge (TOK):** This required course for the diploma programme asks you: 'How do you know what you know?' Language, also referred to in TOK as a 'way of knowing', is an important tool for acquiring knowledge. This coursebook makes connections between the course content and TOK through boxes in the margins, which often include questions and activities for classroom discussion,
- **Creativity, Activity, Service (CAS):** There are several connections between CAS and the English B course. Both encourage you to interact with others in an international setting. Both focus on experience and reflections as ways of learning. Boxes in the margins of this coursebook help you make these connections.

Approaches to Learning (ATL)

The IB encourages you to develop the following approaches to learning throughout your diploma programme. The English B course provides you with many opportunities to explore and develop these in class through features such as tips, activities and questions. The skills you will need to develop are:

- **Communication skills:** Listening, reading, writing, speaking and interacting skills are at the heart of this course.
- **Thinking skills:** This course encourages you to develop thinking skills, by connections to TOK and asking deeper questions.
- **Social skills:** The activities in this coursebook invite you to interact with classmates, by engaging in conversation and playing games.
- **Research skills:** This coursebook includes boxes in the margins labelled 'extra', in which you are invited to research the ideas of the texts and activities in more depth. Furthermore, the marginal boxes on the extended essay give you guidance on how to research typical English B topics.
- **Self-management skills:** What kinds of study habits do you need to develop in order to acquire English effectively? This coursebook encourages you to reflect on your own learning.

HL extensions and literature

Each unit offers activities and texts for higher level students, which offer more depth and breadth to each topic. Furthermore, you will find a passage of literature at the end of each unit. These texts and activities help you develop skills for studying the *two* literary works that your teacher will assign you over the course of two years. The term 'literary works' means works of prose fiction, prose non-fiction, poetry and drama, that are appropriate to your reading level. At higher level, your understanding of one of the literary works will be assessed through an individual oral assessment. Standard level students are not required to read literary works.

How is the course assessed?

There are three assessment components at both higher and standard level. Here is an overview, that will help you understand the differences between the standard and higher levels. As you will see in further explanations of each component, the IB differentiates between standard level (SL) and higher level (HL) in the following ways:

- the amount of time allowed for taking exams
- level of difficulty of tasks
- level of difficulty of stimulus texts and recordings
- number of words for written production
- descriptors of ability levels in the assessment criteria.

Chapters 7–9 offer activities, specimen exam papers and examples of student's work, that will help to give you a more in-depth understanding of the assessment for this course.

The following table summarises the assessment for the course.

	SL	HL	Percent of final grade
Paper 1 (Externally assessed by examiner)	• 1 hour 15 minutes • one writing task from a choice of three • each task based on a course theme • select a text type • 250–400 words • 30 marks	• 1 hour 30 minutes • one writing task from a choice of three • each task based on a course theme • select a text type • 450–600 words • 30 marks	25%
Paper 2 (Externally assessed by examiner)	• 45 minutes listening for 25 marks • 3 audio passages • 1 hour reading for 40 marks • three reading texts • based on themes	• 1 hour listening for 25 marks • 3 audio passages • 1 hour reading for 40 marks • three reading texts • based on themes	50%
Individual oral (Internally assessed by teacher)	• presentation of a photograph • conversation with teacher about an additional theme	• presentation of a literary passage • conversation with teacher about a theme	25%

Paper 1: Productive skills – writing

Paper 1 tests your ability to write for a particular audience, for a specific purpose, using the conventions of a specific text type. At both higher and standard level, you will see three prompts, each of which corresponds to a different theme from the course. You only have to respond to *one* of three prompts, using one of three recommended text types for your response. See the criteria on Paper 1 in the following section of this introduction. Chapter 7 includes student sample work which has been marked according to these criteria.

Paper 2: Receptive skills – listening and reading

Paper 2 is a test of your listening and reading comprehension skills. The exam is based on *three* audio recordings and *three* reading texts, each of which corresponds to a different, prescribed theme from this course. Paper 2 will include a range of questions, including multiple choice, true/false, matching, fill–in–the–gap or short answer. Many of the activities in Chapters 1–5 help develop your listening and reading skills. See Chapter 8 for a practice Paper 2 at both standard and higher level.

Individual oral

The only component of internal assessment at both standard and higher level is the individual oral, which is marked by your teacher and moderated by the IB. This table shows you how this exam differs at higher and standard level.

	Standard level	Higher level
Supervised preparation time	**15 Minutes** Select one of two visual stimuli (photo, illustration, cartoon, poster) each corresponding to a theme. Make notes and prepare a presentation.	**20 minutes** Select one of two literary extracts of 300 words, each from a different literary work. Make notes and prepare a presentation on the extract.
Part 1: Presentation	**3–4 minutes** Give a presentation in which you relate the stimulus to the theme and target culture.	**3–4 minutes** Give a presentation on the extract, commenting on the events, ideas and messages in the extract.
Part 2: Follow-up discussion	**4–5 minutes** Discuss this theme further with your teacher. Expand on your presentation.	**4–5 minutes** Discuss the extract further with your teacher. Expand on your observations.
Part 3: General discussion (5-6 minutes)	**5–6 minutes** Have a general discussion with your teacher about one or more themes of the course.	**5–6 minutes** Have a general discussion with your teacher about one or more themes of the course.

For a more detailed description of the individual oral assessments at standard and higher level see Chapter 9, which includes student sample responses and preparation activities. See the assessment criteria on for the individual oral given in the following section.

Assessment Criteria for IB English B

Paper 1: Assessment criteria SL

Criterion A: Language	Criterion B: Message	Criterion C: Conceptual understanding
How successfully does the candidate command written language?	To what extent does the candidate fulfil the task?	To what extent does the candidate demonstrate conceptual understanding?
1–3 Command of the language is limited. Vocabulary is sometimes appropriate to the task. Basic grammatical structures are used. Language contains errors in basic structures. Errors interfere with communication.	**1–3 The task is partially fulfilled.** Few ideas are relevant to the task. Ideas are stated, but with no development. Ideas are not clearly presented and do not follow a logical structure, making the message difficult to determine.	**1–2 Conceptual understanding is limited.** The choice of text type is generally inappropriate to the context, purpose or audience. The register and tone are inappropriate to the context, purpose and audience of the task. The response incorporates limited recognizable conventions of the chosen text type.
4–6 Command of the language is partially effective. Vocabulary is appropriate to the task. Some basic grammatical structures are used, with some attempts to use more complex structures. Language is mostly accurate for basic structures but errors occur in more complex structures. Errors at times interfere with communication.	**4–6 The task is generally fulfilled.** Some ideas are relevant to the task. Ideas are outlined, but are not fully developed. Ideas are generally clearly presented and the response is generally structured in a logical manner, leading to a mostly successful delivery of the message.	**3–4 Conceptual understanding is mostly demonstrated.** The choice of text type is generally appropriate to the context, purpose and audience. The register and tone, while occasionally appropriate to the context, purpose and audience of the task, fluctuate throughout the response. The response incorporates some conventions of the chosen text type.
7–9 Command of the language is effective and mostly accurate. Vocabulary is appropriate to the task, and varied. A variety of basic and more complex grammatical structures is used. Language is mostly accurate. Occasional errors in basic and in complex grammatical structures do not interfere with communication.	**7–9 The task is fulfilled.** Most ideas are relevant to the task. Ideas are developed well, with some detail and examples. Ideas are clearly presented and the response is structured in a logical manner, supporting the delivery of the message.	**5–6 Conceptual understanding is fully demonstrated.** The choice of text type is appropriate to the context, purpose and audience. The register and tone are appropriate to the context, purpose and audience of the task. The response fully incorporates the conventions of the chosen text type.

10–12 Command of the language is mostly accurate and very effective.

Vocabulary is appropriate to the task, and varied, including the use of idiomatic expressions.

A variety of basic and more complex grammatical structures is used effectively.

Language is mostly accurate. Minor errors in more complex grammatical structures do not interfere with communication.

10–12 The task is fulfilled effectively.

Ideas are relevant to the task.

Ideas are fully developed, providing details and relevant examples.

Ideas are clearly presented and the response is structured in a logical and coherent manner that supports the delivery of the message.

Paper 1: Assessment criteria HL

Criterion A: Language	Criterion B: Message	Criterion C: Conceptual understanding
How successfully does the candidate command written language?	To what extent does the candidate fulfil the task?	To what extent does the candidate demonstrate conceptual understanding?
1–3 Command of the language is limited. Vocabulary is sometimes appropriate to the task. Some basic grammatical structures are used, with some attempts to use more complex structures. Language contains errors in both basic and more complex structures. Errors interfere with communication.	**1–3 The task is partially fulfilled.** Few ideas are relevant to the task. Ideas are stated, but with no development. Ideas are not clearly presented and do not follow a logical structure, making the message difficult to determine.	**1–2 Conceptual understanding is limited.** The choice of text type is generally inappropriate to the context, purpose or audience. The register and tone are inappropriate to the context, purpose and audience of the task. The response incorporates limited recognizable conventions of the chosen text type.
4–6 Command of the language is partially effective. Vocabulary is generally appropriate to the task and varied. A variety of basic and some more complex grammatical structures is used. Language is mostly accurate for basic structures but errors occur in more complex structures. Errors at times interfere with communication.	**4–6 The task is generally fulfilled.** Some ideas are relevant to the task. Ideas are outlined, but are not fully developed. Ideas are generally clearly presented and the response is generally structured in a logical manner, leading to a mostly successful delivery of the message.	**3–4 Conceptual understanding is mostly demonstrated.** The choice of text type is generally appropriate to the context, purpose and audience. The register and tone, while occasionally appropriate to the context, purpose and audience of the task, fluctuate throughout the response. The response incorporates some conventions of the chosen text type.

7–9 Command of the language is effective and mostly accurate.

Vocabulary is appropriate to the task, and varied, including the use of idiomatic expressions.

A variety of basic and more complex grammatical structures is used effectively.

Language is mostly accurate. Occasional errors in basic and in complex grammatical structures do not interfere with communication.

7–9 The task is fulfilled.

Most ideas are relevant to the task.

Ideas are developed well, with some detail and examples.

Ideas are clearly presented and the response is structured in a logical manner, supporting the delivery of the message.

5–6 Conceptual understanding is fully demonstrated.

The choice of text type is appropriate to the context, purpose and audience.

The register and tone are appropriate to the context, purpose and audience of the task.

The response fully incorporates the conventions of the chosen text type.

10–12 Command of the language is mostly accurate and very effective.

Vocabulary is appropriate to the task, and nuanced and varied in a manner that enhances the message, including the purposeful use of idiomatic expressions.

A variety of basic and more complex grammatical structures is used selectively in order to enhance communication.

Language is mostly accurate. Minor errors in more complex grammatical structures do not interfere with communication.

10–12 The task is fulfilled effectively.

Ideas are relevant to the task.

Ideas are fully developed, providing details and relevant examples.

Ideas are clearly presented and the response is structured in a logical and coherent manner that supports the delivery of the message.

Individual oral: Assessment criteria SL

Criterion A: Language

How successfully does the candidate command spoken language?

Criterion B1: Visual stimulus

How relevant are the ideas to the selected stimulus?

1–3 Command of the language is limited.

Vocabulary is sometimes appropriate to the task.

Basic grammatical structures are used.

Language contains errors in basic structures. Errors interfere with communication.

Pronunciation and intonation are influenced by other language(s). Mispronunciations are recurrent and interfere with communication.

1–2 The presentation is mostly irrelevant to the stimulus.

The presentation is limited to descriptions of the stimulus, or part of it. These descriptions may be incomplete.

The presentation is not clearly linked to the target culture(s).

4–6 Command of the language is partially effective.

Vocabulary is appropriate to the task.

Some basic grammatical structures are used, with some attempts to use more complex structures.

Language is mostly accurate in basic structures but errors occur in more complex structures. Errors at times interfere with communication.

Pronunciation and intonation are influenced by other language(s) but mispronunciations do not often interfere with communication.

3–4 The presentation is mostly relevant to the stimulus.

With a focus on explicit details, the candidate provides descriptions and basic personal interpretations relating to the stimulus.

The presentation is mostly linked to the target culture(s).

7–9 Command of the language is effective and mostly accurate.

Vocabulary is appropriate to the task, and varied.

A variety of basic and more complex grammatical structures is used.

Language is mostly accurate. Occasional errors in basic and in complex grammatical structures do not interfere with communication.

Pronunciation and intonation are easy to understand.

5–6 The presentation is consistently relevant to the stimulus and draws on explicit and implicit details.

The presentation provides both descriptions and personal interpretations relating to the stimulus.

The presentation makes clear links to the target culture(s).

10–12 Command of the language is mostly accurate and very effective.

Vocabulary is appropriate to the task, and varied, including the use of idiomatic expressions.

A variety of basic and more complex grammatical structures is used effectively.

Language is mostly accurate. Minor errors in more complex grammatical structures do not interfere with communication.

Pronunciation and intonation are easy to understand and help to convey meaning.

Criterion B2: Message—conversation

How relevant are the ideas in the conversation?

Criterion C: Interactive skills—communication

To what extent does the candidate understand and interact?

1–2 The candidate consistently struggles to address the questions.

Some responses are appropriate and are rarely developed.

Responses are limited in scope and depth.

1–2 Comprehension and interaction are limited.

The candidate provides limited responses in the target language.

Participation is limited. Most questions must be repeated and/or rephrased.

3–4 The candidate's responses are mostly relevant to the questions.

Most responses are appropriate and some are developed.

Responses are mostly broad in scope and depth.

3–4 Comprehension and interaction are mostly sustained.

The candidate provides responses in the target language and mostly demonstrates comprehension.

Participation is mostly sustained.

5–6 The candidate's responses are consistently relevant to the questions and show some development.

Responses are consistently appropriate and developed. Responses are broad in scope and depth, including personal interpretations and/or attempts to engage the interlocutor.

5–6 Comprehension and interaction are consistently sustained.

The candidate provides responses in the target language and demonstrates comprehension.

Participation is sustained with some independent contributions.

Individual oral: Assessment criteria HL

Criterion A: Language

How successfully does the candidate command spoken language?

Criterion B1: Message—literary extract

How relevant are the ideas to the literary extract?

1–3 Command of the language is limited.

Vocabulary is sometimes appropriate to the task.

Some basic grammatical structures are used, with some attempts to use more complex structures.

Language contains errors in both basic and more complex structures. Errors interfere with communication.

Pronunciation and intonation are generally clear but sometimes interfere with communication.

1–2 The presentation is mostly irrelevant to the literary extract.

The candidate makes superficial use of the extract. Observations and opinions are generalized, simplistic and mostly unsupported.

4–6 Command of the language is partially effective.

Vocabulary is generally appropriate to the task, and varied.

A variety of basic and some more complex grammatical structures is used.

Language is mostly accurate for basic structures but errors occur in more complex structures. Errors at times interfere with communication.

Pronunciation and intonation are generally clear.

3–4 The presentation is mostly relevant to the literary extract.

The candidate makes competent use of the literary extract. Some observations and opinions are developed and supported with reference to the extract.

7–9 Command of the language is effective and mostly accurate.

Vocabulary is appropriate to the task, and varied, including the use of idiomatic expressions.

A variety of basic and more complex grammatical structures is used effectively.

Language is mostly accurate. Occasional errors in basic and in complex grammatical structures do not interfere with communication.

Pronunciation and intonation are mostly clear and do not interfere with communication.

5–6 The presentation is consistently relevant to the literary extract and is convincing.

The candidate makes effective use of the extract Observations and opinions are effectively developed and supported with reference to the extract.

10–12 Command of the language is mostly accurate and very effective.

Vocabulary is appropriate to the task, and nuanced and varied in a manner that enhances the message, including the purposeful use of idiomatic expressions.

A variety of basic and more complex grammatical structures is used selectively in order to enhance communication.

Language is mostly accurate. Minor errors in more complex grammatical structures do not interfere with communication.

Pronunciation and intonation are very clear and enhance communication.

Criterion B2: Message—conversation

How relevant are the ideas in the conversation?

1–2 The candidate consistently struggles to address the questions.

Some responses are appropriate and are rarely developed.

Responses are limited in scope and depth.

3–4 The candidate's responses are mostly relevant to the questions.

Most responses are appropriate and some are developed.

Responses are mostly broad in scope and depth.

5–6 The candidate's responses are consistently relevant to the questions and show some development.

Responses are consistently appropriate and developed.

Responses are broad in scope and depth, including personal interpretations and/or attempts to engage the interlocutor.

Criterion C: Interactive skills—communication

To what extent does the candidate understand and interact?

1–2 Comprehension and interaction are limited.

The candidate provides limited responses in the target language.

Participation is limited. Most questions must be repeated and/or rephrased.

3–4 Comprehension and interaction are mostly sustained.

The candidate provides responses in the target language and mostly demonstrates comprehension.

Participation is mostly sustained.

5–6 Comprehension and interaction are consistently sustained.

The candidate provides responses in the target language and demonstrates comprehension.

Participation is sustained with some independent contributions.

Identities

How do you see yourself? When you look in the mirror, who do you see? This chapter explores the theme of identity, asking you to think about how you define yourself and how others influence your self-image.

In this Chapter

- In Unit 1.1, you will explore how our individual identities are shaped by the diverse cultures in which we're raised.
- In Unit 1.2, you will discuss how your identity is shaped by your beliefs.
- In Unit 1.3, you will study how the media and the advertising industry shape people's definition of 'beauty' and impact their sense of self-esteem.

Unit 1.1
Citizens of the world

Guiding questions

- What does it mean to be a 'citizen of the world'?
- How do you develop your sense of identity in a globalised world?
- What kinds of experiences have contributed to your sense of identity?

Learning objectives

- Develop an understanding of international-mindedness.
- To use language effectively to explore the topic of globalisation.
- To develop appropriate language skills to discuss and express your identity.

LEARNER PROFILE

The first part of the IB mission statement reads: 'The International Baccalaureate aims to develop *inquiring, knowledgeable* and *caring* young people who help to create a better and more peaceful world through intercultural understanding and respect.' Two traits of from the learner profile have been written in *italics*. Being an inquirer is also mentioned. What other character traits should you have if you're going to make the world a better place? Make a list as a class.

Have you ever met someone who finds it hard to answer the question: 'Where are you from?' Perhaps you are one of them. Defining who we are in a **multicultural** and mobile world is becoming more and more challenging. You might live in a place where you were not born. Your parents might speak a language that is not your own. Your culture might not be the same as your neighbour's. Thanks to **globalisation** people are moving to other countries, doing business across borders and making friends online. Trying to figure out who we are in a globalised world is not easy.

This unit asks you to think about who you are in the context of where you are from, where you have been and where you are going. You will read several texts about people who have come to understand themselves better by travelling and getting to know other cultures. You could say that these people are more 'citizens of the world' than citizens of any one nation. Through their stories, you might see the value of being a **worldly** person. You might come to understand the ethos of the International Baccalaureate a little better.

Getting started

1.1 For each of the questions below, you are asked to name a country. Without showing your classmates, write your answers on a piece of paper and give them to your teacher.

a In which country were you born?

b Where are your parents from?

c During international sporting events, such as the Olympic games or the World Cup (football), which country are you most likely to support?

d If you could visit any country in the world, which would it be?

e Is there any other country that you feel close to? Which one?

1.2 Your teacher will make one alphabetical list of the countries from your class' answers to the previous activity, and then read the list aloud.

After each country is read aloud, take a few seconds to write down the first **association** that comes to mind. You might use words and phrases such as 'home', 'warmth', 'power', 'poverty' or even 'fish and chips'. There are no right or wrong answers!

1.3 Make a list of everyone's associations with the countries that were mentioned in the previous activity. Everyone could write their associations on the whiteboard, or place sticky notes on a large map. Whichever you choose, display everyone's answers so they are visible to all. Discuss the following questions:

a   How **diverse** is your class?

b   Why do you have these associations with these countries? If these are **stereotypes**, ask yourself where they come from.

c   Were some of the associations very different or was everyone in agreement?

d   Why do such perceived differences exist?

e   How does it make you feel when others view your home country differently from how you view it?

EXTRA

a   Do an online search for 'maps of stereotypes'. You may want to check those of Yanko Tsvetkov, also known as 'Alphadesigner'.

b   Hold a classroom discussion about these stereotypes. Ask yourself why there are different views on countries.

c   How do you think stereotypes originate?

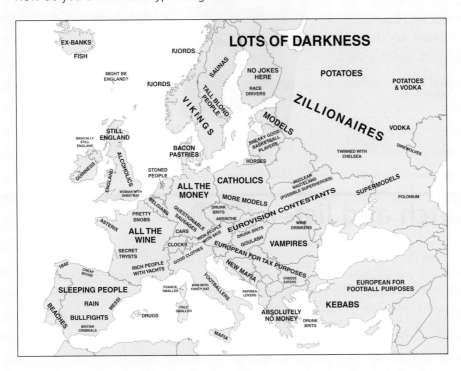

Word bank

multicultural
globalisation
worldly
association
diverse
stereotypes
identity
race
ritual
customs
values
abroad
habits
foreign
heritage
roots
third culture kid
nomad
repatriation
culture clash
communication
appearances

CAS
CAS stands for Creativity, Activity and Service. As you meet your CAS requirements, you will have experiences that help you grow as a person. What's more, you are encouraged to have experiences across different cultures and communities. As you read this unit, think about how you can come into contact with people from other cultures and communities to ensure that you grow as a person.

3

1.4 Read the captions to the images below (a-d), which are quotations from famous people. Then answer the following questions:

a As a class, create a mind map with the word '**identity**' in the middle. What factors contribute to our identity? Where do you see evidence of this in the four quotations?

b What do you already know about these historical figures? Share your knowledge with your classmates.

c Based on each quotation, how closely does each person identify with the country in which he or she was born? What part of the quotation leads you to believe this?

d Looking back at the list of countries from Activities 1.1-1.3, can you name some famous people from these countries? What did these people do for their country? How have they helped to make the world a better place?

A

I am an Albanian by birth. Now I am a Catholic citizen of India. I am also a Catholic nun. In my work, I belong to the whole world. But in my heart I belong to Christ.

Mother Teresa

B

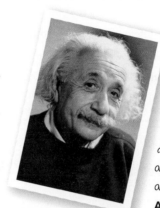

If the Theory of relativity is confirmed, the Germans will say that I am a German, and the French that I am a citizen of the world; but if my theory is disproved, the French will declare me a German and the Germans – a Jew.

Albert Einstein

C

My identity might begin with the fact of my **race**, but it didn't, couldn't end there. At least that's what I would choose to believe.

Barack Obama

D

To be an African in South Africa means that one is politicized from the moment of one's birth, whether one acknowledges it or not.

Nelson Mandela

Watch and listen 🎥 🔊

1.5 Go to TED.com and search for 'Taiye Selasi: Don't ask where I'm from, ask where I'm a local.' Before you watch her presentation, read the words and phrases in the box and list (a–i) at the top of the next page, which will be used in Selasi's talk. Try to match the words and phrases from the box with their synonyms in the list.

to look like	a take away from
it's quicker to say	b to belie
familiar	c it hit me
to not quite work	d fixed point in place and time
milieu	e using a short hand
the penny finally dropped	f overlap
remove	g at home
a constant	h to pass as
layers that merge together	i environment

Taiye Selasi

1.6

a Selasi explains that there is a difference between the questions: 'Where are you from' and 'Where are you a local?' How are these questions different in her mind? What would be your own answers to these questions?

b Selasi suggests that we are defined by our **rituals**. What are some of your daily rituals and how do they define the culture you come from?

c Selasi also says that we are defined by our relationships. If you think about the people you connect with on a weekly basis, where do these connections take place, literally? Consider both your online and physical settings? How do these people and places define you?

d Lastly, Selasi claims that people's identities are often defined by the restrictions they experience. What kinds of restrictions is she referring to? Do you experience such restrictions in your life? How do these restrictions define who you are?

1.7 After you have discussed the questions from the previous activity, copy the table below. Interview a classmate and ask him or her how these things define who they are. Use their responses to complete the table. Then ask your classmate to use the table to interview you. Use your completed tables to introduce each other to your classmates.

Rituals	Relationships	Restrictions

1.8 Discuss your answers to the following questions before listening to Audio track 1.

a What is 'globalisation' exactly? As a class, can you come up with one definition?

b What do you think are *three* main problems in the world today?

c Do you think that globalisation forces people to give up their identity?

d What are the differences between '**customs**' and '**values**'?

TOK

In TOK we ask the question: 'How do we know what we know?' Much of what you know may be defined by where you come from and what kinds of experiences you have had. In her TED Talk, Selasi uses the following logic to persuade the audience:

- All experience is local (Or: our experience is where we're from) (premise 1).
- All identity is experience (premise 2).
- Therefore my identity is defined by where I have been (conclusion).

This form of reasoning, when starting from general premises to a specific conclusion, is known as **deductive reasoning**. Do you agree with Selasi's reasoning?

1.9 In the box below is a selection of words that you will hear in Audio track 1. Look up the meaning of any unfamiliar words and then use them to complete the sentences below. Check your answers with fellow classmates and your teacher before listening to Audio track 1.

	commence	privilege	adapt	esteemed	
adopt	possess		boundaries	aspiration	sacrifice

a   After they moved to a different country, he had to ... to a different culture.

b   After the opening ceremony, the games will ....

c   She had the ... of speaking to the students on the first day of school.

d   They could not have children so they decided to ... a young girl.

e   The war spilled over the ... of the country.

f   It was her ... to become a leader in parliament.

g   The IB Learner Profile encourages students to ... certain character traits.

h   He had to ... his Saturday in order to help at the shelter.

i   The school had an excellent reputation. It was one of the most ... schools in the region.

1.10   As you listen to 🔊 Audio track 1, listen for answers to the following questions. After listening, check your answers with a classmate and then with your teacher.

a   Fill in the gap. The speaker refers to the students of this international school as young and '. . .'

b   What has the speaker been asked to talk about?

c   Fill in the gap. Rather than referring to himself as a '. . .', the speaker would like to think of himself as a 'citizen of the world'.

d   Fill in the gap. The speaker thinks the world would be a better place with more '. . .' citizens.

e   The speaker mentions three main problems that this generation faces. Name one of them.

f   Fill in the gap. Globalisation is a reality which people will have to '. . .'

g   Fill in the gap. People have different customs and '. . .'

h   Name one of the two international organisations that the speaker mentions.

i   Fill in the gap. The speaker asks if people have to sacrifice their '. . .' to make the world a better place.

1.11   Try to make one long, meaningful sentence that includes as many answers as possible from Activity 1.10. Share your sentence with your classmates. Who has included the most words? Does their sentence make much sense? Try to use punctuation accurately.

TIP

For your Paper 2 exam, you will do several text-handling exercises. The 'Exploring texts' sections in Chapters 1–5 should help you prepare for this part of your exam. Notice how the activities in this coursebook ask you to predict what the texts will be about before you read them. During your Paper 2 exam, make predictions based on the text titles. This strategy will help you engage with the texts and to understand them, as you read them.

Exploring texts

1.12   Imagine you were to move abroad and live abroad for over 10 years. How might that affect you? How might that change your perspective on life? What kinds of lessons might you learn? Discuss your answers to these questions with your classmates. If you have anyone in your class who has spent a significant about of time living abroad, ask them to answer these questions.

1.13 The title and the paragraph headings have been removed from Text 1.1. Read through Text 1.1 and find where these lines fit into the text appropriately.

a The life of a new immigrant 2

b We're all just human 6

c Adventures in fitting in 3

d The inevitable pep talk 7

e Questions of belonging 4

f 10 years of living abroad: How moving to Australia changed by my life. 1

g Finding myself 5

READING STRATEGY

Activity 1.13 asks you to read the headings that have been removed from the original text (Text 1.1) and match them with their corresponding paragraphs. When you are faced with a text with lots of sub-headings, it is useful to read these sub-headings *before* reading the whole text. This way you can predict more accurately what the text will be about.

Text 1.1

1... 10 years ago today, I moved abroad for the first time.

I packed two (very heavy) bags and left behind the only home I had known until that point in my life – Calcutta, India.

I came to the Gold Coast in Australia to get a Master's degree and planned to move back to familiarity as soon as I was done.

Little did I know then, that I was taking a step that would go on to be one of the biggest turning points of my life.

2... During my first year in Australia, I hated it. I found it beautiful, but superficial and the people friendly, but distant. I missed my family, my friends, the food and the overfamiliar warmth of India.

I was also terrified of how polite everyone was. Every sentence seemed to be punctuated with a please or a thank you. If you come from a non-Anglo culture, you'll know exactly what I mean.

It wasn't an English language problem because I have spoken English my whole life; but communication in India is a lot more direct.

In Australia however, I realised I had to embellish my sentences with *"Would you mind…"* or *"Could you please…"* before even getting around to the actual point. I lived in mortal fear of losing friends because I hadn't said the right amount of pleases and thank yous.

I make it sound like we're so rude in India. We're not, I promise.

Our politeness is just more centred around gestures and body language (head nods, anyone?) and not so much around minding our Ps and Qs. It's complicated, but if you've ever spent time with anyone from an Asian culture, you'll know what I mean.

Of course when I wasn't terrified of politeness, I spent my time worrying about accents. Back in 2007, I was ridiculously shy and hated having to repeat myself or worse, asking people to repeat themselves.

I struggled a bit with the nasal Queenslander Aussie accents and jargon and in return, I got my share of strange looks for my accent or choice of words that aren't commonly heard in Australia.

3... And of course, despite the majority of people I met, being amazingly nice, I also dealt with my share of racists and bigots. People made fun of my accent, or made me feel like I didn't belong because of skin colour or my ethnicity.

But, through all the ups and downs of immigrant life and adjusting to life abroad, somehow I managed to fall in love with Australia.

At some point, I realised that "fitting in" wasn't up to anyone else but me. If I wanted Australia to embrace me, I was going to have to embrace it first.

I met some incredible people, who I am proud to call my friends today.

I found a job that not only taught me so much about digital marketing, but also about Aussie workplace culture and it gave me a whole new group of friends.

And of course, somewhere in between all my fitting-in, I also met Johnny.

4... Fast forward to 27th February, 2017 and Australia is now my home. I will always be Indian, but I am also very proudly Australian.

Over the years, I have had many variants of *"go back to where you come from"* or *".... in Australia we do it like this"* thrown at me.

It used to upset me because it made feel like I didn't belong but now I honestly just laugh at the ignorance of people who say stupid stuff like that.

Moving to and living in Australia taught me a lot about Australia (obviously) but also a lot about myself. I am still an introvert but I am a much more confident introvert.

10 years of living outside the country of my birth has made me a much more empathetic person. But most importantly, it has taught me that my identity is more than my skin colour, my ethnicity or my accent.

I belong in Australia just as much as the ignorant idiots.

But, I am also proud of not belonging entirely.

I am no longer insecure about that. I embrace it and thrive in it.

I had the courage to give up the familiar and unlike many racists and bigots, I now not only have a deeper understanding of my own culture, but of my adopted country as well.

5... Today, I have embraced *"not belonging"* on a whole new level.

Packing up my life to go live abroad in a brand new city every few months, is now normal for me. I love the thrill of travel and heading off to an unknown place.

Many people go off to travel as a way to find themselves. It makes you want to roll your eyes but there is a grain of truth to it. When you travel outside your home country, you learn things about yourself and see yourself in a completely new light.

Moving to Australia taught me that if I could give up everything that is familiar and create a brand new life when I was 22 – I was capable of a lot more than I gave myself credit for.

It also made me want to learn about different ways of life around the world because travelling and living abroad can teach you much more about the world and people than any school ever could.

So in 2013, when we gave up our life in Australia in exchange for a life of travel – I was nervous as hell but also excited for what lay in store and what we could potentially learn from other countries, other cultures.

6... A very wise man (my dad) once told me that underneath all our differences, we're all the same and want the same basic things from our lives. We're human.

Having lived in many different countries in the past few years, I cannot help but say my dad is right.

If you relate to people on a human level, and stop comparing who's better (or worse) – you will come out with brand new friends and develop a much richer understanding of the world.

I've never liked being put into a box. I refuse to be limited by definition of my nationality or ethnicity alone.

There's more to me than that.

I have left a piece of my heart in every place we've been to and I carry a piece of them in me.

Today, I am part Indian, part Australian but also part Colombian, part Mexican, part Thai & much more — all of which combine to make me wholly global — fitting in everywhere yet not belonging anywhere.

And I love that.

7... I'll just end with this: I moved to Australia to study and with a plan to take on the world of journalism. But instead, I ended up with a brand new, completely different life. I will forever be grateful for that.

Have the courage to give up the familiar. Have the courage to grow.

Have the courage to willingly put yourself in situations that make you uncomfortable.

Good things never came out of comfort zones.

Travel. Go see the world. Leave the comforts of your home behind and go live abroad if you can.

It can be scary as hell but NOTHING else can change you the way travel and living abroad can. It's not all rainbows and unicorns (real life doesn't work that way.) It will be tough and uncomfortable but you will never, ever regret it.

Oh and P.S.: Be nice to immigrants. We're all fighting battles – internally and externally and a little kindness goes a long way.

www.fulltimenomad.com

1.14 Can you find synonyms from Text 1.1 for the following words? They appear in the same order as they do in the text.

a	insincere	b	detached
c	well-mannered	d	adorn
e	timid	f	slang
g	extremists	h	obliviousness
i	compassionate	j	excitement
k	~~evidently~~	l	~~worry about~~ *not in text.*
m	bravery		

9

1

1.15 What does the author of Text 1.1 mean by the following phrases?

a to mind your Ps and Qs

b all the ups and downs

c to roll your eyes

d to be put into a box

e its' not all rainbows and unicorns

f good things never came out of comfort zones

1.16 What has the author of Text 1.1 learned from her experiences living abroad? Return to your answers from Activity 1.12 and compare her experiences to you answers. What does living abroad teach you? Find references from the text to support your answers.

Form and meaning

1.17 Read Text 1.2, below about an American-born Chinese (ABC) woman, who lives in Beijing. She writes about her life and her daily activities. Here are two groups of sentences taken from Text 1.2. For each group of sentences explain why the particular verb tense (underlined) has been used.

1 When do you use 'to be' with '-ing' (the present continuous verb tense)?

    a My friends <u>are</u> constantly <u>asking</u> me …

    b But I don't feel like <u>I'm</u> <u>missing</u> out.

    c … <u>we're</u> <u>living</u> abroad.

    d It would've been very different from what <u>I'm</u> <u>experiencing</u> now.

    e <u>I'm</u> just <u>enjoying</u> my life.

2 When do you use the present simple verb tense?

    a I <u>believe</u> that the term applies to me.

    b We always <u>have</u> a home to go back to.

    c The culture <u>doesn't</u> <u>make</u> sense sometimes.

    d I <u>have</u> no idea what my future holds.

    e I <u>don't like</u> the thought of settling.

1.18 Do you need help describing the difference between the present simple and the present continuous verb tenses? Look at the sentences in Activity 1.17 again. Make a copy of the table below, and decide which of the descriptions (a–g) go in the 'present simple' column and which in the 'present continuous' column.

a General statement

b Something temporary

c Something happening right now

d A state of being

e Something annoying

f Something permanent

g Something that happens again and again

Present simple	Present continuous

1.19 Test your understanding of the present simple and the present continuous by selecting the correct verb tense in each sentence below.

a   Studies prove that many TCKs (suffer/are suffering) from depression.

b   (I live/I'm living) in this flat until the end of the month.

c   The USA (grants/is granting) 50,000 Green Cards every year.

d   TCKs usually (speak/are speaking) more than one language.

e   Most military families (live/are living) on bases during their time abroad.

f   We (run/are running) out of time to talk about the immigration bill.

g   He (constantly makes/is constantly making) that slurping noise with his soup!

h   My psychiatrist thinks I (suffer/am suffering) from reverse culture shock.

i   Some people (find/are finding) the term 'third culture kid' offensive.

1.20 Think about the use of verb tenses in Text 1.2, a blog by Michelle Lai- Saun Guo.

a   How long do you think the author plans to live in Beijing?

b   Does she feel she has come 'home' to her roots in China, or is she only a long-term visitor?

c   Where in the text do you see evidence to support your answers?

ATL

The IB encourages five skills or approaches to learning (ATL):

- thinking skills
- communication skills
- social skills
- self-management skills
- research skills.

Texts 1.1–1.3 are about people who have lived abroad. How did their experiences help them develop one or more of these skills? Where in the texts do you see evidence of these skills?

Text 1.2

My Beijing Survival Diary

My friends are constantly asking me, 'When are you coming home?' Although I understand it's because they miss me, and obviously I miss them, it's a difficult question to answer for several reasons. The first is the state of the US economy. I feel like being in China gives me many opportunities to network and create opportunities that people back home may not have. The second is quite simply because I've learned that even if I make plans for my life, God's going to shake a finger and say 'Nuh uh! That's not how I see it going down.'

Although the Urban Dictionary definition of a **Third Culture Kid [TCK]** is typically someone whose parents have moved him/her around to different countries during childhood, I believe that the term applies to me and my Beijing expat friends as well; especially those of us who are of Chinese heritage.

Sidenote: for those ABCs who have never been to China but think you understand Chinese culture, you'd be amazed at what you discover actually living here. As much as we TCKs complain to each other about the lack of lines outside subway trains, baby poop on the sidewalk, or getting scammed by housing agents, we understand that there's something that still draws us to China despite all those things.

Having spent my first year and a half in Beijing with only close Chinese friends, it's nice to finally have friends here who understand what I miss most about America, and also understand what I go through here in China, such as visa issues, looking for housing, getting sick from the lack of quality dairy, even my cross-cultural relationship. Although I didn't study abroad, I feel like it would've been very different from what I'm experiencing now, which is living abroad.

One thing that TCKs share (at least the ones I know) is spending a good portion of their mid-20's not partying in Vegas, but hitting up Sanlitun or other bar areas. When I see pictures of my friends from home together in Vegas, of course I wish I could be there. But I don't feel like I'm missing out by being here. Last weekend, I went to Xiu with some friends. I was standing on the rooftop terrace, looking up at the tall, chic Jianwai SOHO buildings that surrounded the bar. It was an awesome view, and I thought to myself, 'This is the epitome of life in your 20's, of living in this city where the culture doesn't make sense sometimes, but you just go with it.'

In a way, living overseas doesn't bring as much pressure as I imagine the 'real world' back home would have. One reason is that we always have a home to go back to, even if we're living abroad. I've always been a **nomad**, and I love the feeling of not knowing where I'm going to 'settle,' if I do settle at all. To be completely honest, even if I moved back home, I'd be open to moving back to China in the future, or even another country. I don't like the thought of settling in one place and planning out my entire future based around that one location.

So while I have no idea what my future holds, I'm just enjoying my life of hanging out in artsy cafes, eating *chuan'r* outdoors, and playing basketball with guys whose names I can never remember because three Chinese characters are harder to remember than one English name.

Blog by Michelle Lai-Saun Guo

READING STRATEGY

We usually read with a purpose in mind. If you are looking for information you might quickly glance over the text to find key words (scanning). Similarly, when reading texts for exams or in the classroom, make sure you always know what you are looking for. In other words, *read the question before reading the text*. Keep the following guiding questions in mind as you read Text 1.2.

- What do we know about the author?

- What is she doing in Beijing?

- How long does she plan to live there?

TEXT AND CONTEXT

- The term 'ABC' (paragraph 3) stands for 'American-born Chinese', describing someone born in America to first generation Chinese immigrants.

- This term can be used jokingly (as seen in this text) or in a negative way to describe Chinese-Americans who have given up their parents' traditions and culture.

EXTRA

The author of Text 1.2 is not the first migrant to go back to her roots. Immigrants and their descendants have frequently gone back to their country of origin – a process known as **repatriation**. Try to find other texts about people who have 'gone home' to a place that might no longer feel like home. Prepare a brief presentation on one of your texts and the story that it tells. You may use one or more of the examples below:

- The Back-to-Africa movement and the history of Liberia

- Mexican repatriation in the 1930s

- The Law of Return, giving all Jews the right to return to Israel

- Skilled non-resident Indians (NRIs) returning to India.

The `Back to Africa' movement, which began in the early 19th century, encouraged African Americans to return to their roots in Africa.

Discussion

1.21 Do you agree or disagree with some of these statements made by the author of Text 1.2? Give reasons for your answers.

a 'If I make plans for my life, God's going to shake a finger and say, 'Nuh uh! That's not how I see it going down.'

b 'The epitome of life in your 20's [is] living in [a] city where the culture doesn't make sense sometimes, but you just go with it.'

c 'I love the feeling of not knowing where I'm going to 'settle'.'

d 'I don't like the thought of planning out my entire future based around that one location.'

1.22 Edward T. Hall was a famous anthropologist who likened culture to an iceberg in 1976. He claimed that 'external' culture was like the tip of an iceberg that is visible above water. It includes people's 'outward' behaviour, such as their customs and art. Under the water lies people's 'internal' culture, that includes their ways of thinking, values and norms. See the image below for a more detailed understanding. Using this iceberg model of culture, discuss the similarities and differences between two cultures with which you and your classmate(s) are familiar. Present your findings to your classmates.

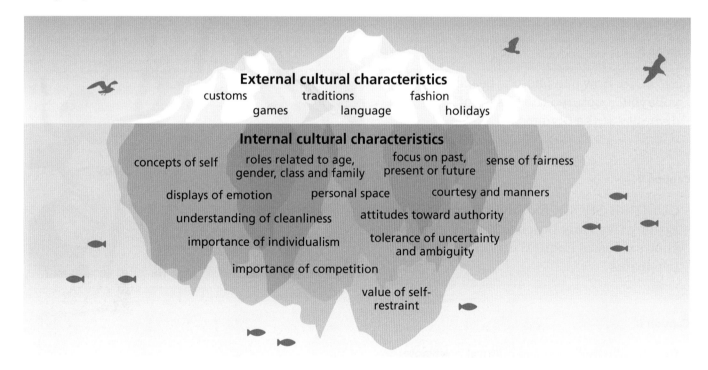

EXTRA

If you are interested in how cultures work and the iceberg model, you might like to investigate the research of Geert Hofstede on 'cultural dimensions'. *The Culture Map* by Erin Meyer is a more recent best-seller on this topic. Do more research on Geert Hofstede or read Erin Meyer's book (or parts of it) and tell your classmates more about the 'science' of culture in a presentation.

1.23 The photograph below was taken at the 2016 Olympic Games in Rio de Janeiro. It is accompanied by four headlines from four different newspapers (Captions A-D) and a Tweet from a journalist (Caption E). Answer the following questions after studying Captions A-E, that are below the picture:

a For each of the five captions, what is the author's intention?

b Which one of the first four captions best captures the way you feel about this image? Why would you say this?

c How are these terms different: 'cultural divide', 'cultural contrast', and '**culture clash**'? What do they mean and what is the effect of using each term?

d Do you agree with Ben Machell's message in his tweet (Caption E)? Is there really much difference in culture between two teams that compete in the same sport?

e To what extent does the sportswear of these two women reflect their cultural identity?

Caption A

'The cover-ups versus the cover-nots: Egyptian and German beach volleyball players highlight the massive cultural divide between Western and Islamic women's teams

Daily Mail

Caption B

Rio 2016: How one photo of beach volleyball captured the beauty of diversity at the Olympics

Global News

Caption C

CULTURE SHOCK Rio Olympics 2016: Egypt v Germany beach volleyball clash shows colossal cultural divide between two teams

The Sun

Caption D

Beach volleyball displays cultural contrasts coming together at the Olympics

Report UK

Caption E

Hijab vs bikini thing aside, how much of a 'culture clash' is it really if you are both playing women's beach volleyball at the Olympics?

Tweet by Ben Machell (*The Times* and *Evening Standard*)

Writing

1.24 Do an online search, using the headlines (captions A-E) from Activity 1.23. Read one of the articles that follows one of these headlines. Write a letter to the editor in response to their reporting of the Egypt versus Germany women's volleyball match from the 2016 Olympics. Voice your opinion, that you expressed in the discussion from Activity 1.23. For more information on how to write a letter to the editor, see Unit 6.1.

1.25 Texts 1.1 and 1.2 are both blogs about living abroad. While there are many different types of blogs, these texts are like public diaries or journals, open to friends, family and anyone who is interested in the writer's personal experiences. Try writing your own blog entry about an experience that you have had while traveling or even living abroad. Try using terms from the word bank in this unit. For more information on blog writing see Unit 6.3.

Extended Essay

If you would like to write an extended essay for English B, you can do so in one of three categories:

1 A specific analysis of the language (its use and structure), normally related to its cultural context or a specific text.

2 a A socio-cultural analysis of the impact of a particular issue on the form or use of the language based on an examination of language use.

 b An essay of a general cultural nature based on specific cultural artefacts.

3 An analysis of a literary type, based on a specific work or works of literature exclusively from the target language.

Talk to your supervisor about the IB's specifications. You can write about how language reflects culture and how culture shapes identity, which is in the spirit of this unit. Be sure to focus on a particular Anglophone culture and a particular set of language, as expressed in various texts or 'cultural artefacts', that can be anything concrete such as newspapers, magazines, articles, books, cartoons, advertisements, websites, policies or speeches.

Higher level extension

1.26 We started this unit by studying the opening lines from IB's mission statement. The final lines of this statement read:

> 'These [IB] programmes encourage students across the world to become active, compassionate and lifelong learners who understand that other people, with their differences, can also be right.'

Identities

In order to think about the phrase 'other people, with their differences, can also be right,' study the list of famous individuals. Research them online and answer the following questions:

- Who were these individuals?
- How were they different?
- How were they right?

a   Marie Curie

b   Mahatma Gandhi

c   Alan Turing

d   Rosa Parks

e   Dick Fosbury

f   Steve Jobs

Rosa Parks in 1955

Dick Fosbury at the Olympic games in 1968

1.27 Have you ever experienced situations when travelling or living abroad, where people did things differently?

- What did they do differently?
- Could you consider these differences 'right' or 'wrong'?
- Discuss your experiences and opinions with your classmates.

1.28 The following words have been removed from Text 1.3. Study the list before reading Text 1.3 and look up the meaning of any words that you do not know. Then read Text 1.3 and insert the missing words from the list below.

a   mundane   b   reexamine

c   ulterior   d   rubs

e   blunt   f   sense

g   reconfigure   h   apology

i   funny   j   self-development

k   deception   l   niceties

m   abundance   n   superficially

o   outspokenness   p   repercussion

Text 1.3

In 2011 I travelled to Saint Petersburg, Russia. The food sucked. The weather sucked. My apartment sucked. Nothing worked. Everything was overpriced. The people were rude and smelled ...1.... Nobody smiled and everyone drank too much. Yet, I loved it. It was one of my favorite trips.

There's a bluntness to Russian culture that generally ...2... Westerners the wrong way. Gone are the fake ...3... and verbal webs of politeness. You don't smile at strangers or pretend to like anything you don't. In Russia, if something is stupid, you say it's stupid. If you really like someone and are having a great time, you tell her that you like her and are having a great time. It doesn't matter if this person is your friend, a stranger, or someone you met five minutes ago on the street.

The first week I found all of this really uncomfortable. I went on a coffee date with a Russian girl, and within three minutes of sitting down she looked at me funny and told me that what I'd just said was stupid. I nearly choked on my drink. There was nothing combative about the way she said it; it was spoken as if it were some ...4... fact – like the quality of the weather that day, or her shoe size – but I was still shocked. After all in the West such ...5... is seen as highly offensive, especially from someone you just met. But it went on like this with everyone. Everyone came across as rude all the time, and as a result my Western-coddled mind felt attacked on all sides. Nagging insecurities began to surface in situations where they hadn't existed in years.

But as the weeks wore on, I got used to the Russian frankness, much as I did the midnight sunsets and the vodka that went down like ice water. And then I started appreciating it for what it really was: unadulterated expression. Honesty in the truest ...6... of the word. **Communication** with no conditions, no strings attached, no ...7... motive, no sales job, no desperate attempt to be liked.

Somehow, after years of travel, it was in perhaps the most un-American of places where I first experienced a particular flavour of freedom: the ability to say whatever I thought or felt, without fear of ...8.... It was a strange form of liberation *through* accepting rejection. And as someone who had been starved of this kind of ...9... expression most of his life – I got drunk on it like, well, like it was the finest vodka I'd ever had. The month I spent in Saint Petersburg went by in a blur, and by the end I didn't want to leave.

Travel is a fantastic ...10... tool, because it extricates you from the values of your culture and shows you that another society can live with entirely different values and still function and not hate themselves. This exposure to different cultural values and metrics then forces you to ...11... what seems obvious in your own life and to consider that perhaps it's not necessarily the best way to live. In this case, Russia had me re-examining the fake-nice communication that is so common in Anglo culture, and asking myself it this wasn't somehow making us more insecure around each other and worse at intimacy.

I remember discussing this dynamic with my Russian teacher one day, and he had an interesting theory. Having lived under communism for so many generations, with little to no economic opportunity and caged by a culture of fear, Russian society found the most valuable currency to be trust. And to build trust you have to be honest. That means when things suck, you say so openly and without ...12.... People's displays of unpleasant honesty were rewarded for the simple fact that they were necessary for survival – you had to know whom you could rely on and whom you couldn't, and you needed to know quickly.

But, in the 'free' West, my Russian teacher continued, there existed an ...13... of economic opportunity – so much economic opportunity that it became far more valuable to present yourself in a certain way, even if it was false, than to actually *be* that way. Trust lost value. **Appearances** and salesmanship became more advantageous forms of expression. Knowing a lot of people ...14... was more beneficial that knowing a few people closely.

This is why it became the norm in Western cultures to smile and say polite things even when you don't feel like it, to tell little white lies and agree with someone whom you don't actually agree with. This is why people learn to pretend to be friends with people they don't actually like, to buy things they don't actually want. The economic system promotes such ...15....

The downside of this is that you never know, in the West, if you can completely trust the person you're talking to. Sometimes this is the case even among good friends or family members. There is such pressure in the West to be likeable that people often ...16... their entire personality depending on the person they're dealing with.

Extract by Mark Manson

CONCEPTS

Purpose

So far, you have read three accounts from people living abroad (Texts 1.1-1.3). Discuss your answers to these questions with your classmates.

a Why do the authors of these texts feel a need to share their experiences with others?

b What is their intention or *purpose*?

c Why have they chosen these text types to achieve their *purpose*?

d Have you ever felt the need to write about your experiences abroad? How have you shared these with others?

1.29 Answer the following questions, using complete sentences and making reference to Text 1.3.

a Despite bad weather and terrible food, why does Mark Manson say that his trip to Russia was one of his favourite trips?

b What, according to Mark Manson, is the main cultural and behavioural difference between Americans and people in the West?

c What do Russians think of this behaviour of people in the West? And how do people in the West, like Mark Manson, usually respond to this Russian behaviour?

d Why, according to Mark's Russian teacher's historical reasons, do these cultures behave differently?

1.30 To what degree has your identity been shaped by experiences that you've had with people who were 'different'? Discuss how 'other people' have influenced who you are today.

Literature

1.31 In the spirit of this chapter's theme, identity, you will read a passage from Richard Wright's novel, *Black Boy* (Text 1.4). Before you read the text, discuss your answers to the following questions:

a To what degree does the colour of your skin determine your sense of identity?

b Do you live a society that is racially diverse or homogeneous (meaning all the same)? How does this affect your view on people from other cultures?

c Do you think racism is a problem in the place where you live? How does this problem express itself in day-to-day relationships?

1.32 The words in the vocabulary box below are used in Text 1.4. For each sentence that follows, decide which of these words is being referred to.

| nuisance | trivial | tardiness | circulated | naïvely | paternal | kin | stoutly | brooded |

a This word is used to describe how news travelled through Richard's community about a white man who beat a black boy.

b Richard uses this word to describe the right that he thought fathers had to beat their children.

c Richard uses this word to describe how annoying he once was for asking too many questions as a child.

d This word describes how Richard says, in a very firm and resolute way, that he would not let anyone beat him.

e This word is used to describe how Richard thought for a long time about the relationships between whites and blacks.

f This word is used to describe a family relative. Richard is surprised to learn that the black boy was not beaten by a member of his own family.

g In this way, Richard assumed that a 'black' boy could be beaten by a 'white' father, meaning that he was quite inexperienced and immature.

h Richard uses this word to describe how he was rather slow or late in his understanding of racial relationships in the South in the 1920s.

i This word describes the small and seemingly insignificant news and happenings of Richard's neighbourhood.

TEXT AND CONTEXT
- *Black Boy* is a memoir by Richard Wright, published in 1945.
- It is about Richard, growing up in the 1920s in the South of the USA.

Text 1.4

I soon made myself a nuisance by asking far too many questions of everybody. Every happening in the neighborhood, no matter how trivial, became my business. It was in this manner that I first stumbled upon the relations between whites and blacks, and what I learned frightened me. Though I had long known that there were people called 'white' people, it had never meant anything to me emotionally. I had seen white men and women upon the streets a thousand times, but they had never looked particularly 'white.' To me they were merely people like other people, yet somehow strangely different because I had never come in close touch with any of them. For the most part I never thought of them; they simply existed somewhere in the background of the city as a whole. It might have been that my tardiness in learning to sense white people as 'white' people came from the fact that many of my relatives were 'white'-looking people. My grandmother, who was white as any 'white' person, had never looked 'white' to me. And when word circulated among the black people of the neighborhood that a 'black' boy had been severely beaten by a 'white' man, I felt that the 'white' man had had a right to beat the 'black' boy, for I naively assumed that the 'white' man must have been

the 'black' boy's father. And did not all fathers, like my father, have the right to beat their children? A paternal right was the only right, to my understanding, that a man had to beat a child. But when my mother told me that the 'white' man was not the father of the 'black' boy, was no kin to him at all, I was puzzled.

'Then why did the 'white' man whip the 'black' boy?' I asked my mother.

'The 'white' man did not **whip** the 'black' boy,' my mother told me. 'He **beat** the 'black' boy.

'But why?'

'You're too young to understand.'

'I'm not going to let anyone beat me,' I said stoutly.

'Then stop running wild in the streets,' my mother said.

I brooded for a long time about the seemingly causeless beating of the 'black' boy by the 'white' man and the more questions I asked the more bewildering it all became. Whenever I saw 'white' people now I stared at them, wondering what they were really like.

Extract from Black Boy by Richard Wright

Would Richard Wright have been a good IB learner? What IB learner traits apply to Richard, as the main character of this passage? Give evidence from the text for each trait that applies to him:

- Inquirers
- Thinkers
- Principled
- Caring
- Balanced

- Knowledgeable
- Communicators
- Open-minded
- Risk-takers
- Reflective

1.33 Here are several questions about Text 1.4 and the context in which it was written. Discuss your answers with classmates.

a How is Richard's understanding of 'black' and 'white' different from other people's understanding of 'black' and 'white' in the American South in the 1920s?

b How are people's views on racial differences in the American South in the 1920s similar or different from modern-day views on racial differences where you live?

c Besides race, what other values are different, when comparing your world to Richard's world of the 1920s?

REFLECT

This unit has explored the topic of identity in light of globalisation. Discuss your answers to the following questions to reflect on what you've learned.

a The texts, quotations, audio file and video were mainly stories. Could you relate to the experiences that these authors described? Describe how you have had similar or different experiences when travelling or living abroad.

b The title of this unit is 'Citizens of the world'. What does this phrase mean to you?

c Do you consider yourself a 'citizen of the world'? Why or why not?

Unit 1.2
Belief and identity

Guiding questions	Learning objectives
• To what extent is your identity defined by what you believe? • How have you come to believe what you believe? • How do people express their beliefs through language?	• Become more aware of different beliefs and more conscious of how they shape identity. • Develop a command of language that enables you to discuss religion and faith appropriately.

Belief is a powerful force in the world. Your beliefs might be the underlying **principles** that guide you in life. Your beliefs might reflect your **values**. They might determine your daily rituals. They might even influence the way you vote. While beliefs are hard to prove right or wrong, they have a lot to say about what is 'right' and 'wrong'. Challenge someone about their beliefs and you have challenged their very identity.

This unit invites you to think about what it means to believe, whether you believe in God or in a designer label. By the end of this unit you should have a better understanding and appreciation of **religion**, **faith** and **spirituality**.

2.1 As you begin to discuss belief and identity, it helps to know topic-related vocabulary. Using some of the words from the word bank, fill in the blanks in the sentences below. Look up any words that you do not already know.

a A ____ is system of religious devotion directed at a figure or person.

b Someone who is _____ is critical and not easily convinced.

c Something that is not associated with religion or spiritual matters is called ___.

d A ____ is a song that is sung to express religious devotion.

e ____ is like a sixth sense or a 'gut feeling'.

f When one changes their belief system, they can _____ to a religion.

g Your _____ are the rules that you believe in and live by.

h A _____ is a person who does not believe in god.

i _____ are rules laid down by a religious authority.

j _____ is the act of spreading Christianity by telling others about it.

k ____ people practise their religion regularly.

l _____ is a state of being, where one is blessed and saved from one's sins.

On the right is a photograph of Pope Francis, the 266th Pope of the Catholic Church and the spiritual leader of Catholics around the world.

Word bank

principles
values
religion
faith
spirituality
intuition
dogmas
cult
sceptical
self-determination
mysticism
atheist
agnostic
convert
epiphany
secular
fate
reconcile
devout
holy
hymn
evangelism
ritual
disciples
grace

Organisational skills

Each unit in Chapters 1–5 of this coursebook has a list of vocabulary called the 'Word bank'. You need to get to know these words by reading them in the contexts in which they appear, using them for activities and including them in your writing or speaking assignments. How are you going to master these words? You might want to create a vocabulary journal where you write down, define, translate, memorise and use these words to improve your proficiency. Organising a method for vocabulary building is part of the learning process.

CAS

Whether you have a religious faith or not, you might want to find out how local places of worship (i.e. churches, mosques or temples) are running projects to help the community. How can you contribute to these projects and activities? What can you learn about your own faith and values by working with such organisations?

2.2 Would you agree or disagree with the following statements? Discuss your answers with a classmate. Take a poll in your class.

a   Religious people are happier in life.

b   People need spiritual leaders to inspire them to lead better lives.

c   It is possible to believe in both evolution theory and God.

d   Some people have the 'faith gene', meaning they are genetically more inclined than others to believe in an organised religion.

e   Psychologically, there is not much difference between people who practise a religion and people who are loyal to a product brand.

f   You are more likely to be religious if your parents are religious.

2.3 Look at the four images below.

a   Explain how your own beliefs are relevant to each image.

b   How do these images represent a set of beliefs?

c   Use words from the word bank to describe your beliefs.

For example:

In response to Image A: 'I do not trade options or stock on the market, but I believe in the effectiveness of capitalism. I think that if no one believed in the value of their stocks, their value would probably drop.'

Image A – A stock market

Image B – US President Donald Trump

Image C – The power of meditation

Image D – An Apple Store

EXTRA

Conduct a small role-playing game as a class. One of you is an alien who has just arrived on planet Earth. The rest of you have to explain to him or her why humans practise organised religion. The alien should ask lots of questions. Use words from the word bank in your conversation.

LEARNER PROFILE

Principled or Spiritual

The 'learner profile' outlines ten traits that define an IB learner. For one of these traits, schools can encourage students to become 'principled' or 'spiritual'.

- Which of these two character traits has your school adopted?
- What do you think of this choice?
- What are the differences between these two words?

Watch and listen

2.4 Below is a list of words taken from an online video that you are about to watch. Based on these words, what do you think the video will be about? Share your predictions with your classmates.

perpetrate	unease	temple	faith	abandon	transcend	suffering	journey
	fervor	crossroads	cauldron	devout	progressive		

2.5 Do an online search for a video called 'Rainn Wilson's Spiritual Journey', published by Big Think. Watch Rainn Wilson (right) talk about his faith and experiences. As you watch, listen for ways in which he uses the words from the list in Activity 2.4. Decide which is the correct word for each of the following questions:

a Rainn Wilson uses this word synonymously with religion.

b This word is used to describe the social values of the Baha'i.

c Rainn Wilson uses this word to describe how religions and ideas came together in his household.

d This word describes what he did with his religious principles when he moved to New York.

e Wilson thought that there could not be a god with so much of this in the world.

f Wilson uses this word to describe how religion spreads evil.

g Wilson uses this word to describe how he went his own way.

h Wilson uses this word to describe the energy he put into his acting career.

i Wilson says he 'came to a ___', which is synonymous with making a decision.

j Wilson uses this word to describe how he felt after hitting 'rock bottom'.

k Wilson claims that there is no difference between being ___ and being an artist.

l Wilson uses this word to describe a yearning to seek something higher.

m This is a place where one can worship.

TOK

Faith and intuition are two 'ways of knowing' in the IB Theory of Knowledge syllabus. Which of these two – faith, **intuition**, or both – are relevant terms for 'knowing' the following things. Explain your answers.

a Your team is going to win next week's match.

b The president of your country will do a good job leading the country.

c It's better to overdress than to underdress on your first day at a new job.

d Humans will travel to Mars eventually.

e Reflecting on your wrongdoings will most likely lead to self-improvement.

TEXT AND CONTEXT

- In his talk on Big Think, Rainn Wilson uses the word 'catholic' in the original Latin and Greek sense of the word, which means 'universal', 'on the whole' or 'in general'.

- SoulPancake is a media and entertainment company.

2.6 Discuss your answers to the questions below as a class. There are no right or wrong answers.

a To what extent have you adopted the beliefs of your parents?

b Do you agree with Rainn Wilson that there is no difference between creativity, spirituality and philosophy? Explain your answer.

c Have you ever abandoned your beliefs? What happened? Did you ever have a 'rock bottom' experience that changed your thinking?

2.7 Listen to 🔊 Audio track 2. Before you listen, discuss your answers to the following questions:

a Is religion good for the economy?

b Can you suggest some characteristics or traits that 'happy' people have in common? List five traits that define 'happy' people.

c Do you think spiritual people spend their income differently than non-spiritual people? In what ways?

2.8 Read the questions below and answer them after listening to Audio track 2. Be thorough with your answers. Check your answers with your teacher.

a What is this podcast usually about?

b How many people did Jason Botswain survey in total?

c Who spend more money in general: Atheists or spiritual people?

d Give one example of how religion acts as an economic boost, according to the interviewee?

e Fill in the gap: 'Spiritual people are _____ and compassionate.'

f Fill in the gap: 'They _____ and self-actualise.'

g Fill in the gap: 'And they take time to _____ life experiences.'

h Name one thing that spiritual people are less likely to spend their money on, according to Jason Botswain.

i What 'drives' spiritual people, according to him?

2.9 Revisit your answers to the three questions from Activity 2.7.

a Listen to 🔊 Audio track 2 again to find answers to these three questions.

b Compare your answers to the ones from the recording. How are they different?

c Do you agree with the claims that are made in the podcast? Explain your answers.

Exploring texts

2.10 Below is a list of words (a–q) taken from Text 1.5. Match these with their synonyms in the box. The words appear in the same order in this activity as they appear in the text. They have been underlined so that you can spot them more easily.

> degree contentment outgoing situation confused passion
> irreligious tendency show surprise frenzy part
> instinctive obvious ability precious intolerance

a reveal	**b** extent
c dear	**d** component
e scenario	**f** unavoidable
g extrovert	**h** innate
i capacity	**j** fulfillment
k tantrum	**l** predisposition
m bigotry	**n** bemused
o revelation	**p** secular
q fervour	

Text 1.5

What Twins Reveal About The Science Of Faith

I am frequently asked by journalists to recall the most surprising finding of our twin studies. The study of religion and belief in God is the one that always comes to mind, and the results are not easily accepted by many people. Most people can accept diseases or height and even weight being genetically heritable to some <u>extent</u>, but when it comes to our personal beliefs we tend to be more **sceptical**. For many, the idea that there is a genetic component to our faith (or lack of it), is a stretch too far and damages the concept of **self-determination** that we hold so <u>dear</u>.

Nevertheless science has shown us clearly that one level of belief in God and overall spirituality is shaped not only by a mix of family environment and upbringing (which is not surprising), but also by our genes. Twin studies conducted around the world in the U.S., the Netherlands and Australia as well as ours in the U.K. show a 40 to 50 percent genetic <u>component</u> to belief in God.

What is striking is that these findings of a genetic basis for belief are consistent even across countries like the U.S. and the U.K., with their huge differences in beliefs and church attendance. For example, in the latest surveys in the

U.S., when asked, 61 percent of white Americans say they firmly (i.e. without any doubt) believe in God, compared with only 17 percent of firm believers in similar populations in the U.K. (greater than a threefold difference). The opposite scenario of non-belief is also true: only a tiny 3 percent of the U.S. population report being firmly atheist compared with 18 percent in the U.K. As well as belief, participation follows separate trends in the two countries. Some form of weekly church attendance is now nearly three times higher in the U.S. than the U.K.

Sceptics among you might say that the twin studies showing similarity for belief are just reflecting some cultural or family influence that wasn't properly corrected for in the study design. However in one study of adopted twins, the researchers looked at religious belief in a number of adopted twins raised apart. They found exactly the same result: greater similarity in identical twin pairs, even if raised apart. The conclusion is unavoidable: faith is definitely influenced by genes.

To uncover in more detail exactly what part of belief or religion was genetic, an unlikely research partnership was formed between two academic twin experts: Nick Martin, an extrovert atheist Australian and Lindon Eaves, a British lay preacher originally from Birmingham.

In an attempt to separate the '3 Bs'-- belonging, behaving, and believing, the three elements that make up religiosity, they asked a range of questions attempting to get a handle on individual differences in spirituality. They defined this as 'the capacity to reach out beyond oneself and discover or make meaning of experience through broadened perspectives and behavior.' The scale is based on three main factors: self-forgetfulness,

transpersonal identification and **mysticism**. Questions in the test they designed included:

- 'I believe that all life depends on some spiritual order or power that cannot be completely explained' True or false?

- 'Often when I look at an ordinary thing, something wonderful happens: I get the feeling that I am seeing it fresh for the first time' True or false?

They estimated the heritability of spirituality to be around 40 to 50 percent, which is quite high considering how tricky it is to measure. Other U.S. studies using even more detailed questions in larger numbers have found similar or even stronger genetic influences. These studies demonstrate our variable but innate inherited sense of spirituality, which affects how we perceive the world, ourselves and the universe. This is independent of our formal religious beliefs and practices and, strangely, largely independent of family influence.

The positive feedback and inner reward we get from these spiritual or religious thoughts could also account for some differences. One individual during prayer or meditation may feel a rush of immense joy and fulfillment from the reward centers of the brain (in the hypothalamus), and someone else may feel only the uncomfortable chair and be worrying about the shopping list. While the spiritual side is important for some, others find great comfort in religious practice and attendance.

Studies show that for twins living at home, there is no clear genetic influence or difference from their parents in their practice. However, genes start to play a role, once the twins leave the nest.

Elizabeth and Caroline were identical twins who came from an academic

middle-class English family with an **atheist** father and **agnostic** mother. The sisters were very similar in appearance and character, both admitted to being stubborn, although Elizabeth was the naughtier of the two. At primary school, they both became interested in Christianity and much to their father's surprise and displeasure they were baptised and prayed regularly. Their parents split up soon after and their father left home. They went through the normal teenage tantrums and slowly lost interest in organized religion and prayer.

After school they went to different universities. Caroline quickly rediscovered her faith; she became an even more committed Christian and joined student societies and church groups. Elizabeth began discussions with an Islamic group, initially arguing against religion, read the Quran to dismiss it and then found herself being drawn to and then **converted** to Islam. Both married and had two kids: Caroline with an English Anglican husband, and Elizabeth with a Pakistani Muslim (from then on she wore the veil, hijab in public).

After leaving home, children with the right predisposition can often switch religions. As she now says: 'I strongly believe that Islam is the one true faith and Christianity is wrong. I endured many taunts and bigotry about my style of dress and beliefs and was often frightened to go outside. I once had to witness my 3-year-old disabled son being spat at.' Caroline is similarly strongly opposed to her sister's Islamic views and 'her lack of belief in Jesus being the Messiah really upsets me.' She has had an easier time socially, but misses being close to her sister and having a drink with her. She says: 'I will never forget the fact that she very pointedly refused to sing hymns at my big day, a Christian wedding.' Both twins admit being saddened that neither could bear to act as a guardian of the other's children because of their faith, although ironically they have much more in common genetically with each other's children than other aunts and share the same proportion of genes with them.

Sadly their mother, Annie, developed terminal metastatic lung cancer, which had the positive side effect of briefly bringing the family back together. The closeness and bonding was short-lived. She admitted: 'I was initially <u>bemused</u> and then distressed by their fierce disagreements over faith, which being

a self-confessed agnostic I just couldn't relate to. My main hope was to live long enough to see the birth of my two new grandchildren.' When, against medical odds, she did, and was still alive nine months later, she had a <u>revelation</u>. 'I think I've found God,' she told her daughter Caroline as she recounted an **epiphany** moment she had while out walking. 'I felt his presence all around me, a spiritual presence. It's not just because I'm about to die: I'm not afraid of death. But I've changed my mind, there is more to life than just the current one.' She died shortly afterward. Annie's genetic predisposition for faith, likely suppressed by her **secular**

surroundings and her dominant atheist husband, may have been the crucial factor that influenced her daughters' uncompromising beliefs.

Where did this religious <u>fervor</u> come from? Neither had religious parents, and it is unlikely that the school alone could have had such an influence. Other twin studies have shown that after leaving home, children with the right predisposition can often switch religions, and that which form they then choose is not down to the genes but to life events or some mysterious unknown force.

www.popsci.com

TEXT AND CONTENT

- Self-determination is the opposite of **fate** or destiny. It is the notion that people can determine their own future through their own decisions and actions.

- Mysticism is the belief that we can become unified with a higher being through spiritual contemplation.

- To be baptised means to go through a religious rite, involving water, in which a person is admitted to the Christian Church.

- Agnostic people believe that nothing is known or can be known about the existence of a god. They are different from atheists, who claim that there is no god.

- Epiphany is a moment in which we suddenly realise something, gain more insight or have a deeper understanding of the world.

TIP
You might also come across true/false questions in your Paper 2 exam. It might ask you to justify your answers with evidence from the text. This means that you have to write out exact phrases or sentences from the source text that clearly prove the statement true or false. Paraphrasing is not sufficient.

2.11 According to Text 1.5 are the following statements true or false? Justify your answers with evidence from the text.

a   The journalist who wrote this article predominantly studies religion. (true/false)

b   The researcher studied the percentage of white people who were religious in both the U.S. and U.K. (true/false)

c   The researcher's test on twins took cultural differences into account. (true/false)

d   The research partners defined spirituality as the ability to have meaningful experiences through worship. (true/false)

e   The researchers concluded that people inherit 40–50 per cent of their parents' spirituality genes. (true/false)

f   Once children move out of their parents' house, their genes start to determine their spirituality instead of their parents' influence. (true/false)

g The article tells a story about identical twins, whose parents separated after the children entered the Christian faith. (true/false)

h Elizabeth was drawn to the Islamic faith from the first moment she came into contact with it. (true/false)

i Because Elizabeth and Caroline are twins, their children's genetic makeup is very similar to theirs. (true/false)

j The twins' mother, Annie, was probably a carrier of the 'faith' gene, but because of circumstances, this was only expressed very late in life. (true/false)

k Studies on twins have shown how genetics can determine the religion to which one identifies. (true/false)

2.12 Text 1.5 claims that 'religiosity' (the experience of religion) consists of '3 Bs': belonging, behaving, and believing. How might these three ideas be relevant to people outside organised religion? Use a few words to fill in the table below. Discuss your answers with classmates. The first one has been started for you.

	belonging	behaving	believing
Sport	playing in a team / supporting a team	work out / cheering	believing in winning
Money			
Family			
School			
Politics			

To what degree is cheering for your favourite sports team like worshipping in a church or temple?

Form and meaning

2.13 Below are several sentences taken from Text 1.5. In the left column are sentences that use *adverbs*. In the right column are sentences that use *adjectives*. Study these examples and answer the following question:

When do we use adjectives and when *do* we use adverbs?

Try explaining these rules to a classmate or your teacher.

Adverbs	Adjectives
The results are not <u>easily</u> accepted.	The research was <u>easy</u> to conduct.
Science has shown us <u>clearly</u> that belief in God is shaped by our genes.	It is <u>clear</u> that our genes influence our predisposition toward religion.
They <u>firmly</u> believe in God.	They share a <u>firm</u> belief in God.
She adapted <u>incredibly</u> <u>quickly</u>.	It was <u>incredible</u> how <u>quick</u> they were to adapt.

2.14 To help you discuss your findings from Activity 2.13, six explanations (a–f) have been provided. On a copy of the table below, write the letter of each explanation in the correct column.

Adverbs	Adjectives

a These are used to describe nouns, i.e. people, places or things.

b These are used to describe verbs, i.e. *how* somebody does something or *how* something happens.

c These are used with some verbs, such as *to be, to look, to feel* and *to sound*.

d These are used to describe adjectives.

e These are used to describe adverbs.

f These are used before past participles, for example: *written, held* or *organised*.

2.15 Select the correct word from those in parentheses.

a I will never forget the fact that she very (pointed/pointedly) refused to sing hymns at my big day.

b She walked (terrible/terribly) slowly.

c My faith is something (personal/personally) to me.

d She died (short/shortly) thereafter.

e I was (initial/initially) bemused and then distressed by their (fierce/fiercely) disagreements over faith.

f Some people feel (uncomfortable/uncomfortably) discussing religion.

g Annie's genetic predisposition for faith, (like/likely) suppressed by her secular surroundings and her dominant atheist husband, might have been the crucial factor that influenced her daughters' (uncompromising/uncompromisingly) beliefs.

1

TOK

In your TOK class, you might be asked to define the term 'knowledge'. A popular definition claims that 'knowledge' is justified true belief. In other words you can only really *know* that something is true if:

- it is actually true
- you believe it is true
- you have justification to believe that it is true.

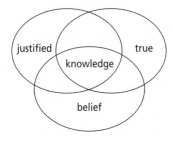

Here is a short list of things some people *believe* to be true. How can they not *know* them to be true? Do they have evidence that they are true?

- There is life on other planets.
- Your birth date determines your identity.
- Your behaviour today influences what happens to you tomorrow. (Karma)
- Ghosts exist.

Discussion

2.16 Read the Calvin and Hobbes cartoon below and discuss your answers to the following questions:

a Why do children stop believing in Santa Claus?

b How is believing in Santa Claus different from believing in God?

c To what degree do secrecy and mystery play a role in a religion with which you are familiar?

d Perhaps you are familiar with the expression 'seeing is believing.' To what extent is 'seeing' an important part of 'believing' for you?

2.17

Many currencies in the world have coins, which read 'In God we trust'. Prepare and give a five-minute talk on one of these captions, that could accompany the image below.

a 'In God We Trust' and 'In Capitalism We Believe', but 'In Spiritualism We Lack'. In other words, an obsession for money is bad for the soul.

b People need religion to guide them in what is right and wrong. Therefore, integrating religion into politics, economics and education is good for most individuals in society.

c Phrases such as 'God bless America' in political speeches or 'In God We Trust' on coins are not appropriate, because they confuse politics and economics with religious values.

CONCEPTS

Meaning and Context

You might not have noticed any references to 'God' on coins or bills in the country where you live (see image). Why would these references be there? What do they mean? One of the key concepts in your English B course is *meaning*. Another is *context*. In the English B course, you should constantly ask yourself how *meaning* is created by the placement of a text in a certain *context*. The *phrase* 'In God We Trust' has a different meaning when it's on a coin or if it's on a sign above a bus driver's head (which is common in some countries). Be sure to notice how meaning is affected by context as you study texts in your English B course.

Writing

2.18 Re-read Text 1.5. Imagine you are Caroline or Elizabeth. You have disagreed with your sister about your religious differences for years. You have read this article about your family and realise that you actually have more in common with your sister than you thought. Taking the article into consideration, write a personal letter to your sister, which tries to **reconcile** your differences and find common ground. You might want to use the following phrases in your letter:

- After reading the article about our shared predisposition for faith...
- Despite our differences, I believe that we...
- Although we practise a different religion, we share...
- After reflecting on past events in our lives, I would like to suggest that we...

2.19 Listen to Audio track 2 again. Several statements are made that you can research further online. For example, 'spiritual people are happier than non-spiritual people' or 'religion is good for the economy'. Take notes on your findings and use them as evidence for an opinion piece that you write for a newspaper, entitled 'Spiritualism, happiness and money.' You can use words from the wordbank for your opinion piece.

Extended Essay

Category 1 extended essays for language acquisition ask you to analyse how language is used in a particular cultural context. Religious texts are perfect to analyse for this purpose. Most relevant might be the analysis of the sermons of a popular preacher in your own country, or another country where religion influences many people. Through an online search you can find out more about pastors and preachers with celebrity status who give inspiring sermons.

Higher Level Extension

2.20 Are there certain brands that you 'believe' in? These could be fashion, food, car or computer brands.

a Make a collage of several logos of brands that you identify with. Place them on one page, and submit this anonymously to your teacher.

b When your teacher displays your collage of logos, along with those from other students, try to guess who has created each collage.

c What does this tell you about how well you know your classmates?

2.21 After Activity 2.20, take a moment to present your collage to your classmates in a small presentation. In your presentation answer the following questions:

a Besides various products and services, what do these brands 'stand for'?

b Why do you 'believe' in these brands?

c How do these brands make you believe in them?

2.22 In the box below you find words that have been removed from Text 1.6. Decide which of the words below should be used to fill each of the gaps (a–p) in the text. Look back at Activities 2.13-2.16 for help with when to use adverbs and adjectives.

possibly	vibrant	firm	fast	considerable	valuable
particularly	coincidentally	easily	unambiguously	emotionally
modest	entire	uniquely	deliberately	oral

Text 1.6

Nine Components That Powerfully Engaging Brands Share With Religion

Mark couldn't wait. Thoughts of it had kept him awake nights. He'd spent most days preparing for the big day. And it had cost him his (a)...... fortune. It was the opening of the Apple Store in Sydney, Australia.

He had flown 15 hours from his hometown of Palo Alto, Calif., and camped out overnight to be near the head of the line of 4,000 people. And this wasn't the first time he had gone to such lengths. He'd also flown to Tokyo for the opening of the Apple Store there. But Sydney was Apple's 40th store, so Mark was sharing a special anniversary with the brand he loved. What did he expect to get out of it? 'A T-shirt,' he said.

(b)......, the opening took place a week before the Catholic Church's World Youth Day and the arrival of Pope Benedict. If you had just landed on Earth, with no idea of what humans worship, you might (c)...... have drawn comparisons between the thousands of Apple fans and the thousands of Catholics who converged on Sydney.

Having spent years talking with brand fans; from obsessed Harley-Davidson riders to devoted Guinness drinkers to young Hello Kitty admirers (one of whom owns more than 12,000 pieces of Hello Kitty merchandise), I've been struck by the power brands have over their followers. But can the apparent parallels between brands and religion (d)...... hold up?

Have some brands actually managed to create their own religions by, coincidentally or (e)......, adopting triggers and tactics from the world of religion?

To find out, I partnered with neuroscientists, who used MRI to compare the brain activity of **devout** Christians to that of brand fans. It turned out that brand iconography activated the same region in the brains of fans that was activated in the brains of Christians when they were exposed to faith-related triggers. But that was the case only with (f)...... powerful brands such as Apple, Harley and Guinness. Brands not among that rarified group, such as BP and KFC, provoked less activity and engaged fewer regions of the brain than brands with dedicated fan bases.

What is it that sets these emotionally engaging brands apart? As part of the study, we also interviewed 14 religious leaders from across the world to establish the components of a powerful religion, and a powerfully engaging brand.

A clear vision

This is the cornerstone of religion. It can inspire great action and (g)...... conviction. To see how this translates into branding, take L'Oréal's mission: 'We sell hope.' Then there's Apple's 1982 brand vision: 'Man is the creator of change in this world. As such he should be above systems and structures, and not subordinate to them.' These companies' visions drive them and guide them.

A sense of belonging

What do Tupperware, Harley-Davidson, Lego and Apple have in common? They're all based on communities. Considering Lego's (h)...... brand equity, you might expect that the company's marketing budget would count in the billions. Not so. In fact, it is so (i)...... that if I recorded it here, you'd probably think it was a typo. Lego doesn't do the talking. It lets Lego maniacs do it instead.

An enemy

Imagine Pepsi without Coke. Impossible, right? A competitor is a (j)...... foil that unites a company from within and pushes the brand's boundaries. The enemy shapes the brand.

Sensory appeal

If you were to close your eyes and walk into a place of worship, the sounds and smells would still tell you where you were: ringing bells, incense, the rumble of a massive organ. Most brands are lacking here. Visit any supermarket or retail chain, and you'll struggle to experience any sensory stimulus, other than visual, that tells you, (k)......, where you are.

Storytelling

The world's **holy** texts are built on (l)...... traditions. Storytelling has driven faith and religious practice, keeping them alive for millennia. Just as every **hymn** and window in a church is linked to an all-embracing story, brands have the potential to build holistic identities.

Grandeur

It's all about thinking big; really big. Cathedrals are massive in scale. This attribute is (m)...... relevant for brands and perhaps more accessible than other religion-related characteristics. Think about the Fifth Avenue Apple Store in New York, the latest Prada store in Tokyo or Burj Al Arab, the world's first seven-star hotel.

Evangelism

This phenomenon has lived for centuries and now takes place via chat rooms and viral videos. Word-of-mouth is powerful, trusted and cheap. Brands must make use of the inclination of consumers to be persuaded by friends. Brazilian cosmetics brand Natura deploys a direct-sales force of more than 718,000 to win converts. Just by knocking on doors, it has established a (n)...... network of brand supporters.

Symbols

Imagine a smashed stained-glass window, a page loosed from a Bible, a snippet of choral singing. Would you recognise where they came from? Most likely. Few brands, however, reflect this consistency. Not many can be recognised without their logos. Examine an iPod, and you'll have problems finding the Apple logo. Yet its design is so in tune with the brand's identity and so (o)...... original that you know an iPod when you see and feel it.

Rituals

Rituals build brands. The act of placing a wedge of lime in the neck of a Corona bottle helps sell those beers. And where did it come from? As one story goes, it was invented by two bartenders in California to see how (p)...... a ritual could spread.

www.adage.com

2.23 Review your answers to Activity 2.22 with your classmates and your teacher. Re-read the text and answer the questions below.

a Why does the author begin his article with the story of Mark?

b How did the author, Martin Lindstrom, conduct his research into brands and religion?

c How are brands such as Apple and Harley different from BP and KFC?

d Why is Lego's marketing budget so small?

e How are hymns and church windows relevant to brand awareness?

f How does the word 'grandeur' relate to both religion and brands?

g How, according to the author, is holding an iPod like picking up a torn page from a Bible?

h How has the act of placing a slice of lime in the neck of a Corona beer helped sell that beer?

2.24 Go back to your presentation of your favourite brands from Activity 2.21. Review your notes and ideas. Now select your favourite brand and compare it to a major world religion with which you have some familiarity. Complete a copy of the table below.

	Your favourite brand	A major world religion
a clear vision		
sense of belonging		
an enemy		
sensory appeal		
storytelling		
grandeur		
evangelism		
symbols		
rituals		

READING STRATEGY

Activity 2.26 is a 'thinking routine' called 'see, think, wonder', made popular by the book *Making Thinking Visible*, by Karin Morrison, Mark Church, and Ron Ritchhart. As you learn in the Diploma Programme, applying this routine will help you connect abstract thoughts and ideas to concrete images or things. Making predictions and asking questions about a text will help you engage more with the text and be a better reader.

Literature

2.25 Discuss your answers to the following questions with a classmate or as a class.

a What is your answer to the question: 'What is humankind's main purpose in life?'

b Do you believe that, by nature, people are imperfect and need a god or a higher being to reach a more perfect state?

c Do you believe that the natural world is evidence of a higher being?

2.26 Text 1.7 is the opening passage from the novel *A River Runs Through It* by Norman Maclean. Before reading the passage, read the three questions below. Make a large copy of the following table in the front of your class. Write your answers to these questions so that they are visible for everyone to discuss.

a   Write one or two words to describe an image or images that come to mind after reading this passage. These words should be concrete nouns, including physical things that you can *see*, *touch* or *hear*.

b   Write one or two words to describe the abstract ideas that this passage makes you *think* about. These should include concepts that are intangible (that you cannot see or hear).

c   Write a question that could be answered by reading the rest of the novel. This question should be about something that you *wonder* or a prediction that you can make.

See	Think	Wonder

Text 1.7

A River Runs Through It

In our family, there was no clear line between religion and fly fishing. We lived at the junction of great trout rivers in western Montana, and our father was a Presbyterian minister and a fly fisherman who tied his own flies and taught others. He told us about Christ's **disciples** being fishermen, and we were left to assume, as my brother and I did, that all first-class fishermen on the Sea of Galilee were fly fishermen and that John, the favourite, was a dry-fly fisherman.

It is true that one day a week was given over wholly to religion. On Sunday mornings my brother, Paul, and I went to Sunday school and then to 'morning services' to hear our father preach and in the evenings to Christian Endeavor and afterwards to 'evening services' to hear our father preach again. In between on Sunday afternoons we had to study *The Westminster Shorter Catechism* for an hour and then recite before we could walk the hills with him while he unwound between services. But he never asked us more than the first question in the catechism, 'What is the chief end of man?' And we answered together so one of us could carry on if the other forgot, 'Man's chief end is to glorify God, and to enjoy Him forever.' This always seemed to satisfy him, as indeed such a beautiful answer should have, and besides he was anxious to be on the hills where he could restore his soul and be filled again to overflowing for the evening sermon. His chief way of recharging himself was to recite to us from the sermon that was coming, enriched here and there with selections from the most successful passages of his morning sermon.

Even so, in a typical week of our childhood Paul and I probably received as many hours of instruction in fly fishing as we did in all other spiritual matters.

After my brother and I became good fishermen, we realised that our father was not a great fly caster, but he was accurate and stylish and wore a glove on his casting hand. As he buttoned his glove in preparation to giving us a lesson, he would say, 'It is an art that is performed on a four-count rhythm between ten and two o'clock.'

As a Scot and a Presbyterian, my father believed that man by nature was a mess and had fallen from an original state of **grace**. Somehow, I early developed the notion that he had done this by falling from a tree. As for my father, I never knew whether he believed God was a mathematician but he certainly believed God could count and that only by picking up God's rhythms were we able to regain power and beauty. Unlike many Presbyterians, he often used the word 'beautiful.'

By Norman Maclean

2.27 Give informed answers to the following questions, referring to Text 1.7.

a How old do you think the narrator is, as he describes himself in the early passages of this novel? What evidence do you have from the text to support this answer.

b How intent is the narrator's father on making the narrator recite long passages from The Catechism?

c What were Sundays like for the narrator, his brother and his father? What actually happened on these days?

d How good is the father at fly fishing?

e Why is it important for the narrator's father to have a rhythmical and beautiful method of casting his fishing rod?

2.28 Compare the opening passage from *A River Runs Through It* (Text 1.7) to the opening passage of the novel or literary work that you are reading for higher level. Discuss your answers to the following questions:

a How is the narrative voice similar or different in these two works? Narrative voice includes the use of verb tense, the level of subjectivity (can you trust him or her?), the use of dialogue and reported speech. Furthermore you can ask yourself: to whom does the narrator direct his or her story?

b How do the opening lines from these two works set a similar or different mood or atmosphere? Note: the 'mood' of a text is often set by the tone of the narrator and his or her choice of words (also known as diction).

c To what degree is a problem or conflict introduced in the opening lines of both works? How does the author create tension from the start of these works?

d How are the main characters already taking shape in the opening lines of both works?

REFLECT

a Reflect on what you have learned from this unit on belief and identity.

b Revisit Activity 2.2, where you were asked to agree or disagree with various statements about religion, faith and belief.

c Re-read the three texts (1.5-17), and listen to Audio track 2 again or watch the suggested video.

d Have you changed your mind about your responses to any of the statements from Activity 2.2?

e Has what you have studied in this unit helped you to define your beliefs and identity? Explain your answer.

Unit 1.3
Beauty and health

<table>
<tr><td>

Guiding questions

- To what extent is your definition of 'beauty' shaped by the media, including advertisements, movies and TV commercials?
- What are the effects of the media's narrow definition of 'beauty' on people's mental and physical health?

</td><td>

Learning objectives

- Become more aware of the adverse effects of the beauty industry on people's physical and mental health, caused by an unrealistic depiction and narrow definition of 'beauty' in the media.
- Be able to articulate ideas about the beauty industry and the pressures on people to look 'beautiful'.

</td></tr>
</table>

We see images of beautiful, happy and successful people in the media every day. Subconsciously we tell ourselves: if we can be like them, we will be happy and successful too.

But what if we cannot be like the people in the advertisements and movies? What if we are bigger, smaller, taller or shorter? What if the image we see on the billboards is not what those people are really like, because an editor has **airbrushed** the images? It then becomes impossible for us to be like the people we see in the ads. We can try to be like them by exercising, dieting and having cosmetic surgery, but this can have an adverse effect on both our mental and physical health.

This unit asks you to question your own definition of beauty and how it is influenced by the beauty industry. You will study images from advertising campaigns, watch a commercial, listen to a radio show and read several articles to gain a better understanding of the beauty industry and its effects on people's **self-esteem**.

Word bank

airbrushed
self-esteem
self-image
fashion
expectations
models
diet
anorexia
media
bulimia
celebrities
whitening
awareness

Getting started

3.1 On the following page you see an advertisement for an Estée Lauder product called 'Even Skintone Illuminator'. What is the effect of the language of this advertisement on its audience? Complete the sentences below.

a   The phrase 'imagine having nothing to hide' makes the reader feel...

b   The inclusion of ticked boxes for 'blotchiness', 'blemish marks', 'discolourations' and 'uneven skin tone' implies that...

c   The name of the product 'Even Skintone Illuminator' makes the reader believe that the product...

d   By referring to a statistic that '79% of women saw an immediate improvement', people are more likely to...

e   The look of the woman in the advertisement suggests...

f   Generally speaking, this advertisement creates a sense of...

In our quest for knowledge a good question is 'What is beauty?' This unit asks to what extent the media have shaped your definition of beauty. In groups, discuss the following questions:

- Is beauty in the eye of the beholder, as the saying goes?
- Or is beauty something universal and timeless, that transcends cultures?
- How might your definition of beauty be defined by your culture?
- How do the media play a role in shaping your definition of beauty?

3.2 Here are several sentences taken from this unit. Write down the words from the word bank, that you would use to fill the gaps in sentences a–e. Not all of the words from the word bank are used.

a How aware are you and your classmates about the way the _____ portray false representations of beauty?

b For years, magazines and the _____ industry and Hollywood said that glamour was just fun.

c They can feel they need to change themselves, to _____ away their natural shape, exercise compulsively and have cosmetic surgery to feel acceptable.

d Meeting our own beauty _____ is difficult because we just don't look like the models we see all around us.

e After reading too many fashion magazines, she had low_____ because she felt she could never look as good as the girls she read about.

Watch and listen 📹 🔊

3.3 Do an online search for 'Dove Real Beauty Sketches – You're more beautiful than you think (3 minutes)'. Dove is a popular brand of beauty products. Before you watch this three-minute video read the list of nouns below. They appear in the same order as they are spoken in the video.

- As you listen and watch the video (without subtitles), write down the adjectives that you hear before the nouns a-k listed below.
- Compare your answers with those of a classmate.
- Are there any words you do not understand? Watch the video a second time if necessary.

a　… artist
b　… board
c　… jaw
d　… feature
e　… face
f　… forehead
g　… questions
h　… chin
i　… eyes
j　… nose
k　… beauty

3.4 In response to the video, 'Dove Real Beauty Sketches', discuss your answers to the following questions as a class.

a　What do you think of this 'experiment'?

b　In this video, how do women use words to describe their own features compared to the words they used to describe other women's features?

c　What is the main message of this video? Do you think it's true?

d　How would you describe your own **self-image**?

e　If you feel comfortable doing so, ask a friend or classmate to describe your facial features. How does their description differ from your own description?

3.5 Study the words in the box below, which have been taken from Audio track 3. Predict what you think the recording will be about.

psychology	self-esteem	advertising	research
insecure	confidence	subtle	blatantly

3.6 Listen to 🔊 Audio track 3, an interview with a psychologist.

- Read the questions below. Judging from the questions, to what extent were your predictions from Activity 3.5 correct?
- Now play Audio track 3 and listen out for information that will help you to answer questions a-g below.
- When you are finished, share your answers with a classmate. Listen again and check your answers together.
- If you are uncertain about the spelling or meaning of any words, discuss them as a class with your teacher.

TIP

- In your Paper 2 exam there will be a listening activity. It might include a question such as Activity 3.5, where you are asked to write down specific words that you hear.

- It's important to read the questions before listening and then make predictions.

- As you listen and write down answers, do not worry about spelling, as this slows down your ability to listen. You can go back later and correct mistakes.

a What is the name of the radio show?

b The interviewer refers to advertising and self-esteem as what kind of problem?

c Fill in the gap. It's always been assumed that women become more insecure or even '. . .' at seeing skinny models in magazines.

d Fill in the gap. Subtle ads, according to the researcher, include pretty models together with '. . .', or where women are in the background of a photograph.

e Fill in the gap. If you take ads that blatantly focus on the bodies and faces of supermodels, where their beauty is clearly dominating the ad, readers become '. . .' confident, paradoxically.

f Fill in the gap. Many women seem to have a defense '. . .' when viewing unrealistic body shapes.

g Fill in the gap. Women begin to '. . .' their own self-image in response to ads that depict sexy models with unrealistic body shapes.

3.7 In the interview, the researcher contrasts ads that subtly and blatantly depict beautiful women. Together with a classmate study images A–C. Rank these advertisements from subtle to blatant. Discuss your answers to the following questions together as a class.

a Do you agree on which ad most blatantly focuses on beauty and the female body? Explain your reasons for ranking the ads in your order.

b Notice that all three ads include a handbag. How focused is each text on the product that it aims to sell? If it is not about a product, what else is it selling?

Image A

Image B

Image C

c   Do you agree with the researcher from Audio track 3 that blatant images of beauty cause women to feel *more* confident about their self-image? Do you think that subtle images of beauty cause women to feel more insecure? How are these ads examples of the claims that she makes?

d   Do you think these ads target men or women? What makes you say this?

e   How do the young men in your class respond differently to these ads than the young women?

CONCEPTS

Variation

One of the main concepts that you explore in this course is 'variation'. Images A-C are different *variations* of the same text type, a print advertisement, with the same purpose – to sell a handbag.

- How are these three variations different?
- How might their differences be received differently by audiences?

Exploring texts

3.8 You are going to read a transcribed interview about Dove's 'Campaign for Real Beauty'. Below is a list of questions that are asked in the interview, but not in the correct order.

- Before you read the interview (Text 1.8), try to work out the order in which the questions will be asked.
- After you have read the interview, check to see if your answers were right. Complete a copy of the table below. The first answer has been given for you.
- The numbers in the text indicate the gaps where the questions (a–h) belong.

Order in which the questions appear 1-8	Question
1	g
2	
...	

a   What's the downside of this kind of pressure to look beautiful?

b   What can I be doing to help myself? I don't always feel good.

c   What about pressures outside the family?

d   Are you saying the narrow standards for beauty are hurtful to girls and women?

e   Do you think Dove's Campaign for Real Beauty is helping to change things?

f   How sure are we that society out there plays a destructive role in the beauty agenda?

g   Where do we get this idea first?

h   What other kinds of harmful things are happening because of the narrow definitions of beauty?

Extended Essay

A collection of advertisements from a single campaign would serve well as a 'cultural artefact' for a Group 2 extended essay.

To what extent is the Dove's Campaign for Real Beauty, effective in raising awareness about the adverse effects of the beauty industry and helping young women build self-esteem?

Text 1.8

Expert Susie Orbach answers questions about the negative effects of culture on self-esteem and body image

Girls grow up knowing that how they look is important. And while girls and women enjoy beauty and **fashion**, they can also worry about their looks, their hair, their tummies, their breasts, their legs, their size and their shape.

(1) …

We get our sense of how important this is as we watch our mums and hear their sighs or, less frequently, see their smiles of pleasure as they look at themselves in the mirror. That's not to say it is our mum's fault. It is just that, as young girls, we absorb from them how very crucial it is to focus on our bodies.

(2) …

Of course we get the idea that beauty is important from other girls, from dads, from TV shows, pop videos and ads. We want to enjoy our beauty and be playful with it but often, too often, meeting our own beauty **expectations** is difficult because we just don't look like the **models** we see all around us.

(3) …

Girls can grow up feeling inadequate, fret about their bodies and their looks and feel bad if they don't conform to the pictures of beauty they see projected on them from TV screens, billboards and ads. They can feel they need to change themselves, to **diet** away their natural shape, exercise compulsively and have cosmetic surgery to feel acceptable. Every girl and woman recognises that beauty is important. But often they do not see themselves as attractive because their uniqueness has not been reflected back to them. What they see in their mirror is someone who is unlike the models.

(4) …

For years, magazines, the fashion industry and Hollywood said that glamour was just fun. No negatives. Girls and women, so it went, like to dress up. They like to press their bodies into different shapes. Just look at the corsets of a hundred years ago. We aren't doing anything special, say the fashion industry.

And of course they are right; women have always been involved in decorating themselves. But it was never imperative before. And it never involved so many women for so much of their lives. In our grandma's time it was important to be beautiful for a few years. Now girls as young as six and women in their seventies and eighties worry if they aren't sufficiently beautiful – and beautiful

today means skinny, big breasted, long legged and so on. Some 6-year-olds already don't go to the beach because they feel they are too chubby. 70% of 9-year-old girls are dieting, even if many of them are quite slim and most aren't by any means podges. In some old people's homes, there are cases of **anorexia** because the older women feel too fat.

(5) …

Yes. I think we know they are. If we look at Fiji, a country without the kind of **media** we are all exposed to, we discover that in 1998, just three years after TV had been introduced to Fiji, 12 out of 100 teenage girls had **bulimia**. The girls were so affected by the US TV shows that they tried to change their bodies so that they would mirror what they saw on TV.

(6) …

Recently we've seen the rise of early caesarean births. A few **celebrities** elected to have their babies at 36 weeks because of the myth that this would make it easier for them to return to their pre-pregnancy bodies. It ignores the importance of those extra pounds for the mother and the good nutrition of the baby and it turns the attention away from mums being able to just settle in with their babies.

(7) …

We don't want to give up the quest to be beautiful. I think Dove's promotion of the gorgeousness of ordinary women is important. It is giving women such a lift to see a version of themselves portrayed on the billboards and allowing them to appreciate their own appearance.

(8) …

You probably have friends who you think are beautiful but they don't feel it. See if that applies to you too. If it does, consider just for a few seconds a day (and build up to a few minutes) that you too are seen as beautiful.

You probably have pictures of yourself from a few years ago, that when you look at them, you think how lovely you looked then. Now ask yourself, did you feel lovely then? If the answer is not often enough, then try to appreciate yourself now. It would be awful to look back again next year and realise how pretty you looked and yet how you missed it again.

www.dove.co.uk

READING STRATEGY

When reading a transcribed interview, like Text 1.8, it is important to consider both the interviewer and interviewee. Who are these people and why are they taking part in this interview? Below are some questions you can apply to Text 1.8 or any transcribed interview. (Hint: To make this interesting, do not read the 'Text and context' feature or the 'Source' of the text until you have answered these questions. You might want to hear the text read out loud first.)

- For whom do the interviewer and interviewee work and what do they stand to gain by doing this interview?

- What makes the interviewee an authority on a particular matter?

- Who is the target audience for this interview?

- Where would this interview appear?

EXTRA

Watch *Killing Us Softly 4* by Jean Killbourne or *Miss Representation* by Jennifer Siebel. These are two interesting films that are useful to discuss as a class. Your guiding question for these discussions could be: 'How do the media shape your definition of 'beauty'?'

3.9 In the left column of the table below are the stems of sentences that comment on Text 1.8. Match these with the sentence endings in the right-hand column to make meaningful complete sentences about the text.

First half of sentence	Ending of sentence
I Girls learn to be critical of their bodies from a young age …	a because they are ashamed of their bodies.
2 The fashion industry says that it is not to blame …	b because they focus too often on how good they looked in the past.
3 The media are to blame for women's insecurities …	c because they see their mothers doing the same.
4 Some 6-year-olds do not wear bathing suits in public …	d because they want to regain their slim figure quickly.
5 Since the introduction of TV to Fiji, many girls suffer from bulimia …	e because they encourage ordinary women to feel confident about their bodies.
6 Several celebrities have caesarean births at 36 weeks …	f because they want to be as thin as the American women they see.
7 Susie Orbach thinks Dove's campaign is good …	g because they portray an unrealistic image of beauty.
8 Orbach suggests women do not appreciate their looks today …	h because they are giving women what they want.

TEXT AND CONTEXT

- Susie Orbach is a British psychotherapist and journalist who helped found Dove's 'Campaign for Real Beauty'.

- Dove's 'Campaign for Real Beauty' started in 2004 after a study (carried out by Dove) revealed that only 2% of women around the world described themselves as 'beautiful'.

- Anorexia is an eating disorder where a person does not eat enough because they are afraid of gaining weight.

- Bulimia is an eating disorder where a person eats a large amount of food in a short period of time, followed by self-induced vomiting, and a lot of exercise and fasting to control their weight.

- 'Podges' comes from the word 'podgy', which is an insensitive term used to describe overweight people.

Identities

Thinking skills

Throughout the IB Diploma Programme, you are encouraged to develop *thinking skills*. As you explore texts that make claims about the adverse effects of the advertising industry on people's self-esteem, adopt a critical approach. Ask questions such as:

- 'Who are the people behind these ads?'
- 'Why would they want consumers to feel insecure?'
- 'Where would this advertisement appear?'

3.10 Until now, you have focused on the beauty industry and its effects on women. But what about men? Look carefully at the image below. Then discuss your answers to the following questions.

a Whom does this target: men, women or both? Explain your answer.

b What impression do you receive from the man's appearance in this advertisement?

c What is the effect of using the following words in this advertisement: charcoal, hydra energetic X, fight, 'magnetic' effect, black, expert?

d The slogan at the foot of the advertisement reads: 'Expert at being a man'. What do you think this means?

e In brief, what message is this advertisement sending?

f How is this advertisement similar to or different from advertisements that sell women's beauty products and accessories such as Images A, B and C in Activity 3.7?

g Do you think this ad might make some men feel insecure, in the same way other ads might make women feel insecure? Why do you think this?

3.11 In the box below is a list of words taken from Text 1.9. Look for these words as you read the text. Match them with the definitions a–i listed below the box. The definitions do not appear in the same order in which the words appear in the text.

pigmentation	texture	rash	dermatologist	bleach
blister	domain	reaction	deteriorating	

a a skin doctor

b an area

c an effect or response

d a small pocket of fluid under the skin

e a chemical substance that removes colour or whitens

f an irritation of the skin

g the physical structure of something; how it feels

h the colour of one's skin

i when something becomes worse than it was

Text 1.9

Addicted to fairness creams?

With the fairness market booming with men too now wanting to become 'fair and lovely', I wonder if anyone stopped to think of its side-effects!

First it was Shah Rukh Khan who created a buzz with his Lux soap commercial and now it's Shahid Kapoor who's hit the headlines for promoting Vaseline men's face **whitening** lotion. While fairness creams had remained the domain of women, we have men who have taken them up rather seriously.

Resultantly, the 'fairness' market is booming what with men too getting in line to become 'fair and lovely'. But in the bid to look good, has anyone thought of its side-effects?

Dermatologist Dr Amit Vij, says, 'Face whitening creams are harmful for all – be it man or woman. They might be in great demand for the fair look they promise but the only ones who've been regular in using it would know the harm that the creams have caused to their skin. That's not to say that the person didn't achieve his goal – of looking fair, but at what cost?'

But going by the texture of men's skin and presuming that their fairness creams have a higher quantity of bleach, are men at a higher risk of skin damage? 'Like I said, these fairness creams are bad for men and women alike. And as for men, their skin is only slightly rough on the beard area, the rest is as sensitive and prone to reactions.'

He continues, 'The main ingredient of these fairness lotions is bleach, so you can understand how people turn fair. And it is just that, causing all the harm.'

Warning of the use of these fairness creams in the long run, Dr Vij says, 'The obvious side-effect is thinning of the skin. Daily use of these creams leads to the skin losing its tightness and becoming thinner in return. Growth of acne is another harm that these creams cause to the skin.'

Elaborating further, he says, 'Also, most fairness cream consumers are unaware of the photosensitive reaction which these creams cause. Due to this the more exposed one is to the sun, [the] worse one's skin condition becomes. This would mean anything from getting pink and red rashes – the degree of which would vary from person to person – to sun burns, blisters, itchiness to burning sensations, each time the person steps out in the sun.

'Such a skin, that has become photosensitive, could also lead to one having problems if he went in for any kind of packs or massage treatments, for those oils or packs could further react on the skin.'

So how much time do these reactions take to show up? 'It varies. For one person, it could react immediately, for another it could take months to show signs of deteriorating skin,' he says.

In that case, the best way to acquire fair skin is 'by doing away with the pigmentation,' advises Dr Vij. 'Fairness creams only hide them, but that's definitely not a permanent treatment and that's the reason why people are tempted to use them regularly. It's important that people realise that bleach can never avoid photosensitivity, which is a big problem once one is struck with it.'

Times of India

TEXT AND CONTEXT

- Shah Rukh Kahn and Shahid Kapoor are both famous film stars in India.

- Fairness creams are popular in India and other Asian cultures, where lighter skin is considered by some to be more attractive than darker skin.

3.12 Answer the following questions to test your understanding of Text 1.9. Give a short quote from the text to support each of your answers.

a   Do fairness creams actually make your skin lighter, according to dermatologist Dr Amit Vij?

b   Are fairness creams more harmful for men than women?

c   What makes fairness creams harmful according to dermatologist Dr Amit Vij?

d   What happens to one's skin when too much fairness cream is used?

e   If skin becomes photosensitive, what can happen to it?

f   Why are men tempted to use fairness creams regularly?

CONCEPT

Audience

How does the advertisement for fairness creams target its audience effectively? How does it appeal to people who want to buy this product? What do they value when looking for a new fairness cream? How might this advertisement reflect values of a culture that is similar or different to yours?

3.13 Text 1.9 explores the harmful side-effects of fairness creams.

a   Does the text convince you that they are ineffective? How reliable is this source? Explain your answers.

b   Together with a classmate study the image above, packaging for two brands of fairness creams. Does it convince you that the products are effective? Why?

c   Do an online search for an advertisement for men's fairness creams. Study the advertisement that you find and present it to your classmates. Explain why you find the language of the advertisement convincing or unconvincing.

Form and meaning

3.14 In Unit 1.3, you have read texts that use parallelisms. Parallelisms are sentences that repeat a particular structure to effectively convey a list of ideas. Here are some examples of parallelisms from Texts 1.8 and 1.9. Notice how the verb tenses in each list of ideas are all similar.

First part of sentence	List of ideas	End of sentence
They can feel they need to change themselves, to …	**1** diet away their natural shape **2** exercise compulsively and **3** have cosmetic surgery	to feel acceptable.
But	**1** going by the texture of men's skin and **2** presuming that their fairness creams have a higher quantity of bleach	are men at a higher risk of skin damage?

Below are four incomplete sentences. They each contain three ideas 1–3, which are *not* parallel. Change the verb forms and add new words, to form a parallel sentence.
Example: *a* Women who suffer from bulimia diet regularly, binge eat and vomit to lose weight.

a Women who suffer from bulimia … **1** They are always dieting. **2** Binge eating is common among them. **3** Vomiting is a way for them to lose weight.

b Men are not spared by the beauty industry, since … **1** The beauty industry targets them just as much as women. **2** They are exposed to unrealistic images of male body types. **3** Financial success is paired with the perfect body.

c Adbusters spreads awareness about the beauty industry, by … **1** They create spoof ads. **2** Events are organised by them. **3** Many articles are written in their magazine and on their website about this topic.

d Dove has received criticism for their campaign, for … **1** Their full-figured models are also airbrushed. **2** They do not include large women. **3** They show their models in their underwear.

3.15 In Text 1.9 you read 'The more exposed one is to the sun, [the] worse one's skin condition becomes'. This type of sentence is known as a *correlative comparative*. It shows a cause and effect relationship and follows a simple pattern.

First half of sentence	Second half of sentence
The more	the more
The faster	the faster
The worse …,	the worse ….
(etc.)	(etc.)

Join the two sentences below, using correlative comparatives. You will need to use superlatives (more, faster, worse, etc.) to connect the two sentences.

Example: **a** The more ads show younger models, the more the number of cosmetic surgeries increases.

a   Many ads show very young models. The number of cosmetic surgeries is increasing.

b   Beauty pageants are becoming more and more popular in West Africa. Weight problems, such as anorexia, are becoming an issue in these countries.

c   Many advertisements are banned for sexual content. These ads receive a lot of attention in the media.

d   Many Bollywood stars promote skin-whitening cream. Many Indians suffer from the side-effects of these creams.

e   Parents talk to their children from a young age about the portrayal of 'beauty' in the media. These children are more likely to have a strong self-esteem.

f   New innovations in beauty products come out all the time. Women are made to feel that they need to keep up with these trends to look beautiful.

g   Awareness campaigns sometimes show anorexic people to shock viewers. These ads actually stimulate anorexic behaviour in patients with anorexia.

Discussion

3.16 So far in this unit, you have considered the ways in which the media define beauty. What is the role of airbrushing in creating this narrow definition of beauty? 'Airbrushing' describes how pictures are 'touched up' or manipulated, using computer software. Look at Image A, an advertisement for eyeliner by L'Oréal, and Image B, a photograph of Aishwarya Rai Bachchan, an Indian actress and model who appears in Image A. Discuss the differences between the two pictures and consider the following questions.

Image A

Image B

a   In which picture do you think she looks more beautiful?

b   What has been airbrushed?

c   Why has she been airbrushed?

d   What effect might this airbrushing have on its target audience's definition of beauty? How does this relate to Text 1.9?

e   How could this definition affect the physical and mental health of women in India?

3.17 Do you think that Dove's 'Campaign for Real Beauty' is effective in helping women increase self-esteem and broadening the definition of 'beauty'? Or do you think that some cosmetics companies are making a lot of money from their beauty products by giving the impression they are doing good? Discuss your answers with regards to Text 1.8 and the image on the right.

3.18 Study the cartoon and discuss your answers to the following questions.

a   Who do you think the man and woman are? What kinds of roles do they have? Where might this situation take place?

b   To whom is the man referring by saying 'we'?

c   What does their body language tell you about their attitudes?

d   What is the main issue that this cartoon is commenting on?

e   Do you agree or disagree with the main message that this cartoon explores? Explain why.

3.19 Study images A and B below. Each image has two captions ('a' and 'b').

a   For each caption state whether you agree or disagree.

b   Organise several mini-debates between groups in the class that take opposing views on each caption. Each group has a few minutes to state their arguments and another few minutes to respond. There could be as many as four debates and eight groups (see the plan below). You may be a member of one or more groups (depending on your class size).

Debate 1		
Group I Image A / Caption A AGREE	versus	Group 2 Image A / Caption A DISAGREE
Debate 2		
Group 3 Image A / Caption B AGREE	versus	Group 4 Image A / Caption B DISAGREE
Debate 3		
Group 5 Image B / Caption A AGREE	versus	Group 6 Image B / Caption A DISAGREE
Debate 4		
Group 7 Image B / Caption B AGREE	versus	Group 8 Image B / Caption B DISAGREE

TIP

At standard level for your individual oral, you will be asked to talk about a visual stimulus for 3-4 minutes with a 4-5-minute discussion. Although there will be no captions, as in Activity 3.19, you should look for points of contention or debate to help you discuss the topic with your teacher. Furthermore, you can write notes like these captions during your 15 minutes of preparation.

Image A

a   The advertising industry supports the cosmetic industry at the cost of women's self-esteem.

b   Thanks to cosmetic surgery women can feel better about themselves.

Image B

a   Both men and women are negatively affected by unrealistic depictions of 'beauty' in advertisements.

b.   Advertisers simply give people want they already want to see: ideal beauty.

Writing

3.20 Imagine you have been given Image C as a stimulus for your individual oral at standard level on the theme 'identities' and the topic 'beauty and health'. You are allowed to write '10 bullet-pointed working notes' in 15 minutes. These working notes may be like the captions from from Activity 3.19. You have 15 minutes to write these notes. When you are done, compare your notes to your classmates' notes. Which notes were the most effective in preparing this oral? Why do you say this? (Hint: you might want to explore the topic of anorexia, self-esteem and the adverse effects of advertising.)

Image C

3.21 After discussing the Dove 'Campaign for Real Beauty' in this unit, write a letter to the company commending them or criticising them on their efforts to promote self-esteem. Refer to Text 1.8 or other images from this unit. You might want to research Dove's campaign in order to inform your opinion further. Find out more about letter writing by turning to Unit 6.1. Some phrases that you might find useful include:

- In response to your recent advertisement, I would like to...
- The underlying message of your advertisement seems to tell audiences that...
- For future campaigns, I would like to suggest that Dove considers...

Extended Essay

For an extended essay on English B you can write about culture and language with specific reference to 'cultural artefacts' (Category 2b). A series of advertisements from a particular campaign could be considered artefacts for analysis. An appropriate research question might read: 'How did the language of the 'Stupid' campaign from Diesel Jeans encourage irresponsible, reckless and loose behaviour among youth in the early 2010s?' As always it is important to study both the original advertisements as primary sources and also other texts and articles as secondary sources.

1

Higher level extension

3.22 Study the image below and discuss your answers to the following questions:

a Is this advertisement for jewelry harmless or harmful? What makes you say this?

b How might this ad make an anorexic boy or girl feel when viewing it?

c Are eating disorders a problem among the people you know? What reasons do they have for having these?

d How big is the problem of eating disorders in your country? Do a quick online search to find out more about this topic. What search terms did you use? What did you discover?

3.23 Imagine a famous fashion model has just died of anorexia. You are a journalist, and have been asked to write a report on this.

- What kinds of questions would you ask? List as many relevant questions as possible.
- As you read Text 1.10, check to see if your questions have been answered by the text.

3.24 Complete the sentences below with reference to Text 1.10.

a Isabelle Caro worked as a …

b When she posed for Nolita in 2007, she …

c The Nolita campaign shocked many people because …

d Caro decided to participate in the campaign because …

e Fabiola De Clercq felt that the Nolita campaign …

f Isabelle Caro's TV career included …

g Isabelle's mother kept her out of school because …

h During her self-imposed diets, Isabelle would …

i After talking to a psychologist, Isabelle …

Text 1.10

Isabelle Caro, anorexic model, dies at 28

1   Isabelle Caro, a French model and actress who became the international face of anorexia when she allowed her ravaged body to be photographed nude for an Italian advertising campaign to raise awareness about the disease, died on November 17. She was 28.

2   Her friends and family initially kept her death secret. Danièle Gouzard-Dubreuil-Prevot, Ms. Caro's longtime acting instructor, informed The Associated Press on Wednesday that she died after returning to France from a job in Tokyo.

3   Though her anorexia was almost certainly a factor in her death, its exact role was not clear, and her weight at her death was not known. But Ms. Caro weighed only about 60 pounds when she posed, reclining and staring balefully over her right shoulder, for an advertising campaign for the Italian fashion label Nolita in 2007. She was 5 feet 4 inches tall and had battled anorexia since the age of 13.

4   The image, displayed on billboards and in newspapers as Fashion Week got under way that year in Milan, was shocking. Ms. Caro's face was emaciated, her arms and legs mere sticks, her teeth seemingly too large for her mouth. In large letters, 'No – Anorexia' ran across the top of the photograph.

5   The photo was taken by Oliviero Toscani, celebrated in the fashion industry for his Benetton campaigns in the 1980s and 1990s, which included such provocative images as a close-up of a man dying from AIDS and prisoners on death row.

6   The Nolita campaign came as the fashion industry was under a spotlight over anorexia, after a 21-year-old Brazilian model, Ana Carolina Reston, died from it in 2006.

7   'The idea was to shock people into awareness,' Ms. Caro said at the time. 'I decided to do it to warn girls about the danger of diets and of fashion commandments.'

8   Some groups working with anorexics warned, however, that it did a disservice to those with the disorder. Fabiola De Clercq, the president of Italy's Association for the Study of Anorexia and Bulimia, said that Ms. Caro should be in hospital and pronounced the image 'too crude.'

9   The ads were eventually banned by an Italian advertising watchdog agency, which determined that they exploited the illness.

10 The campaign gained Ms. Caro widespread attention in Europe and the United States. She subsequently served as a judge on the French version of the reality show 'America's Next Top Model' and worked periodically as a film and television actress.

11 Ms. Caro often spoke out about her anorexia and her efforts to recover, including an appearance on the VH1 reality series 'The Price of Beauty,' starring Jessica Simpson.

12 Ms. Caro's Facebook page said that she was born on Sept. 12, 1982. In her 2008 memoir, 'The Little Girl Who Didn't Want to Get Fat,' she described a tormented childhood dominated by the profound **depression** that gripped her mother, an artist, when Isabelle was 4. **Obsessed** with protecting Isabelle, her mother kept her out of school until the age of 11 and forbade her to play with other children, lest she pick up an illness. She often criticised her daughter for being too fat.

13 'She wanted me to be her little girl forever,' Ms. Caro told Italian Vanity Fair in 2007. 'So as I started puberty I hated the idea that my body was going to change. I wanted to have the body of a child forever, to make my mother happy.'

14 As a result of her self-imposed diet, she would often lapse into comas and awake delirious, not knowing who she was. At one time, she survived on one square of chocolate a day with a cup of tea that she consumed a teaspoon at a time, to make it last.

15 Ms. Caro's long struggle with her disease had alarming ups and downs. In 2006, when her weight dwindled to 55 pounds, she sank into a coma. After months in intensive care, she was advised by a psychologist to break free of her parents, and she moved to Marseille. She also began a blog documenting her struggle with anorexia.

16 'I still eat almost nothing, but I've stopped vomiting,' she said after her photo shoot for Nolita. 'I have started to distinguish tastes of things. I have tried ice cream – it's delicious.'

17 This March, she announced with pride that her weight had risen to 93 pounds.

The Swiss singer Vincent Bigler had been working with Ms. Caro on a video for a song he wrote about anorexia called 'J'ai Fin,' a wordplay in French that means roughly 'I am the end' but has the same pronunciation as 'I am hungry.' He said he wrote the song after being so moved and worried by seeing Ms. Caro on television.

18 Mr. Toscani said that he had visited several hospitals in France, Italy and Germany to find the right model and chose Ms. Caro because she exhibited the classic physical characteristics of advanced anorexia and because her eyes were haunting.

New York Times

3.25 Below is a list of more difficult words taken from Text 1.10. Look back to the context in which they can be found in the text (use the paragraph numbers given) and state whether these words are used as nouns, verbs, adverbs or adjectives. On a copy of the table below, write the words in the appropriate boxes.

Nouns	Verbs
Adjectives	**Adverbs**

a   ravaged (paragraph 1)   b   balefully (paragraph 3)
c   battle (paragraph 3)   d   emaciated (paragraph 4)
e   provocative (paragraph 5)   f   commandment (paragraph 7)
g   disservice (paragraph 8)   h   pronounce (paragraph 8)
i   crude (paragraph 8)   j   ban (paragraph 9)
k   exploit (paragraph 9)   l   dominate (paragraph 12)
m   lest (paragraph 12)   n   delirious (paragraph 14)
o   dwindle (paragraph 15)   p   exhibit (paragraph 18)
q   haunting (paragraph 18)

3.26 Match the words from Activity 3.25 with their synonyms in the box below.

obscene	control	thin	take advantage of	darkly	rule
show	harm	in case	say	decrease	fight	forbid
	shocking	devastated	confused	unforgettable	

3.27 The image below comments on the main ideas from this unit. Discuss the following questions about this image with your classmates:

a   Who do you think is the producer of this text?

b   Who is the receiver or the target audience?

c   Where might this ad appear?

d   What is the effect of writing the text in white boxes across the woman's face? How important is the placement of each sentence on the page?

e   Why do you think some words are in capital letters and others are underlined?

f   Do you agree or disagree with the underlying message of this text? Give reasons to support you answer.

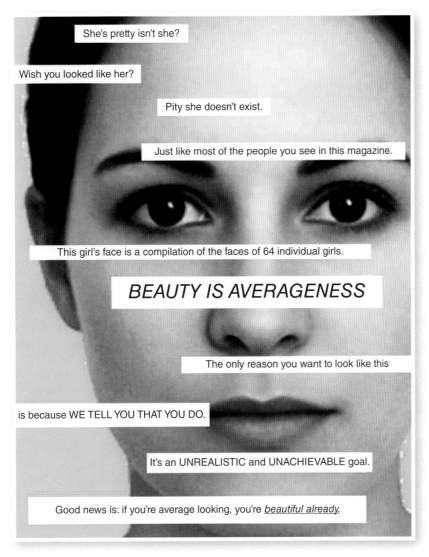

Literature

3.28 As you begin to study literary works for your English B course, it helps to understand more about *figurative language*. Figurative language is the opposite of *literal language*, where people write exactly what they mean. Figurative language can be found in many forms or 'stylistic devices', which are described below. Make yourself familiar with these devices.

a   Assign small groups of students in your class a device.

b   Then read Text 1.11, 'The Diet', by Carol Ann Duffy. Each group should identify an example of their concept or term.

c   Why do you think Duffy used these stylistic devices?

Imagery – Appealing to the readers' sense of sight, sound, smell, touch and taste
Personification – Referring to an abstract idea as if it is a person
Metaphor – Comparing one thing, person or idea to another thing, person or idea without using the words 'like' or 'as'
Simile – A comparison of two things, using the words 'like' or 'as'
Synecdoche – Referring to a thing or person by the name of one of its parts
Hyperbole – An exaggeration for the sake of emphasis
Expression – A common way of saying something, often using figurative speech
Fable – A story, not always meant to be taken literally, with a moral or lesson

Text 1.11

The Diet

The diet worked like a dream. No sugar,
salt, dairy, fat, protein, starch or alcohol.
By the end of week one, she was half a stone
shy of ten and shrinking, skipping breakfast,
lunch, dinner, thinner; a fortnight in, she was
eight stone; by the end of the month, she was skin
and bone.

She starved on, stayed in, stared in
the mirror, svelter, slimmer. The last apple
aged in the fruit bowl, untouched. The skimmed milk
soured in the fridge, unsupped. Her skeleton preened
under its tight flesh dress. She was all eyes,
all cheekbones, had guns for hips. Not a stitch
in the wardrobe fitted.

What passed her lips? Air,
water. She was Anorexia's true daughter, a slip
of a girl, a shadow, dwindling away. One day,
the width of a stick, she started to grow smaller - ~
child-sized, doll-sized, the height of a thimble.
She sat at her open window and the wind
blew her away.

Seed small, she was out and about,
looking for home. An empty beer bottle rolled
in the gutter. She crawled in, got drunk on the dregs,
started to sing, down, out, nobody's love. Tiny others
joined in. They raved all night. She woke alone,
head splitting, mouth dry, hungry and cold, and made
for the light.

She found she could fly on the wind,
could breathe, if it rained, underwater. That night,
she went to a hotel bar that she knew and floated into
the barman's eye. She slept for hours, left at dawn
in a blink, in a wink, drifted away on a breeze.
Minute, she could suit herself from here on in, go
where she pleased.

She stayed near people,
lay in the tent of a nostril like a germ, dwelled
in the caves of an ear. She lived in a tear, swam
clear, moved south to a mouth, kipped in the chap
of a lip. She loved flesh and blood, wallowed
in mud under fingernails, dossed in a fold of fat
on a waist.

But when she squatted the tip of a tongue,
she was gulped, swallowed, sent down the hatch
in a river of wine, bottoms up, cheers, fetched up
in a stomach just before lunch. She crouched
in the lining, hearing the avalanche munch of food,
then it was carrots, peas, courgettes, potatoes,
gravy and meat.

Then it was sweet. Then it was stilton,
roquefort, weisslacker-kase, gex; it was smoked salmon
with scrambled eggs, hot boiled ham, plum flan, frogs'
legs. She knew where she was all right, clambered
onto the greasy breast of a goose, opened wide, then
chomped and chewed and gorged; inside the Fat Woman now,
trying to get out.

By Carol Ann Duffy

3.29 Discuss your answers to the following questions as a class.

a   What do you think is the author's purpose in writing this poem?

b   Who is 'she'? Why has the author chosen for this name for the main character in her poem?

c   Why has the author told a story that is a fantasy or unrealistic? How might fiction comment on reality in this case?

d   Why are the words Fat Woman capitalised (in the penultimate line)?

e   Do you like the poem? Why or why not?

CAS

Text 1.11 makes a connection between mental health and physical health. Is there a CAS project that enables you to raise awareness about physical and mental health problems in your community? What will you do to meet your 'activity' requirement of CAS? How will this help you grow physically and mentally?

REFLECT

Reflect on what you learned in this unit by completing the following sentences. Share your sentence endings with your classmates and teacher to discuss what you've learned.

a The next time I see advertisements that feature 'beautiful' people I will...

b The sketches from the forensic artist in the Dove video (Watch and listen section) made me realise that...

c I learned that the fairness of one's skin is important to some men in India, because...

d Young, skinny models in the fashion industry feel pressure to...

e I understand that people with bulimia and anorexia have difficulties with...

f This unit has raised my awareness about...

Experiences

In the previous chapter, you discussed how one's identity is shaped by one's culture and experiences. This chapter continues to explore the importance of experience in defining who we are.

In this Chapter

- In Unit 2.1, you will learn about various modern-day pilgrimages, asking yourself what it means to go on a journey of self-exploration.
- In Unit 2.2, you will learn about the wonderful world of extreme sports, where people push themselves to their limits.
- In Unit 2.3 you will explore the topic of migration, a powerful force in a globalised world.

Unit 2.1
Pilgrimage

Word bank

reflect

journey

retreat

custom

commemorate

dedication

memorial

experience

goal

accomplishment

adventure

traditional

destination

momento

rite

CAS

Many schools organise CAS trips. While finding a project close to home can be an advantage, you might want to go somewhere further away where people need your help more. There are advantages to organising a trip like this: you have to commit yourself to a goal and learn how to plan ahead, and you might have to do a fundraising activity. A CAS trip, in a sense, could be seen as a kind of pilgrimage.

People who go on pilgrimages usually aim to achieve a goal. What might that goal or purpose be? What do you associate with the word 'pilgrim'?

In this unit, you will learn about American veterans returning to Vietnam to remember and **reflect**; why, every year, young Australians and New Zealanders travel to Gallipoli, in Turkey; and how fans of Elvis Presley consider a trip to his mansion, Graceland, a kind of spiritual **journey**.

You will explore two religious examples. You will learn about a popular European pilgrimage to Santiago de Compostela, in Northern Spain, which for many pilgrims is as much about the journey as the destination. At a higher level, you will turn your attention to the Hajj, the sacred pilgrimage that Muslims hope to make at least once in their lifetime.

Getting started

1.1 What do you think of when you hear the word 'pilgrimage'? Look up the word in a dictionary, if you are not already familiar with it. Create a spider diagram around the word 'pilgrimage', using the words from the word bank on this page. You might have to look up the definitions of these words.

1.2 The four images, A–D show people on different kinds of pilgrimage. What is the purpose of the pilgrimages in these images? Use language from the word bank to describe what you think is going on in each picture.

A

B

C

D

1.3 Try listing some modern-day examples of pilgrimages that you know of. Compare your list with a classmate's. Is there a trip that you do not consider a pilgrimage but which someone else does? Would you ever consider going on one of these pilgrimages? Explain your answer.

1.4 How are the following trips similar to, or different from your definition of pilgrimage? Explain why you would or would not include these on your list of pilgrimages in Activity 1.3:

a   A visit to your grandmother

b   A visit to a war or military memorial

c   A mountain climbing expedition that's physically challenging

d   A trip to Mecca, also known as the 'Hajj'

e   An evening at a stadium concert by a famous pop star

f   A safari trip in South Africa

g   A visit to Stonehenge in England (see 'Extra')

h   A visit to your favourite author's house

i   A weekend **retreat** to a spa and yoga centre

1.5

a   Explain the difference between the two words in each of the pairs a–g below. You might need to check the definitions of some words.

b   How are the terms 'connotation' and 'denotation' helpful in defining these words (see TOK box)?

c   How do these words relate to our pilgrimage theme?

a	trip	journey
b	look for	search
c	habit	**custom**
d	important	sacred
e	place	destination
f	religious	spiritual
g	story	legend

Thinking skills

Activity 1.1 asks you to create a spider diagram, that is also known as a 'mind map'. To make a spider diagram, write a concept in the middle of a large sheet of paper. Then branch out from this concept, by connecting a few more concepts or key words. Continue to create branches with more specific associations on the outer nodes. Much research has been done on the effectiveness of spider diagrams in developing *thinking skills*.

TOK

Words have both literal *denotations* and emotional *connotations*. 'Denotation' refers to a word's most literal sense. 'Connotation' refers to a word's emotional value, which is different for everyone. For example, 'home' may denote a building with a roof where one lives. The connotation of 'home', however, may include family dinners, seasonal celebrations and warmth. What do you think are the denotation and connotation of the word 'pilgrimage'? What are the connotations and denotations of the words from Activity 1.5?

Principled

One of the main reasons for going on a pilgrimage is to remind oneself of important principles in life. As you define 'pilgrimage' in Activity 1.1, ask yourself what these principles are for each trip. This might help you to determine whether or not each trip can be described as a pilgrimage. Think of some principles that you value. What sort of pilgrimage might you go on to remind yourself of these principles?

Stonehenge in Wiltshire, England.

EXTRA

Stonehenge is a mysterious collection of large stones in Wiltshire, England, thought to have been a place of healing or burial from 3000 to 2000 BC. It is not known exactly how the stones got there or how the site was constructed, although there are many theories.

a Find out more about Stonehenge.

b Would you consider a trip to this site as 'a pilgrimage? Why?

c What is the difference between visiting a historic site and going on a pilgrimage?

Watch and listen 📷 🔊

1.6 You are going to listen to Audio track 4, a recording of an American veteran from the Vietnam War, telling his story about revisiting Vietnam with his son.

Here are some words, names and phrases from the recording that you might not be familiar with. Research each item online before listening to the recording. Copy the table below and complete the first two columns.

	What do I already know?	**What have I learned about this online?**
Fall of Saigon		
Nixon		
Military-Industrial Complex		
Agent Orange		
G.I. (military)		

1.7 Read the crossword puzzle clues below and make a copy of the puzzle. Listen carefully to  Audio track 4 to find words that match the definitions in the crossword clues. Note that the verb tenses might be different in the crossword puzzle from their use in the recording. See how many you can answer, then ask your teacher for a copy of the audio transcript to help you complete any that you missed.

Across

4 to be left behind

5 to think about an experience after it has happened

6 When you've travelled across time zones, you may have had problems with jet ___.

9 to be hesitant or unwilling

11 to be scattered about

12 the remainders or the things left over

Down

1 closed building used to house aircraft

2 a person employed in an office to keep records and do other administrative duties

3 pure or harmless

4 to be flown out or transferred by air

7 flaws or imperfections

8 one does something in ___ time, when the time is right for it

10 to put in the ground and cover with earth

CONCEPTS

Context

In order to understand Audio track 4, you need to understand some of the *context* of the war in Vietnam from 1955–1975. Activities 1.6 and 1.8 should help you with this. As you learn more about other pilgrimages in this chapter, ask yourself how much contextual knowledge you need to understand the texts better.

TIP

On your Paper 2 exam you will most likely not be asked to find words for a crossword puzzle. Nevertheless, you can make educated guesses about the answers to the listening comprehension questions, even before you listen to the recording. This will help you listen with purpose, which is necessary for the exam.

1.8 After listening to Audio track 4, discuss your answers to the following questions:

a Why has this radio station featured Tom Carter's story on its programme?

b Why is Tom not very eager to answer his son's questions about the war?

c How does Tom feel about returning to Vietnam after so many years? What makes you think this?

d How do Tom and his son travel to Chu Lai?

e What do the Vietnamese people think of American veterans who return to Vietnam, according to Tom?

f What did Tom do during the war, and how does this make him feel?

1.9 Do an online search for the video 'American veterans reflect on their return to Vietnam' by CBS Evening News.

a Judging from the title of this video, describe the types of images you expect to see. List your ideas with your classmates.

b Then watch the video and see which images match those that you listed.

c How accurate were your predictions?

1.10 Watch the video again and listen for the correct words to fill the blanks in the following sentences:

a But for many who fought there was no … .

b The toll that it took on the people of this country was pretty … .

c Being here helps him write an end to a … chapter in his life.

d Is there … here for some of these men?

e His job was trying to … civilians to support the US.

f A bomb … his hut. He would have been killed.

g The war … massive anti-war demonstrations.

h And took a toll on a whole … .

LEARNER PROFILE

Courageous

IB learners are expected to be *courageous* (or risk-takers). How are Vietnam veterans being *courageous* by going back to Vietnam long after the atrocities of that war?

1.11 There are more videos about Vietnam veterans that you can find online. Do an online search for 'Vietnam vets return to Vietnam'. Choose a video that you find particularly interesting. Describe the relevance of one or more of the following words to your video:

a healing
b responsibility
c haunt
d forgive
e reconcile
f courage

CONCEPTS

Purpose

Text 2.1 gives you information about ANZAC Day and the services at Gallipoli. Generally speaking, texts aim to inform, persuade or entertain their readers. In practice though, the *purpose* of a text is often more complicated than this. Besides informing readers about Gallipoli, what else is Text 2.1 doing? What single word suggests this? How does the *purpose* of Text 2.1 compare to the *purpose* of the poster depicted here below.

Exploring texts

1.12 Before you read Text 2.1, try matching the following adjectives, a–e below with the correct noun from the box. You can check your answers as you read the text.

emotions	services	pilgrimage	hours	onlookers

a early
b unforgettable
c memorial
d interested
e strong

1.13 Find the words in Text 2.1 that go together with these synonyms a–f. They do not appear in the text in the same order as shown here:

a bravery
b well-known
c remember
d makes you feel
e authentic
f most important

Text 2.1

● ● ●

Anzac trips: Trips for 18–30 somethings

- Anzac Tour Options
- Anzac Gallipoli
- Turkey Highlights
- Turkey Map
- Anzac Tour Photos
- Request a Brochure
- Why Choose Topdeck
- Anzac Tour Testimonials
- Tour FAQs
- Contact Us
- Sign up for Newsletter
- Home

Anzac Gallipoli

On the 25th April 1915 Australian and New Zealand soldiers were a part of the British invasion force to capture the strategically important Dardanelles region of Turkey. The courage shown by these men and the equally courageous Turkish defenders is now legendary.

Every year a large group of Aussies, Kiwis and interested onlookers gather in the early hours of the morning at Gallipoli to **commemorate** the bravery and **dedication** of the soldiers of the ANZAC forces. Many have slept out under the stars only to waken to the haunting memory of the thousands of men arriving on the beaches at ANZAC Cove. A dawn service on ANZAC Day, attended by Australian, New Zealand and Turkish officials provokes strong emotions amongst the thousands of spectators nearly 100 years later. A track is carved out of the landscape from the cove to the top of the very hills the troops had to climb and **memorial** services are held at Lone Pine for Australian servicemen and Chunuk Bair for New Zealanders during the rest of the day.

Topdeck has been privileged to operate tours to ANZAC Day services at Gallipoli for 30 years and the commitment to offering a genuine **experience** is paramount. Join Topdeck on an unforgettable pilgrimage.

Topdeck Anzac Tours

- Guided tour Istanbul
- Guided tour Gallipoli
- Coach transport
- Experienced Turkish guide
- Aussie/Kiwi Trip Leader
- Trip hoodie
- Anzac Ceremony Parade Participation and more ...

www.anzactrips.com

Extended Essay

Category 2 extended essays may be 'of a general cultural nature based on specific cultural artefacts'. For example, First World War propaganda posters from Australia and New Zealand, such as the one shown on the right, may be considered 'cultural artefacts'. A good guiding question might read, 'How did the language of propaganda posters convince young Australians and New Zealanders to go and fight in the First World War?' For a Category 3 extended essay on literature, you might want to study the Alan Seymour play (1960), titled *The One Day of the Year*, which questions the value of ANZAC Day. A good guiding question would read, 'Are Seymour's criticisms of ANZAC Day justified?'

A typical propaganda poster from World War I, calling on Australians and New Zealanders to enlist.

TEXT AND CONTEXT

- 'Kiwi' (paragraph 2) is a nickname for New Zealanders.

- ANZAC is an acronym. It stands for 'Australian and New Zealand Army Corps'.

- The battle for Gallipoli was one of the bloodiest in the First World War, lasting eight months before Allied (British, French and Russian) forces succumbed to the Ottoman Army, commanded by Mustafa Kemal, later known as Ataturk, the founding father of Turkey.

1.14 When you have read Text 2.1, decide whether the following statements are true or false. Support your answers with evidence from the text.

a Turkish, Australian and New Zealand soldiers all fought bravely, according to the writer.

b Australians and New Zealanders hold memorial services together at Gallipoli.

c Tourists like to camp on the beaches near ANZAC Cove.

d Topdeck is a travel agency that organises trips for Australians and New Zealanders to come to Turkey.

e This text is an advertisement by Topdeck.

1.15 You are going to read Text 2.2, which is about the Camino de Santiago. Some words have been removed from the text. Study the words below and decide which of the blank spaces they belong in.

a discomfort   **b** revival

c sheer   **d** substantially

e modest   **f** coveted

g secular   **h** picturesque

Text 2.2

In the footsteps of a thousand years of pilgrims

Heading into northwestern Spain, paved roads, stony pathways, wooded trails and cobbled streets all seem to lead to the medieval city of Santiago de Compostela. It has been a (1) … destination for travellers from many walks of life and many levels of European society since the ninth century. Millions of people have walked, ridden donkeys and horses, or been carried to this most famous Christian pilgrimage site after Jerusalem and Rome, often taking months or even years to reach their **goal**.

While recent pilgrimage sites such as Lourdes in France, Fatima in Portugal and Medjugorje in Bosnia might now surpass Santiago for (2) … volume of visitors, the history-steeped Camino de Santiago (Road of St. James) across northern Spain has experienced an enthusiastic (3) … since the early 1980s. This has not only drawn new generations of believers but a global clientele of active travellers with a

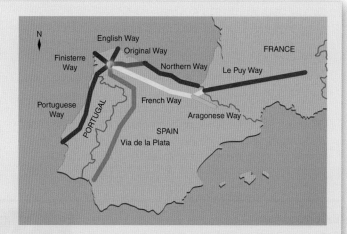

largely (4) … agenda of walking, cycling or even horseback riding through the (5) … , often challenging, countryside and historic townscapes, unchanged in many parts from the days of the earliest pilgrims.

Most people have a life list of **accomplishments** they hope to check off before they wind down; for me, walking a (6) … piece of the Camino de Santiago has been near the top for a while. Feeling the early stages of wind-down coming on, I figured it was time to get going on this one.

Now, I didn't long to hike 750 kilometres or more from the French/Spanish Pyrenees border all the way to Santiago de Compostela, nor carry even a portion of my worldly goods on my back, nor share communal nights in the free pilgrim dormitories spaced out along the Camino. I am, after all, a North American for whom the term "soft **adventure**" has a nice ring, and a Baptist whose motivation to blend a high degree of (7) … into my pilgrim walk was (8) … less than **traditional** Catholics may have thought acceptable. […]

www.travelwithachallenge.com

1.16 Read Text 2.2 again and look for answers to the following questions. Be sure to support your answers fully with reference to the text.

a What kinds of people walk the Camino de Santiago?

b How is the storyteller different from most people who walk the Camino de Santiago?

c How does the Camino de Santiago compare with other pilgrimages?

d How is Text 2.2 different from Text 2.1 in its purpose?

Form and meaning

1.17 Different words have different functions. Learning to identify the differences between nouns, adjectives and verbs will help your reading skills. Use words from Text 2.2 to complete a copy of the table below.

Noun	Adjective	Verb
	Believable	to believe
Challenge		to challenge
	Accomplished	to accomplish
Commune		to commune
Acceptance		to accept

1.18 The gerund form of a verb (the '-ing' form) can help you make longer and more varied sentences. Here are two examples of gerunds from Text 2.2. Notice how the gerund is used to combine two ideas. Make sentences using the gerund form to connect the ideas in the examples below.

Idea 1: I head into northwest Spain.	**Idea 2:** Paved roads, stony pathways, wooded trails and cobbled streets all seem to lead to the medieval city of Santiago de Compostela.

Combined: Heading into northwestern Spain, paved roads, stony pathways, wooded trails and cobbled streets all seem to lead to the medieval city of Santiago de Compostela.

Idea 1: I want to walk a piece of the Camino de Santiago.	**Idea 2:** This has been on the top of my list of things to do for a while.

Combined:

Idea 1: I took up bungee jumping.	**Idea 2:** This has helped me become a better risk-taker.

Combined:

Idea 1: I visit my grandmother's grave every year.	**Idea 2:** This is a family tradition.
Combined:	

Idea 1: We fast during Ramadan.	**Idea 2:** This reminds me that others are less fortunate than me.
Combined:	

Discussion

1.19 After reading Texts 2.1 and 2.2, compare and contrast the reasons for these two pilgrimages. How are they similar or different? You might have to carry out some further research to find out more about ANZAC Day and the Camino de Compostela.

1.20 The three cartoons below make humorous comments on the idea of a spiritual journey or pilgrimage. It is said that there is an element of truth in all humour. What truth about human nature do you think these cartoons reveal? Start your response with the words, 'Sometimes people have the tendency to …'

a

Are we there yet?'

b

OUR COMPATRIOTS IN PARIS

*'Well, now we've seen that, Augusta.
Cross it off the list.'*

c

*'Don't you get it? It was never about the stick —
I sent you there to find yourself.'*

1.21 Below you see an image of the 'Western Wall' in Jerusalem. Do some research online to find out why it is important to Jewish people. Then prepare a 3–5 minute presentation based on one of the statements below.

a   The Jewish practice of visiting the Western Wall is not dissimilar from other popular pilgrimages in the world.

b   To help spread cross-cultural understanding, Mecca, the holy site of Muslims, should be opened to secular tourists, like St. Peter's Cathedral in the Vatican City or the Western Wall in Jerusalem.

c   Whatever the culture or nation, people need pilgrimages to find meaning in life and spiritual satisfaction.

EXTRA

Research in detail one of the pilgrimages from the list below. Hold a question-and-answer session in which you imagine you have just come back from your chosen journey. Classmates ask you questions about your travels and experience.

- The Char Dham pilgrimage circuit in India

- Lourdes, France

- Mecca, Saudi Arabia (*Hajj*)

- The Wailing Wall in Jerusalem, Israel (see image)

- Flanders Fields, Belgium

- A concert by your favourite group or singer

Writing

1.22 Do some research to find out more about the ANZAC Day memorial at Gallipoli, Turkey, which was described in Text 2.1. Imagine you have gone on this pilgrimage. Write a text similar to Text 2.2, in which you tell your audience why this journey was so important to you, in an effort to persuade people to go there. In preparation for this assignment, you might find it helpful to turn to Unit 6.3 on blog writing. Text 1.1–1.3 in Chapter 1 might also be useful examples of travel blogs. Here are some phrases that you can use:

- If you are going a trip to Gallipoli for ANZAC Day, you might want to consider...

- For those who aren't afraid of camping under the stars, you will find...

- I had always wanted to make this pilgrimage because...

- At the outset of the journey I had ambitions to...

1.23 Write an essay in which you argue that pilgrimages are important for everyone, whether religious or non-religious. Explain why you believe that people should go on a pilgrimage of some sort at least once in their lifetime. You may refer to the examples of pilgrimages from this unit, such as Gallipoli (Text 2.1), Santiago de Compostela (Text 2.2), Graceland, Tennessee (Text 2.3) and the Hajj (Text 2.4 higher level extension).

- Research shows that people who go on pilgrimages generally feel...

- In order to understand the value of pilgrimages, one should...

- While the term is not easily defined, a pilgrimage, for the sake of this essay, is considered...

- According to the one study, the increasing numbers of religious pilgrims can be attributed to the fact that...

Text 2.3

Experience Elvis Presley's Graceland

This is the perfect year to bring your family to Elvis Presley's Graceland in Memphis. Graceland, the ultimate rock 'n' roll pilgrimage, will take you on an unforgettable journey that showcases why, 35 years later, Elvis is still the king.

The Graceland experience includes:

Walk in Elvis' Steps at Graceland Mansion

Step inside Graceland Mansion and follow in the same steps as Elvis himself as you enjoy an audio-guided tour featuring commentary and stories by Elvis and his daughter Lisa Marie. See where Elvis lived, relaxed and spent time with his friends and family. The Graceland Mansion tour includes Elvis' living room, music room, parents' bedroom, dining room, kitchen, TV room, pool room and the famous Jungle Room.

After touring the Mansion, check out the other great parts of the 14-acre estate as you tour Vernon Presley's business office and Elvis' racquetball building. Also part of the Mansion tour you'll visit Elvis' trophy building that houses an amazing collection of his gold and platinum records, as well as other great memorabilia from Elvis' early career, his movies, his charitable endeavors and more.

The final stop on the tour of Graceland Mansion is Meditation Garden where Elvis and members of his family have been laid to rest.

Stroll Through The Elvis Presley Car Museum

Elvis loved cars and the **Elvis Presley Car Museum** displays some of his favorites. Stroll down a tree-lined street with a drive-in theatre and see over 33 vehicles owned by Elvis. Highlights include his famous Pink Cadillac, Harley-Davidson motorcycles, Stutz Blackhawks, a 1975 Dino Ferrari, a 1956 Cadillac Eldorado Convertible, the red MG from Blue Hawaii and more. Also, see some of Elvis' favorite motorized toys, including a go-cart, dune buggy, motorised three-wheelers and a pedal car. Some newer additions to the Elvis Presley Car Museum include his Rolls Royce sedans, 6-door Mercedes Benz limousine and Elvis' John Deere 4010 tractor that he used on his ranch and at Graceland.

VIP TOUR ONLY EXHIBIT

Elvis ... Through His Daughter's Eyes

This exhibit is included only as part of the Graceland VIP Tour.

Born in 1968, Lisa Marie Presley became the center of Elvis' world. "Elvis... Through His Daughter's Eyes," looks at Lisa Marie's experience of growing up with a famous father and features 200 items assembled by Lisa Marie and the Graceland Archives team. Home movies, toys and rarely-seen family **mementos** are among the many items that are on display.

www.elvis.com

READING STRATEGY

How might two people read a text differently? You could explore texts by breaking your class up into groups, where each group reads a text from a different perspective. For example, imagine you had to convince a friend to come with you on a trip to Graceland, Tennessee to see the mansion of your favourite rock idol, Elvis Presley. How might you read Text 2.3 differently from your friend? How might a member of Elvis's family read Text 2.3? How might a neighbour of Graceland Mansion read this text? How might a car collector read this text? Reading texts from different perspectives can be an engaging activity.

1.24 After reading Text 2.3, taken from the official Elvis Presley website *http://www.elvis.com*, imagine you have taken the Graceland tour. Write a 250–400 word text, with the same purpose as Text 2.2, in which you share your experience with others to try to persuade them to visit Elvis Presley's Graceland. Your text should be both general, in your explanation of Elvis Presley, and specific in retelling your experiences at his mansion. You might want to research more information about this tour, perhaps from the Elvis Presley website, to support your written work.

Higher level extension

1.25 One of the largest pilgrimages in the world is the Hajj, the journey that Muslims make to the city of Makkah (or Mecca). What do you already know about the Hajj? How is the Hajj similar to or different from a pilgrimage to a military remembrance site such as Anzac Gallipoli (Text 2.1)? Draw a Venn diagram to compare and contrast these two pilgrimages.

1.26 Photographs, a–f below depict various **rites** that occur during the Hajj. Rites are ceremonious, religious acts that usually take place in a certain order. The rites depicted in these photographs do not appear in the correct order. Before reading Text 2.4, try organising these pictures in the order you think is correct. Then after you have read the article, which explains the various rites of the Hajj, look back to see if your order is correct.

TEXT AND CONTEXT

- In 1956, Elvis Presley hit American pop charts with a style of music that became known as 'rock and roll'.

- His music was heavily inspired by African-American music from the American South.

- In the history of music, he is second only to the Beatles in music sales.

a

b

c

d

e

f

Text 2.4

The Story of Hajj

In commemoration of the trials of Abraham and his family in Makkah, which included Abraham's willingness to sacrifice his son in response to God's command, Muslims make a pilgrimage to the sacred city at least once in their lifetime. The Hajj is one of the "five pillars" of Islam, and thus an essential part of Muslims' faith and practice.

Muslims from all over the world, including the United States, travel to Makkah (in modern-day Saudi Arabia). Before arriving in the holy city, Muslims enter a state of consecration (dedication), known as ihram, by removing their worldly clothes and donning the humble attire of pilgrims: two seamless white sheets for men, and simple white dresses and scarves for women. The white garments are symbolic of human equality and unity before God. Since all the pilgrims are dressed similarly, money and status are no longer a factor for the pilgrims – the equality of each person in the eyes of God becomes paramount.

Upon arriving in Makkah, pilgrims perform the initial tawaf, which is a circular, counter-clockwise procession around the Ka'bah. All the while, they state "Labbayka Allahumma Labbayk," which means, "Here I am at your service, O God, Here I am!" The tawaf is meant to awaken each Muslim's consciousness that God is the center of their reality and the source of all meaning in life, and that each person's higher self-identity derives from being part of the community of Muslim believers, known as the ummah. Pilgrims also perform the sa'i, which is hurrying seven times between the small hills named Safa and Marwah, re-enacting the Biblical and Quranic story of Hajar's desperate search for lifegiving water and food.

Next, on the first official day of Hajj (8th of Dhul-Hijjah), the two million pilgrims travel a few miles to the plain of Mina and camp there. From Mina, pilgrims travel the following morning to the plain of Arafat where they spend the entire day in earnest supplication and devotion. That evening, the pilgrims move and camp at Muzdalifa, which is a site between Mina and Arafat. Muslims stay overnight and offer various prayers there.

Then the pilgrims return to Mina on the 10th, and throw seven pebbles at a stone pillar that represents the devil. This symbolises Abraham's throwing stones at Satan when he tried to dissuade Abraham from sacrificing his son. Then the pilgrims sacrifice a sheep, re-enacting the story of Abraham, who, in place of his son, sacrificed a sheep that God had provided as a substitute. The meat from the slaughtered sheep is distributed for consumption to family, friends and poor and needy people in the community. After the sacrifice, the pilgrims return to Makkah to end the formal rites of Hajj by performing a final tawaf and sa'i.

Muslims believe the rites of the Hajj were designed by God and taught through prophet Muhammad. Muslims believe that since the time of Adam, there have been thousands of prophets, including such well-known figures as Noah, Abraham, Moses, Jesus and David, and that Muhammad was the final prophet of God.

The Hajj is designed to develop God consciousness and a sense of spiritual upliftment. It is also believed to be an opportunity to seek forgiveness of sins accumulated throughout life. Prophet Muhammad had said that a person who performs Hajj properly, "will return as a newly born baby [free of all sins]." The pilgrimage also enables Muslims from all around the world, of different colors, languages, races and ethnicities, to come together in a spirit of universal brotherhood and sisterhood to worship the one God together.

www.islamicity.com

1.27 Look again at images a–f. Did you place them in the correct order? Which of the following captions would you give to each image?

a   Performing the sa'i between the small hills of Safa and Marwah.

b   Making a sacrifice.

c   Attaining ummah by walking the tawaf.

d   Wearing the Ihram.

e   Throwing stones at the devil.

f   Camping at Mina.

1.28 Are the following statements true or false? Justify your answers with evidence from the text.

a Pilgrims wear white garments, so that others can easily see that they are on a pilgrimage.

b Ummah is the idea that every Muslim's identity is connected to an Islamic community with Allah at the centre.

c Muslims believe that Muhammad created the Hajj.

d In the history of Islam, there have been many great prophets since Muhammad.

1.29 From your understanding of Text 2.4, what do Muslims value most highly? For each of the words and phrases below, state whether these are Muslim values and where you find evidence of these in Text 2.4. You may also refer to the 'Text and context' box.

a Devotion

b A sense of adventure

c Equality

d Caring for the poor

e Obedience

f Discipline

1.30 The words in the box below are taken from Text 2.4. Use these words to fill in the gaps in sentences a–i.

> consecration   attire   supplication   paramount   re-enact
> consumption   consciousness   dissuade   earnest

a When a new Pope is selected a … service is held in Rome.

b It is … that you prepare spiritually before setting out on the Hajj.

c His efforts to help her were … . He wanted to see her go on the pilgrimage.

d Buddhist monks wear modest, dark red or orange … .

e Muslims who carry out the Hajj are more in tune with God. Supposedly, they achieve a higher level of … .

f After months of praying and … , the people of the village had gathered enough funds to send him on the pilgrimage.

g She tried to … me from going to the place where the accident happened.

h At that restaurant, the fish in the aquarium is for … .

i Every year, Americans dress up as soldiers and … battles from the Civil War.

1.31 Do you think you know everything there is to know about the Hajj after reading Text 2.4?

• Think of a list of questions that go unanswered in this text.

• Combine your questions together with those of classmates, and produce a final list of the questions that you think are the best.

• Make sure you have enough questions for everyone in the class. Write these questions on cards and hand out one question for each classmate to research.

• Write down the answer to the question that you have received on a new card.

• Then shuffle the question cards and hand them out to classmates again.

• Find the person who holds the answer card to the question that you are now holding.

TEXT AND CONTEXT

• Abraham is an important prophet for Jews, Muslims and Christians. They believe that God commanded him to kill his son, Isaac, as a test of his faith, but an angel was sent by God to stop him from carrying this out.

• The 'five pillars' of Islam are 1 the shahada (a declaration of faith), 2 daily prayers, 3 giving to charity, 4 fasting during Ramadan and 5 the Hajj (pilgrimage to Mecca).

• Hajar was Abraham's wife. As another test of faith, God told Abraham to leave her in the desert with their infant son. In a frantic attempt to find water and keep an eye on her son, she ran between the hilltops of Al-Safa and Al-Marwah.

LEARNER PROFILE

Inquirer

An IB learner is an inquirer. What does this mean? Even after reading a text and learning more, it is challenging but useful to go back and ask yourself: 'What remains unanswered?' Activity 2.30 encourages you to do this. It is a skill that you can apply to any text.

Literature

1.32 In the spirit of this chapter's theme of experiences and the topic of pilgrimages, you will read an extract from *Wild* by Cheryl Strayed. It is about a woman who hikes the Pacific Crest Trail, which is 2663 miles (4285 kilometres) long. The story starts with a dilemma. She is in the middle of the wilderness and one of her boots has fallen off a cliff.

Before reading the text, discuss the following questions:

a What would you do in her situation, after you have lost one of your hiking boots in the middle of the wilderness?

b Why would anyone want to walk 2,663 miles?

c Do you think a 26 year-old woman should be walking that distance through the wilderness alone? Why or why not?

1.33 The words below, a–k, appear in the same order as they do in Text 2.5. As you read the text, match these words with their synonyms listed in the box below.

forgiveness	sway	grasp	propel	grief	carry
inhale	stray	recover	useless	knock over	

a catapult   **b** topple   **c** retrieve   **d** gasp

e clutch   **f** futile   **g** orphan   **h** mercy

i lug   **j** stagger   **k** sorrow

Text 2.5

Wild: From Lost to Found on the Pacific Crest Trail

The trees were tall, but I was taller, standing above them on a steep mountain slope in northern California. Moments before, I'd removed my hiking boots and the left one had fallen into those trees, first catapulting into the air when my enormous backpack toppled onto it, then skittering across the gravelly trail and flying over the edge. It bounced off of a rocky outcropping several feet beneath me before disappearing into the forest canopy below, impossible to retrieve. I let out a stunned gasp, though I'd been in the wilderness thirty-eight days and by then I'd come to know that anything could happen and that everything would.

But that didn't mean I wasn't shocked when it did.

My boot was gone. Actually gone.

I clutched its mate to my chest like a baby, though of course it was futile. What is one boot without the other boot? It is nothing. It is useless, an orphan forevermore, and I could show no mercy to it. It was a big lug of a thing, of genuine heft, a brown leather Raichle boot with a red lace and silver metal fasts. I lifted it high and threw it with all my might and watched it fall into the lush trees and out of my life.

I was alone. I was barefoot. I was twenty-six years old and an orphan too. *An actual stray*, a stranger had observed a couple

of weeks before, when I'd told him my name and explained how very loose I was in the world. My father left my life when I was six. My mother died when I was twenty-two. In the wake of her death, my stepfather morphed from the person I considered my dad into a man I only occasionally recognised. My two siblings scattered in their grief, in spite of my efforts to hold us together. Eventually, I gave up and scattered as well.

In the years before I pitched my boot over the edge of that mountain, I'd been pitching myself over the edge too. I'd ranged and roamed and railed – from Minnesota to New York to Oregon and all across the West – until at last I found myself, bootless, in the summer of 1995, not so much loose in the world as bound to it.

It was a world I'd never been to and yet had known was there all along; one I'd staggered to in sorrow and confusion and fear and hope. A world I thought would both make me into the woman I knew I could become and turn me back into the girl I'd once been. A world that measured two feet wide and 2,663 miles long.

A world called the Pacific Crest Trail.

Extract by Cheryl Strayed

1.34 When studying literature, you are really commenting on how meaning is constructed through language. Below are several lines taken from the text. For each line state how the author, Cheryl Strayed, uses language to have an effect on the reader. What does each line really mean to the reader? How does the language construct this message?

TEXT AND CONTEXT
Raichle is the name of a hiking boot brand.

a   The trees were tall, but I was taller, standing above them on a steep mountain slope in northern California.

b   My boot was gone. Actually gone.

c   I was alone. I was barefoot. I was twenty-six years old and an orphan too.

d   In the years before I pitched my boot over the edge of that mountain, I'd been pitching myself over the edge too.

e   I'd ranged and roamed and railed.

f   At last I found myself, bootless, in the summer of 1995, not so much loose in the world as bound to it.

1.35 Return to your answers from Activity 1.32.

a   How was the main character's response to her shoeless situation different from your response to this situation? What does this response say about her experiences? What does your response say about who you are?

b   Would you ever travel that distance alone? Why or why not?

c   After reading the extract, do you still think it is safe or unsafe for a 26 year-old woman to make this trip alone?

1.36 The term 'plot' describes the series of events in a story. A helpful explanation is given below in this model by Gustav Freytag, known as Freytag's Pyramid.

Where in the plot of the novel *Wild* do you think Text 2.5 appears? Is it part of the exposition, rising action, climax, falling action or resolution? Give evidence from this passage to support your answer. In relation to one of the literary works that you are reading in class, discuss how you think the five points of Freytag's Pyramid are relevant.

- **Exposition:** The main characters and their main goals are introduced.
- **Rising action:** A conflict is introduced.
- **Climax:** The conflict becomes very clear. The main character wants to achieve a goal and someone or something is trying to stop him or her.
- **Falling action:** This stage often includes the greatest moment of tension, where everything seems to go wrong and the main character might not be able to achieve his or her goal.
- **Denouement:** After a confrontation between the main character and his or her opponent, the conflict is resolved.

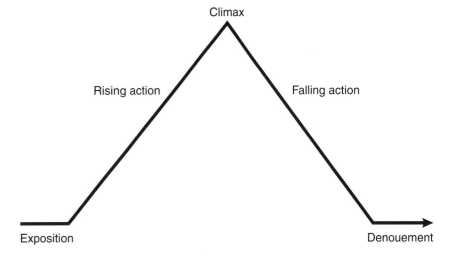

Extended Essay

The Category 3 extended essay for Language B is concerned with a literary text or texts. Note that not all literature has to be fiction. *Wild*, is a literary but autobiographical text. As with all extended essays, it is important that you have a good research question. A good question about *Wild* might read 'In the autobiography, *Wild*, how does the author's use of language inspire her readers to overcome challenges in life?

EXTRA

If you like novels that follow young individuals on a journey, here are a few 'coming of age' novels that you might enjoy:

- Call of the Wild, Jack London

- The Catcher in the Rye, J.D. Salinger

- A Curious Incident of the Dog in the Night Time, by Mark Haddon

- The Hobbit, J.R.R. Tolkien

- The Road, Cormac McCarthy

- On the Road, Jack Kerouac

REFLECT

To finish this unit about pilgrimages and experiences, hold a discussion with classmates to answer the following questions:

a What have you learned from this unit?

b How and why has your definition of `pilgrimage' changed throughout this unit?

c Which text, photograph, audio file or online video did you find the most interesting and for what reasons?

d Have you had any experiences similar to those described in this unit?

e What experiences have shaped who you are today?

f What kinds of experiences do you hope to have in your lifetime? Make a short `bucket list' of things you would like to do. (Note: a `bucket list' is a list of things you hope to do before you die.)

Unit 2.2
Extreme sports

The American author, Ernest Hemingway, once said 'There are only three sports: bullfighting, motor racing, and mountaineering; all the rest are merely games.' People take sports seriously. What's more, dangerous sports like bullfighting, motor racing and mountaineering suggest that people like taking unnecessary **risk**.

What are the world's most dangerous sports? Why are these popular? Should these dangerous sports be part of the Olympic Games? These are the questions we will ask in this unit.

Word bank

risk

thrill

injuries

fatal

hazards

obstacles

competitions

winner

rescue

mortality rates

adrenaline [American spelling; adrenalin -English spelling]

contenders

athlete

gear

77

2

Getting started

2.1 The Hemingway quote in the introduction raises an interesting question: What is the difference between a sport and a game? Before you explore the world of extreme sports, it might be useful to define a few key words. What is the difference between the two words in each of the following pairs? You might have to look up some of these definitions.

a	game	sport
b	fun	adventure
c	risk	danger
d	exciting	**thrill**
e	great	extreme

2.2 Below is a list of 'extreme sports'.

a As a class, assign each person a different sport from the list. Take a moment to research and read more about your sport online.

b Then set up your classroom so that you can speak to every classmate individually about your sport. Explain how it originated, how it is practised, where it is practised, what kind of equipment is involved and why it can be considered dangerous or 'extreme'. Take no more than two minutes for this.

c Form new pairs and explain your sport again, then listen to someone else explain his or her extreme sport to you.

d As a class, discuss your answers to the questions below:

aggressive inline skating	ice canoeing	scuba diving
truck racing	ice jumping	skateboarding
BMX racing	kitesurfing	skydiving
BASE jumping	land windsurfing	skimboarding
bungee jumping	mixed martial arts	slacklining
cave diving	motocross	snowboarding
freediving	mountaineering	snowmobiling
freeflying	mountainboarding	snowskating
freeskiing	mountainbiking	street luge
freerunning	paragliding	surfing
flowriding	powerbocking	wakeboarding
gliding	rallying	waveski
hang gliding	rafting	whitewater kayaking
hardcourt bike polo	rock climbing	windsurfing
ice climbing	sandboarding	wingsuit flying

When describing an extreme sport (Activity 2.2) it might help you to have a (mental) picture of someone practising the sport. How would you describe such a wingsuit to someone who could not see this image?

- What words or phrases did you find yourself using again and again, each time you explained your sport? Make a list of useful phrases for explaining sports.
- Which sport has the most likelihood of **injuries**?
- Which sport has the most likelihood of a **fatal** accident?
- Which sport is the most 'extreme', with the highest level of risk?
- Can you think of an entirely new sport? If so, explain it to your classmates.

Watch and listen 📹 🔊

2.3 You are about to listen to an interview with Alex Weisman, a sports researcher who lectures on Extreme Sports Management at a university. Before you listen to the interview, try to predict what he will answer in response to the following questions. Write your answers in the first column of a table like the one that follows.

a What is the definition of an 'extreme sport'?

b Name two of the top five extreme sports, according to Alex Weisman.

c Why have extreme sports, like kitesurfing, become so popular?

d Name two things that students might study on a degree in extreme sports management.

e Why does the host find it strange to offer a degree in 'extreme sports management'?

f Why, according to Mr. Weisman, is it not strange to offer a degree in extreme sports management?

Predictions (Activity 2.3)	Actual answers (Activity 2.4)
a	
b	
c	
d	
e	
f	

2.4

a Listen to 🔊 Audio track 5 for answers to questions a–f in Activity 2.3. Write the answers in the right-hand column. Be sure to be thorough and complete in your answers.

b Compare your answers to both your predictions and a classmate's answers. Whose predictions were closest to the actual answers?

In Audio track 5, Alex Weisman explains springbocking, as shown in this image. How would you explain this to someone? How does he explain it to the radio host?

2.5 Below are several sentences with phrases underlined. What words or expressions were used in Audio track 5 to express the underlined ideas? If you cannot remember them, listen to the audio track again.

a May I call you by your first name? <u>Yes, you may</u>.

b Sales have gone up <u>every year</u> for the past 20 years.

c So many people are <u>moving over to</u> new sports all the time.

d For a sport to be classed as extreme there has to be some element of <u>risk</u>.

e Some extreme sports are now considered more <u>'normal'</u>.

f The number of wearable cameras being sold has gone <u>up drastically</u>.

g People want to keep their <u>arms and legs whole</u>.

h People want to <u>explore remote places</u>.

i Such <u>contradictions</u> are part of human nature.

2.6 You are going to watch a video about Mike Horn, an explorer, describing his 'Pole to Pole expedition'. This is how his journey is introduced on his website.

'Mike will begin this ground breaking expedition from Europe, then sail his boat, the Pangaea, south to Cape Town, South Africa, the nation where Mike was born. From there it's across the Southern Ocean to Antarctica, where he will cross Antarctica on skis. Crossing finished, he will sail the Pacific from south to north, ending up in the Arctic. From there, he will travel by ski and kayak to Greenland, where he returns to his boat and finishes his trip by sailing back to Europe.'

After reading this introduction, predict which 10 out of the following 15 words will be used in the video. Check the meanings of any words you do not already know.

ice	circle	solution	unaccompanied	nuclear	ship	patience
oxygen	Amazon		jeopardise	expedition	rudder	
	SUV (Suburban Utility Vehicle)			knowledge	unfamiliar	

Mike Horn is famous for exploring some of the remotest parts of the planet.

TEXT AND CONTEXT

- In his video 'Pole to Pole' (Activity 2.6), Mike Horn refers to the 'roaring forties', the 'fifties' and the 'screaming sixties'. These are references to the strong winds that can be found at each latitude below the equator.

- 'Shackleton' is a reference to Sir Ernest Shackleton who led three British expeditions to Antarctica from 1901–1917.

- Shackleton's first expedition was with Sir Robert Scott, who is also mentioned in the video.

2.7 Do an online search for a video with the following title: 'This Explorer Has Seen More Of The World Than Anyone Currently Alive'. As you watch, listen carefully to hear which 10 out of the 15 words listed above are used in the video. Which five words were not used? Write them down. Share your answers with your classmates. Ask your teacher to confirm the right answers.

2.8 Now that you have a list of five words that were NOT mentioned in the video, watch the video again. Listen carefully for synonyms of these five words. What other words are used to describe these ideas?

2.9 Now that you have watched the video twice, what do you remember about it? Write out complete answers to the following questions, without watching the video again. Discuss your answers with your classmates. Then watch the video one final time to see how correct your answers are.

a Where is Mike Horn, as he introduces himself and his expedition in the video?

b What other types of adventures has Mike had in his career as an explorer?

c How long will the expedition take and how many kilometres will it cover?

d What will he do once he arrives in Antarctica?

e Why does he need to arrive in Antarctica as soon as possible?

f What kinds of problems have his team encountered?

g What motivates Mike Horn to go on such a journey?

Exploring texts

2.10 Text 2.6 presents a 'top ten' list of the world's most dangerous sports, but they are not in the correct order. After reading the text, rank the paragraphs in the correct order from 1 to 10, with 1 being the most dangerous sport, and 10 the least dangerous. Use your criteria from Activity 2.2. After you have completed this activity, see how your ranking of these sports compares with a classmate's ranking. How is your list similar to or different from theirs?

2.11 Some of the more challenging vocabulary from Text 2.6 is defined below. Based on your understanding of these words, decide which words belong in the gaps in Text 2.6. You might have to change the form of some words.

a **hazards** = dangers or threats

b deploy = to release

c faeces = excrement, poop

d queue up = form a single line

e itching = eager, excited

f devolve = the opposite of 'evolve', meaning that something grows worse

g deceleration = slowing down

h submerged = underwater

i entice = lure, tempt

j **obstacles** = hindrances

k corpses = dead bodies

l virgin = untouched

m contusions = bruises

n spinal = related to the backbone

o hurl = to throw

Text 2.6

● ○ ○

Top 10 Incredibly Dangerous Sports

You might not remember it, but there was a time when sport had a purpose greater than entertainment and advertising. Early fencing, wrestling, archery, and pentathlon **competitions** trained troops in the practical arts of war. Later, sport refocused to improve physical fitness. But the following list shows places where modern sport has (1) … into novel death wishes.

A) Base jumping

You know, we used to call this behaviour "attempted suicide". BASE jumpers willingly (2) … themselves from buildings, antenna, spans, or earth with nothing but a hand-(3) … parachute to prevent "(4) … trauma." In this game, there's no need to keep score: the **winner** is the one who DOESN'T DIE. Lucky losers get slammed back into the object they just jumped from or break everything they are made of, say, bone. Between 5 and 15 people die each year, according to Harry Parker of The International PRO BASE Circuit. This sport is illegal almost everywhere, and with good reason.

B) High altitude climbing

Today, about one death occurs for every six successful summits on Everest, and each victim had to pass (5) … on the way up. Real mountaineers face every threat you can imagine, up to and including drowning. Gravity must (6) … for its chance to kill you, as hypoxia, hypothermia, frostbite and pneumonia all have prior reservations. Even a regular injury can be fatal, as **rescue** helicopters simply can't get to you and your buddies might be too gassed to help. But if you do summit (you'll probably have to wait in line), keep those glasses on or you'll burn up your corneas from excess UV radiation. It kind of defeats the purpose, huh? To date, 179 out of 1,300 different Everest climbers have died, but **mortality rates** have started to decline since 1990.

C) Heli-skiing

There's a reason some things are so inaccessible – it's God's way of saying, "Don't be stupid". Still, people pay top dollar to be helicoptered (at $500 a pop) to untouched snowcaps, where they leap onto (7) … slopes and ski far from crowds but very close to avalanches. Even the helicopter ride can be dangerous, and many have died en route to untouched powder.

D) Street luging

Climb a big hill on an open-for-business highway, lie supine on an elongated skateboard and roll down. Gather speed and try not to die. That's going to be difficult because you have no brakes, you're an inch from a road surface (8) … to see what bone marrow looks like, and you present a visual profile to passing vehicles that's only slightly larger than a puddle. Which is what you'll be if you have anything close to a lapse in concentration or luck.

E) Bull riding

Rodeo started as the gymnastics of ranching: a series of highly specific competitions taken from key aspects of cattle ranching in the Old West. But there never was and never will be any reason to ride a bull: its only practical application is to make you appreciate your own job – even if you're unemployed. Straddling 1800 pounds of leaping beef routinely results in the rider being thrown 10 feet into the air, with a landing cushioned by a mere inch of dirt and (9) … . And if you don't break your jaw, ribs, or collarbone on re-entry, you still have that bull to worry about (he's still bitter).

F) Cheerleading

Forget the wimps wearing pads and helmets – the real danger is on the sidelines, where estrogen and **adrenalin** combine in one of the newest recognised sports. It has been estimated that there are over 20,000 reported cheerleading injuries a year, making cheerleading the most injury-prone sport in the world for women. Many common injuries include broken legs and (10) … injuries. Think about it – it's like diving on land, with easily distracted co-eds serving as the water. This sport has a lot of catching up to do, safety-wise.

G) Cave diving

The idea for this sport came as somebody was disposing of a body. Take all the regular (11) … of diving (itself a dangerous activity), and add exploring uncharted territory, freezing temperatures, low-visibility conditions, and cramped quarters. And don't forget that ticking clock on your air supply – you can't just go "up" to breathe. On top of that, it's still a wilderness experience, and some of the caves actually have wild animals living in them. According to a recovery team based in San Marcos, there have been more than 500 deaths from this sport since the 1960s. As a result, the National Speleological Society defines a "successful" cave dive as "one you return from." Perhaps they should follow that logic and define an "intelligent" cave dive as "one you don't take".

H) Bull running

The Running of the Bulls ("encierro") is a "sport" that involves running in front of bulls that have been let loose on a course of a town's streets. The purpose is to (12) … or herd the bulls from off-site corrals to the bullring. Any fool over eighteen with more bravado than brains (which would have included me at eighteen) can participate. Every year between 200 and 300 people are injured, mostly with (13) … due to falls. Since 1910, 14 people have been killed in Pamplona's Running of The Bulls.

I) Motorcycle racing

Motorcycling is the most dangerous motorsport in the world. Just one example is The Isle of Man TT event, which has a rich 100-year history. But during that time, there have been over 220 deaths. The drivers in the race are required to maintain their balance while driving through all types of (14) … such as rocks and trees, and even bugs on their windscreens. This is all done while travelling at an extremely high rate of speed.

J) Big-wave surfing

Let's not get crazy here: nobody's saying surfing isn't fun. But any sport with rules for when a shark enters the field of play is not for those with functioning frontal lobes. Big Wave Surfing cranks the dial to 11 by towing surfers into monster 50 ft waves strong enough to crush villages. So if the brute force of the wave doesn't kill you or bury you so far underwater that you drown, you could still bash your head on (15) … rocks or fail to avoid your own board (fickle thing!).

www.listverse.com

2.12 Many words from Text 2.6 are parts of phrases. Match the first part of phrases a–p with the second part of the phrase shown in the box. The phrases are in the same order as they appear in Text 2.6. Explain the meaning of each complete phrase by going back and reading them in the context in which they appear in the text.

Example: a *the arts of war = skills involved in armed battle, such as riding a horse or fighting with a sword*

marrow	suicide	lobes	quarters	force	concentration
territory	dollar	~~war~~	wishes	rate	powder
fitness	business	prone	play		

a the arts of …   **b** physical …

c death …   **d** attempted …

e mortality …   **f** top …

g untouched …   **h** open-for- …

i bone …   **j** lapse of …

k injury- …   **l** uncharted …

m cramped …   **n** the field of …

o frontal …   **p** brute …

2.13 Answer the following questions with short answers based on evidence from Text 2.6.

a Besides being killed, what is one of the risks that BASE jumpers take?

b Why can regular injuries become fatal during a mountain climb?

c What are two dangerous aspects of heli-skiing?

d Do street lugers have to watch out for traffic?

e Where does bullrunning come from?

f Why is cheerleading so dangerous?

g What makes cave diving so dangerous?

h How many people have died in Pamplona from the 'Running of The Bulls'?

i How big are 'big waves'?

2.14 Even though Text 2.6 is about injuries and fatalities in dangerous sports, it is still humorous. Go back and find three humorous quotes from the text. Compare your quotes with those found by a classmate. Why are these parts of the text funny? How does the author use language to make you laugh? Do you think it is acceptable to make a joke of these injuries and deaths?

EXTRA

The author's ranking of these ten sports as 'the most dangerous' is not definitive, as the definition of 'dangerous' will be interpreted differently by different people. Return to Activity 2.2 and the conversations that you had with your classmates. Create your own ranking of the ten most dangerous sports (where number one is the most dangerous and number ten is the most dangerous). Present your list to your classmates and explain why some sports are more dangerous than others. Compare everyone's 'top ten' lists and discuss their differences.

CONCEPTS

Audience

What type of *audience* is targeted in Text 2.6? How does the use of language indicate the type of people who might read the article? You might want to check out the source of the article online *www.listverse.com* to learn more about the readership.

TEXT AND CONTEXT

- BASE (paragraph A) is an acronym which stands for Building, Antennas, Spans and Earth – the four kinds of object from which BASE jumpers jump.

- Hypoxia (paragraph B) is a condition where (part of) the body does not have enough oxygen. Hypothermia (paragraph B) is a condition in which (part of) the body is too cold. Both conditions can be fatal or lead to amputation.

- 'Co-ed' (paragraph F) is short for 'co-educational', where both male and female participants play together.

ATL

Thinking skills

Exercises that ask you to rank, rate, compare or evaluate help you develop your *thinking skills*. A 'bull's-eye' diagram is useful for ranking the importance of ideas and words in a text. To do this activity draw a diagram like the one below, in which you will write the single most important word from Text 2.7 in the bulls-eye (centre). In the second circle, you will write three of the second most important words. In the outer circle you will write six of the third most important words. Compare your diagram with a classmate's. Discuss your similarities and differences. You can apply the bulls-eye diagram to any text.

Use a bull's-eye diagram like this one to rank the importance of ideas and words in any text.

Use the diagram for group discussion.

2.15 Study the images a–e and answer the following questions.

a   What are the names of these sports? Try to be as specific as possible.

b   What do some of these sports have in common?

c   Which one interests you most? Give reasons for your choice.

d   Which two of the five sports are Olympic sports?

e   Why do you think the others are not Olympic sports?

f   Do you think the others should become Olympic sports?

a

b

c

d

e

2.16 You are going to read a text about the future of extreme sports at the Olympic games. Before you read the article, complete the following sentences:

a   When I think about the Olympics I see images of...

b   The purpose of the Olympics is to...

c   The Olympic games could be improved by...

d   The Olympics could include some extreme sports, such as...

Since the writing of this article skateboarding has become an Olympic sport!

What do you think of its inclusion in the games?

Text 2.7

● ● ●

The Extreme Future of Olympic Sports

[1] Let's be honest, nobody will be staying up until 2 a.m. this summer to watch Olympic racewalkers (joggers pretending to "speed walk") on USA or MSNBC. Not to take anything away from the racewalkers, nor the equestrians, synchronised swimmers and badminton players, either, but these events are for most people … well … boring. Other sports, like soccer and the recently removed baseball, have more prestigious events (the World Cup and the World Series) and are pretty irrelevant as Olympic events. Going forward, the Olympics need a shakeup – an extreme shakeup.

[2] Recently, the IOC has done well to adapt to the modern trends in athletics, adopting sports like snowboarding and BMX for the winter and summer games, respectively. Following this trend, the IOC should continue to link itself with the extreme sports community. With the announcement that the X Games will be expanded to a global market, including Asia, Europe and South America, some of the fastest growing sports among youth today are poised to continue their upswing in popularity. In addition, extreme sports generally attract innovative marketers that could breathe fresh life into Olympic marketing and engage entirely different demographics than the summer games typically do.

[3] More importantly, the Olympics are supposed to represent the best from the sports people compete in, all over the world. Why not include the events to which the masses can actually relate? Walk down the street and you could find five kids who own a skateboard with no problem, but you'd be hard pressed to meet someone who just finished their rhythmic gymnastics routine.

[4] With that said, here are five sports that should make their way into the Olympics sooner rather than later (some **contenders** that were scrapped because of logistical and geographical issues were surfing, free diving, and high lining):

Skateboard Vert (Half-Pipe): The IOC already took the step to include the winter version of skateboard vert ramp (the snowboarding half-pipe). Why not round it off by adding the summer event, too? If the IOC could find a way to incorporate the event while Shaun White, the multi-sport **athlete** and

international brand name, is still competing, it would give the event a huge kick-start from the word "go". Skateboarding takes place all over the world, and unlike its rebellious roots, it's big business now. The hardest thing for viewers would be the terminology; goofy names aside, though, it's easy to admire the acrobatics skaters perform on each flight off the ramp.

[5] **Bouldering:** A form of rock climbing, bouldering is a blossoming sport that requires all the skill of technical rock climbing, but no ropes or harnesses. Rather, a foam pad is positioned below the climber as they scale a relatively short route (usually no more than 20 ft. high). More and more people each year are flocking to bouldering because of the minimal **gear** expense, accessibility in gyms, and the shorter time to complete routes. Able to compete on synthetic rock walls indoors, this could be one of the easiest sports to add to the Olympic line-up, logistically speaking. Plus, with more kids gravitating toward climbing as opposed to traditional sports, the ceiling for bouldering currently looks sky high. Even babies are getting in on the action.

[6] **Parkour:** What's not to love about Parkour, also known as free running? A physically demanding sport, athletes combine martial arts manoeuvres with sheer brass to duck, dive, roll, jump, and overcome everyday obstacles with grace and precision. Parkour has become a dream sport for urban athletes bold enough to take on steel and concrete, but Parkour training grounds and parks have also begun to spring up. If Olympic competitions mimic these training grounds, participants could easily participate without the added city dangers (cars, grumpy old people, police, etc.). Probably most famous for the *Casino Royale* chase scene, Parkour possesses the perfect blend of skill and excitement to reawaken bored Olympic viewers.

[7] **Obstacle Course Racing:** Arguably the biggest trend in sports today is the explosion of obstacle course races. The list of competitions is endless, and growing longer each year. People love this stuff. Suddenly, working out has become a sport, and why not? We gawk at the Olympians' bodies,

strength, speed, and power. Why not put a combination of every aspect of athleticism on full display? Typically, these races range anywhere from 3–15 miles in length and force participants to run through mud, freezing water, fire, over and under logs, up ropes, and just about around anything else possible that will challenge the mind and muscle. You know what's better than watching an athlete run countless miles around a circle? Watching them run through mud and fire. Now that's good television.

[8] **Adventure Racing:** Adventure racing is a team relay event that typically involves 3–5 legs, including sports like orientating, climbing, paddling, cross-country running, and mountain biking. Orientating could be axed for simplicity's sake, and with the addition of bouldering (or rock climbing), every other sport is already included in

Obstacle course racing as a sport has grown in popularity in recent years. Why do you think this is?

the summer games in some form or another. It only seems natural that the sports be combined to form one monster race with the countries' best across multiple sports.

Huffington Post

2.17 Return to Activity 2.16 and comment on how you think the author of Text 2.7 would have completed each of the five sentences a–e. Compare your answers with a classmate.

2.18 Text 2.7 contains some difficult vocabulary. Below are explanations of how these words are used in the text. Match the words in the box with the explanations a–t. The explanations are given in the order that the words appear in Text 2.7. You might need to change the form of some words.

gawk	poised	mimic	round off	flock	masses	rebellious
adapt	innovative	blossom	prestigious	adopt	be hard pressed
axe	incorporate	brass	spring up	scrap	goofy	gravitate

a   This adjective describes how some events are even more important than the Olympics for some sports.

b   This verb describes how the IOC has made some changes to go with the trends in sports.

c   This verb describes how the IOC has included some new sports.

d   This adjective describes how the X Games are in a strong position to grow.

e   This adjective describes how advertisers find new ways to promote extreme sports.

f   This noun describes the majority of people in a population.

g   This verb describes how difficult it would be to find someone who does gymnastics.

h   This verb describes how several sports were rejected from the list suggested by the author.

i   This verb is used to suggest that including skateboarding in the summer Olympics would complete the idea of including snowboarding in the winter Olympics.

j   This verb is used to describe the inclusion of skateboarding in the summer Olympics.

k   This adjective describes the unruly origin of skateboarding.

l   This adjective describes the funny words that are used in the world of skateboarding.

m This verb describes how bouldering as a sport is growing in popularity.

n This verb describes how many people are coming to the sport of bouldering.

o This verb describes how young people are drawn towards climbing over more traditional sports.

p This noun describes the nerve or braveness that is required for parkour.

q This verb describes the way Parkour parks are growing everywhere.

r This verb describes how the Olympic Parkour parks should imitate those that are being built in parks everywhere.

s This verb describes how people stare at competitors' muscular bodies during the Olympics.

t This verb describes how the sport of orientating might not be included in adventure racing for practical reasons.

Form and meaning

2.19 The author of Text 2.7 uses different phrases at the beginning of sentences, which adds variety to the reading experience. Match the opening phrases in the box to the correct sentences below. The sentences are listed in the same order as they appear in Text 2.7.

Rather	In addition	Recently	Suddenly	More importantly
		Plus	With that said	

a the IOC has done well to adapt to the modern trends in athletics

b extreme sports generally attract innovative marketers that could breathe fresh life into Olympic marketing.

c the Olympics are supposed to represent the best from the sports people competing from all over the world.

d here are five sports that should make their way into the Olympics sooner rather than later.

e a foam pad is positioned below the climber as they scale a relatively short route.

f with more kids gravitating toward climbing as opposed to traditional sports, the ceiling for bouldering currently looks sky high.

g working out has become a sport, and why not?

2.20 Use the same phrases from the box for Activity 2.19 to complete the sentences a–g below. The phrases 'In addition' and 'Plus' can be used in two different sentences.

a The fans at the fencing match were not very quiet. … they made a lot of noise.

b The climbers will be met at the base camp with more supplies. … they will have the chance to call home.

c It is believed that all Olympic sports are equally important. … advertisers decide that some sports are on TV more than others.

d The fans were shocked. … the referee changed his call.

e … extreme sports have become very popular.

f Yes, we realise that the cave divers must return by 5 p.m. … they must return alive!

g There were high winds that day. … he had problems with his surf board.

TEXT AND CONTEXT

- 'Equestrians' (paragraph 1) are people who partake in horse-related sports.

- IOC (paragraph 2) stands for the International Olympic Committee, which is the governing body of the Olympics, based in Geneva, Switzerland.

- The X Games (paragraph 2) is an annual event in extreme sports, including skateboarding and motocross racing in the summer, and snowboarding and snowmobiling in the winter.

- Vert ramp (paragraph 4) is short for 'vertical', meaning that the half-pipe goes straight up!.

- Orientating (paragraph 8), better known as 'orienteering', is the skill of navigation with or without a map.

TIP

You might find fill-in-the-blank exercises on Paper 2. It is recommended that you read all of the sentences carefully before filling in the gaps. Furthermore, as you fill in the gaps, cross off the words that you have already used.

2.21 The author of Text 2.7 makes several suggestions. What language is used to suggest that other sports should become Olympic sports? There seems to be a clear structure.

- Why not include the events to which the masses can actually relate?

- Why not round it off by adding the summer event, too?

- Why not put a combination of every aspect of athleticism on full display?

Write several sentences with the same structure that propose or suggest the following ideas:

a You would like to suggest to your principal that your school hosts a skateboarding competition in the school's car park.

b You ask your parents to let you go rock climbing in an area where you can be reached by phone.

c You suggest to your friends that you try mountain biking instead of road biking.

Discussion

2.22 What kind of sport qualifies as an 'Olympic sport'?

- Create a list of criteria to assess new sports that want to participate in the Games.

- Imagine you and your classmates are on the board of the International Olympic Committee (IOC) and one or more of the sports from Text 2.7 is being proposed for the next Olympic Games.

- Discuss the arguments for and against allowing one or more of these sports to become Olympic sports according to your list of criteria.

2.23 Look at images A and B. Read the following captions and state whether they would best accompany image A or B or both. Fill in a table like the one a–f on page 91. Give several reasons why you have made these choices.

A

B

a Practising an extreme sport is a good way to grow as a leader. Not only do you develop your physical skills but your mental skills as well.

b Many people who practise extreme sports take unnecessary risks in an effort to boost their ego.

c Friedrich Nietzsche once said: "That which does not kill us, makes us stronger." This is particularly true to the world of extreme sports.

d Extreme sports have a harsh reality that you never see on social media.

e   It's selfish to do extreme sports, when you consider the people and loved ones who depend on you to be there for them.

f   Oscar Wilde once said: "Experience is simply the name we give to our mistakes." If you consider experience an important part of learning, then extreme sports help you to learn quickly.

Caption	Image A, B or both?	Why are the captions appropriate for these images?
a		
b		
c		
d		
e		
f		

Writing

2.24 Write a letter to the IOC in which you recommend that a particular sport becomes an official Olympic sport. In your letter, give evidence to support your arguments. Here are some sentence structures that you might find useful:

- I am writing to you to nominate ... as a new Olympic sport for upcoming games in ...

- Due to the increased popularity in ... , I would like to recommend that ... becomes an official Olympic sport.

- By including ... as an Olympic sport, the Games will appeal to more people who ...

- In order to keep the Olympic Games relevant to a younger audience, you might want to consider ...

For more information on letter writing see Unit 6.1.

Higher level extension

2.25 Match words a–f below with words from the box to make complete phrases. These phrases can be found in Text 2.8. Do you know what these phrases mean? After reading Text 2.8, check to see if you have understood the phrases and their meanings, by reading them in context.

injury	makeup	rush	level	trait	factor

a   mental   b   serious   c   adrenaline

d   personality   e   fear   f   skill

2.26 As you read Text 2.8, ask yourself which of the four images a–d would be most suitable as an illustration for the article, and why?

a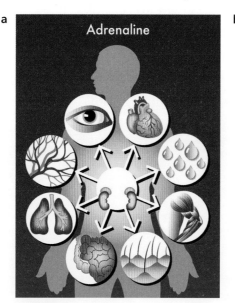

b

c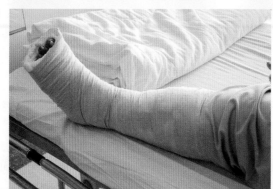

d

Text 2.8

Fear Factor: Success and Risk in Extreme Sports

Yesterday four men were gored during the running of bulls in Pamplona, Spain.

But if you think the risk of serious injury failed to keep hundreds more from running with the 1,300-pound (600-kilogram) behemoths again today during the city's famous multi-day festival, think again.

What it is that drives some to embrace extreme risks, while the rest of us scurrying for the safety of the sidelines?

Lester Keller, a longtime coach and sports-psychology coordinator for the U.S. Ski and Snowboard Association, says that not everyone has the mental makeup to excel in dangerous pursuits.

"It takes a certain kind of person," Keller said. He notes that most of us hit a natural ceiling that limits our appetite for extreme risk and, as a result, our ability to perform well in dangerous conditions.

But others have a much higher tolerance, if not craving, for risk. For example,

Keller points to Daron Rahlves, a top U.S. downhill ski racer who spends the summer off-season racing in motocross competitions. "He enjoys the challenge and the risk," Keller said.

"The high element of risk makes you feel alive, tests what you are made of and how far you can take yourself," Rahlves said in a previous interview with U.S. Ski Team staff. "I'm not looking for danger. I'm in it for the challenge, my heart thumping as I finish, the feeling of being alive," he said. "I definitely get scared on some of the courses. It just makes me fight more. … The hairier the course the better. That's when I do best."

The fear that drives many people away from the risks of extreme sports might be the same ingredient that keeps others coming back for more.

Mountaineer Al Read has logged many notable first ascents over the course of his climbing career. Read now serves as president of the Exum Mountain guides, a pre-eminent guide service based in Wyoming. The company that leads paying clients to the summits of some of the world's toughest – and most dangerous – mountains each year.

Having climbed for over 40 years, Read says he no longer pushes to the extremes as he once did – but the feeling is still vivid.

"I can remember when I was getting into situations where I thought that at any moment I could be killed," he told National Geographic News. "I'm not particularly religious, but I would say, Oh God, don't let me be killed here. I'll never do this again."

But we'd get back down, and when we were safe we'd say, Man was that great!" he recalled. "You forget how scary it was, and you go back again."

Psychologists note that some people seem to have a strong craving for adrenalin rushes as a thrill-seeking behaviour or personality trait.

Like many extreme athletes, Emily Cook's appetite for risk appeared at a young age.

"I was both a skier and a gymnast," said the former U.S. aerials ski champion. "I was one of those kids who enjoyed and excelled at anything acrobatic, anything where you were upside down. It was just kind of a part of Emily."

When Risk Becomes Real

Cook noted that as her expertise grew, so did the stakes. In a sport where skiers perform acrobatic tricks from the height of a five-story building, the consequences of a mistake can be serious.

"As I started doing harder tricks, I was drawn to the fear factor," she said. "There are definitely moments when you're up there doing a new trick and it seems like the stupidest thing in the world. But overcoming that [fear] is just the coolest feeling in the world. Doing something that you know most people wouldn't do is part of it."

Cook was forced to give up her spot on the 2002 U.S. Olympic ski team when risk became reality – she broke both feet during a training jump shortly before the games.

After two and a half years of surgeries and recovery, Cook recently made her first practice jumps into the splash pool at the training facility in Utah Olympic Park. She has set her sights on competing in the 2006 Winter Olympics in Torino, Italy.

How did the injury Cook experienced change her outlook on risk?

"As an injured athlete coming back, generally … my reaction is to stop and reduce the risk a bit," she said. "I've had to change my mentality a little bit now."

"I'm moving up to a jump that was natural before the injury, but now there is a fear of pain, injury, and even the fear of not being able to do it like I could before," she said. "Your body does remember how to do these things. But your mind sometimes gets in the way a bit."

Redefining Risk

Shane Murphy, a sports psychologist and professor at Western Connecticut State University, has worked with Olympians and other athletes. He says he is struck by the way they redefine risk according to their skills, experience, and environment.

"I've worked with groups climbing Everest, including one group without oxygen. To me that just seems like the height of risk. But [the climbers] took every precaution they could think of," he said. "To them it was the next step in an activity that they've done for years. They weren't going out there to get hurt."

Murphy said the perspective of extreme athletes is very different from our own. "We look at a risky situation and know that if we were in [that situation] we would be out of control," he said. "But from the [athletes'] perspective, they have a lot of control, and there are a lot of things that they do to minimise risk."

As Read, of Exum Mountain Guides, is quick to note, climbing and other "dangerous" activities are statistically not as risky as outsiders would assume.

The Zone

Another key aspect of risk perception might be something referred to as "the flow" or "the zone." It is a state in which many athletes describe becoming absorbed in pursuits that focus the mind completely on the present.

"Something that makes you begin climbing, perhaps, is that your adrenalin flows and you become very concentrated on what you're doing," Read said. "After it's over there's exhilaration. You wouldn't have that same feeling if the risk hadn't been there."

People of different skill levels experience "flow" at different times. As a result, some might always be driven to adventures that others consider extreme.

"I can enjoy hitting the tennis ball around, because that's my skill level," Murphy said. "But others might need the challenge of Olympic competition."

National Geographic News

2.27 Answer the following questions with reference to Text 2.8.

a   What is Lester Keller's explanation for why people participate in extreme sports?

b   What is Daron Rahlves' explanation?

c   According to Rahlves, under what kinds of conditions does he perform best?

d   According to mountaineer Al Read, why do climbers go back for more?

e   How do psychologists explain this phenomenon?

f   Why was Emily Cook at a pool in Utah?

g   Emily Cook says: "I've had to change my mentality a little bit now." What does she mean by this?

h   How is the perspective on risk different for those who practise extreme sports? What is Shane Murphy's explanation for this?

i   According to Murphy, what is the importance of skill level in determining one's 'zone'?

2.28   In Text 2.8, several people were asked a number of questions. Using a copy of the table below, try to reconstruct some of the questions each person was asked.

Person questioned	Question asked

TOK
It is not very likely that you have lost a twin brother in a cricket accident. So why read about it? Perhaps a better question is: How can fiction help you understand reality? As a class think of reasons why it might be 'useful' to read works of fiction.

Literature

2.29   You are about to read an extract from *Karoo Boy* by Troy Blacklaws (Text 2.9). **It is about a teenage boy, Douglas or 'Dee', whose twin brother, Marsden, has been killed in a cricket accident. Dee's parents have separated. Dee lives with his mother in Cape Town, South Africa.**

Imagine that you are in his position. Try to think of one word that expresses your feelings in response to these situations. Share your answers with your classmates. Then read Text 2.9 to see if such feelings are expressed.

a   How would you feel if you had a twin brother and he was killed?

b   How would you feel if you saw him killed in a cricket accident?

c   How would you feel if you had to return to school after this accident?

Text 2.9
Karoo Boy

– Oh Dee, life has gone all sour, my mother says to me.

Sour as milk left in the sun.

I begin to cry hard for Marsden dead and gone, and love gone too. But my tears turn to laughter because Chaka dances a giddy dance on the grass, biting at the wind. Crazy bobtail dog, always barking at seagulls and at the coloureds who walk by.

The old coloured man by the lagoon is still watching us, thinking maybe: What a carry-on for folks with a big brick house and grass yard and blackmama maid.

He wanders off with a Masai lamp stand in hand. […] Lips and eyes painted white and wide like the lips and eyes of a clown. Parasols jousting at the sky to the beat of the song that goes: *My geliefde hang in die bos, my geliefde hang in die bos, my gelieeefde hang in die bitterbessiebos.*

My love hangs in the bitterberry bush. The love of my mother for my father hangs in the bitterberry bush. It is as dead as a lizard spiked on a thorn by a butcher bird. It died when the ball hit my brother's head.

I pick up black-eyed, orange seeds from under the coral tree, among the tumbling relics of our front room. I pocket them because my father, teller of myths, told me they are juju seeds, they bring good luck.

– I want you to go back to school tomorrow, my mother says.

I do not want to ride the train without spinning a coin with Marsden for the window seat. I do not want the boys at school staring at me, the undead twin. But then I remember Mister Skinner, who coaches cricket. We schoolboys call him Skin for short. I know Skin will look into my eyes and say:

– Douglas, I'm sorry your brother is dead.

The other teachers will cast sorrowful glances at me and go on as if nothing has changed. I know this because of the time Drew Castle's mother died when a tossed stone flew through her windshield. Skin was the only teacher who went up to him and looked Drew in the eyes and said: I'm sorry.

Cape Town is an unafrican Africa where spears turn into lamp stands, and elephants into foot stools. An Africa of dogs and cats and garden gnomes. Death catches you off guard, lulled by the tunes of Radio 5, or playing cricket on the beach.

So, I will go to school again. I finger the juju seeds of the coral, hoping they will ward death away from me.

Extract from *Karoo Boy* by Troy Blacklaws

TEXT AND CONTEXT

- 'Dee' is short for Douglas, the main character and narrator of this story.

- 'Coloured', in the context of South Africa, is used to refer to people of mixed race.

- *My geliefde hang in die bitterbessie bos* is Afrikaans, which is translated in the following line as 'my love hangs in the bitterberry bush'.

- 'Juju' is a word of West African origin and refers to supernatural powers.

2.30 Using this brief passage from *Karoo Boy*, answer the following questions to the best of your ability.

a Why is Douglas anxious about going back to school?

b What is the importance of the coloured man in this scene?

c How can the reader tell that Douglas misses his brother?

d What is meant by 'it' in the line 'It is as dead as a lizard spiked on a thorn'?

e What is Douglas's opinion of Cape Town?

f Why might Douglas put his faith in the juju seeds?

REFLECT

Look back at the texts, images, video, audio track and activities in this unit, Discuss your answers to the following questions with your classmates:

a Why are sports important for people in general?

b Why do people feel the need to take unnecessary risks in sports?

c Why have extreme sports become so popular in recent years?

d Have you been introduced to any sports in this chapter that appeal to you? Why would you consider (or not consider) taking up some of these sports?

Unit 2.3 Migration

<table>
<tr><td>Guiding questions</td><td>Learning objectives</td></tr>
<tr><td>

• Why do people migrate?

• How is migration changing the world?

</td><td>

• Understand the reasons why people migrate.

• Be able to explain why people migrate and how migration affects the world.

</td></tr>
</table>

Word bank

expat (expatriate)

immigrant

emigrant

abroad

assimilation

integration

refugee

stereotypes

persecution

employment

asylum

resettlement

humanitarian

xenophobia

foreigner

For centuries, people have moved and started new lives elsewhere. While the USA is often called the 'melting pot' of the world, it is not the only country whose population is made up largely of immigrants. For example, there are more Chinese living in Singapore than Malaysians, and more '**expats**' living in Dubai than Emiratis. Remember that every **immigrant** (who has moved to a new country) is also an **emigrant** (who has left his or her home country). Ireland, as you will learn from Text 2.13, is famous for its emigrant population. Did you know that one in every five Irishmen lives outside of Ireland?

In this unit you will ask yourself many questions: 'Why do people move **abroad**?' What risks do immigrants endure? What are the challenges and opportunities for host countries? While questions about immigration can be controversial, they are questions worth discussing. It is important to consider all aspects of the topic before passing judgement. As in all chapters of this book, you are encouraged to keep an open mind.

Getting started

3.1 What do you think of when you hear the word 'immigrant'? Draw a spider diagram in which you explore the associations you can think of for this word. You may use words and phrases from the word bank. Then write a brief definition of 'immigrant'.

3.2 Compare your definition of the word 'immigrant' with the following words and phrases a–d. Compare and contrast by using the following phrase: 'While immigrants are …, migrant workers are …'. You can use words from the work bank if you wish.

a migrant worker

b colonist

c **refugee**

d expatriate (also known as 'expat')

3.3 Match each of the four images a–d with the one of the terms from Activity 3.2. How does each image portray **stereotypes** that we might sometimes associate with these people? Could the people in these images also be 'immigrants'? Why or why not?

a

b

c

d

3.4 For each of the four images a–d, think of a caption or title that best captures the main idea of the photograph. Use one of your captions as the basis for a discussion about migration. You can use words from the word bank.

3.5 Why do people immigrate? Moving from left to right, use one word or phrase from each box in the table below to assemble meaningful sentences. You might need to check in a dictionary for the meanings of some of the words.

People Immigrants Refugees Individuals They	flee from run away from seek refuge from	natural disasters political turmoil unstable economies **persecution** violent situations	in their country at home
	search for seek want to find pursue	better **employment** opportunities relationships family better quality of life **asylum**	abroad in a foreign country away from home
	Immigrate move emigrate		to avoid conflict to be with loved ones to have an adventure

TEXT AND CONTEXT

- The term 'melting pot' suggests that immigrants from different cultures come together to form one common culture. This process is also known as **assimilation**.

- Since the 1970s, many people known as 'multiculturalists' have challenged this idea of assimilation and the melting pot. They believe that it is better to celebrate and encourage cultural differences. They like to speak of the 'salad bowl' or the 'mosaic'. Rather than encouraging assimilation, they speak of '**integration**'. Where individuals, with their differences are accepted as equals.

TIP

At standard level, you will be asked to give an individual oral presentation, based on a photograph and a caption. Images a–d are interesting photographs that could allow you to talk about 'experiences' and 'migration'.

3.6 Immigration is a controversial issue. Brainstorm with classmates and then, in a copy of the table below, list both the benefits and problems associated with immigration. Try to make sure you are balanced in your approach.

Benefits associated with immigration	Problems associated with immigration

EXTRA

On a bulletin board, draw the two-column table from Activity 3.6 in the middle and list 'Benefits associated with immigration' in the left-hand column and 'Problems associated with immigration' in the other column. Include your findings from the activity. Find more texts that comment on the immigration debate in an English-speaking country. These may be webpages, brochures, posters or news features. For each text, highlight their basic arguments and post them on the appropriate side of the table. With pins and string you could connect these arguments to the ideas in the two columns.

TEXT AND CONTEXT

The video refers to a 'Tea Party protest sign'. The Tea Party is a movement in the United States that believes, among other things, that fewer immigrants should be allowed to enter the US.

Watch and listen 📷 🔊

3.7 Do an online search for 'This is Why People Migrate' by AJ+. The video mentions many statistics and numbers, some of which are listed in the box below. Before you watch the video, guess which numbers belong in the gaps in sentences a–i below.

90	83	232	6	11.7	3	1.1	66.6	14

Anti-immigration protester often feel that their way of life and economic stability is threatened by immigrants.

a … million people live in countries that they were not born in.

b … percent of the world's population lives in countries that they are not citizens of.

c … million people from Syria live in Lebanon.

d … percent of the world's refugees live in developed countries.

e … percent of the world's immigrants live in developed countries.

f … million people were born in Mexico but live in the US.

g Wages for manufacturing jobs are … times higher in the US than in Mexico.

h … percent of the private workforce in the UAE comes from Bangladesh, India or Pakistan.

i … thousand Somalis fled to Kenya in early 2011 due to drought.

3.8 Sentences a–g below express the ideas in the video, 'This is Why People Migrate' by AJ+. How does the video's presenter express these ideas using different words and phrases? Replace the underlined words below with her own words.

a   When was the last time you moved to be a refugee or immigrant or a word on a Tea Party protest sign? But <u>please understand</u>: millions of people are living in countries they weren't born in.

b   Every year millions migrate legally and also illegally, voluntarily <u>and against their will</u>.

c   Here are the three major reasons the world is moving <u>in numbers that we haven't seen before</u>.

d   It's a sad fact, but war and persecution are <u>not going to disappear</u>.

e   Lebanon's infrastructure and economy have been <u>pushed beyond capacity</u>.

f   It's not just the West that <u>is drawing people</u>. One big migration trend has people from South Asia moving to the oil-rich Gulf.

g   Those are the reasons why global migration <u>is permanent</u>.

3.9 Listen to 🔊 Audio track 6, an interview with a Syrian refugee who lives in Sweden. The refugee is interviewed shortly after terrorist attacks in Europe.

a   Imagine that you were conducting this interview. Make a list of questions that you would ask.

b   As you listen to the interview, check if your questions are asked. You can use a table like the one below to document your questions and the interviewee's answers.

Questions that you think of before listening	If answered in the interview, what were the interviewee's answers to your questions?

3.10 After having listened to Audio track 6 once for Activity 3.9, decide whether the following statements are true or false. Justify your answers. Then listen to the audio track again and check that your answers are correct.

a   Adad is a Syrian refugee who now lives in Sweden.

b   Adad has personally experienced Swedish people behaving negatively towards him.

c   Adad says that Sweden will continue to welcome refugees, despite the attacks.

d   According to Adad, people in Europe are not prepared for the level of violence that he had become used to while living in Syria.

e   Adad has met terrorists on his journey across the Middle East and Europe.

f   Adad feels that the war in Syria could easily be solved by talking with the terrorists.

g   Adad's brother was angry with him for having his picture taken with the rainbow flag during Gothenburg Pride Week.

h   Adad plans to return to Syria as soon as the war is over.

TEXT AND CONTEXT

- Activity 3.9 asks you to think of questions that you would ask a Syrian refugee. This might be difficult if you do not understand the context of the war in Syria. There are several short videos online that explain this, such as 'The War in Syria Explained in Five Minutes' by Guardian Animations.

- 'Pride Week' is the name of a worldwide festival that celebrates people's rights to their sexual orientation.

LEARNER PROFILE

Open-minded

The IB encourages you to be *open-minded*. How does Adad, the refugee who is interviewed in Audio track 6, show that he is *open-minded*? How do you show people that you are *open-minded*?

Exploring texts

3.11 Read the following short story. It contains several words that have been removed from Text 2.10. After you have read the story, look up any words in italics that you don't know. Then, use the words (a-s) to fill in the gaps 1–19 in Text 2.10.

An older woman was going up the stairs to her apartment, when she paused, with her hand on the *railing (a)*, out of breath. Before her stood a young man, wearing a cap with the logo of some charity *campaign (b)*. At first she was *curious (c)* to know why he stood in front of her apartment door. But she quickly realised that he had been *bothering (d)* people in the building in her flat with brochures. *Instead (e)* of greeting him, she sighed a sigh of *unwillingness (f)* to *engage (g)* in conversation. She was *barely (h)* to the top of the stairs when he asked if he could help her with her shopping bag. 'Did she look that *dire (i)* ?' she wondered. But she let him take her bag, so she could find her keys to the door. Generally speaking, she was *unsuspecting (j)* of strangers.

As she opened her door, she asked what he was collecting money for. 'Don't you remember me?' he asked. He took off his hat and smiled. She was *overwhelmed (k)* . It was her nephew, Jack, whom she hadn't seen for years. He was all grown up, it seemed. There was a *shift (l)* in her voice, as she greeted him: 'Is that you, Jack?' Her mind was a bit *scattered (m)* . She invited him in and showed him a little *hospitality (n)* , serving tea and cookies. She was delighted to talk to him, even though he was indeed collecting money for a good cause. She *pledged (o)* to help refugees who were *fleeing (p)* war-torn areas. Jack didn't have to work hard to *recruit (q)* his aunt for his cause. He said that there were young men, his age, with *struggles (r)* far greater than his in *life (s)*. He only wanted to help others, and it was that kind of empathy that she admired.

TOK

In a discussion on immigration it is important to know the 'truth'. But when reading about immigration, how do you separate 'fact' from 'opinion'. Text 2.10 contains both facts and opinions. Using a copy of the text, use two different coloured highlighter pens to indicate where the author includes facts and opinions. You might find that it is sometimes difficult to separate the two. Compare your results with those of your classmates.

a	railing	b	campaign
c	curious	d	bothering
e	instead	f	unwillingness
g	engage	h	barely
i	dire	j	unsuspecting
k	overwhelmed	l	shift
m	scattered	n	hospitality
o	pledged	p	fleeing
q	recruit	r	struggles
s	life		

LEARNER PROFILE

Caring

An IB learner is someone who cares. How does Text 2.10 show examples of how one message can make others care more? Do you think these examples of caring inspire people to care more for refugees?

Text 2.10

Why people are finding notes in London with messages from Syrian refugees

Elizabeth was walking up some steps when she found a small postcard tied to a cast iron (1)… .

It hadn't been easy to spot with dozens of busy commuters jostling around her but somehow the note had caught her attention.

(2)… , she flipped over the card to find a message from a 16-year-old boy.

It was a cry for help.

'I hope to have a good future. A small family with good work and that is enough,' the words read.

The teenager had run away from home fearing for his (3) … .

Several miles away Selena Victor was about to hop on the Tube when she spotted another message – this time by a mother (4) … violence.

'I just want peace,' it read. 'Without peace, nothing is possible.'

Selena snapped a photo and shared the message on Twitter while others (5)… looked up from their iPhones and walked past without a second glance.

Only a few miles away, another woman called Mollie Yates discovered a note in Westminster from a 17-year-old Syrian girl called Amina.

The teenager was optimistic about the future, despite her (6)… .

'I see a beautiful future… There will be lots of difficulties down the road but they can all be overcome,' it read.

Mollie too snapped a photograph of the note, with the Houses of Parliament in the backdrop, and shared the image on her Instagram account with the hashtag #Human2Human.

People have been finding hundreds of these secret messages from refugees (7)… around London and Edinburgh in the last few weeks.

They've been hidden inside libraries, book stores, coffee shops, museums, tube stations and tied to lampposts and railings for (8)… Britons to find.

The Refugee Crisis: in numbers

13.5 million are in need of humanitarian care in Syria

11 million have fled their homes since the outbreak of civil war in March 2011

4.8 million of those went to Turkey, Lebanon, Jordan, Egypt and Iraq

6.6 million are displaced in Syria

1 million have requested asylum in Europe

300,000 have applied in Germany

100,000 have applied in Sweden

75,000 stranded in (9) … conditions along Syrian-Jordanian border

10,000 refugees rescued from the Mediterranean in 48 hours in Oct 2016

3,502 refugees die attempting to cross the Mediterranean in 2016

43,431 resettlement places offered in Germany

27 other EU countries have offered resettlement places totalling 51,205

0 resettlement places offered in Russia, Singapore, South Korea, Qatar, United Arab Emirates, Saudi Arabia, Kuwait and Bahrain

SyrianRefugees.eu and *https//www.amnesty.org.uk*

It's all part of a campaign by the charity Mercy Corps, a humanitarian aid agency that works in conflict zones and areas of crisis around the world.

The charity specialises in using local people to carry out **humanitarian** work, offering up employment opportunities and not cashing in on sending out 'gap yah' volunteers.

What's different (and refreshing) about this (10) … is that the aid agency isn't asking the public for money.

There's no jingle of coin buckets or dressing up as a giant womble, no stopping people in the streets, and there's no drive to (11) … volunteers.

(12) … , this is a new type of campaign that aims to simply challenge social attitudes. The idea is to show the British public that these are people rather than statistics by leaving messages from refugees for people to find.

The charity is then asking the recipients to share a photograph of the note on Twitter and Facebook.

Amy Fairbairn, from Mercy Corps, explained: 'How we are confronted with this 24 hour news is unrelenting. It is disaster after disaster and people can become a little (13) … by it.

'You see death and destruction in Syria, South Sudan, and North East Nigeria and hear these big numbers and I think you can lose sight of the people at the centre.

'What we want to do is remind people that those at the centre of the crises are just like me and you – and because of that we've got a common human connection.'

'This campaign is about giving people the chance to do something physical, to find the card, to read the quote and to share it online. Then put it somewhere new. It's about bringing refugee's hopes to life and to (14) … people in the debate in a new and different way.'

And the campaign appears to be making a difference.

Elizabeth Cooper, who is 33 and works at Edinburgh University, said she saw one of the cards when walking home from work in the evening.

'I read it, and decided to leave it for others to see,' she told Metro.co.uk. 'In the morning, as I walked to work, it was still there, and other people walking past were not (15) … to stop to look what it was, so I took a picture, tweeted, untied it, and tied it on some railings on Meadow Lane near my office.

'I travelled from France to Syria by bus [in 2005] over a couple of weeks to meet some friends I had met at a conference, and was welcomed to stay with their families. In Syria I experienced such incredible (16) … from so many people.

'It is sad to see what has happened in the country in recent years, and how Syrian refugees are not welcomed in the UK in the same way as I was welcomed there.

'Of course, sharing refugees' stories on cards is not going to solve [all] their problems, but I thought it was a nice idea to make people stop and think.'

Campaigns like this one demonstrate a growing (17) … in how charities are interacting with the public.

While once charities deployed chuggers on every street asking for donations, increasingly many are turning to social media campaigns to spark change at the source.

Part of the problems with the Syrian refugee crisis is the (18) … of nations to open their borders to refugees.

Countries like Saudi Arabia, Qatar, Bahrain and Russia have refused to allow any refugees to settle. In America, the people voted in a president who (19) … to close borders to immigrants.

Closer to home, Britain pledged to take in 20,000 refugees in 2015 as well as giving £100 million of aid but there still remains a core section of the British public who harbour anti-immigration feelings with approximately three-quarters of Britons wanting to impose strict restrictions on immigration, according to a study by the Migration Observatory in November.

Many countries around the world are still closing their borders but with 6.6 million Syrians forced out of their homes since the start of the conflict in 2011, there is growing concern about where these families might end up.

And campaigns like this one might just help shift public opinion in favour of helping.

Metro

CONCEPTS

Purpose

One of the key concepts of IB Language B diploma courses is *purpose*. Text 2.10 is written with a particular *purpose* in mind. Although a news feature, its *purpose* goes beyond informing its audience about facts. Can you find its real *purpose*?

TEXT AND CONTEXT

- Chuggers are people who approach passers-by in the street asking for subscriptions or donations to a particular charity.

- The phrase "gap yah' volunteers' refers to young people who take a year off between secondary school and higher education to volunteer for good causes.

- A 'Womble' is a furry, fictional TV character that appealed to British children in the 1970s.

3.12 After you have checked your answers to Activity 3.11, read Text 2.10 again carefully and give short answers to the following questions:

a   What is the main message that the refugees write on the cards?

b   After studying the box 'The Refugee Crisis: in numbers'. What is the author's purpose in including these numbers?

c   Where are people finding these secret messages from refugees?

d   How is this campaign from Mercy Corps different from most other charity campaigns?

e   Why does Amy Fairbairn believe her campaign will be effective?

f   Why is Elizabeth Cooper more likely to care about the refugee crisis in Syria?

g   What evidence suggests that people in the western countries, like the US and the UK, are reluctant to take in more refugees?

3.13 Text 2.11 is the story of a woman who emigrated from Zimbabwe to South Africa. The eight paragraphs are printed here in the wrong order. Read each paragraph carefully and then, using the letters in the text, list the paragraphs (1–8) in what you think is the correct order. For example, 1 = C.

3.14 In Activity 3.13, you were looking for connections between paragraphs. These 'connections' are the clues for solving the puzzle. Explain how you knew the right order by copying and completing the following sentences.

a   I knew that paragraph … came after paragraph because of the word ' … '.

b   The word ' … ' refers to the word ' … ' in the previous paragraph.

c   The main idea of paragraph ,… is … . This connects to the main idea of the following/ previous paragraph, which states … .

Text 2.11
Zimbabwean immigrants face afro-phobia in South Africa

[A]   All these people were scattered in Zimbabwe – running away from the situation in their home country, South Africa. Our fourth largest city, Mutare, was filled with refugees from other places too, including Mozambique. Over the years we saw many African nationals from different countries come to live in Zimbabwe. If they were to be honest, they could never say they were ill-treated. They were at home. As long as they were on Zimbabwean soil, they were at home. We accepted South Africans or any African as our brothers and still do to this day. No questions asked. Never in Zimbabwe did we dream that our country would be in a situation like we have today.

[B]   Most of us left because we did not agree with the policies in our home country, and there was nothing we could do to change them. Some of us even got into trouble for voicing concerns or disagreeing with those polices. All I know is that it is never easy for anyone to leave home without any plan or a thing to your name to go and start your life all over again. That is why it is called refuge. It's not easy to start all over again and adapt to the changes that you come across in a foreign land.

[C]   Every year as I was growing up, in Harare, Zimbabwe, we celebrated Commonwealth Day at my little school and its community called Sunningdale 1.

[D]   We have stuck it out here in South Africa with all the hostility that we have to tolerate. But never in my wildest imagination did I ever think that it would get to **xenophobia** /afro-phobia attacks. Blacks against blacks. As I am writing this I am very emotional. I cannot stop crying. I can't believe it's happening. I have been displaced, and I find it very hard to trust anyone.

READING STRATEGY

Making a list of questions addressing the author of a text is a very effective way to be an engaged reader. Imagine you could interview the author of Text 2.11. What questions would you ask her?

Once you have placed the paragraphs in the right order (Activity 3.13), read the text again and look for sentences or phrases that you could ask questions about. For example, the author writes: 'Every person who left Zimbabwe left for reasons best known to them.' You might want to ask her: 'Why did *you* leave Zimbabwe?'

TEXT AND CONTEXT

- Because of political and economic problems in Zimbabwe that began in the 1990s, between 1 and 5 million Zimbabweans have emigrated to South Africa.

- Many of these immigrants are considered 'skilled workers', meaning they are educated and have the qualifications to do skilled work. Many South Africans are afraid of losing their jobs to them.

- 'Xenophobia' (paragraph D) is defined as a fear of foreigners. There have been instances of xenophobic violence against Zimbabweans in South Africa. The term 'afro-phobia' is a combination of words, meaning 'a fear of fellow Africans'.

[E] The reaction ranges from a rude insult or mockery, to silence. Imagine you are on the train or taxi and the journey becomes quite unbearable. You are afraid to ask for directions because they will go out of their way to make you lose your way. This is not all of them. There are a few saints who love and respect other people and who are helpful and friendly. But it's always a nine out of ten chance. They will make it worse for you if at work the employer prefers you because you are educated and you understand common sense. Because of where our nation has been, Zimbabweans will work anywhere, regardless of education, just to better our lives and for that, fellow Africans here in South Africa get very jealous.

[F] Little did I know that at this particular school, the majority of pupils were coloured people from a place called Cape Town in South Africa and that some words that they were speaking or putting into our vocabulary were Afrikaans words. I did not know that next door to me in the township of Mbare, not so far away from Sunningdale was a Xhosa family, The Tutanis, from the Eastern Cape; they live there up to this day. I meet some of the people that I went to school with here in South Africa, and they speak the same language and they are not afraid to call my home their home.

[G] We had the best of everything until one day, without expecting it, we found ourselves in an economic situation that is difficult to endure. After much deliberation we decided to come here to South Africa not because we had accommodated them before but because we needed help with our situation. Every person who left Zimbabwe left for reasons best known to them and why they chose wherever they went is a long story.

[H] It's even harder when you are rejected because you are a **foreigner**. What foreigner? I am an African. From a distance I look like one of the black South Africans. It's only when the locals speak to me and I answer back either in the same language or in English that they pick it up that I am a 'foreigner' and the reaction thereafter leaves one stunned to say the least.

Extract from *We Have Done Nothing to Them* by Cynthia Chitongo

3.15 Once you have placed the paragraphs in Text 2.11 in the correct order, write brief answers to the following questions, with examples from the text.

a Who were the author's classmates, neighbours and friends when she was growing up in Harare, Zimbabwe?

b Why did the author have to leave Zimbabwe?

c What kinds of problems does she experience in South Africa?

d Why are South Africans 'jealous' of her?

e Why does the woman cry as she writes this text?

Extended Essay

Notice that the author of Text 2.11 writes: 'It's only when the locals speak to me and I answer back either in the same language or in English that they pick it up that I am a "foreigner".'

One of the Category 2 types of extended essays can be an 'essay of a sociocultural nature with an impact on the language'. Such essays might focus on how discrimination is often based on differences in language use. For your extended essay you can explore a particular variety of English in a particular context, such as the Zimbabwean accent in South Africa, an Irish accent in England or an English accent in the USA. Be sure to include examples of language in use, either in films, on websites or in radio programmes. A good research question might read: 'How does language play a role in stereotyping people in the film *Snatch* by Guy Ritchie?'

CAS
The author of Text 2.11 is both a skilled immigrant and an asylum seeker. How are asylum seekers and refugees treated in the country where you live? What could you do to reduce the stress that they experience? Contact local authorities and find out if you can help by offering language lessons, building homes or collecting information. You might not know how you can help until you have visited a centre for asylum seekers, which can be recommended as a worthwhile experience in itself.

Form and meaning

You are about to read Text 2.12 from Immigration Watch Canada, a group of activists who want to reduce the number of immigrants coming into Canada each year. The text uses different verb tenses to describe the present and the past.

3.16 Read the following sentences a–j from the text. Complete a copy of the table below, placing each sentence letter in the appropriate column.

a Immigration Watch Canada is an organisation of Canadians.

b But immigration has become those two things.

c Why has Canada's 250,000 per year immigration intake remained in place for 20 years?

d These politicians claim that this is a superior moral position.

e They have also pretended that these policies are in the interest of Canada.

f This shameless betrayal of Canada and the promotion of political party self-interest began in 1990 …

g … when one political party (the Progressive Conservatives) increased immigration levels to 250,000 per year.

h Since then, all other parties have adopted the same policy.

i All pretend that their actions are helping people in the rest of the world.

j The reality is that Canada's 250,000 per year immigration intake since 1990 has been far too high.

Category I	Category II	Category III
These sentences describe the present, i.e. the way things are today.	These sentences describe the past. These events are over and complete.	These sentences describe the effects of past events in the present. These events or actions are not over or done.

3.17 After placing sentences a–j into the appropriate categories, underline all of the verbs that are used in these sentences. Do you notice a trend? Can you explain how we use these three forms of verbs to talk about the past and the present?

The timeline below might help you.

- The verb tense from Category I is called the 'present simple'.
- The verb tense from Category II is called the 'past simple'.
- The verb tense from Category III is called the 'present perfect'.

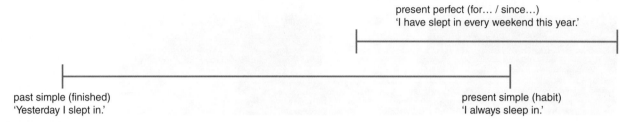

present perfect (for… / since…)
'I have slept in every weekend this year.'

past simple (finished)
'Yesterday I slept in.'

present simple (habit)
'I always sleep in.'

3.18 Here is an exercise to help you practise using these three verb tenses. Select the most appropriate verb tense from those shown in the brackets.

a In Singapore, the Chinese (always outnumbered/have always outnumbered/always outnumber) any other ethnic group.

b Even since the end of slavery, 'human trafficking' (continued/has continued/continues) to be a global issue.

c For hundreds of years, the Irish (emigrated/have emigrated/ emigrate), leaving their home behind.

d The text on the Statue of Liberty (read/has read/reads) 'Give me your tired, your poor, your huddled masses yearning to breathe free.'

e The militia known as the 'Minutemen' regularly (patrolled/have patrolled/patrol) the US/Mexico border these days.

f On 26 January 1788 ships full of British prisoners (arrived/have arrived/arrive) at the penal colony in Port Jackson, now known as Sydney, Australia.

g Since economic turmoil hit Zimbabwe in 2000, many people (left/ have left/leave) the country.

h Religious immigrants called Puritans (came/have come/come) to America between 1629 and 1642.

3.19 The authors of Text 2.12 believe that too many immigrants enter Canada each year. Look back to Activity 3.6 and see if any of the arguments from Text 2.12 relate to your own ideas in the column 'Problems associated with immigration'.

Text 2.12

A Serious Look at Canada's Immigration Policies

Immigration Watch Canada is an organisation of Canadians who believe that immigration has to serve the interests of its own citizens. It cannot be turned into a social assistance job-finding program for other countries. It should not be a method to suppress wages and provide employers with an unending supply of low-wage labour. It should never be a social engineering experiment that is conducted on Canadians without the consent of Canadians.

But immigration has become those three things.

Why? In particular, why has Canada's 250 000 per year immigration intake remained in place for 25 years?

The answer is that for many decades, Canada's major political parties have assumed that, on the immigration issue in particular, they know better the average Canadians.

TEXT AND CONTEXT

- Canada has one of the highest per capita immigration rates in the world, meaning the ratio of immigrants to citizens is relatively high. This has led to high population growth in urban areas.

- Immigration is high for several reasons. The government supports 'family reunification', meaning that once one immigrant has been granted citizenship, other family members may join him or her in Canada.

- The largest number of immigrants come for economic reasons. Skilled workers make up a part of this group. From 1998 to 2012, most immigrants came from China, India and the Philippines.

These politicians imply that the primary purpose of immigration is to help people in other countries, whether this help is to protect them from persecution or from unemployment. These politicians claim that their position is morally superior, and that this is why they support current immigration policies. They have also pretended that these policies are in the interest of Canada. But, in reality, the policies are intended solely to help each of the political parties get a share of the immigrant vote.

This shameless betrayal of Canada and the promotion of political party self-interest began in 1990 when one political party (the Progressive Conservatives) increased immigration levels to 250 000 per year. At the time they did this, they announced they were doing it in order to capture more of the immigrant vote. This might sound hard to believe because it is so brazen, but it is a fact. Since then, all other parties have adopted the same policy. All pretend that their actions are helping people in the rest of the world and that this immigration flood is literally and figuratively enriching Canadian society.

The reality is that Canada's 250 000 per year immigration intake since 1990 has been far too high. In fact, Canada's intake

(a) … the highest per capita in the world. And, contrary to the claims of our political parties, it (b) … destructive and senseless.

What are some examples of the destruction and senselessness? Our high intake (c) … major negative economic consequences for Canadians who are looking for work. In fact, it (d) … many of Canada's own unemployed to compete with immigrants for a limited number of jobs and it (e) … many Canadians. Absurd as it may sound, employed Canadians have actually launched "Hire An Immigrant" campaigns to give immigrants a hiring advantage over unemployed Canadian-born.

In addition, it (f) … many Canadians (especially those in Canada's larger centres) to feel that this social engineering project amounts to the country being ethnically cleansed and re-colonised. Finally, it has turned many areas of the country into crowded, grid-locked, environmental disasters-in-progress.

We (g) … one basic question : Why Is Canada bringing in 250 000+ immigrants per year?

Immigration Watch Canada

3.20 As you read Text 2.12, you will notice that verbs a–g have been removed from the last few paragraphs. Conjugate the verbs below, so that they fit into the context of each sentence. Use either the present perfect or present simple form of each verb.

a   (to be) …

b   (to be) …

c   (to have) …

d   (to force) …

e   (to impoverish) …

f   (to cause) …

g   (to ask) …

Discussion

3.21 According to Text 2.12, immigration is a very political issue, used by politicians to win votes.

a   Think of a country that you know well. How do the politicians of that country try to win votes or popularity by discussing immigration?

b   Are their arguments always fair and balanced?

c   Carry out some research to find information about this topic before organising a discussion on it.

3.22 Have you or anyone in your family ever had to emigrate to another country? Explain the reasons for this move. How is your family's story similar to or different from the stories of other immigrants you know?

3.23 Do an online search for a video called 'Most Shocking Second a Day Video' by the charity Save the Children.

a   Each student in your class is assigned a different moment in the film. Freeze the video and explain what you think is going on. Each person should only take about one minute to explain what he or she thinks is happening in their assigned frame.

b   As a class, answer the following question:

Do you think this video is effective in spreading awareness about the refugee crisis? Why or why not?

3.24 Irony is a mismatch between what is said and what is expected. Using this definition, explain why the cartoon on the left is ironic. How do you think the cartoon comments on human nature, politics and immigration? (Note: In order to understand this cartoon, you might need to know that US President Donald Trump wants to build a wall between the US and Mexico.)

"You fellas need a job?"

3.25 Look at the map below, which shows the movement of people around the world. Are there any immigration patterns on this map that you know about? Why are people moving in these directions? Research one migration pattern and explain the direction of one of these arrows to your fellow classmates.

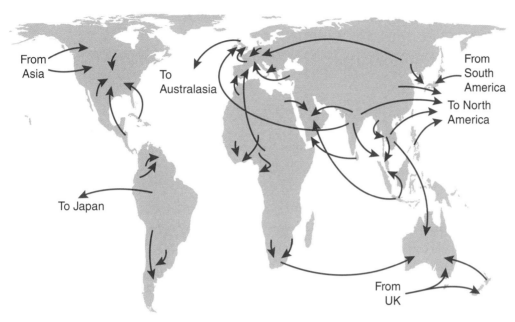

Writing

3.26 Write a blog post on an immigration issue by taking the following steps:

a   Read Unit 6.3 on blogs as a text type. Find out what features they typically include.

b   Re-read Text 2.11 and find evidence of these features.

c   In this chapter we have touched on immigration issues in the UK, South Africa and Canada. Research immigration issues one of these countries further. Find several reliable resources and highlight any facts, figures or data that you can use for your own blog.

d   Think of a context for your blog. Find an existing blog on a global politics site. Write your post in the spirit of this blog, using a similar structure and style.

e   Submit your blog post to your teacher for review.

f   Rewrite your blog, taking your teacher's comments into consideration.

3.27 After reading Text 2.12, you might want to carry out more of your own research about the effects of the high rate of immigration in Canada. For example: Is there high unemployment in that country? Is there a correlation between crime and immigration? Are the cities 'overcrowded' as the authors suggest? Write a letter to Immigration Watch Canada, responding to their claims with facts and evidence.

Higher level extension

3.28 Make a KWL (Know, Want, Learn) table like the one below. Ask yourself: 'What do I know about Ireland and emigration?' and 'What do I want to find out about it? Then, after reading Text 2.13, ask yourself: 'What did I learn about Ireland and emigration?'

What I already <u>know</u>	What I <u>want</u> to find out	What I <u>learned</u>

3.29 Four headings have been removed from Text 2.13. After reading the article, select the heading that is most appropriate for each of the four sections (1–4).

a 'It's like the famine remittance days'

b 23,000 Irish arrived in Australia in 2009

c Ireland has reared a lost generation

d 'What's the point of going back to Ireland?'

Text 2.13

Irish emigration worse than 1980s

Kerry is the home of Gaelic football (GAA) and local businessman Jimmy Banbury runs one of five local teams in the Dingle Peninsula. He usually has no problem producing players sufficiently good to make the selection for the county senior team.

But this year he will struggle.

Unemployment levels are so high that men in their late teens and early twenties can't afford to hang around. GAA, although played like a professional sport, is amateur. And the chance of national football glory in Croke Park is no substitute for a living.

"Eight of our best players have emigrated and more of them are going after Christmas either to Australia or Britain," Banbury told me before Christmas.

For him the return of the dark days of emigration, which Ireland does in regular cycles, is leaving another indelible mark on the community.

"Only eight boys started in junior infants this year. In a 10-year period that has dropped 50 per cent," he says. Dingle is a substantial town but relies on tourism for business and the downturn is evidently driving away those with young families.

Banbury, like everyone else in Ireland, will be unsurprised by today's news that emigration is now running at levels higher than the 1980s.

While Fianna Fáil wastes time playing deckchairs on the *Titanic*, the rest of the country is hanging its head in despair and anyone who has a chance – mainly single men and women – are getting out in the latest wave of emigration.

Today it was predicted that emigration in Ireland this year will be worse than the 1980s. The Economic and Social Research Institute predicts 100,000 Irish will be emigrating in the next two years – 50,000 this year and 50,000 in 2012.

It means more Irish people will emigrate this year than in 1989, when emigration last peaked and 44,000 left Ireland.

This figure is tethered to another timebomb – unemployment. As ESRI's Dr Alan Barrett says, the figures are of course uncertain but "If migration is lower, unemployment will be higher". That's Hobson's choice for young graduates and for thousands of twenty- and thirty-somethings who haven't left the country already.

(1) ...

The figure confirms what every family in Ireland knows: the country has reared a "lost generation" of twenty-something semi-skilled workers and graduates who have no choice but to leave to find a job. Australia is one of the most popular for the Irish and earlier this week I spoke to the authorities in Sydney and to one 26-year-old who had already made the move to Oz.

There are two types of émigrés – those who are making a permanent move to the country with their families, and younger 20-somethings who are going on working holiday visas which, provided they work for three months in a rural area, can last for two years. Five years ago, the department of immigration says, the numbers of Irish on this holiday visa stood at 12,500.

(2) …

This steadily rose year on year and peaked in 2008/9 when 23,000 arrived in Australia seeking a break in fortune. Last year numbers fell slightly, back to 15,000 – although the figures are recorded from June to June, so we don't know yet how many arrived in Australia for the second half of 2010. Migrants with certain types of skills, carpenters, electricians, nurses and other medical workers are the lucky ones. They can get permanent visas. The numbers here have swollen from 1,700 in 2005/2006 to 3,000 in 2009/10. A further 2,000 "temporary visas" were granted to workers with these skill sets who got sponsors.

"If you look at the trends, 2,000 is not an insubstantial number. It's an increase of 65 per cent on the same numbers in 2009 when there were 700. The carpenters, electricians, resident medical officers – these are not trades or professions that any country would like to lose," said Sandi Logan, communications manager with the department of immigration and citizenship.

(3) …

Richie Bohan, 26, left for Australia in November 2009. He couldn't get a job so decided to take a year out. I caught up with him last night and he told me he had no intention of coming back. His dad, a painter, hasn't had work since November and is about to close his business after 43 years.

"I try not to think about what's happening at home too much. It's funny, when I was leaving, my dad was screaming at me not to go and now he's screaming at me not to come back."

"My dad will be alright. I remember when I was about nine he sat me and my siblings down – there are six of us – and told us we would have to move into our gran's, but the boom came along and we never did. He will find something. But it's almost sort of coming back to the days of the famine remittance when those who left sent money home," says Bohan.

(4) …

Bohan tried his hand as a journalist at the *Irish Times* and wrote a blog for me in a previous incarnation. Now he has decided to switch tack completely and is working in sales in Melbourne and loves it. He says the increase in volume of Irish is really noticeable.

"The Irish usually go to Sydney, not Melbourne, but now you see the GAA jerseys everywhere and the Irish rugby jerseys and it's really noticeable when you go to a bar, you just hear the accents. When I went to the Melbourne Cup in November it was like being at the Punchestown races; just Irish accents everywhere," he says.

He keeps in touch with Irish affairs but not too much. It's too depressing, he says.

Will he go back to Ireland? "No, absolutely not. I don't think there is any future in Ireland. I miss my family and friends but I have got to look at the bigger picture.

"What's the point of going back to be with family and friends when you are on the dole?"

Quite.

The Guardian

TEXT AND CONTEXT

- Ireland has had a history of emigration, often referred to as the 'Irish diaspora' ('diaspora' means a scattering or displacement of people away from their homeland). There might be as many as 80 million Irish descendants outside Ireland.

- The reference to the days of 'famine remittance' (section 3) goes back to the Great Famine in Ireland between 1845 and 1852 in which over a million Irish died due to poor potato crops, disease and hunger. The famine sped up a process of emigration that was already happening, where millions of Irish were leaving, mostly for the United States. They sent 'remittance' (money) home to Ireland to support the families they left behind.

- Text 2.13 claims that 'Fianna Fáil wastes time playing deckchairs on the *Titanic*' Fianna Fáil was the political party in power during the time of this article. The phrase suggests that their in-party fighting is insignificant to the bigger problem of emigration, which is like the sinking of a large ship, the *Titanic*.

- 'On the dole' (section 4) refers to unemployment assistance or welfare. It comes from the verb 'to dole out', meaning to give money.

3.30 Read Text 2.13 carefully. Which of the following statements are true or false? Support your answer with evidence from the text.

a   The Dingle Peninsula's county senior team for Gaelic football has been halved due to emigration.

b   People are leaving Dingle because its main industry, tourism, is in decline.

c   Within a period of two years (2011–2012) 100,000 people left Ireland, making it the worst wave of emigration since 1989.

d   Entire families are packing up and moving from Ireland to Australia.

e   The Australian government extends working holiday visas for up to two years if immigrants are willing to work on farms and ranches.

f   Only immigrant workers with a sponsor can apply for a permanent visa in Australia.

g   Richie Bohan is considering sending money home to support his unemployed father in Ireland.

h   Richie Bohan misses Ireland, but would not want to live there and be unemployed.

3.31 Look at photographs a–d which depict ideas described in Text 2.13. Think of a caption that connects each photograph to the article. Explain to a classmate why you felt your caption was suitable.

a

b

c

d

3.32 What would you do? Imagine you are 20-something, educated and from Ireland. Would you emigrate to Australia or another country? Would you stay at home, look for work, start a business, raise a family or receive unemployment benefits?

Literature

3.33 As you have noticed throughout this unit, racism is closely connected to immigration. People hold certain prejudices about immigrants and refugees. Acts of discrimination against foreign-born people occur every day. As a class, share any experiences that you have had with racism or discrimination. How do you think such acts of racism could be prevented?

3.34 You are about to read the opening lines from the novel *House of Sand and Fog* by Andre Dubus III (Text 2.14). Read the following questions and look for answers to them as you read Text 2.14. Discuss your answers as a class.

a   Why do you think the narrator is doing this kind of work?

b   Why is Tran shaking his head in disappointment?

c   Why does Mendez laugh?

d   Why does the narrator stare at Mendez' scar?

e   Why does the narrator call the other men '*goh*'?

f   Why does the narrator write out his entire name in the second to last line?

g   Why does Torez say that he is 'general' in the last lines?

h   How do you think this text comments on the challenges of immigrating to another country?

Text 2.14

The fat one, the radish Torez, he calls me Camel because I am Persian and because I can bear this August sun longer than the Chinese and the Panamanians and even the little Vietnamese, Tran. He works very quickly without rest, but when Torez stops the orange highway truck in front of the crew, Tran hurries for his paper cup of water with the rest of them. This heat is no good for work. All morning we have walked this highway between Sausalito and the Golden Gate Park. We carry our small trash harpoons and we drag our burlap bags and we are dressed in vests the same color as the highway truck. Some of the Panamanians remove their shirts and leave them hanging from their back pockets like oil rags, but Torez says something to them in their mother language and he makes them wear the vests over their bare backs. We are up on a small hill. Between the trees I can see out over Sausalito to the bay where there are clouds to think I cannot see the other side where I live with my family in Berkeley, my wife and son. But here there is no fog, only sun on your head and back, and the smell of everything under the nose: the dry grass and dirt; the cigarette smoke of the Chinese; the hot metal and exhaust of the passing automobiles. I am sweating under my shirt and vest. I have fifty-six years and no hair. I must buy a hat.

    When I reach the truck, the crew has finished their water and the two Chinese light new cigarettes as they go back to the grass. The Panamanians have dropped their cups upon the ground around their feet and Tran is shaking his head, and saying something in his language as he stoops to pick them up with his hands. Mendez laughs. He is almost as big as the radish and there is a long burn scar the color of sand upon one of his fat arms. He sees me looking at it as I drink my ice water and he stops his laughing, no longer does he even smile, and he to me says: "What are you looking at, *viejo*?"

    I drink from my cup and let him look at my eyes. His brothers have started to go back to work but now they stop to watch.

> "Old *maricón*," says Mendez. He takes us his trash spear from the orange tailgate, but my eyes look at the burn again long enough for him to see. His face becomes more ugly than it already is and he yells something at me in his language and his teeth are very bad, like an old dog's. I don't give him rest from my eyes and so now he steps to me, yelling more, and I smell him, last night's wine and today's sweating of it, and now Torez is yelling louder than Mendez. Again it is in their mother tongue and it is over quickly because Mendez knows this crew can manage very fine without him, and he needs money for his *sharob*, his wine. He is *goh*, the shit of life. They are all *goh*.
>
> "*Vamonos*, Camello." Torez moves by me and closes the tailgate. Tran is already working ahead of the truck while the smoking Chinese and the lazy Panamanians walk to the shade of the trees, pretending there is trash there.
>
> I pull my sack over my shoulder and to Mr. Torez I say, "In my country I could have ordered him beaten."
>
> "*Si*, Camello? In Mendez' country he would have beaten you himself."
>
> "I was colonel, Mr. Torez. I was colonel in the Imperial Air Force. Do you know this, Mr. Torez? I was *colonel*."
>
> He hands to me my garbage spear and looks me in my eyes. His are gavehee, brown as coffee, like all his people, like my people also. But I see he has made up his mind about me.
>
> He says to me, to Genob Sarhang Massoud Amir Behrani: "Okay, Colonel, but today I'm Señor General. *Comprende?*"
>
> Extract from *House of Sand and Fog* by Andre Dubus III

3.35 Look back on the texts, audio files, images and activities from this unit and discuss your answers to the following questions:

a In the beginning of this unit you were asked to write down the benefits and challenges of immigration. Did you have a more positive or negative outlook on immigration?

b How have your ideas about immigration changed since you started this unit?

c Do you know any immigrants? How might this affect your attitude on immigration?

d Do you think you will ever immigrate to another country? Why or why not?

REFLECT

In this chapter you have explored the theme of 'experiences' through three different angles, focusing on:

- pilgrimages
- extreme sports
- migration.

These three topics are very different, but what do they have in common? John Dewey, an American philosopher, once said that learning is experience plus reflection. Even though your life experiences have been different than those you've studied in this chapter, ask yourself:

What have you learned by reflecting on other people's experiences?

Human ingenuity

This chapter explores the theme of human ingenuity. One important characteristic that distinguishes humans from other species is our desire to create and invent. Why do we do this? How do science and technology affect our lives? What can we learn from art? These are a few of the guiding questions for this chapter.

In this Chapter

- In Unit 3.1, you will explore the topics of cloning, nanorobotics, genetically modified food and gender selection.
- In Unit 3.2, you will consider the effect of technology on human interaction.
- In Unit 3.3 you will ask yourself: 'What is art?' 'What is the purpose of art?' and 'How is art changing?'

Unit 3.1
Future humans

Word bank

eradicated

clone

genetically modified

in vitro fertilisation

sex selection

family balancing

nanorobots

controversial

fertility

reproduction

taboo

genes

species

technological singularity

clinic

People now live longer than they did 100 years ago. Some diseases, such as polio and tuberculosis, have been nearly **eradicated**. Prosthetic limbs have allowed disabled people to run marathons. Much of modern science is devoted to improving human health. If scientific developments continue for the next 50 years as they have for the last 50 years, what benefits will that make to our lives?

As you will read in Text 3.1, one scientist is already trying to **clone** human beings. Who knows, perhaps there maight be a cloned version of you one day! You might also eat food that is **genetically modified (GM)**, such as a 'golden rice'. In Text 3.2 you will learn more about the pros and cons of GM foods. Finally, in Text 3.3, you will learn about couples who are able to select the sex of their child, as they travel from Australia to clinics in Thailand that conduct a special form of treatment – **in vitro fertilisation (IVF)**. What would happen to the world's population if everyone could choose the sex of their child? Why not select the colour of the child's eyes and hair as well?

These new and developing technologies raise many questions. This unit might not give you all the answers, but it offers much food for thought!

Dolly the sheep, the first cloned mammal (1996)

Getting started

What is cloning? There are three types of cloning:

- molecular cloning – the process of copying a single DNA molecule and adding it to the DNA of other organisms
- cellular cloning – the process of making more cells from a single cell
- organism cloning – the process of creating an organism that's identical to another organism (Dolly the sheep was the world's first cloned mammal).

1.1 What are some of the arguments for and against cloning? Make a copy of the table below, then write the following statements into one of the two columns, after discussing them with classmates. Remember: there are no right or wrong answers, only well-argued ones.

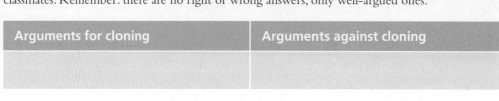

Arguments for cloning	Arguments against cloning

116

a   Cloning could allow humans to take on a God-like role.

b   Human cloning could allow couples to determine the sex of their child.

c   Many religious leaders are against cloning.

d   Human cloning could allow infertile couples to have a child that is made up of their combined DNA.

e   Cellular cloning already allows scientists to grow organs and tissue.

f   In the future, cloning may provide entirely new bodies for existing brains.

g   Human cloning would allow new generations of 'successful' people to be born.

h   Investing in cloning research to advance what we know about the human body.

1.2 What if you could genetically modify fruits, vegetables or even animals? Imagine for a moment that you were an engineer of genetically modified food. How and why would you alter produce or meats? Begin your answer to this question with: 'I would … because …'.

With genetic manipulation it is possible to change the colour of fruits

1.3 Consider a situation where a happy couple have a lovely little daughter. They would like to have a son as well. They are wealthy and can afford to pay a special clinic to perform IVF (in vitro fertilisation) treatment that will allow them to select the sex of their child (also known as '**sex selection**' or '**family balancing**'). One of the couple is eager to undergo this treatment; the other is reluctant. Imagine a discussion they might have on this topic, using the vocabulary from the table below. You may also refer to the word bank.

Producing a test-tube baby

Eager to have IVF for sex selection	Reluctant to have IVF for sex selection
family balancing	test-tube baby
reproductive rights	unnatural
modern	favouritism
feels right	feels wrong
appropriate	inappropriate
deserving	elitist
must have male heir	fear of breaking government policy

3

Thinking skills

Activity 1.4 makes use of the 'Connect, Extend, Challenge' routine. This was designed by Harvard Project Zero as one of several ways to develop *thinking skills*. It is a useful way of connecting new knowledge to existing knowledge. As an IB learner, you should try to become more conscious of how you acquire knowledge. Are there any other ways you remember, understand or apply new things that you learn?

TEXT AND CONTEXT

• 'Sci-fi' is an abbreviation for science fiction.

Watch and listen

1.4 Listen to Audio track 7, which is about **nanorobots**. What you hear might:

• 'connect' with what you already know

• 'extend' your knowledge on the subject

• 'challenge' your understanding of it.

As a class, listen to Audio track 7 and do a 'Connect, Extend, Challenge' routine using a table like the one below. You might find it helpful to draw your table on a whiteboard and use three sticky notes per person to share everyone's ideas with the class.

Connect	Extend	Challenge
How does the information about nanorobotics <u>connect</u> to what you already know?	What new ideas about nanorobotics extended or pushed your thinking in new directions?	What is still <u>challenging</u> or confusing about nanorobotics? What questions or wonderings do you have?

1.5 After listening and discussing your answers to the 'Connect, Extend, Challenge' exercise (Activity 1.4), listen to Audio track 7 again. Decide whether the following sentences are true or false. Justify your answers with phrases from the recording if you can remember them.

a The speaker's main aim is to get more money for his team's research.

b The speaker believes that robots are more intelligent than humans.

c Nanorobots are different from other robots.

d Nanorobots, according to the speaker, have a mind of their own.

e Nanorobots can prevent people from ageing.

f The speaker and his team spend as much time and money gathering cell material as they do on the rest of their research.

g According to the speaker, progress in the field of chemotherapy is slow.

h The speaker would like to run tests on live organisms.

1.6 You are going to watch a short video titled 'Human Clones, Through the Wormhole'. Make a list of images and video footage you would expect to see in a video with this title.

1.7 Do an online search for the video titled 'Human Clones, Through the Wormhole' by the Science Channel.

a   Watch the video and then return to your list of images that you expected to see (Activity 1.6). How many of these did you see in the video?

b   What other images were included that you did not expect to see?

1.8 Listen carefully to what is said in the film to answer the questions below.

a   What is the primary thing you need to clone an individual?

b   Why can't geneticists currently implant a human embryo into a uterus?

c   Why is it difficult for geneticists to obtain funding for their research?

d   Even if Robert Lanza could easily get more human embryos (or human 'eggs'), why might he need hundreds of them?

e   How does Robert Lanza explain the chances of have successfully cloning a human being?

f   Why does the narrator believe that humans will be cloned?

g   How is cloning a person not the same as duplicating a person?

h   Complete the final sentence of the video: 'Perhaps the key to life after death is not to grow an entirely new body, but to...'

Exploring texts

1.9 If you were a doctor developing the technology to clone humans, how would you answer the following questions?

a   Where would you conduct your cloning of humans?

b   What kinds of people would you clone?

c   What is more important: creating the first human clone, or creating a *healthy* cloned child?

d   Would you want the world to know about your experiments, or would you want to keep them a secret? Give reasons for your answer.

1.10 Read Text 3.1 and ask yourself 'How would Dr Zavos answer the questions from Activity 1.9?' Then compare your answers with his.

EXTRA

This article on Dr Zavos is a little out of date. What has happened to him since it was written? What are the latest developments in (human) cloning? Do some research on this topic and present your findings, along with a few discussion questions, to your classmates.

READING STRATEGY

The title of Text 3.1 has been removed. After reading the article, try to decide on an appropriate title. You can use this 'information-gap' activity with other texts as well.

Text 3.1

1   A **controversial fertility** doctor claimed yesterday to have cloned 14 human embryos and transferred 11 of them into the wombs of four women who had been prepared to give birth to cloned babies.

2   The cloning was recorded by an independent documentary filmmaker who has testified to *The Independent* that the cloning had taken place and that the women were genuinely hoping to become pregnant with the first cloned embryos specifically created for the purposes of human **reproduction**.

3   Panayiotis Zavos has broken the ultimate **taboo** of transferring cloned embryos into the human womb, a procedure that is a criminal offence in Britain and illegal in many other countries. He carried out the work at a secret laboratory, probably located in the Middle East where there is no cloning ban. Dr Zavos, a naturalised American, also has fertility clinics in Kentucky and Cyprus, where he was born. His patients, three married couples and a single woman, came from Britain, the United States and an unspecified country in the Middle East.

4   None of the embryo transfers led to a viable pregnancy but Dr Zavos said yesterday that this was just the 'first chapter' in his ongoing and serious attempts at producing a baby cloned from the skin cells of its 'parent'.

5   'There is absolutely no doubt about it, and I may not be the one that does it, but the cloned child is coming. There is absolutely no way that it will not happen,' Dr Zavos said in an interview yesterday with *The Independent*.

6   'If we intensify our efforts we can have a cloned baby within a year or two, but I don't know whether we can intensify our efforts to that extent. We're not really under pressure to deliver a cloned baby to this world. What we are under pressure to do is to deliver a cloned baby that is a healthy one,' he said.

7   His claims are certain to be denounced by mainstream fertility scientists who in 2004 tried to gag Dr Zavos by imploring the British media not to give him the oxygen of publicity without him providing evidence to back up his statements. Despite a lower profile over the past five years, scores of couples have now approached Dr Zavos hoping that he will help them to overcome their infertility by using the same cloning technique that was used to create Dolly the sheep in 1996.

8   'I get enquiries every day. To date we have had over 100 enquiries and every enquiry is serious. The criteria is that they have to consider human reproductive cloning as the only option available to them after they have exhausted everything else,' Dr Zavos said.

Dr Zavos

9   'We are not interested in cloning the Michael Jordans and the Michael Jacksons of this world. The rich and the famous don't participate in this.'

10   It took 277 attempts to create Dolly but since then the cloning procedure in animals has been refined and it has now become more efficient, although most experts in the field believe that it is still too dangerous to be allowed as a form of human fertility treatment. Dr Zavos dismissed these fears saying that many of the problems related to animal cloning, such as congenital defects and oversized offspring, have been minimised.

The Independent

TOK

Science, as an area of knowledge, is based on what is known as the scientific method. Below are the steps 1-6 that scientists follow.

- How do you think they apply to Dr Zavos's work on human cloning?
- Why do you think he inserted 11 embryos in four women?
- What is the importance of Dolly the sheep?
- Why might it be better to clone animals before humans?

Use terms from the scientific method below to answer these questions.

Steps in the scientific method:

1 Observe a phenomenon and ask a question.
2 Do background research.
3 Form a hypothesis.
4 Perform one or more experiments and collect data.
5 Analyse the data.
6 Interpret the data to make conclusions.

> **TEXT AND CONTEXT**
> - Michael Jordan (paragraph 9) is an American basketball star.
> - Michael Jackson (paragraph 9) was a famous pop star, who died in 2009.
> - Congenital defects (paragraph 10) are diseases or physical abnormalities that occur to babies in the womb.

1.11 Below is a list of words taken from Text 3.1. Match these words with their synonyms in the box.

improve	reject
censor	insert
try	declare
move	increase
create	sustainable
ask	criticise

a	Inject	b	transfer
c	testify	d	viable
e	deliver	f	intensify
g	denounce	h	gag
i	implore	j	exhaust
k	refine	l	dismiss

1.12 Answer the following questions on Text 3.1. Give evidence from the text to support your answers.

a Has Dr Zavos tried to clone humans before?

b Did Dr Zavos succeed in cloning four humans?

c Why is the word 'parent' in quotation marks?

d What does Dr Zavos mean when he says, 'There is absolutely no way that it will not happen.'

e Why did scientists tell the British media to ignore Zavos?

f Why do couples seek Dr Zavos' help?

1.13 What do you already know about genetically modified (GM) food and crops? What questions do you have about this? As a class, complete a Know, Want, Learn (KWL) table, like the one below. Fill in the third column after reading Text 3.2.

What I already *know* about GM food and crops	What I *want* to learn about GM food and crops	What I *learned* about GM crops

1.14 As you read Text 3.2, notice how the words a–m in the list below are used in context. Match each of these words with a synonym from the box. The words in the list are in the same order as they appear in the text.

poisonous	arrival	prolonging	start	challenging
returns	problems	characteristic	first	filtering
suggested		changes	disappearance	

a	sorting	b	daunting
c	proposed	d	initial
e	extending	f	fluctuations
g	yields	h	issues
i	trigger	j	trait
k	toxic	l	extinction
m	emergence		

Genetically modified (GM) rice

Text 3.2

GM Foods: Pros and Cons

With all of the controversy around genetically modified (GM) foods, sorting through huge volumes of information can seem like a daunting task. Many members of the public are asking questions about GM foods and they are also raising concerns about the effects these foods might have on their health or the environment. There are different advantages and disadvantages of GM foods, although to what extent they can help or harm humans and the environment is a debatable aspect of this technology.

Benefits of GM Foods

A proposed benefit of GM foods is that they can potentially produce higher crop yields, which could help by feeding more people in developing countries. They are also cited as more economical, despite the initial higher cost of the seeds. The rationale is that they reduce the need for pesticides and herbicides as well as reducing the manpower needed to successfully grow the crops, which should translate into improved financial gains.

Improved food quality is another benefit associated with GM foods. A tomato, for instance, can be engineered to stay fresher for longer, thereby extending its shelf life in the supermarket.

Yet another benefit that is believed to occur from GM technology is that crops can be engineered to withstand weather fluctuations and extremes. This means that they can provide sufficient yields and quality despite a severe, poor weather season.

Issues With GM Foods

A worrisome issue in GM foods is the ability of a food to trigger an allergy in humans. Some of the **genes** used in GM technology might be taken from a food that causes allergies in some people. Inserting that gene into another organism could cause the host organism to express that allergen as a trait. Alternately, a new allergen could be produced when genes are mixed across different **species**.

Another potential downside to GM technology is that other organisms in the ecosystem could be harmed, which would lead to a lower level of biodiversity. By removing one pest that harms the crop, you could be removing a food source for an animal. Also, GM crops could prove toxic to an organism in the environment, leading to reduced numbers or extinction of that organism.

Given that some GM foods are modified using bacteria and viruses, there is a fear that we will see the emergence of new diseases. The threat to human health is a worrisome aspect of GM technology and one that has received a great deal of debate.

www.geneticallymodifiedfood.co.uk

1.15 In the table below are several statements that express the ideas of Text 3.2. Match the first half of the sentence in the left column with its second half in the right column.

First half of sentence		Second half of sentence	
I	One advantage of GM crops is that …	a	they could cause new human diseases.
2	Although GM crops might be more expensive …	b	they are engineered to be stronger and withstand extreme conditions.
3	From the supermarket's perspective, GM crops are advantageous, because …	c	they can cause unexpected allergic reactions.
4	GM crops are more likely to survive storms, because …	d	they can produce more food on less soil, which is good for developing countries.
5	One disadvantage of GM crops is that …	e	they can be toxic for other organisms or destroy the food supply of other organisms.
6	In fact, the problem with combining two plant species is that …	f	they can be engineered to stay fresher for longer.
7	GM crops might harm the diversity of an ecosystem, because …	g	they can create a new, unknown allergen.
8	Because some crops are altered using bacteria or viruses, there is a worry that…	h	they are economically cheaper in the long run, because they do not require as much maintenance.

> **TEXT AND CONTENT**
> Pesticides (paragraph 2) are the chemicals that farmers put on crops to protect them from insects and diseases.

1.16 Return to your KWL diagram in Activity 1.13. Were all of your questions about GM food and crops from your 'What I want to learn' column answered? If not, search for these answers online. As a class, discuss which key words you should use in an online search to answer your questions. Some examples are given below.

Questions	Key search terms
What crops and food are most often genetically modified?	'top GM crops', 'most produced GM food'
Are GM crops and food bad for me?	GM foods health concerns'
…	…

Form and meaning

1.17 How certain is the author of Text 3.2 of the advantages and disadvantages of genetically modified foods? He writes that they 'can potentially produce higher crop yields'. But have they? He also uses words such as 'might' and 'could', which create a sense of uncertainty. Using these words and others in the vocabulary box on the next page, decide which words are needed to fill the gaps in the sentences that follow.

seem	might	could	tend	would	should	try	decide

a The data … to show a trend in disease treatment.

b Governments … invest more in GM food, if they want to see advancements.

c People … to become more ill in the colder months.

d Eating GM food regularly … expose you to new allergies.

e He … consider being the first cloned human, if the magazine promises to run an article about him.

f Genetically modified fish … be found in the average supermarket in the near future.

g Every year they … to break their old record.

h If they … to test the technology before it is ready, the professor will be angry.

If you look closely at the sentences in Activity 1.17 above, you will see that there are two kinds of verbs:

- those that are followed by an infinitive verb ('the data *seems* <u>to show</u>')
- those that are followed by an infinitive verb without 'to' ('nanotechnology *could* <u>be</u> just around the corner').
- 'Could' is called a modal verb. Modal verbs are different for the following reasons:
  - They do not take on an 's' in the third person. 'He *can* invent the cure.'
  - They are used to make questions. '*Should* she <u>test</u> the medicine?'
  - They are followed by an infinitive verb without 'to'. 'They *must run* the experiment again.'

We use modal verbs for several reasons:

- Probability – something *might/may/could* happen, though it is not certain.
- Ability – someone *can* or *could* perform a task, because they have the ability to.
- Obligation or advice – someone *must/should* do something, because they are told to.
- Permission – someone *may/could/*can be allowed to do something, if they are given permission.
- Habit – in the past tense, you can say that people *would* do something regularly. In the
- present and future, you can say that someone *will* always act in a certain way.

1.18 In the box below are several modal verbs. Use these verbs to fill in the gaps in the sentences that follow. Some of the verbs are interchangeable, meaning that they can go into one or more of the gaps. You may use the same word twice. You might not need to use all of the verbs.

can	could	may	might	will	would
	must	shall	should		

a Many people believe that genetically modified crops … change the world of farming.

b Scientists … be aware of the ethical issues, before they start cloning humans.

c He asked the head of the lab if he … experiment on mice.

d He asked the head of the lab, ' … I experiment on mice?'

e She … not conduct the experiment because she did not have the right tools.

f If cloning humans is possible, scientists … do it.

g At our old school, the Biology teacher … always bring in dead animals off the road for dissection.

Discussion

1.19 Do you think scientists should be allowed to clone humans? Why, or why not? What are the ethical implications? In your discussion refer to the cartoon below. How does this cartoon present an argument for or against cloning?

'The lab has come up with a neat solution to our staffing problem. These are junior executives in the larval stage.'

1.20 Below are several statements about the future, that accompany the image below. Which statement do you agree with the most? Give a 3-4-minute talk in which you explain why you agree with this statement the most. Do research to find supporting arguments.

a Robots will one day enhance our mental capabilities, just like they already enhance our physical abilities. Software for the brain is like construction tools for the hands.

b There is something inherently wrong with placing a computer chip into the human body.

c Nanobots are the fountain of youth. They will help us live longer.

d With an ability to upload existing memories and intellectual abilities into new bodies, humans will, in a sense, become immortal.

e The invention of artificial intelligence will abruptly trigger runaway technological growth, resulting in unthinkable changes to human civilisation. (Note: This hypothesis is known as **'technological singularity'**.)

TOK
The discussion questions in Activities 1.20 and 1.21 relate to *ethics*, which is considered an 'area of knowledge' in the TOK course. The underlying knowledge question here is: 'How do we know what is right or wrong?' One theory of ethics, known as *utilitarianism*, suggests that people should be free to do what they want, as long as they do not harm anyone else. How successful is this theory in relation to technological singularity or genetically modified food?

3

Research skills

Activity 1.21 suggests you do research before giving a short presentation. Many of the statements relate to the concept of technological singularity. Before making claims about the future of technology, you might want to research current trends and topics. Many students turn to online encyclopedias, such as Wikipedia, that serve as good starting points for research. It is recommended, however, that you go beyond these sources and find scientific articles from (online) journals and other publications. Check the reliability of your sources before presenting your ideas.

1.21 Discuss your answer to the following questions with classmates:

a Do you think that genetically modified (GM) crops are the solution to world hunger?

b Do you think it is morally wrong to change the natural world by genetically modifying crops?

c Would you eat GM food? If so, are there limits to what you would eat?

d If you would not eat GM food, what are your arguments against it?

e How are the issues surrounding GM crops similar to, or different from, your discussion about human cloning in the previous activity?

Extended Essay

In your extended essay there should be an emphasis on culture and language. If you are going to write about a topic that relates to the theme of 'Human ingenuity', make sure that it is not too broad or general. For example, stem cell research has been more controversial in the USA than in many other countries. A good extended essay could explore arguments made by politicians for or against stem cell research in various US media. What do these arguments tell us about American culture and values? Support your essay with articles from newspapers and other sources.

Writing

1.22 Below is an image that could be used as a stimulus for a standard level individual oral assessment on genetically modified (GM) food and the theme of human ingenuity. Look ahead to Unit 9.1 to learn more about the requirements for working with visual stimuli in the standard level individual oral. Think back to the discussion you had in Activity 1.21 on GM food. Write a set of working notes that you could use for an individual oral on this visual stimulus. You have 15 minutes to write these notes. When you are done, compare your notes with those of your classmates. What were some of the most effective notes? What makes you say this?

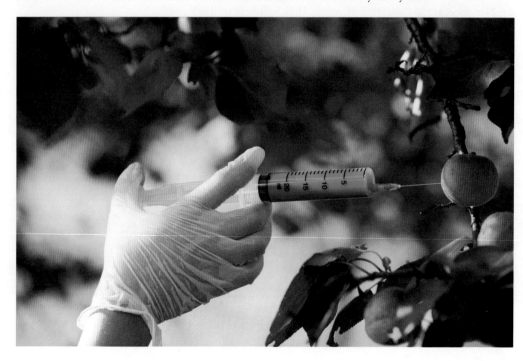

1.23 Imagine that Dr Zavos (Text 3.1) has just succeeded in cloning the first human. You are the reporter to break this news story to the world.

a What would you include in this news report?

b Who would you interview and what would they say?

c See Unit 6.5 on news reporting to help you write your report. Here are a few phrases that you might find useful:

- 'Reliable sources have reported that ...'
- 'According to a recent study ...'
- 'When asked about ... Dr Zavos responded by saying that ...'
- 'Witnesses have confirmed reports that ...'

Higher level extension

1.24 What if you could select the gender of your child? Discuss your answers to the following questions to help you think about the issues in Text 3.3.

a If you could select the gender of your child, would you want a girl or a boy? Why would you select a boy or a girl?

b Should gender selection be something for the wealthy, everyone or no-one?

c What if everyone could select the gender of their child? How might this change the make-up of the world's population in 50 years' time?

d What is to stop people from selecting more than gender? Do you think couples should be allowed to select the colour of their child's hair and eyes?

e Look at the image. Is this the ideal family? Why might many people think this?

1.25 Here are some of the main ideas from Text 3.3. Do you agree or disagree with these statements? Give arguments to support your answers.

a   It is all right to break the law if you feel the law is unethical.

b   Whether or not an embryo becomes a baby should not be a matter of whether it is a boy or a girl.

c   People should be happy that they can simply have children without being able to determine their gender.

d   Ensuring that something happens safely, does not ensure that it is necessarily ethical.

e   If you want to do something that is illegal, it is all right as long as you do it in a country where it is considered legal.

f   Public opinion should weigh more than the opinions of IVF experts.

1.26 Find sentences in Text 3.3 that express the same ideas as those in Activity 1.25, but using different words.

Text 3.3

IVF parents travel overseas to pick baby's sex

A LEADING IVF clinic is helping clients choose the sex of their baby by sending them to an overseas **clinic** it co-owns, avoiding Australian rules which allow the practice only for medical reasons.

Sydney IVF, that has several clinics in NSW as well as in Canberra, Perth and Tasmania, is part-owner of Superior ART, a Thai clinic that will provide IVF for 'family balancing' – when families with children of one gender are seeking another child of the opposite sex.

It costs $11,000 including flights and accommodation, a spokesman for Sydney IVF said.

Australian fertility clinics are prohibited from offering sex selection for non-medical reasons by national ethical guidelines by which they must abide to be accredited.

But Sydney IVF maintains it is not doing anything wrong, arguing the rules banning the procedure are hurting Australian families.

The National Health and Medical Research Council's health ethics committee developed the guidelines. Its chairwoman, Sandra Hacker, said Australians generally believed parents should not be allowed to choose their child's gender to 'balance' out their family.

'The right to life should not be determined by gender,' she said. 'There is a view that you should be happy with whatever gender you bring into the world, as long as they are well and happy'.

However, it would breach people's rights to ban them from travelling overseas to have the procedure. If they did, she could understand Sydney IVF wanting to ensure they used a reputable provider. 'But that doesn't make it any more ethical, it just makes it safer,' she said.

The chief executive of Sydney IVF, Kylie de Boer, said that when the company had stopped offering sex selection in early 2005 families were left 'devastated'.

'These were people who loved children,' she said. 'They had a lot of children already and they wanted to have more.'

She said the clinic still received about 15 phone calls a week from parents seeking the procedure, despite openly explaining on its website it was banned and the only option was to travel overseas.

Dr de Boer said when Sydney IVF had done the procedure clients were often mothers wanting a daughter.

'The desire for a mother–daughter relationship was very strong,' she said.

She believed the decision was a highly personal one which should be made between doctors and patients.

'I think the guidelines are due for review and I think the guidelines are wrong,' she said.

The medical director at Sydney IVF, Mark Bowman, said the sense of 'loss and grief' felt by couples who could not conceive a child of the gender they desired was as strong as that felt by infertile couples.

The president of the Fertility Society of Australia, Peter Illingworth, did not have a problem with Sydney IVF providing sex selection overseas, so long as it complied with the rules of the country it operated in.

Public debate on whether the national guidelines were right and enforceable was needed.

'What is important is the community view about these matters, not necessarily the views of IVF specialists,' he said.

The National Health and Medical Research Council said the guidelines would be reconsidered after a legislative review into the use of human embryos. That review, chaired by the former Federal Court judge Peter Heerey, is open for submissions.

Sydney Morning Herald

1.27 Below are a list of synonyms for words from Text 3.3. Find the words in the text that have similar meanings to the words below. The synonyms appear in the order that the words appear in the text.

a customers

b offer

c forbidden

d follow

e break

f well thought of

g distressed

h become pregnant

i childless

j obey

k able to control

1.28 Imagine you were to interview an Australian couple who had selected the gender of their child at a clinic in Thailand. What kinds of questions would you ask this couple and what kinds of answers would you expect? Write a transcribed interview for a popular Australian magazine.

1.29 In this unit, you have learned about controversial scientific advances. You have explored issues that relate to cloning, nanorobotics, genetically modified food and gender selection. Do you think there will be cloned humans in 50 years' time? Will people regularly eat genetically modified food? Will all couples be able to select the gender of their child? What other controversial scientific advances might the future bring us?

Literature

1.30 This unit has raised several questions about science, health and the future of human beings. Some of the topics seem to come straight out of science fiction novels. As a class, discuss your answers to the following questions:

a   What do you associate with the term 'science fiction'?

b   Are there any examples of science fiction movies or books that you particularly like? Explain why you like them.

c   Are there any examples of science fiction that you dislike?

d   Why do you like or dislike science fiction?

e   What makes science fiction different from other literary genres?

1.31   Read Text 3.4, a passage from *Ender's Game*, the science fiction novel by Orson Scott Card.

- If you have already read this novel, it is best to wait until your classmates have completed this activity before taking part in the activities that follow.
- For those who have *not* read the novel, make a list of questions that you have about the characters, the setting, or the storyline. For example, your first questions might be: 'How old is Andrew?' or 'Why is he called 'Ender'?'
- Once you have written your list of questions, share them with your classmates. Then, as a class, think of answers to these questions.

Text 3.4

The monitor lady smiled very nicely and tousled his hair and said, 'Andrew, I suppose by now you're just absolutely sick of having that horrid monitor. Well, I have good news for you. That monitor is going to come out today. We're going to just take it right out, and it won't hurt a bit.'

Ender nodded. It was a lie, of course, that it wouldn't hurt a bit. But since adults always said it when it was going to hurt, he could count on that statement as an accurate prediction of the future. Sometimes lies were more dependable than the truth.

'So if you'll just come over here, Andrew, just sit right up here on the examining table. The doctor will be in to see you in a moment.'

The monitor gone. Ender tried to imagine the little device missing from the back of his neck. I'll roll over on my back in bed and it won't be pressing there. I won't feel it tingling and taking up the heat when I shower.

And Peter won't hate me anymore. I'll come home and show him that the monitor's gone, and he'll see that I didn't make it, either. That I'll just be a normal kid now, like him. That won't be so bad then. He'll forgive me that I had my monitor a whole year longer than he had his. We'll be – not friends, probably. No, Peter was too dangerous. Peter got so angry. Brothers, though. Not enemies, not friends, but brothers - able to live in the same house. He won't hate me, he'll just leave me alone. And when he wants to play buggers and astronauts, maybe I won't have to play, maybe I can just go read a book.

But Ender knew, even as he thought it, that Peter wouldn't leave him alone. There was something in Peter's eyes, when he was in his mad mood, and whenever Ender saw that look, that glint, he knew that the one thing Peter would not do was leave him alone. I'm practising piano, Ender. Come turn the pages for me. Oh, is the monitor boy too busy to help his brother? Is he too smart? Got to go kill some buggers, astronaut? No, no, I don't want your help. I can do it on my own, you little bastard, you little Third.

'This won't take long, Andrew,' said the doctor.

Ender nodded.

'It's designed to be removed. Without infection, without damage. But there'll be some tickling, and some people say they have a feeling of something missing. You'll keep looking around for something. Something you were looking for, but you can't find it, and you can't remember what it was. So I'll tell you. It's the monitor you're looking for, and it isn't there. In a few days that feeling will pass.'

The doctor was twisting something at the back of Ender's head. Suddenly a pain stabbed through him like a needle from his neck to his groin. Ender felt his back spasm, and his body arched violently backward; his head struck the bed. He could feel his legs thrashing, and his hands were clenching each other, wringing each other so tightly that they ached.

Extract from *Ender's Game* by Orson Scott Card

1.32 After you have read Text 3.4, written your questions and tried to answer them as a class, do an online search to find and read a synopsis of the novel. Wikipedia is a good option for this exercise. Can you answer your questions from Activity 1.31 now?

REFLECT

In this unit you have explored topics about advances in science and human life. Discuss your answers to the following questions as a class:

a What ideas from this unit did you find most interesting?

b Do you think that government organisations should put limitations on the progress of science? Are there some developments, such as the cloning of humans, that should be forbidden?

c What is the future for humans? Based on the developments of recent years, predict what the future will be like.

Unit 3.2
Technology and human interaction

Guiding questions	Learning objectives
• How has technology affected the way people interact with each other? • How can people best engage in meaningful relationships without technology getting in the way?	• Become more aware of the effects of technology on social interaction. • Be able to discuss and debate issues associated with technology and social interaction.

Word bank

technology
devices
millennials
internet
tweeting
narcissism
chat
collaboration
empathy
conversation
screens
connected
phubbing
creative
gadget
boredom
distracted driving
surfing
intelligent

Technology has changed the way we interact with other people. Much of your social life probably takes place online. Most likely you use apps, sites and **devices** to keep in touch with friends, make appointments, exchange ideas or find out the latest news. With all of these technological possibilities, it is worth asking: Are our devices changing the ways we communicate? Or are they changing who we are? Winston Churchill once said: 'We shape our buildings, thereafter they shape us.' Is the same true about our digital devices such as phones, tablets and laptops?

This unit explores this question through a study of several texts. You will:

- watch a video about how younger generations (**Millennials**) act and interact with colleagues and technology at work
- read an opinion piece about how the iPod once changed the social landscape of New York
- read the introduction to a book titled '*Reclaiming Conversation: The Power of Talk in a Digital World*'
- read about someone who lived offline for a year
- explore, at a higher level, the the effect that Google is having on our mental capacities.
- study a literary text taken from a humorous memoir about the role of television in the family life.

2.1 After reading the title of this unit and the brief introduction above, predict which words you will hear and read in the unit by creating a spider diagram. In the middle of your spider diagram, write the title 'Technology and human interaction' and add branches to it. Share your mind maps with your classmates. Then look at the wordbank for this unit. Which words appear in your spider diagram?

2.2 In order to understand the changes that technology has brought us, think about how people have changed the ways they've done things since the arrival of the **internet**. Make a copy of the table below. For each of the situations, comment on how these developments have changed the way people interact.

Situation	How people did this before the Internet?	How people did this after the Internet?	What effect has this had on how people interact with each other?
a Listening to your favourite music in the car			
b Shopping			
c Planning a holiday			
d Preparing a nice meal			
e Finding a new job			
f Dating			
g Finding someone to provide a service			
h Sharing pictures with friends			

2.3 Share your findings from Activity 2.2 with your classmates and hold a group discussion on the following question:

How has the arrival of the internet changed people's behaviours, attitudes and personalities?

Watch and listen 🎥 🔊

2.4 You are going to watch an interview with Simon Sinek on Inside Quest, in which he answers the questions below. Before you listen to his answers to these questions, ask yourself how you would answer them.

a   Who are Millennials and how would you describe the character traits of this generation?

b   What do younger generations look for in an ideal job these days?

c   Why might younger people find it difficult to work for an employer, after they've experienced years of bad parenting?

d   Would you say that mobile phones have an addictive quality, rather like alcohol? Explain your answer.

e   Are people more impatient today than they were before the arrival of the internet? Explain your answer.

f   What kinds of things in life can technology *not* help you with?

g   Do companies have a responsibility to help younger employees find more fulfillment in work *and* in life? Explain.

Communication skills
One of the skills that you should develop is communication. As you can see in his video 'The Millennial Question', Simon Sinek has very effective *communication skills*. He really engages his audience. What can you learn from him? What kinds of good *communication skills* is he using?

2.5 Do an online search for the video 'The Millennial Question' by Simon Sinek.

a How do you think Simon Sinek might answer the questions from Activity 2.4? As you listen and watch, write down some rough notes.

b After watching the video, write out complete sentences that answer the questions from Activity 2.4. Compare your answers to your classmates. Watch the video again if necessary.

Simon Sinek

2.6 In the video, Simon Sinek uses various verbs in combination with different nouns. Use the verbs from the box below to fill in the blanks in sentences a–l.

check	articulate	form	overcome	rely on	binge	wander
	waft through	attack	fail at	cope with	thrust into	

CONCEPTS

Audience

Simon Sinek's speech on 'The Millennial Question' is fascinating to watch online because his *audience* is also filmed. What's more, his *audience* seems to be the age group that he is talking about. Watch the video again carefully and comment on the reactions and the facial expressions of the *audience*. How do they respond and why do you think this is?

a Every business should be able to … their purpose.

b Millennials feel uncomfortable when employers … their self-image.

c Sinek say that parents sometimes … parenting strategies.

d After they leave school, young people are … the real world.

e During your adolescent years, you learn to … your friends.

f Alcohol is sometimes used by people to help them … stress and anxiety.

g Young people find it difficult to … deep, meaningful relationships.

h Many people … their messages right after waking up.

i Some people skip entire seasons of TV series, so that they can …. watch it at the end.

j People who are plugged in all the time, tend to… life.

k Many people need help to… the challenges of the digital world.

l Ideas and innovation happen when our minds … .

EXTRA

- Simon Sinek's video 'The Millennial Question' was viewed by millions of people within a few months and it received much criticism. Find an article that was published in response to the video. Give your classmates a copy of the article and give a small presentation in which you either defend or attack the article's position on the video.

- Do an online search for Joel Stein's article from 2013 for Time Magazine, entitled 'Millennials: The Me Me Me Generation'. Read the article and write a letter to the editor, which includes your response to its main claims.

2.7 The video 'The Millennial Question' created some controversy and Simon Sinek received much criticism for saying the things that he said. The interviewer in the video says very little. If you could ask Simon Sinek anything in response to the video, what would you ask? Make a list of questions as a class.

2.8 Now listen to 🔊 Audio track 8. Are the questions that you asked in Activity 2.7 asked in this short interview?

2.9 Listen to 🔊 Audio track 8 again. Which phrases or words are used to express the ideas underlined in phrases a–i? They appear in the same order below as in Audio track 8.

a   Rayna Rainman has recently received a lot of <u>media attention</u> for some things she said.

b   She has said some <u>provocative</u> things about Millennials.

c   The interviewer says he is going to <u>cite</u> a few words Rayna has used in a recent talk.

d   Many young people felt like they were being accused of <u>bad behaviour</u>.

e   Research suggests that failed parenting <u>methods</u> combined with hand-held technologies may be to blame.

f   People use platforms like Facebook to <u>boast</u> to their friends in an artificial way.

g   The interviewer challenges Rayna, asking 'Why <u>victimise</u> the youngest generation?'

h   People do not <u>switch jobs frequently</u> because they have a Twitter account.

i   Do we want to have <u>fake</u> friendships?

Exploring texts

2.10 You are going to read Text 3.5, called 'Society is Dead: We Have retreated into the iWorld'. The paragraphs do not appear in the correct order.

Read each paragraph and then place them in what you think is the correct order. After you have done this, check your answers with a classmate and your teacher. Discuss why you chose for your order by using these phrases. Replace 'w', 'x', 'y' and 'z' with letters, words and phrases from Text 3.5.

- 'I think [w] comes before [x], because the phrase [y] introduces the ideas that are explored in [z].
- '[x] appears after [w], because [z] refers back to what was mentioned earlier in [y].'
- 'The words [x] suggest that this paragraph comes after [w], since [z] elaborates on what was already stated in [y].

TOK

In Audio track 8, the interviewer and interviewee refer to the phrases 'causal relationship' and 'correlation'. In TOK, as you learn how knowledge is acquired, it is important to learn the difference between these two ideas.

- A 'correlation' is where two things behave similarly.
- A 'causal relationship' is where something behaves a certain way *because* of something else.

Do you think there is a causal relationship or a correlation between **Tweeting** and job hopping?

Text 3.5

Society is Dead: We have retreated into the iWorld

a   Yes, I might as well own up. I'm one of them. I witnessed the glazed New York looks through my own glazed pupils, my white wires peeping out of my ears. I joined the cult a few years ago: the sect of the little white box worshippers. Every now and again I go to church: those huge, luminous Apple stores, pews in the rear, the clerics in their monastic uniforms all bustling around or sitting behind the 'Genius Bars,' like priests waiting to hear confessions.

b   And like all addictive cults, it's spreading. There are now 22m iPod owners in the United States and Apple is becoming a mass-market company for the first time. Walk through any airport in the United States these days and you will see person after person gliding through the social ether as if on autopilot. Get on a subway and you're surrounded by a bunch of Stepford commuters staring into mid-space as if anaesthetised by technology. Don't ask, don't tell, don't overhear, don't observe. Just tune in and tune out.

c   I was visiting New York last week and noticed something I'd never thought I'd say about the city. Yes, nightlife is pretty much dead (and I'm in no way the first to notice that). But daylife – that insane mishmash of yells, chatter, clatter, hustle and chutzpah that makes New York the urban equivalent of methamphetamine – was also a little different. It was quieter.

d   Even without the white wires you can tell who they are. They walk down the street in their own MP3 cocoon, bumping into others, deaf to small social cues, shutting out anyone not in their bubble.

e   Others began, as I did, with a Walkman – and then a kind of clunkier MP3 player. But the sleekness of the iPod won me over. Unlike other models, it gave me my entire music collection to rearrange as I saw fit: on the fly, in my pocket.

What was once an occasional musical diversion became a compulsive obsession. Now I have my iTunes in my iMac for my iPod in my iWorld. It's Narcissus heaven: we've finally put the 'i' into Me.

f   Manhattan's downtown is now a Disney-like string of malls, riverside parks and pretty upper-middle-class villages. But there was something else. And as I looked across the throngs on the pavements, I began to see why.

g   Every now and again some start unconsciously emitting strange tuneless squawks, like a badly tuned radio, and their fingers snap or their arms twitch to some strange soundless rhythm. When others say 'Excuse me' there's no response. 'Hi,' ditto. It's strange to be among so many people and hear so little. Except that each one is hearing so much.

h   There were little white wires hanging down from their ears, or tucked into pockets, purses or jackets. The eyes were a little vacant. Each was in his or her own musical world, walking to their soundtrack, stars in their own music video, almost oblivious to the world around them. These were the iPod people.

The Sunday Times

EXTRA

In Text 3.5 you read the word 'Narcissus' (paragraph e). You have also heard the word narcissist and **narcissism** earlier in this unit. Do you know where this word originates and what it means? Do an online search to find out more and share your findings with your classmates in a short presentation.

2.11 In your own words explain what the author means by the following phrases from Text 3.5. They are not in any particular order.

a I joined the cult a few years ago: the sect of the little white box worshippers.

b Don't ask, don't tell, don't overhear, don't observe. Just tune in and tune out.

c It's strange to be among so many people and hear so little. Except that each one is hearing so much.

d We've finally put the 'I' into Me.

2.12 You are going to read Text 3.6, titled: 'Reclaiming conversation: The Power of Talk in a Digital Age'. Before you read the text, discuss your answers to the following questions with a classmate.

a What do you think is meant by the phrase 'the power of talk'?

b Why do you think the author has titled her book 'Reclaiming conversation'?

c What is the value of having face-to-face conversations over digital contact?

2.13 Some of the more difficult words from Text 3.6 have been removed. Fill the blanks in the text using the words below.

implicated	mediated	revise	spontaneous	devices	**chat**
contact	**collaborations**	development	**empathy**	cure	feed
		irresistible			

TEXT AND CONTEXT

- 'Stepford' a reference to the novel The Stepford Wives, about submissive wives who are secretly robots.

- Chutzpah is a Yiddish word for 'audacity', 'insolence' or 'boldness'.

- Methamphetamine is an illegal drug which causes hallucination.

3

Text 3.6

Reclaiming Conversation: The Power of Talk in a Digital Age

Why a book on **conversation**? We're talking all the time. We text and post and (1)....... We might even begin to feel more at home in the world of our **screens**. Among family and friends, among colleagues and lovers, we turn to our phones instead of each other. We readily admit we would rather send an electronic message or mail than commit to a face-to-face meeting or a telephone call.

This new (2)....... life has gotten us into trouble. Face-to-face conversation is the most human – and humanising – thing we do. Fully present to one another, we learn to listen. It's where we develop the capacity for (3)....... It's where we experience the joy of being heard, of being understood. And conversation advances self-reflection, the conversations with ourselves that are the cornerstone of early (4)....... and continue throughout life.

But these days we find ways around conversation. We hide from each other even as we're constantly **connected** to each other. For on our screens, we are tempted to present ourselves as we would like to be. Of course, performance is part of any meeting, anywhere, but online and at our leisure, it is easy to compose, edit, and improve as we (5).......

We say we turn to our phones when we're 'bored.' And we often find ourselves bored because we have become accustomed to a constant (6)....... of connection, information and entertainment. We are forever elsewhere. At class or at church or business meetings, we pay attention to what interests us and then when it doesn't, we look to our (7)....... to find something that does. There is now a word in the dictionary called '**phubbing**.' It means maintaining eye (8)....... while texting. My students tell me they do it all the time and that it's not that hard.

We begin to think of ourselves as a tribe of one, loyal to our own party. We check our messages during a quiet moment or when the pull of the online world simply feels (9)....... Even children text each other rather than talk face-to-face with friends – or, for that matter, rather than daydream, where they can take time alone with their thoughts.

It all adds up to a flight from conversation, at least from conversation that is open-ended and (10)......., conversation in which we play with ideas, in which we allow ourselves to be fully present and vulnerable. Yet these are the conversations where empathy and intimacy flourish and social action gains strength. These are the conversations in which the **creative** (11)....... of education and business thrive.

But these conversations require time and space, and we say we're too busy. Distracted at our dinner tables and living rooms, at our business meetings, and on our streets, we find traces of a new 'silent spring' – a term Rachel Carson coined when we were ready to see that with technological change had come an assault on our environment. Now, we have arrived at another moment of recognition. This time, technology is (12)....... in an assault on empathy. We have learned that even a silent phone inhibits conversations that matter. The very sight of a phone on the landscape leaves us feeling less connected to each other, less invested in each other.

Despite the seriousness of our moment, I write with optimism. Once aware, we can begin to rethink our practices. When we do, conversation is there to reclaim. For the failing connections of our digital world, it is the talking (13).......

By Sherry Turkle

2.14 Return to Activity 2.12 and ask yourself how the author of Text 3.6 would answer the three questions.

2.15 Before you read Text 3.7, look at the list of words below. On your own or with a classmate, group the words into categories and label these categories to say what they have in common. You might find it helpful to check the meaning of some of these words. Compare your word categories to those of other people in your class.

technology	interruption	producer	device	connectivity	office
distraction	school	driver	rendezvous	social engagement
PC	cab	temptation	information	phone	prison
conversation	friend	**gadget**

2.16 Use the words from Activity 2.15 to predict what you think Text 3.7 will be about. After reading the article, come back to these predictions. Were you right or wrong in what you predicted?

Social skills

The author of Text 3.6 believes that the ability to hold a meaningful conversation is an import life skill. She also believes that devices like phones are interfering with our ability to practise this skill. Think about the actual places in your life where you can practise your *social skills*. Where do you engage in meaningful conversation with others? How can you be more 'in the moment' during these conversations and not distracted by devices?

LEARNER PROFILE

Reflective

Text 3.6, an introduction to a book on 'conversation', raises an interesting point. In its second paragraph, it states that conversation encourages self-reflection. As an IB student you are most likely aware that reflection plays an important role in learning (and assessment). For this reason, you are encouraged to have frequent, meaningful conversations with classmates, teachers and your extended essay supervisor.

3

CAS

Not everyone has someone to talk to. To fulfill your CAS requirement, you might want to volunteer at a home for elderly people. You might find that by simply talking with older people, showing empathy for them and actively listening to them, you can brighten up their day. What's more, you will learn about life from their wealth of experience, and you will become a better conversationalist.

TEXT AND CONTEXT

- 'Dumbphone' (paragraph 2) is jokingly referred to as the opposite of a 'smartphone', which has internet capabilities.

- String cheese (paragraph 4) is popular in the United States. You can pull strings off it before eating it.

- The cache (paragraph 10) on one's computer is the storage of information, such as passwords, which can be called up by the computer for future requests.

- Occupy Wall Street (paragraph 12) was a movement that started in New York in 2011, where angry citizens demonstrated against banks and businesses that were believed to promote social and economic inequality.

- Base-jumping (paragraph 14) is an illegal sport in which people jump off buildings or structures with a parachute.

- Luddites (paragraph 14) were a group of workers in the clothing industry in the nineteenth century. They protested violently against the machinery that replaced them during the Industrial Revolution.

Text 3.7

Offline: day one of life without internet

Dear Diary,

I just spent 24 hours entirely without the Internet for the first time I can remember in my adult life.

1 I think there are two kinds of people who live with technology constantly in their face: people who freak out when they're forcefully separated from their devices or connectivity, as if their arm has been cut off, and people who feel really chill when they're forcefully separated from their devices or connectivity, as if they've been let out of prison. I've spoken to many of both kinds as I've prepared for leaving the Internet, and thankfully I fall in the latter camp.

2 I've lost my phone for weeks at a time before (in my pre-iPhone days), and let my current dumbphone run out of charge numerous times, and I always feel at peace knowing nobody can call me and demand anything of me. I know it's really frustrating for people who do want to reach me, and I'm always in danger of missing out on a party or failing to make a rendezvous, but overall I feel like it's a positive.

3 The moment I reached down and unplugged the Ethernet cable from my computer, I felt like school was out for the summer, and the simultaneous relief and **boredom** that last bell brings. I stood up, and I realised that I'd been anticipating this moment for ages, but for some reason I hadn't made any plans. It was a stark contrast to the hectic day I'd just experienced, which had culminated in a 3-hour, ultra-insane livestream of myself playing *StarCraft* and *Minecraft* simultaneously while Skyping with friends and playing jams in Turntable.fm.

4 I stood up, stretched, and then played local-multiplayer video games in the office for a couple hours, naturally. All that was missing was a beanbag and string cheese and I would've been 12 again.

5 To get my PC rig home I took a cab. Since Jordan, one of our video producers, was following me with a camera, recording this momentous evening, my cab driver asked me what we were shooting.

6 'Oh, I'm leaving the Internet for a year,' I said.

7 'Why?' he asked.

8 It was a good question, and he didn't seem to find my answer very interesting. Our conversation ended there.

9 At home I listened to records with my roommate and the peaceful boredom continued. I found myself really engaging in the moment, asking questions and listening closely, even more than if I'd just closed my computer or locked my phone, because I knew neither of those things could demand anything of me. Not tonight, and not for another 364 nights.

10 My first major temptation came the next morning, when I pulled out my iPad. I had forgotten to turn my iPad's Wi-Fi off for about five minutes after midnight, so I knew there were post-disconnect tweets cached on there. They'd be about me. They would stoke my ego, or maybe deflate it. I was very curious.

11 I deleted the app, tweets unseen. In fact, I've been keeping my Internet-reliant apps in a folder on my iPad, so I deleted all of those. Twitch.tv: I'll miss you most of all.

12 I went into the office a couple times for various errands, and heard snippets of news, but didn't stay long. I'll let the secondhand information stream start some other day. I heard something about a 'BlackBerry 10' and something about Diet Coke that I plan on searching for in the next issue of my daily paper. More interesting to me was hearing Joshua Kopstein talk about some of his first-hand experiences that day with the Occupy Wall Street crowd. I guess I'm a bit of a first-hand fanboy right now.

13 I spent much of the day catching up with a friend from out of town. He's actually a major authority on limiting phone-based distraction. He doesn't text, and his phone is often off. While I had to field a bunch of calls the whole time we were hanging out, he wasn't interrupted a single time by any of his gadgets. It's almost intimidating to have someone be that attentive to you.

14 The whole day was really refreshing. All my Internet-based social engagement the day before had been about how what I was doing was 'brave' or 'insane' or 'inspirational' or a 'publicity stunt' or 'stupid' or 'a waste of everyone's time,' as if I was planning on going on a hunger strike or basejumping off the Empire State Building. But while hanging out with a fellow Luddite, it felt like my undertaking is the perfectly natural thing.

15 I haven't settled into a rhythm yet. In fact, I haven't even made a new schedule for myself. I've done a little writing, a little reading, and a lot of chilling. I don't really know what the next days and weeks are going to look like. All I know is that so far I'm loving it.

16 *Paul Miller will regularly be posting dispatches from the disconnected world on The Verge during his year away from the Internet. He won't be reading your comments, but he'll be here in spirit.*

www.theverge.com

A 'dumb-phone' without Internet-enabled applications

2.17 Words a–m listed below are taken from Text 3.7. Match these words with a synonym from the box. The words in the list appear in the same order as in the text.

attraction	expect	film	frighten	chore	small bit	busy
answer	at the same time		liberation	end	important	reduce

a simultaneous   b relief

c anticipate   d hectic

e culminate   f momentous

g shoot   h temptation

i deflate   j errand

k snippet   l field

m intimidate

LEARNER PROFILE

Risk-takers

IB learners are encouraged to be risk-takers. As the poet T.S. Eliot once claimed: 'Only those who will risk going too far can possibly find out how far one can go'.

- How might Paul Miller's year without internet involve certain risks?
- What does he stand to gain by switching off his devices?
- Is this a kind of risk that you would be willing to take? Why or why not?

TOK

In TOK we ask ourselves how knowledge is gained. One way we learn is through experience.

- What do you think Paul Miller will learn by living for a year without the internet? His method of research ('going native') is sometimes used in the social sciences, such as anthropology.

- Do you think you could learn the same lessons as Paul Miller, without actually living for a year without the Internet?

2.18 Fill the gaps in the sentences below using words from phrases found in Text 3.7. The sentences are based on the phrases as they appear in the text.

a I'm annoyed by loud advertisements that are constantly in your … .

b There are two kinds of people: optimists and pessimists. Fortunately I … into the first camp.

c I have been looking forward to this big moment for … .

d Our weekend in the country was in … contrast to our busy city lives.

e Please don't give me too many compliments. You're … my ego.

f I discovered this to be true through … experience.

g We hadn't talked in such a long time. It was nice to … up.

2.19 Answer the following comprehension questions which refer to Text 3.7.

a What did Paul Miller do after he unplugged the Ethernet on his computer?

b What did the cab driver think of his plan to live without Internet?

c How was the author's evening at home with his roommate different from his usual evenings at home?

d Where does Paul Miller work? What kind of work does he do?

e What did Paul Miller do while hanging out with his friend from out of town?

f In the days leading up to Paul Miller's experiment, what kind of responses did he receive from people about his choice to live without the Internet?

g How does Paul Miller plan to live without the Internet?

Form and meaning

2.20 Could you live without Internet? How would you survive without your phone? What would happen? In order to answer questions like these you will need to use the 'future unreal conditional' tense. This type of grammatical structure consists of two parts (or clauses):

- an 'if' clause
- a 'would' clause.

Notice from the examples below that the 'if' clauses take the past simple verb, such as 'had'. The 'would' clause can also use 'could' (from 'can') or 'might' (from 'may'). Here are a few examples:

'If' clause	'Would' clause (or 'could' or 'might')
If I had to live without Internet for a day	I would go crazy.
If I didn't have access to Google Maps	I could get lost easily.
If my phone plan included more data	I might be able to steam video.

The following sentences a–g are missing a clause. Make up your own clause to complete the following sentences, using the future unreal conditional.

a If people still had a dial-up connection, …

b If there were no censorship of the Internet, …

c … then I might be able to work from home.

d … then citizens would be more informed voters.

e If our city introduced free wireless, …

f … students might not listen to their teachers anymore.

g If the public library ceased to exist, …

Research skills
Imagining a life offline might be difficult, especially when you think about doing research. For example, how would you write your extended essay without the Internet? While using the Internet as a research tool is advisable, it is also worth considering other useful, offline *research skills,* such as brainstorming, interviewing, reading books and articles or the making and organising of notes.

Research suggests that you are more likely to remember something if you have written it by hand

Discussion

2.21 Imagine you had to live for one week without the Internet. How would your life be different? You might want to use words and phrases from the following table to respond to this question.

If I could not access the Internet	I would not be able	to chat with my friends.
If I couldn't check my email	it would be impossible	to check my homework.
During a week without the Internet		to see what's going on in the news.
If I were not allowed to go online		
If the Internet had been disconnected for a week		

2.22 Prepare a short presentation on the topic of **distracted driving**. You can use the left-hand image below as a stimulus. Include answers to the following questions in your presentation.

• How common is texting whilst driving your country?

• How many injuries or deaths are caused yearly by distracted driving in your country?

• What initiatives have been taken to discourage distracted driving?

Texting whilst driving might seem harmless, but it couldn't be more dangerous

To support your presentation, you might want to show your classmates an example of an advertising campaign that aims to discourage distracted driving. Discuss how effective you think these ads are.

2.23 Here are several quotations. What is each quotation saying about the Internet? Do you agree or disagree with these statements? Explain why. Discuss your answers with classmates.

a 'The Internet is becoming the town square for the global village of tomorrow.' – Bill Gates

b 'Getting information off the Internet is like taking a drink from a fire hydrant.' – Mitch Kapor

c 'The Internet is just a world passing notes in a classroom.' – Jon Stewart

d 'The Net treats censorship as a defect and routes around it.' – John Gilmore

e 'The Internet is like alcohol in some sense. It accentuates what you would do anyway. If you want to be a loner, you can be more alone. If you want to connect, it makes it easier to connect.' – Esther Dyson

f 'The Net is a waste of time, and that's exactly what's right about it.' – William Gibson

2.24 Can you relate to the character in the cartoon on the right? Have social media and online communication tools made you more or less communicative? Discuss your answer with your classmates.

"I used to call people, then got into e-mailing, then texting, and now I just ignore everyone."

Writing

2.25 Imagine if you are going to write an opinion piece about the future of information technology and human interaction.

a Start by reading an article that predicts the future of information technology and human interaction. This might be in a magazine that comments frequently on this topic, such as *Wired* magazine.

b What are the main points in this article with which you agree or disagree?

c Check Unit 6.3 on how to write a blog. What structural and stylistic features should you include in your opinion piece?

d Check the assessment criteria for Paper 1 in Unit 7.1 (SL) or Unit 7.2 (HL).

e What are your predictions for the future? Why do you think this? Make a spider diagram to collect your ideas. Be sure to refer to the importance of technology in education, business and government.

f Now write your opinion piece In your piece try writing one or two sentences that use the future unreal conditional (Activity 2.20). For example, you could start a sentence with: 'If entire cities had free wireless everywhere, then …'.

g Ask a classmate and your teacher to assess your piece according to the assessment criteria for Paper 1.

h Based on the feedback you have received, re-write your piece and submit it to your teacher.

2.26 This unit has introduced criticisms of an over-mediated lifestyle. Write a letter to Simon Sinek ('The Millennial Question') or Sherry Turkle (*Reclaiming Conversation*) in response to their concerns about the role of technology on relationships. You can criticise or praise these authors on their points of view, using examples from your own life as evidence. Go to Unit 6.1 to find out more about how to write a letter.

EXTRA

- Nicholas Carr's book *The Shallows* was one of the first to raise concerns about a generation growing up with so much information technology. Read this book or extracts from it, and write a letter to the author with your response.

- Watch the movie *Her*, about a man who falls in love with his personal computer. How likely is something like this to happen in the future? Use this as a source of inspiration for your opinion piece in Activity 2.25.

Extended Essay
If you decide to write your extended essay on an English B topic, you have three 'categories' of essay to choose from (see Unit 1.1). On the topic of the Internet, you might decide to write a category one essay on language. This could be about how the Internet has introduced new vocabulary into our everyday lives. Your research question might read, 'To what extent have information technology and social media corrupted or contributed to the English language?' You might find that one of David Crystal's books or articles on this subject is a good source of inspiration.

Higher level extension

2.27 Text 3.8 is titled: 'Google Effect: Is technology making us stupid?' What do you think the 'Google Effect' is?

a Write a definition on a sticky note and place it on a wall for your classmates to read.

b Read everyone's definition. Where do you see similarities?

c Now do an online search for the term 'Google Effect'. How close were you to the actual meaning?

d Does the Google Effect apply to you and your life? Do you experience this phenomenon often?

2.28 Several words have been removed from Text 3.8. Decide where you think the following words fit into the gaps 1–15 in the text. You might have to look up their definitions first.

a	cognitive	**b**	safeguard
c	store	**d**	connections
e	stick	**f**	innovation
g	danger	**h**	engagement
i	memory	**j**	distraction
k	amnesia	**l**	intelligence
m	concern	**n**	raft
o	bear		

Text 3.8

Google Effect: Is technology making us stupid?

Can't remember phone numbers or birthdays? You may be suffering from the 'Google Effect' – a theory that we've outsourced our memories, safe in the knowledge that answers are just a click away. Genevieve Roberts investigates.

"Is the internet making us stupid?" I type. Press enter. Almost instantly, a (1)....... of answers and articles on screen. It's an unsettling feeling that my first instinct – to Google my own stupidity – may be the root of my increasing daftness.

A recent study (you've probably forgotten it by now) suggests 90 per cent of us are suffering from digital (2)........ More than 70 per cent of people don't know their children's phone numbers by heart, and 49 per cent have not memorised their partner's number. While those of us who grew up in a landline-only world may also remember friends' home numbers from that era, we are unlikely to know their current mobiles, as our phones do the job. The Kaspersky Lab concludes we don't commit data to (3)....... because of the "Google

Effect" – we're safe in the knowledge that answers are just a click away, and are happy to treat the web like an extension to our own memory.

Dr Maria Wimber, lecturer at the University of

Birmingham's School of Psychology, worked with the internet security firm on their research. She believes the internet simply changes the way we handle and store information, so the Google Effect "makes us good at remembering where to find a given bit of information, but not necessarily what the information was. It is likely to be true that we don't attempt to (4)....... information in our own memory to the same degree that we used to, because we know that the internet knows everything."

These findings echo Columbia University Professor Betsy Sparrow's research on the Google Effect on memory, which concluded, "Our brains rely on the internet for memory in much the same way they rely on the memory of a friend, family member or co-worker. We remember less through knowing information itself than by knowing where the information can be found."

[...]

But is this making us more stupid? Anthropologist Dr Genevieve Bell, a vice-president at Intel and director of the company's Corporate Sensing and Insights Group, believes not. She says technology "helps us live smarter" as we're able to access answers. "Being able to create a well-formed question is an act of (5)......., as you quickly work out what information you want to extract and identify the app to help achieve this. To me, this suggests a level of (6)....... with the world that's not about dumbness." She gives the example of a new mother trying to work out whether their baby not sleeping is bad – and when to start worrying. "These are all questions that technology may be able to address quicker than calling your own parents," she says. "This isn't making consumers dumber, instead it's helping them to think smarter."

She believes our biggest (7)....... should be our mindset towards technology. "My suspicion is it isn't that the use of technology is making us dumber; instead it's a very human set of preoccupations and anxieties," she says. "Ultimately it's the anxiety about what technology means for us, what it means for our humanity, our bodies, our competency – and what it means to have new technologies in some ways threaten some of those things."

In contrast, Nicholas Carr, author of The Shallows: How the Internet is Changing the Way We Think, Read and Remember and The Glass Cage: Where Automation is Taking Us, believes we should be alarmed. "We're missing the real (8)......., that human memory is not the same as the memory in a computer: it's through remembering that we make connections with what we know, what we feel, and this gives rise to personal knowledge. If we're not forming rich (9)....... in our own minds, we're not creating knowledge. Science tells us memory consolidation involves attentiveness: it's in this process that you form these connections."

He believes the combination of the Google Effect and the constant (10)....... of smartphones, constantly delivering information, is concerning. A Microsoft study found the average human attention span fell from 12 seconds in 2000 to eight seconds today.

"There is a superficiality to a lot of our thinking," Carr says. "Not just the (11)....... side, but also the emotional side. That not only reduces richness in one's own life and sense of self, but if we assume that rich, deep thinking is essential to society then it will have a detrimental effect on that over the long run. There will always be people who buck those trends, but I think it will have an effect of making ourselves and our culture a little shallow."

[...]

Andrew Keen, author of The Internet is Not the Answer, [...] agrees with Carr that "technology is making us shallower thinkers, multi-tasking, unable to digest speeches, even songs, perpetually flicking". In response, he says what we need now is creativity and (12)......... . "We need to think eclectically and daringly," he says. "The big issue is how to teach creativity. We don't need to learn facts, to remember stuff is less important, so the nature of professions are shifting; teachers should (13)....... this is mind. The question is, how do you teach children to think differently?"

Dr Wimber advises people to spend time offline to (14)....... their memories. "We know from memory research that we only remember information we pay attention to," she says. "If we spend all our time online, or experiencing our lives through a smartphone camera lens, we might miss important experiences, and not commit them to long-term memory. Constantly looking up information online is not an effective way to create permanent memories. The best way to make information (15)....... is to sometimes sit back, and mentally refresh what you learnt or experienced a minute, an hour or a day ago."

The Independent

2.29 Re-read Text 3.8 and look for arguments to go into each of the columns in the table below. Then, after you have completed the table, divide your class in two and have a small debate on the matter. Articulate the ideas from the article in your own words. Add arguments, referring to your own experiences, where relevant.

Google is making you more stupid	Google is not making you more stupid

2.30 After your debate, try writing a Paper 1-style response to the prompt below in 450-600 words. Use one of the three suggested text types for your written response. Depending on your level of experience, you may wish to write this response under exam conditions, by hand in 1 hour and 30 minutes. See Unit 7.2 for further advice on Paper 1 at higher level.

Imagine that several teachers at your school have complained that the attention span of students has decreased over the years. They blame this lack of focus on the distractions that students experience from digital devices. Using one of the text types below respond to their complaints and address the problem.

editorial letter speech

2.31 Find out more about Sergy Brin and Larry Page, the founders and inventors of Google.

- What were their intentions when creating Google?
- To what extent have they accomplished these goals?
- What criticisms are made of Google today?

After reading about Google and its founders, hold a 'press conference' in which you or another classmate are interviewed in the role of either Sergy Brin or Larry Page. Try to answer all questions as if you were those people.

Sergy Brin and Larry Page, founders of Google

TOK

One of the aims of TOK is to help you develop critical thinking skills. Define the following TOK terms and explain their relevance to the cartoon below.

- critical thinking
- wisdom
- knowledge
- certainty
- authority workshop
- reliability

Literature

2.32 Imagine two families. In one family the children grow up watching a lot of TV. In the other family children grow up without a TV at all. In the table like the one below make a list of the possible effects of these different upbringings on the children.

Effects of raising children with a lot of TV	Effects of raising children without TV

2.33 You are about to read Text 3.9, the opening lines from a short story about growing up with television. Much of the text is meant to be humorous. After you have read the text, discuss why the following lines are funny. The paragraph number has been placed after each line, so that you can read them in context.

a   I hoped that in walking around after dark I might witness a murder, but for the most part our neighbors just sat in their living rooms, watching TV. [1]

b   When my mother reported that Mr. Tomkey did not believe in television my father said, 'Well, good for him. I don't know that I believe in it either.' [2]

c   It was speculated that just as the blind man develops a keener sense of hearing, the family must somehow compensate for their loss. [4]

d   Because they had no TV, the Tomkeys were forced to talk during dinner. [6]

e   They did not know what attractive was or what dinner was supposed to look like or even what time people were supposed to eat. [6]

f   What must it be like to be so ignorant and alone? Could a normal person even imagine it? [7]

Text 3.9

1   Back in New York State, we had lived in the country, with no sidewalks or streetlights; you could leave the house and still be alone. But here [in North Carolina], when you looked out from the window, you saw other houses, and people inside those houses. I hoped that in walking around after dark I might witness a murder, but for the most part our neighbors just sat in their living rooms, watching TV. The only place that seemed truly different was owned by a man named Mr. Tomkey, who did not believe in television. This was told to us by our mother's friend who dropped by one afternoon with a basketful of okra. [...]

2   To say that you did not believe in television was different from saying that you did not care for it. Belief implied that television had a master plan and that you were against it. It also suggested that you thought too much. When my mother reported that Mr. Tomkey did not believe in television my father said, 'Well, good for him. I don't know that I believe in it either.'

3   'That's exactly how I feel,' my mother said, and then my parents watched the news, and whatever came on after the news.

4   Word spread that Mr. Tomkey did not own a television, and you began hearing that while this was all very well and good, it was unfair of him to inflict his beliefs upon others, specifically his innocent wife and children. It was speculated that just as the blind man develops a keener sense of hearing, the family must somehow compensate for their loss. 'Maybe they read,' my mother's friends said. 'Maybe they listen to the radio, but you can bet your boots they're doing something.'

5   I wanted to know what this something was, and so I began peering through the Tomkey's windows. During the day I'd stand across the street from their house, acting as though I were waiting for someone, and at night, when the view was better and I had less chance of being discovered, I would creep into their yard and hide in the bushes beside their fence.

6 Because they had no TV, the Tomkeys were forced to talk during dinner. They had no idea how puny their lives were, and so they were not ashamed that a camera would have found them uninteresting. They did not know what attractive was or what dinner was supposed to look like or even what time people were supposed to eat. Sometimes they wouldn't sit down until eight o'clock, long after everyone else had finished doing the dishes. During the meal, Mr. Tomkey would occasionally pound the table and point at his children with a fork, but the moment he finished, everyone would start laughing. I got the idea that he was imitating someone else, and wondered if he spied on us while we were eating.

7 When fall arrived and school began, I saw the Tomkey children marching up the hill with paper sacks in their hands. The son was one grade lower than me, and the daughter was one grade higher. We never spoke, but I'd pass them in the halls from time to time and attempt to view the world through their eyes. What must it be like to be so ignorant and alone? Could a normal person even imagine it?

Extract from Us and Them *by David Sedaris*

2.34 Return to your answers from Activity 2.32, where you listed the effects of growing up with or without television.

a How many of your original ideas were reflected in Text 3.9?

b After reading Text 3.9, do you have any new effects to add to this list?

c Use your completed lists to have a classroom discussion on the value of television in the family life.

2.35 Try writing your own short story in which you describe a family that raises their children without mobile phones or Internet-connected devices. You can take the perspective of a child, parent or neighbour (like Text 3.9). Compare your story to that of a classmate who has written from a different perspective.

REFLECT

Take some time to reflect on the ideas from this unit. Answer the following yes/no questions as a class.

- After your teacher reads out each question, decide whether you will stand in the 'yes' or 'no' half of your classroom.
- After each question, explain why you chose 'yes' or 'no'.
- Use this format to have a constructive conversation on technology and human interaction.

Refer to the ideas and texts in this unit as you give your answers.

a Are you a Millennial?

b Do you behave like the Millennials that Simon Sinek described in his video 'The Millennial Question'?

c Are you addicted to your phone?

d Do you have meaningful, face-to-face conversations with your friends every day?

e Are you sometimes guilty of phubbing?

f Have you been affected by the problem of distracted driving?

g Do you think that Google is making you 'stupid'?

h Do you think that textbooks will eventually 'die'?

i Do you think that television has made you less ignorant?

Unit 3.3
Redefining art

'What is art?' 'What is the purpose of art?' 'How is art changing?' Art is a never-ending conversation about identity, values and beliefs.

This unit encourages you to both define and redefine 'art' for yourself, and to consider the value that people attach to art. It provides you with lots of opportunities to challenge you, and your own definition of art!

Getting started

3.1 'Is this art?' Below are several images a–l. For each one, discuss with a classmate whether or not each qualifies as 'art', according to your definition of art. In your discussion, feel free to compare images. Use the words from the word bank.

a The Lascaux Cave paintings, France

b A photograph of the Milky Way, taken by the Hubble Telescope

c A flash mob performance (a seemingly random performance by a group of people in a large public place, often organised through social media)

d A sonnet by William Shakespeare

e The Taj Mahal in Agra, India

f A marble bust of Julius Caesar made recently, for sale on Etsy.com

Word bank

value

technique

skill

intention

novelty

aesthetic

beauty

interpretation

context

authorship

collect

exhibit

imagination

experience

vision

iconic

criticism

appreciate

imitate

curate

a

b

c

d

e

f

In your TOK class, you will explore the arts as an area of knowledge (AoK). Activity 3.1 asks you to answer the question 'This is art?' As you define art, you may discuss:

- the **value** that people attach to an art work
- the **technique** of the artist
- the artist's ability to apply a **skill** or technique
- the artist's **intention** or purpose
- the **novelty** of the work
- the art work's **aesthetic** qualities, or its sheer **beauty**
- the viewer or reader's emotional response or **interpretation**.

Make sure you know the meaning of each of these words. Check in the glossary at the end of the book for the meaning of any you don't know.

g   Marcel Duchamp's 'Fountain'

h   A Coca-Cola advertisement

i   A chair designed by Charles and Ray Eames

j   Street art by Banksy, which has been removed from a wall and placed in a museum

k   A basketball player making a three-point shot from centre court just before the buzzer to win a game by one point

l   'The John Lennon Peace Wall', a place in Prague where everyone can draw peace and love themed graffiti.

g    h    i

j    k    l

LEARNER PROFILE

Open-minded

The IB encourages you to be *open-minded*. This trait is particularly relevant to this unit, where you are asked to redefine your ideas about art. As the IB states in their learner profile, you should 'seek and evaluate a range of points of view, and [be] willing to grow from the experience.' Analysing, evaluating and even creating art are all activities that help you to become more *open-minded*.

3.2 The images from Activity 3.1, ask you about the relation between art and other fields of expertise. Using the list of words a–j below, discuss your answers to the following question:

'*What is the difference between art and…?*'

Are these forms of art, or do they have something in common with the arts?.

a	design	b	architecture
c	graffiti	d	engineering
e	craft	f	sport
g	photography	h	desktop publishing
i	graphic design	j	performing arts

3.3 Take a look at the images from Activity 3.1 that you did NOT consider to be art. Ask yourself: 'Under what circumstances, or in which **context** might this item be considered as art?'

EXTRA

Activities 3.1–3.4 ask you to define art through a study of examples. Perhaps the definition of 'art' is not black or white. There might be many graduations of grey in between.

a Try rating images a–l on a scale of 1–10, where 10 indicates that the image is most definitely art, and 1 that the image is most definitely *not* art.

b When you have done this, make your own list of examples that 'might be art', and which fall into this grey area between 'art' and 'not art'.

c Share your list with a classmate and see how he or she rates each item.

3.4 After your discussions in Activities 3.1-3.3, write a definition of art that expresses your own opinion. Write your definition on a sticky note and place it on a wall along with those of your classmates, for everyone to read. Compare and contrast everyone's definitions and leave them on the wall as a reminder while you work on this unit.

CAS
The 'C' in CAS is for *creativity*. Being creative helps you grow as an individual. Displays of *creativity* can enrich the lives of others. To fulfill part of your CAS requirement, consider how you yourself can develop and enrich the lives of others by being *creative* or encouraging others to be creative. If you have a talent, how can you share it?

Watch and listen 🎥 🔊

3.5 In the previous activities, you made your own definition of what art is. Now take a moment and write a short answer to the question: 'What is art for?' Share your answers with your classmates. As a class, decide on the *five* best reasons why people need to create and consume art.

3.6 In the box below are several words taken from the video 'What is art for?'. Before you watch the video, use the words from the box to fill in the blanks in the sentences that follow. Look up the meanings of any words that you do not already know.

stifle	ascribe	energise	aggravate	weigh	condition	drawn to
flock to	visible	tease out	extraordinary	close	glamorous	
regret	awkward	depress	false	stiff	rounded	vital

a People ... museums

b There was a(n) ... silence.

c Maybe we can ... purposes to art.

d We need pretty things ... to us.

e Problems ... so heavily on people.

f There is a lot of sadness and ... that we cannot express.

g Art makes our pain more ... and accessible.

h Sad works do not have to ... us.

i Pain is part of the human ... .

j Art fights the ... optimism of commercial society.

k Every good life has ... amounts of suffering.

TIP

Activity 3.6, a 'fill in the blank' activity, can be made easier for you. Study all of the words in the box and label them 'verb', 'noun', 'adjective', or 'other' (if you do not know). Then read the questions and ask yourself what kind of word is missing from each sentence? Now your list is much shorter, and if you don't know the meaning of a word, you now have a much better chance of guessing correctly! Applying this method to this type of question in an exam situation can help make the questions easier for you.

l   We should not ... sadness by thinking we are losers.

m   We are ... art because is compensates us for what we lack.

n   Art helps us feel more ... .

o   Art helps us get in touch with the pain and drama that we have had to ....

p   What a society calls 'beautiful' is a ... clue to what it is missing in society.

q   Some artists can make grass or oranges look ... .

r   Artists can ... something that has been neglected in society.

s   Art can ... people for a cause.

t   People sometimes get ... and lose their spontaneity around famous people.

3.7   Search for the film 'What is art for? Alain de Botton's animated guide, Art and design' by Guardian Culture. As you watch the film, take notes on your answers to the questions below. When it is finished, write out your answers thoroughly.

a   Why are people scared to answer the question: What is art for?

b   Why does prettiness matter?

c   Why are somber works of art important?

d   Why does the video include a scale?

e   According to Alain de Botton, why do whole societies sometimes fall in love with a particular art style?

f   Why do Van Gogh's oranges appear on the red carpet in the video?

g   How is art like propaganda?

h   Why should we 'relax' around art? And how should we 'use' it?

CAS

If you agree with Alain de Botton that art is something *needed* by people, then you might want to organise an art exhibition for 'people in need'. These do not have to be poor people, but people in a place without much art. Perhaps there is a drab part of town that would benefit from a mural. Perhaps there is a home for senior citizens that could be brightened up for the residents. Perhaps the hallways of your school look bare and uninteresting. Think of opportunities, together with your CAS coordinator, to liven up somewhere with some inspiring artwork.

3.8   After watching Alain de Botton's video, return to your answers from Activity 3.5. How similar were his ideas to your reasons for why people need art?

Alain de Botton is a popular, contemporary philosopher who writes and speaks about topics such as art and love.

3.9   You are going to listen to Audio track 9, about a fictional 'vlogger' (a video blogger) who pulls a prank on exclusive art dealers in London, by selling them prints from a leading furniture store as important works of art. Before you listen to the recording, discuss your answers to the following questions with your classmates:

a   Might prints from the 'art' department of any large home-decorating store, have artistic value?

b   How would you convince an exclusive art dealer that a print from a furniture store is valuable?

c   Is it ethically permissible to film someone and post the film on the Internet without his or her consent?

d   Are art dealers better at assessing the value of artwork than you?

e   Are art dealers entitled to earn more on the sale of an artwork than the artist?

f   Can pranks or stunts be considered as performing arts?

g   Could something be considered as 'art' if it serves a commercial purpose, like spreading brand awareness?

h   What does the word 'hypocrisy' mean to you?

Audio track 9 asks you to think about the value of art. How scientific is this process of attaching a price tag to an artwork?

3.10 Listen to 🔊 Audio track 9. Listen carefully for words with the meanings in sentences a–j. These meanings are listed in the same order as the words appear in the recording. Read the meanings before listening to the recording, and make guesses where you think you already know the answer. As you listen to the recording, write your answers. You do not have to spell the words correctly at first. You can correct them later. Share your answers with your teacher and classmates. Listen to the recording again to check your answers.

a   This is a term used to describe a video or commercial that has travelled the internet quickly, like a virus.

b   This is an adjective to describe an act that makes fun of human behaviour.

c   This word is used for people who create their own business.

d   This word is an antonym (or opposite) of 'fake'.

e   This is another word for a mastermind or incredibly clever person.

f   This word is used to refer to an entire system that has been in place for years.

g   This verb means having copied content and distributed it for free, or a lower price than the original.

h   This is what you call people who are fake or phony.

i   This word describes someone who is honourable.

j   This word means informative or educational.

3.11 After listening to Audio track 9, return to your answers from Activity 3.9. Have your answers to those questions changed at all? If so, how? Discuss the questions again with your classmates.

Exploring texts

3.12 You have exactly 30 seconds to read Text 3.10. Then close your coursebook and write down *three* bullet points that sum up the main ideas of the text. You do not have to understand or even read every word of the piece. You should simply aim to reduce the whole article to three short bullet points. Are you ready? Go!

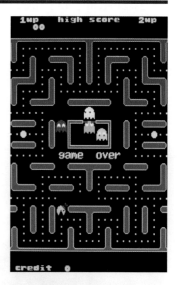

Pac-Man was on display at New York's MoMA in 2013.

Text 3.10

Sorry MoMA, video games are not art

Exhibiting Pac-Man and Tetris alongside Picasso and Van Gogh will mean game over for any real understanding of art

There needs to be a word for the overly serious and reverent praise of digital games by individuals or institutions who are almost certainly too old, too intellectual and too dignified to really be playing at this stuff. Gamecrashing? [Gamebollocks? Spiellustfaken?]

I first encountered this trope of the inappropriate elder's interest in the newest games a few years ago at a philosophy conference in Oxford University (I was an interloper in those hallowed groves). An aesthetician – a philosopher who specialises in aesthetics – gave a talk on his research into games. He defended them as serious works of art. The art of games, he argued, if I understood him right, lies in their interactive dimension and liberation of shared **authorship**. But he never answered the question: what was a professor doing playing all these games?

Now the Museum of Modern Art in New York is up to the same manoeuvre. MoMA has announced that it is to **collect** and **exhibit** games from Pong to Minecraft. So, the same museum that owns such great works of art as Ma Jolie by Picasso, Starry Night by Vincent van Gogh and Vir Heroicus Sublimis by Barnett Newman is also to own SimCity, Portal and Dwarf Fortress. MoMA claims these games belong in its collection because they are art. Really? Is that so?

Casting my mind back to the philosophical debate I spied on in Oxford, I remember a pretty good argument for why interactive immersive digital games are NOT art. Walk around the Museum of Modern Art, look at those masterpieces it holds by Picasso and Jackson Pollock, and what you are seeing is a series of personal visions. A work of art is one person's reaction to life. Any definition of art that robs it of this inner response by a human creator is a worthless definition. Art may be made with a paintbrush or selected as a ready-made, but it has to be an act of personal **imagination**.

The worlds created by electronic games are more like playgrounds where experience is created by the interaction between a player and a programme. The player cannot claim to impose a personal vision of life on the game, while the creator of the game has ceded that responsibility. No one 'owns' the game, so there is no artist, and therefore no work of art.

This is the essential difference between games and art, and it precedes the digital age. Chess is a great game, but even the finest chess player in the world isn't an artist. She is a chess player. Artistry might have gone into the design of the chess pieces. But the game of chess itself is not art nor does it generate art, it is just a game.

And so is Dwarf Fortress.

The Guardian

3.13 Activity 3.12 asked you to read the Text 3.10 in 30 seconds and write down three bullet points that summarise the text. Share your three bullet points from this activity with a classmate. How are your points similar or different? Now take time to read the article *without* time pressure. Return to your three points and those of your classmate. Whose points were more accurate?

3.14 Below is a crossword puzzle, based on the vocabulary from Text 3.10. Look up the meanings of any words that you don't know before you make the puzzle.

Across

5 a person who comes to a place where they do not belong
6 a discussion or argument
8 to deny, deprive or cheat
9 a series of moves requiring skill and care
12 creative skill or ability
13 an adjective to describe someone who is respected or honourable
14 to be surrounded by a sensation or stimulus
15 a verse from a song that was sung in Mass in medieval times
16 the ability of the mind to be creative
17 the sense of ownership held by a creator of art

Down

1 a meeting for lectures and discussion
2 an adjective to describe something that is holy or worshipful
3 an aspect or feature
4 to give up or give away
7 a small wood or group of trees
10 the study of beauty or artistic tastes
11 a public display

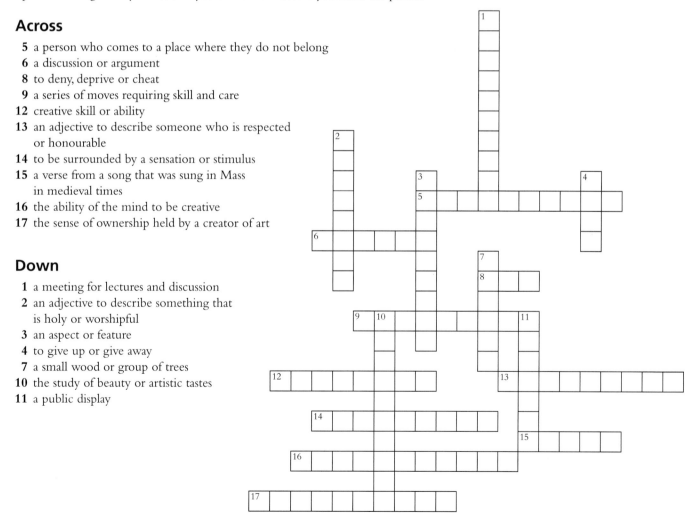

3.15

a   Select *three* words that were answers to your crossword puzzle in activity 3.14 and try to make a meaningful sentence with them.

b   Then, try to make a meaningful sentence with *four* words from the puzzle.

c   Finally, try to make a meaningful sentence using *five* words from the puzzle. Share and compare your sentences with your classmates and teacher.

3.16   The paragraphs below, from Text 3.11, do not appear in their correct order.

a   Together with a classmate, read each paragraph and place them in an order that makes more sense.

b   Check your order with other classmates and ask your teacher for the correct order.

c   What clues and words from the text helped you re-order the paragraphs correctly?

d   Which paragraphs did you find difficult to place? Why?

Extended Essay

Jill Greenberg's End Times photographs would be excellent 'cultural artefacts' for a Category 2b extended essay. A research question might read: 'To what extent do Jill Greenberg's photographs from her End Times series give the viewer an understanding of the political climate in the United States in the early 2000s?' As you can see, works of fine art are perfect vehicles for an essay that explores culture and language.

Text 3.11

Paragraph A

She said that the specific photographic techniques used to heighten the drama, a special recipe of studio lights combined with some postproduction effects that she often uses in her commercial work, might have intensified the outcry.

© Evan Kafka / Getty images

'I think the lighting and the whole approach shooting slightly from below it makes the subject heroic and **iconic** and intense, and it sort of overly dramatises the emotion,' she said.

Paragraph B

But **criticism** of her series, 'End Times,' hasn't focused on Greenberg's political views. Instead, it has focused on the crying faces in the photographs, prompting accusations that Greenberg abused the children to get them to show emotion.

'It's upsetting to get emails sort of randomly saying that I'm a horrible person,' Greenberg said. 'I have two children of my own. Crying is not evidence of pain or any real suffering. It's really just the way children communicate.'

Paragraph C

Jill Greenberg created portraits of crying children in 2006 to reflect her frustration with the politics of the Bush era. 'The most dangerous fundamentalists aren't just waging war in Iraq; they're attacking evolution, blocking medical research and ignoring the environment,' she wrote in a statement. 'It's as if they believe the apocalyptic End Time is near, therefore protecting the earth and future of our children is futile. As a parent I have to reckon with the knowledge that our children will suffer for the mistakes our government is making. Their pain is a precursor of what is to come.'

Paragraph D

Greenberg enlisted her daughter, her friends, and a few child models to participate.

Their mothers came along for the shoots, and together they'd work to get the children to start crying. 'The moms would hand them a lollipop in some cases, or they would offer them their cellphone, and then just sort of ask for it back. And basically the child was throwing a tantrum to try to get this candy or toy back, sort of putting on a show in a way,' Greenberg said.

Paragraph E

But in general, Greenberg said the controversy is overblown. 'Making children cry for a photographer can be considered mean. But I would say that making children laugh and show off their jeans for an apparel ad is just as exploitative and less natural. Toddlers' natural state, like 30 percent of the time, is crying, and it doesn't indicate pain or suffering,' Greenberg said.

Paragraph F

But in other ways, Greenberg said, the series has had a life of its own that she didn't expect and doesn't **appreciate.** She said she continues to get hate mail about the photographs, and in one case, an agency refused to hire her for a job because of the controversy surrounding the series. Further, Greenberg said the images are often **imitated** and regularly stolen for use in advertising and political campaigns. 'What's weird about the images is they seemingly can be applied to all these random disparate causes. My husband was saying they're like emoticons,' she said.

Paragraph G

Though the series has caused her plenty of headaches, Greenberg said she doesn't regret doing it. 'It's sort of bizarre how it's become such a focal point in my career,' Greenberg said. 'It's just this double-edged sword. I did so much work before it, and I did so much after. It's hard as an artist when you become known for one thing. It's really, really hard to fight your way out of that box.' The series is now collected in a book, published by TF Editores/D.A.P.

Paragraph H

In a way, Greenberg said, the photographs are serving their intended purpose by inciting a strong emotional reaction from viewers. 'The still image continues to have a ton of strength,' Greenberg said. 'An image taken out of context from one fraction of a second to the next can tell a story, and if photographers are looking to tell a certain story, they can **curate** those slices of time to their advantage.'

www.slate.com

CONCEPTS

Meaning

Perhaps what gives Jill Greenberg's photographs from *End Times* so much meaning are the captions, which turn the images into political commentary. Images can create meaning. Words can create meaning. Words combined with images can often create a new dimension of meaning. This is important to remember with analysing text with images.

3.17 After you have read Text 3.11 in its original order, think of a heading or title for the article. Post every classmate's heading on a board for everyone to read. Which one do you think is most appropriate and for what reasons? Ask your teacher to give you the original heading. How similar or different was yours to the original?

Form and meaning

3.18 The following three sentences were taken from Texts 3.10 and 3.11. What do they have in common? How are they similar in form and syntax?

- Art may be made with a paintbrush.

- Making children cry for a photographer can be considered mean.

- The images are often imitated.

Compare the above sentences to the ones below. How have they been changed? What words have been added? What words have been removed? How has the meaning slightly changed?

- Many artists make art with a paintbrush.
- Some people consider making children cry for a photographer mean.
- Other photographers often imitate the images.

3.19 In Activity 3.18, you might have noticed that the first three sentences were 'passive' and the last three sentences were 'active'. Notice how the last sentences include 'agents' or subjects that *do* the things the verbs suggest. In the first set of sentences there are no 'agents', 'artists', 'people' and 'photographers' have been added to the last sentences.

How can a sentence be made 'active' or 'passive'?

Active	Passive
• Include an 'agent' or subject (i.e 'photographers').	• Exclude an 'agent' and include an object (i.e. 'images')
• An active verb (i.e. 'imitate')	• Use a form of the verb 'to be' (i.e. 'are')
• Include an object (i.e. 'images')	• Use the past participle of another verb (i.e. 'imitated')

When should the active or passive form be used?

The active form is often used to sound stronger and emphasise '*who* did what'. The passive form is often used to avoid 'who' and focus on 'what'. (Note: It is possible to say *who* did what in a passive sentence by adding a 'by' phrase. For example:

> *Images are often imitated <u>by photographers.</u>*

Change the following sentences to make them either active or passive. You will have to create your own 'agents' where necessary. You may add a 'by' phrase. The first sentence has been done for you.

	Active	Passive
a	Art dealers sell street art these days.	Street art is sold by art dealers these days.
b	Jill Greenberg made children cry for her photographs.	
c		Art dealers were lied to by ProPrankster.
d		Paintings of landscapes are loved by people all over the world
e	Not everyone considers video games art	
f		In video games, an experience is created by both players and programmers.
g	People should use art to discover themselves.	

h	Some dealers acquire street art without the artist's permission.	
i		Some works of art have been over analysed by critics.
j	In the end, art collectors determine the value of art.	
k		The artist's sketches were exhibited by the museum.

Writing

3.20 Have you ever written a review of an art show?

a See Unit 6.2 on how to write a review. What are the key features of this text type?

b Find a review of an art show in a newspaper. Does this article contain all of the features described in Unit 6.2.

c Go and visit an art show at a museum or gallery near you. If you cannot find a show, try to find a series of photographs or works online by one artist.

d Write a review of the show for your teacher and classmates. Use the assessment criteria and requirements for Paper 1 as a guideline.

e Have a classmate and your teacher assess your review according to the assessment criteria for Paper 1.

f Taking their feedback into consideration, rewrite your review and submit it to your teacher.

Discussion

3.21 This unit has asked you to consider the question 'what is art?' Your answer to this might depend on who you are. Is beauty in the eye of the beholder, as the saying goes? This suggests that everyone is entitled to have an opinion about what is beautiful or not. Or is there such a thing as 'absolute beauty' with its own rules and principles? Find examples of art in art books or online to debate these opposite positions on art.

3.22 Do you agree with the author of Text 3.10? Have a mini-debate as a class in which one group defends and the other group rejects the following statement: 'Video games should be considered as art and placed on exhibit in the Museum of Modern Art (MOMA) in New York.' Keep in mind the arguments given by the author of Text 3.10.

3.23 Jill Greenberg (Text 3.11) suggests that art has a responsibility to incite an emotion from its viewers. But at what cost should this come? Is it unethical to make toddlers cry in the name of art? What if an animal dies in creating art? Is it unethical for graffiti artists to deface public property? Together with your classmates, try to come up with a set of ethical rules for artists.

TOK

Activity 3.21 asks you to think about the nature of art. Essentially it asks you if art is *relative* or *absolute*. Is art only about opinion or is it a human endeavor to discover a truth and reality? The English Romantic poet John Keats once wrote: 'Beauty is truth, truth beauty.' Pablo Picasso once said: 'Art is a lie that tells the truth.' What do you think these artists meant? Are their observations accurate?

EXTRA

Activity 3.23 asks you to explore ethics and art. There are many examples of art that seem to break any rules of ethics. For example in 2007, Guillermo Vargas tied a famished dog to a wall in the Codice Gallery in Nicaragua. The artist had placed dog food just out of reach of the dog. By the end of the exhibit, the dog had died because viewers did not feel it was their responsibility to feed it. Do an online search for more examples of art installations and pieces that push the boundaries of what is ethically acceptable and use these examples for your discussion in Activity 3.23.

3.24 Prepare a 3–4-minute oral presentation, using one of the two stimulus images below. You may include one or more of these statements in your oral presentation. In your presentation, refer to the ideas discussed so far in this unit.

a Beauty is in the eye of the beholder.
b 'Art' is something that will constantly need redefining, as people continue to change.

a Art is an essential part of the human condition. People must create and experience art to live meaningful lives.
b One of the purposes of art is to break boundaries and make people ask what is legal, ethical and meaningful.

Higher level extension

3.25 As a class, discuss your answers to the following questions:

a What would you do if you discovered a piece of art by a famous street artist, which could easily be removed from its public space and kept safely in your home?

b What would you do if a famous street artist painted a piece of art on a building that you owned, and the municipality sent you a letter, insisting that you remove it before they do?

c What would you do, as the director of a museum, if someone offered you a piece of street art that was acquired without the artist's permission?

d What would you do, as a famous-but-anonymous street artist, if someone removed one of your works from the street and tried to donate it to a museum?

e What would you do if you were offered $700 000 for a piece of street art that you acquired without the artist's permission?

3.26 Some of the more difficult vocabulary has been taken from Text 3.12 and listed below. Match the words a–o from the text with their synonyms in the box below.

careful	problem	unintended	honour	dilemma
profit	foolish	example	widespread	argument
story	dollar	recognisable	hero	promise

a saga	**b** iconic	**c** issue
d integrity	**e** rampant	**f** protagonist
g misguided	**h** painstaking	**i** inadvertent
j clash	**k** gain	**l** precedent
m quandary	**n** pledge	**o** buck

Text 3.12

'What would you do if you were offered a small fortune for a painting the artist didn't want sold?'

This is the thorny moral question that drives the newly released documentary 'Saving Banksy.' It follows the saga of one man's quest to save an iconic graffiti work by the infamous street artist Banksy from being whitewashed by the city government or being ripped from the streets and sold at auction. In doing so, the film pulls back the curtain on an issue plaguing many street artists and the integrity of their work: the rampant dislodging and sale of street-art works against the will of artists.

'These pieces show up in galleries and at auction, and the public doesn't generally know that the artist didn't intend for the pieces to be sold, or that none of the money is going to the artist,' explains the film's director, Colin Day, shortly after the film's release in San Francisco. In addition to raising awareness of the challenges street artists are dealing with, the film also aims to 'get people to appreciate street art, in its intended form,' says the film's executive producer, Brian Greif.

Greif, who is also the story's protagonist, is a street art collector, albeit a 'misguided' one, as the film's press release admits. His intentions were pure: to remove Banksy's *Haight Street Rat* mural from its high perch on the wall of a Victorian hotel in San Francisco in order to rescue it from being whitewashed by the city government. He'd then donate the work, that depicts one of the artist's signature rats wearing a Che Guevara-style cap and wielding a spray can, to a museum. However, after painstakingly extracting the piece, Greif learns that his plan will be impossible to realise. He inadvertently finds himself in the middle of a heated clash between a community of street artists and a group of individuals who remove street art work for personal gain, and being

schooled in the complex politics of the sale of street art in the process.

'The thing is, artists like Banksy make pieces in their studios that they designate for sale,' explains Greif. 'But the works they're making on the street aren't intended to be sold, or even saved.' It's precisely this question of intent that first thwarts Greif's plans. In one scene, he offers the painting as a gift to SFMOMA. But while John Zarobell, the museum's assistant curator at the time, admits it's a strong piece, he explains that he can't accept the donation without a note from Banksy approving the removal of the painting and its placement within a museum context.

Zarobell also outlines another requirement by the museum: the delivery of a certificate of authenticity from Banksy himself, to ensure that he created the painting. But while the *Haight Street Rat* was listed on the artist's website as an original, Banksy's studio wouldn't provide the document. It might seem like an odd decision for an artist to block their work from entering a prominent museum collection. So why would he do it?

As Greif explains, if Banksy were to authorise the work it would set a precedent, 'that works intended for the street, after they're removed, still have value.' And that's not a precedent, as we learn through the documentary, that artists like Banksy want to support. Day elaborates: 'There's kind of a black market that's emerged for paintings removed from the street, and artists don't want to encourage it by legitimising those paintings.' While selling works uprooted from the streets isn't technically illegal, the process does pose some serious ethical quandaries. Not only do most street artists disapprove of the removal of their works from their original context, but they also don't see any of the profit made from the sales.

Stephan Keszler is one of several dealers

TEXT AND CONTEXT

- Banksy is a famous but anonymous street artist, who has made art illegally in cities all over the world.

- Che Guevara was a revolutionary leader in Cuba in the mid-twentieth century. He often wore a beret with red, communist star.

- SFMOMA is an acronym for 'San Francisco Museum of Modern Art'.

- Banksy's works are often 'stencilled', meaning they are made with spray paint and patterns or designs that have been pre-cut from sheets of cardboard.

known for ignoring the intentions of artists like Banksy whose street work he sells. He shows up in one of the film's more memorable scenes, showing a series of Banksy street paintings he maintains 'aren't for sale' at a 2012 Miami art fair. The presentation includes the *Haight Street Rat*, which Greif had lent in frustration after his unsuccessful attempts to return the work to a public context. However, Grief begins to regret his decision the moment he sees the work on the wall of the fair: 'I don't know how I feel about this. It's like when you see a deer in the wild, it's cool, but when you see a deer's head on the wall, it's not so cool.'

To confuse matters further, Greif's piece is hung alongside two works that were originally stenciled by Banksy on a wall separating Palestine and Israel. The artist placed them there, as artist Glen E. Friedman points out in the film, in an attempt to 'make a positive impact' in the war torn region. Friedman goes on to express a frustration shared by numerous artists across the film, when 'some fucking asshole takes the shit off the wall and tries to sell it to someone. What sense does that make?' Street artist Ben Eine, a friend of Banksy who accompanied him on the trip to Palestine, echoes the sentiment, referring to Keszler in particular: 'In the street-art world he's considered a shyster, a villain.'

After the fair closes its doors, Keszler ends up selling all of the works he

presented, except Greif's. Despite receiving a $500,000 offer from the dealer, which is a significantly higher figure than those typically drawn by similar works authenticated by Banksy selling at major auctions, Greif stayed true to his pledge to return the work to the public.

These days, Greif still struggles to find public platforms to exhibit *Haight Street Rat*, but he'll never sell it. Like Banksy and a dedicated community of street artists, Greif refuses to fuel the market for paintings pulled from the streets. But beyond refusing to engage with operations like Keszler's, a big question remains: how can activity of this sort be quelled? 'Well, it's a hard question,' Greif says. 'If a piece is painted illegally, without the owner of the building's or the city's permission, there's not much that can be done. The building owner legally owns the painting and can do whatever they want with it.' And that might mean selling it to a dealer like Keszler to make a quick buck, or more.

'Again, many of these people removing the works and the collectors buying them don't know the damage they might be doing to an artist's career or the work's integrity,' Greif concludes. 'So that's why we made this film, to inspire more respect for this work, the artists who make it, and their wishes.' As 'Saving Banksy' kicks off its tour, Greif and Day are hopeful that their goals, this time around, will become a reality.

www.artsy.net

3.27 Are the following statements true or false? Justify your answers with statements from the text.

a The film, 'Saving Banksy' is about someone who rescues a   piece of street art before it is removed by the municipality or art dealers.

b The film aims to spread awareness about the illegal practices of galleries and auction houses that sell the work of street artists.

c Brian Greif, who removed Banksy's *Haight Street Rat*, intended to sell the work to SFMOMA, but they refused it because he could not authenticate the work or acquire permission from the artist.

d Banksy frequently gives permission for his works to be sold.

e SFMOMA refused to accept Banksy's piece because they did not believe it was an original work.

f Banksy and other street artists do not feel it's fair that they are not included in profits from the sale of their street art.

g Brian Greif allows Stephan Keszler to show *Haight Street Rat* at an art fair in Miami.

h *Haight Street Rat* does not sell at the art fair in Miami, because Keszler clearly states that none of the Banksy works on display are for sale.

i Even though the creation of street art is illegal, building owners are free to sell what is painted on their buildings to art dealers.

3.28 Return to your answers for Activity 3.25. After reading Text 3.12, how have your answers to these questions changed? Do you think that people should have the right to acquire and deal in street art without the artist's permission? Do you think museums should exhibit works without the artist's permission?

TIP

On your assessment 2/Paper 2 exam you might also find true/false statements like those in Activity 3.27. Be sure to justify each answer with phrases from the source text. Be careful of statements that might be true in real life but not necessarily proven true by the text you are reading!

Literature

3.29 This unit has asked you to define art and its purpose. Now ask yourself: How should 'art' be taught in school? Here are several questions for you to explore and discuss as a class:

a To acquire your IB Diploma, you must take six subjects: one from each of the six 'Groups'. However, Group 6, called 'The arts' is optional. You can take an additional subject from another group in its place. Do you agree with this system? Or should you be *required* to take one of the following subjects currently offered by the IB: Visual Arts, Film, Dance, Theatre, Music, or Literature and Performance?

b You might be taking a Group 1 subject that teaches you about literature. One of the aims of your English B course is to instill an appreciation of literature. *How* are you learning to appreciate literature? What kinds of activities do you do to help you appreciate literary works?

c Have you ever tried writing a work of fiction: a short story, poem, novel or play? Why did you do this? Or why have you never done this? If you have tried creative writing, what did you learn from the process?

d What literary works are you reading or have you read for your English B course? Why were these selected for you? What have you learned from them? What *value* do these works have for you?

Have your ever prepared a theatrical performance with others? What kinds of things did you learn from the experience?

3.30 Read the poem 'Introduction to Poetry' (Text 3.13) and answer the questions below. Discuss your answers with your classmates.

a Who do you think the people are in this poem? Who is 'I' and 'them'?

b Why has the author chosen for these particular uses of imagery, that include a 'color slide', a 'hive', a 'mouse', a 'waterski' or a 'chair'?

c What do you think is the author's message? What is he trying to say about poetry and the way it is taught or read?

d How does the poem make you feel about studying poetry?

Thinking Skills

Some types of thinking skills are more challenging than others. For example understanding something is more challenging that remembering something. Like art, the ability to analyse or evaluate something is a prerequisite for creating something. In other words, artists often study art before creating art themselves. Activity 3.31 asks you to create a drawing, which might not at first seem relevant to your English B course. But by making a drawing, you will have to read the poem critically. Similarly, the more you write in English, the more you will read critically in English.

Text 3.13

I ask them to take a poem
and hold it up to the light
like a color slide

or press an ear against its hive.
I say drop a mouse into a poem
and watch him probe his way out,

or walk inside the poem's room
and feel the walls for a light switch.

I want them to waterski
across the surface of a poem
waving at the author's name on the shore.

But all they want to do
is tie the poem to a chair with rope
and torture a confession out of it.

They begin beating it with a hose
to find out what it really means.

Introduction to Poetry by Billy Collins

3.31 Make a drawing or artwork that depicts one or more ideas that you find in this poem. You do not have to be an artist to do this activity. Share your drawings with your classmates and discuss what decisions you made when you made your drawing. How does it depict your understanding of the poem?

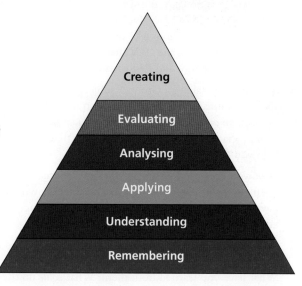

Bloom's taxonomy, revised by Anderson and Krathwohl in 2001, suggests that creativity is a higher-order thinking skill.

REFLECT

Return to the first few activities in this unit, in which you defined art. In particular, return to Activity 3.4, where you posted your definition of art on a board for others to read.

After having read several texts, listened to the audio recording and watched a short film, has your definition of art changed? Consider how and why.

You were also asked to comment on the purpose of art. How has your understanding of the purpose of art changed over the course of this unit?

Social organisation

This chapter explores the theme of social organisation. While this theme is very broad, this chapter has focused on three aspects: work, school and love. How do institutions like marriage, business and school affect who we are and how we behave? What kinds of rules regulate us? What roles do we adopt? What kinds of jobs do we desire? Questions like these help us understand our place in the world and how we can make the world a better place.

In this Chapter

- In Unit 4.1, you will learn more about minority groups around the world and their struggle to fit into systems of education.
- Unit 4.2 asks you to think about what it means to be 'partners for life' with someone.
- In Unit 4.3 you will consider how the 'future of jobs' is changing with the rise of technology and immigration.

Unit 4.1
Minorities and education

Guiding questions	Learning objectives
• What problems do social minorities face? • How can education help alleviate these problems?	• Become more aware of the problems encountered by social minorities around the world. • Develop skills that enable you to discuss social minorities and education.

Word bank

meritocracy

graduation

public schools

enrolled

attendance

diploma

motivation

entry requirements

application

dropout

illiterate

citizen

inclusive

differentiate

mainstream

compulsory

Many countries have social 'minorities', who can be defined in terms of race, culture, wealth, class or privilege. These social minorities often struggle to access mainstream education, because their values or beliefs are not understood or appreciated in schools, where the values of the dominant cultures are taught.

This unit explores the relationship between minority cultures and education, and asks questions about this. You will learn about the experiences of minority cultures in the US, Australia, the UK and Africa.

You might want to consider your own position in society and your access to education and opportunity. You might ask yourself what values and beliefs your school is teaching you, and how they fit with your own cultural background.

Getting started

1.1 Using the words from the word bank, fill in the blanks in the sentences below. You might need to look up their definitions.

a He was … on the course, so he knew how much it cost.

b At the beginning of the lesson, the teacher took … to see if all were there.

c The … ceremony was wonderful. The principal gave a great speech.

d … culture is often considered 'normal' or 'standard'.

e She did not meet the … , so she could not register.

f It was difficult to find a job as a highschool … .

g Because they were … , they did not know the instructions.

h Even if you are the brightest student, if you lack … , your grades may drop.

i Every … of this country is entitled to a good education.

j … are underfunded in many countries.

k After she filled in the … , she decided not to attend.

l After she was awarded her … , she went on to study medicine.

m For any student who wants to go on to study medicine, biology and chemistry are … .

n A … is a system where those who are rewarded most are the ones who perform the best and achieve the most.

o 'To …' means that one takes people's differences into account when teaching or assigning activities to pupils.

p An … education is one that does not select and filter people according to ability level.

1.2 Do you agree or disagree with the following statements? Discuss your answers with others.

a In my country, no matter where you go to school, everyone has an equal chance at becoming successful in life.

b The best way to help the poor is to give them access to good education.

c Ethnic minorities should be given easier access to higher education.

d Good exam results have nothing to do with a student's cultural background and everything to do with their ability to work hard.

e There is no good reason for dropping out of school.

f If your parents were successful at school, it is likely that you will be too.

g Everyone should be able to take the IB Diploma or an IB course.

1.3 Do schools ignore individual differences in the process of testing? To what degree is education a **meritocracy**?

Watch and listen 🎥 🔊

1.4 Words often come in pairs. Make word pairs using the words a–n below with the words in the box. The pairs are taken from the video 'A teacher growing green in the South Bronx' that you will watch shortly. If you do not know what some of the words mean, look up their definitions. Compare your answers to a classmate's. Ask your teacher for the final answers.

a learning	abatement
c foster	benefits
e affordable	nutrition
g international	housing
i tax	stamp
k pumpkin	account
m health	love
b prenatal	care
d 21st-century	disabled
f bank	technology
h farmer's	community
j food	market
l living	patch
n unconditional	wage

1.5 Based on the pairs of words from Activity 1.4, what do you think the video that you are going to watch will be about?

1.6 Do an online search for a TED Talk called: 'A teacher growing green in the South Bronx' by Stephen Ritz. He is a passionate teacher who talks very quickly. It is not important that you understand every word of his talk. But as you watch and listen, try to find answers to the following questions.

a Why does Steve Ritz refer to the South Bronx as a desert?

b What does Steve mean when he says that he hopes his reach exceeds his grasp?

c What does Steve mean when he says: 'This is my harvest, people!'

d 'Triple bottom line' means that something has a positive social, environmental and financial effect. How do Steve's students achieve a triple bottom line?

e Steve often refers to a 'sí se puede' moment, which means 'yes, you can' or 'it is possible' in Spanish. It is the motto of the United Farm Workers. Why does Steven continuously use it in his TED Talk?

f Steve explains: 'As my kids learned to get, they learned to give.' What does he mean by this?

g What do you think Steve means when he says: 'when you expand their palates, you expand their vocabulary.'

Stephen Ritz is a teacher, speaker and innovator, who is changing the landscapes of New York and the 'mindscapes' of young individuals through urban farming

h What, according to Steve, is the 'biggest bully in school'? Why is this a problem for the youth and the community?

i One of Steve's final remarks is: 'We are all tadpoles, but I urge you to become a big frog and take that big, green leap.' What do you think he means by this?

CAS

If you are enjoying an IB education, you are rather fortunate. What can you do to make education (or an IB education) more accessible to others? As a CAS project, think of a way to improve the quality of education in your country by making it more accessible to everyone.

CONCEPTS

Variation

Steve Ritz's English might be a different *variation* of English that what you are used to hearing. It is characteristic of New York, an accent that has been influenced by many minorities over the years, including Irish and Italians. As you explore minorities and education, ask yourself why 'different' language variations are often seen as 'less' or 'inferior'. Where do these notions come from? Are these prejudices fair to those who speak a 'different' variety of language?

Listen

1.7 You are going to listen to Audio track 10, a discussion with an Aboriginal leader about education in Australia. The following words have been taken from the recording. Before listening to the audio track, place these words into groups that have something in common. Label each group with the theme they have in common.

farming	bush	unemployment	exam	metalwork	situation
abuse	scores	rural	context	bushcraft	dire	poor
remote	abandoned	suffering	crime	violence	woodwork
		tests	background		

1.8 Listen to 🔊 Audio track 10. Read the incomplete sentences a–k below before listening to the recording. As you listen, make rough notes to help you complete the sentences. After listening to the audio track, fill in the gaps so that the sentences closely reflect the ideas that you heard in the recording.

a   According to Tom Anderson, Aboriginal children are failing NAPLAN tests because '…'

b   According to Tom Anderson, teenage girls get pregnant deliberately because '…'

c   Tom points out that even though small improvements have been made in rural aboriginal schools, '…' has gone up.

d   Tom believes that the NAPLAN tests fail to '…'

e   In order to train students how to use the powers of observation, Tom suggests that they '…'

f   Tom thinks the idea of 'preserving' Aboriginal languages is wrong because it suggests that '…'

g   Tom believes that private sponsors are necessary for his vision of education because '…'

h   The host, Mike, does not think Tom's suggestion for Aboriginal education is very 'revolutionary' because it includes: '…'

i   The part of Tom's plan that Mike *does* find revolutionary includes the teaching of '…'

j   Tom wants to get rid of the NAPLAN tests for Aboriginal children because '…'

k   Tom is suggesting that instead of serving an exam board, aboriginal schools should serve their '…'

After listening to Audio track 10, do you think the indigenous people of Australia should have their own curriculum?

TIP

As you listen to Audio track 10, you will only have time to take rough notes to complete the sentences in Activity 1.8. After listening, you can go back and read your notes to write complete sentences that fully answer the questions. Apply this skill on Paper 2 when you listen to audio recordings and answer exam questions (see Unit 7.2).

4

Self-management skills
As an IB learner, you should aim to develop self-management skills. What are these? Besides organising yourself, bringing the right materials to class and planning ahead, you are expected to work on your affective skills. These include your ability to show resilience and perseverance in the face of challenges at school. Challenges that are too easy or difficult de-motivate. Are you tackling challenges at school that are achievable with hard work? As you read about minorities and education, think about the kinds of challenges that minorities face at home and in school. Why do they struggle to overcome these?

Exploring texts

1.9 What do you associate with the following words (a–e)? For each word write the first one or two words that come to mind. Do not think about them for a long time. Write your responses on a board, together with your classmates' responses. Why do you think you associate these things with these words? Discuss as a class.

a Indians

b Native Americans

c Indian reservation

d Tribe

e South Dakota

1.10 Before you read Text 4.1, read the statements below. Then, based on your reading and understanding of the text, decide whether the following statements are true or false. Give evidence from the text to support your answer.

a In South Dakota, between 25 and 30 per cent of Native Americans graduate from high school.

b Janessa Driving Hawk gave birth to her daughter, Neleigh, when she was 15 years-old.

c Many Native American children do not attend school because their parents are struggling with alcoholism and cannot take care of them.

d Joe Garcia and Janessa Driving Hawk have something in common.

e Janessa is grateful to her mother for quitting her job, so that the she (Anita) can look after Neleigh, while Janessa goes to school.

f Basic utilities seem to be a problem for Native American children.

g The author of Text 4.1 is confident that the number of Sioux Indian graduates will increase.

READING STRATEGY
Who are the people in Text 4.1? Draw a diagram, such as a family tree, that depicts the relationships between them. Compare your diagram to a classmate's. How is your understanding of the text similar or different?

Text 4.1

The fleeting promise of education

1 Lower Brule: Every week day morning, 3-year-old Neleigh Driving Hawk steps on a Head Start bus, giggling, smiling, excited to drive off to a day of learning and fun with all her friends.

2 Most days, her teenage mother tries to chase the education dream as well. But Janessa Driving Hawk's smile isn't nearly as broad.

3 At 18, she is still struggling to finish her freshman year at Lower Brule High School. It's difficult, to be a mother and student both on the reservation, she says.

4 'I'm trying to go back,' Janessa said. 'But not always having a babysitter, it's tough.' The **graduation** numbers for Native American students in South Dakota's public and tribal schools suggest she doesn't struggle alone. Lower Brule's graduation rate was only 25 percent in the spring of 2009, according to the Bureau of Indian Education. The Flandreau Indian School was 21.78 percent; Marty on the Yankton Reservation, 26.47 percent.

5 Few tribal schools finish very far above the 50 percent mark; Cheyenne-Eagle Butte was the exception at almost 89 percent. But even among South Dakota's **public schools**, Native American youth graduate at a 67 percent rate, compared to almost 90 percent for all public school students.

6 Keith Moore, national director of the Bureau of Indian Education and an **enrolled** member of the Rosebud Sioux Tribe, said one only need look at conditions on the reservations to understand the poor school numbers.

7 'There are so many factors. This is a systemic issue,' Moore said. 'There are social factors. There are economic factors. There are nutrition factors. There is sexual abuse. There are so many factors that affect kids outside of school.'

8 Sleeping in poorly insulated housing when the propane tank goes empty affects school **attendance**. Searching for something to eat among countertops strewn with empty beer cans does too.

9 When he was 15, Joe Garcia said his mother moved their family back to Pine Ridge from Boise, Idaho, so she could be closer to her ailing mom. They lived in a shack, Garcia, 31, recalled, with no running water or electricity.

10 'I didn't get a high school **diploma**,' he said. 'My parents didn't push us kids. There was a lack of **motivation** on their part.'

11 'Instead of going to school, I stayed home and babysat my nieces. It was get up, clean up and play with the kids. I had no social life. I hated it.'

12 The babysitting situation has kept Janessa Driving Hawk out of school for most of the past three years as well, though she and her mother disagree about why that is.

13 Anita Driving Hawk said she quit her job to stay home and watch her granddaughter. 'Then she stays home from school because she says she's got no babysitter,' Anita said.

14 Janessa rolls her eyes. 'Yeah, right, that's why I'm not going to school,' she said. 'I'm not going to school ... because she's never around to babysit.'

15 For some children on the reservation, getting to school is never an issue, though it's clear that many of them aren't likely to ever graduate.

Extract from Growing Up Indian, by Steve Young

4

- 'Freshman' (paragraph 2) is an American term for first-year high school students, usually between the ages of 14 and 15.

- Many Native Americans live on 'reservations' (paragraph 2), which are lands managed by tribes, with limited sovereignty and varying laws.

- 'Public school' (paragraph 4) might have a different meaning in different parts of the world. In the USA, it refers to state-funded schooling.

- It is estimated that 1 million of the 2.5 million Native Americans live on reservations in the USA.

1.11 Copy the table below, changing the words in the 'Noun' column into adjectives, as they appear in Text 4.1.

Noun	Adjective
system	
society	
economy	
sex	

EXTRA

You might find the concept of 'reservations' difficult to understand. Compile a list of questions that you might have about Indian reservations, carry out some research, and present detailed answers in a presentation. Here are some questions you might want to explore:

- When and why were reservations founded?

- How different are they from national US land?

- Why do so many Native Americans live outside the reservations?

- Do reservations help preserve tradition and culture?

1.12 Find the following words in Text 4.1

a   an adjective that describes how something can be wide or big (paragraph 2)

b   a verb meaning 'to work hard' (paragraph 3)

c   a noun used to describe something that is different from the norm (paragraph 5)

d   a noun that means 'circumstances' or 'situation' (paragraph 6)

e   the past participle of a verb that means 'scattered' or 'cluttered' (paragraph 8)

f   an adjective to describe someone's poor health (paragraph 9)

g   a verb that means 'to encourage' or 'to motivate' (paragraph 10)

1.13 If you could meet Janessa Driving Hawk today, what would you ask her? Write your questions on a piece of paper and do not show it to anyone. Collect your class's questions, and ask one classmate or your teacher to read them out. Vote on which question you find most appropriate to ask Janessa, considering her circumstances.

1.14 Before reading Text 4.2, discuss these questions with classmates:

a   Imagine you had never spent a day in a classroom in your life. How might your life be different, today, if you were not attending school?

b   Besides reading, writing and arithmetic, what are some of the life skills that you learn at school?

c   What reasons can you think of to explain why many children in the world do not go to school?

1.15 Scan Text 4.2 to find answers to the following questions:

a   Why did the author leave a blank space under 'educational history' on her college application form?

b   How many Gypsies, both nomadic and permanently housed, are there in the UK?

c   How many siblings and half-sisters did Roxy Freeman grow up with?

d   What sorts of things did she learn growing up?

e   How did the author learn to read?

f   How were Gypsies depicted in the magazines and books that she read?

Text 4.2
My Gypsy Childhood

Roxy Freeman never went to school. But, at the age of 22, she decided to get a formal education, forcing her to face up to the prejudices that blight her Gypsy community – and to shackle her wandering spirit.

The receptionist looked at me with disdain when I walked into Suffolk College asking to enrol. Their access course for mature students didn't have any **entry requirements** as such, but the receptionist warned me it was an advanced, intensive course, and there seemed to be a blank space under 'educational history' on my **application** form. When I explained that I wasn't a **dropout**, I just hadn't gone to school, she looked even more scornful.

I was 22 and had never spent a day in a classroom in my life; an alien concept for many people, but common in Gypsy and Traveller families. There are more than 100,000 nomadic Travellers and Gypsies in the UK, and 200,000 who live in permanent housing. Many, like me, never attend school, while others are **illiterate** because formal education is not a priority in our culture.

My upbringing was unusual, but not unique. Until I was eight, my family lived on the road, travelling around Ireland by horse drawn wagon. I was one of six children, with three more half-sisters, and our family was considered small. Having 12 or 13 children was common among Travellers in Ireland.

Instead of going to school, my siblings and I, like many children from travelling families, were taught about the arts, music and dance. Our education was learning about wildlife and nature, how to cook and how to survive. I didn't know my times tables but I could milk a goat and ride a horse. I could identify ink caps, puff balls and field mushrooms and knew where to find wild watercress and sorrel. By the age of eight or nine, I could light a fire, cook dinner for a family of 10 and knew how to bake bread on an open fire.

Unlike some of my siblings, I learned to read when I was quite young. My mother and grandparents bought me books and, with mum's help, I could read by the time I was about nine. By the age of 12 or 13, I had devoured all of F Scott Fitzgerald, EM Forster, Louisa May Alcott and Emily Brontë. I bought them in charity shops or asked for them as birthday presents; together, books and cards gave me an understanding of words and numbers in the absence of any formal education.

TEXT AND CONTEXT

• The author of this text refers to herself as a 'Gypsy'. While many Gypsies in Ireland and England have Irish and English blood, their ways of living stem from the Romani people, an ethnic group that is found throughout Europe.

• 'Ink caps' and 'puff balls' are types of wild fungus.

If it hadn't been for literature, maybe I would have remained unaware of the way we were described. But a love of books evolved into an interest in magazines and newspapers, and that exposed a world of prejudice and ignorance to me. In my early teens, I realised for the first time that there's a widely held view that everyone who lives in a caravan or on the road is a dirty, thieving Gypsy, never contributing to society while living for free on land that doesn't belong to them.

Gypsies and Travellers are the only social group that it is still acceptable to insult. In part, I think this stems from our levels of illiteracy and lack of social involvement; if people are unaware of what is being written about them, they're not going to dispute it. And if they don't dispute it, it will carry on.

Adapted from *My Gypsy Childhood* by Roxy Freeman

LEARNER PROFILE

Reflective

An IB learner is *reflective*, and reflection plays an important role in your IB education. Roxy Freeman is being very *reflective* in this autobiography. She is looking back on events from her past and drawing conclusions. What conclusions does she come to? Reflect on your own experiences from your school career. What important lessons have you learned?

TOK

What judgements did you make about the Gypsy lifestyle described by Roxy Freeman in Text 4.2? In TOK we learn that it is difficult to make objective observations without a degree of cultural bias. 'Cultural bias' describes how we tend to prefer our own culture, values and beliefs to those of others. Do you value the skills of reading and writing over those of milking a goat and riding a horse? How does this affect your perception of the Romani people?

1.16 Match the words from Text 4.2 in the box below with their synonyms (a–o) in the list a–o on the right. The words in the text box are in the same order in which they appear in the text.

blight	**a** brothers and sisters
shackle	**b** wandering
disdain	**c** disagree with
intensive	**d** offend
scornful	**e** disapproval
alien	**f** importance
nomadic	**g** stain
priority	**h** the only one
unique	**i** opened up
siblings	**j** hold back
exposed	**k** unawareness
prejudice	**l** rigorous
ignorance	**m** contemptuous
insult	**n** strange
dispute	**o** discrimination

1.17 Text 4.2 only presents part of Roxy Freeman's story. She was 22 years-old when she enrolled in college and 30 years old when she wrote this piece. What do you think happened to her in between? Write an imaginative piece in which Roxy decides to go to school for the first time in her life.

Form and meaning

1.18 What is the difference in meaning between the words *affect* and *effect*?

Below are four sentences, of which the first two are taken from Text 4.1 'The fleeting promise of education'. After reading all of the sentences, try to explain to a classmate the difference between these two words.

a   There are so many factors that *affect* kids outside of school.

b   Sleeping in poorly insulated housing when the propane tank goes empty *affects* school attendance.

c   The investment in education had a great *effect* on the economy.

d   The scientist wanted to see the *effects* of sleep deprivation on the students.

1.19 If you need more help in explaining the difference between *affect* and *effect*, read the explanations a–e. On a copy of the table below, write the letter of each explanation in the appropriate column.

Affect	Effect

a   usually used as a verb

b   usually used as a noun

c   is similar to the word 'to influence'

d   is like the word 'result'

e   is usually used in combination with the prepositions 'of' and 'on'

1.20 Choose the word *effect* or *affect* to fill the blanks in the sentences below. You might have to conjugate the verb *to affect*.

a   After taking so many of them, the pills began to lose their… .

b   The introduction of after-school activities … the students' grades. They improved!

c   In… by opening a day care centre for the children of teenage mothers, school attendance improved.

d   The noisy atmosphere at home… his ability to learn.

e   The… of proper lighting in the classroom can be measured by looking at the students' results.

1.21 In Text 4.1, you will see the words *poor* and *poorly* used as in the two following examples:

*   'Look at conditions on the reservations to understand the *poor* school numbers.'

*   'Sleeping in *poorly* insulated housing when the propane tank goes empty affects school attendance.'

Poor is an adjective and *poorly* is an adverb. On the next page are two more examples from Text 4.2. Look carefully at the words *open* and *widely*. Which one is an adjective and which one is an adverb?

a   'I could light a fire, cook dinner for a family of 10 and knew how to bake bread on an *open* fire.'

b   'There's a *widely* held view that everyone who lives in a caravan or on the road is a dirty, thieving Gypsy.'

When do we use adjectives and when do we use adverbs? Try explaining these rules to a classmate or your teacher.

1.22   Explain the rules for using adjectives and adverbs. Six explanations are given below a–f. On a copy of the table, write the letter of each explanation in the correct column.

Adjectives	Adverbs

a   These are used to describe nouns, i.e. people, places or things.

b   These are used to describe verbs, i.e. *how* somebody does something or *how* something happens.

c   These are used with some verbs, such as *to be, to look, to feel* and *to sound*.

d   These are used to describe adjectives.

e   These are used to describe adverbs.

f   These are used before past participles, for example *written, held* or *organised*.

1.23   Select the correct word from those in brackets in the following sentences.

a   Romani people are (common/commonly) stereotyped as thieving, dishonest vagabonds.

b   After missing school for so long, he could not read (good/well).

c   His school attendance record is (poor/poorly).

d   The Maasai have (colourful/colourfully) dress.

e   Individuals from ethnic minorities are (frequent/frequently) stopped by the police without reason.

f   The local authority is (remarkable/remarkably) helpful in finding housing for Romani who want to settle.

g   He will be (sore/sorely) missed by his fellow Travellers.

h   After years of living abroad, she spoke (perfect/perfectly) English.

i   Once she enrolled in school, she learned (incredible/incredibly) quickly.

j   I don't think she was joking. She sounded quite (serious/seriously).

Discussion

1.24 Return to Activity 1.9, in which you listed the associations that you had with Native Americans and Indian reservations. Now study the three photographs a–c below. Discuss the following questions.

a How are the photographs of these Native Americans similar to, or different from, your description of Native Americans and Indian reservations from Activity 1.9?

b Where and how in these photographs do you see a clash between traditional and modern culture?

a

b

c

1.25 The reservations that Steve Young describes in Text 4.1 are some of the poorest places in the USA. Conditions are comparable to some of the poorest countries in the world, with very high rates of infant mortality, unemployment and teenage pregnancy. Do you agree or disagree with the following statements?

a Before the USA spends more on space exploration, more should be spent to alleviate poverty on Indian reservations.

b If Indian reservations are some of the poorest places in the USA, then they are not functioning. Reservation lands should be nationalised.

c Many Native American reservations now have large casinos that earn a lot of money from non-Native Americans. These casinos often help finance health and educational services on the reservation. The poorer reservations in South Dakota should have casinos. (Note: you can find out more on this topic from the US National Bureau of Economic Research.)

1.26 Use one of the visual stimuli A or B to conduct a mock individual oral. In your oral, reflect on the ideas that you have discussed in this unit. You can use points a–d as working notes.

a In many countries, schools have been an extension of a colonial system that makes indigenous people conform to a Western lifestyle.

b Too many schools are 'Westist, testist and bestist', and this needs to change by creating more inclusive schools that **differentiate**.

c Schools should focus more on making positive change for everyone in a community and less on the test results or academic achievements of an elite few.

d 'Education for a better world' (the IB's slogan) suggests that we need to learn to live in harmony with the planet and each other. So why are we not teaching urban farming as part of the school curriculum?

Extended Essay

'How is a social group portrayed by the media?' This question could lead to a good Category 2, type B extended essay in which a documentary or film serves as a 'cultural artefact' for the exploration of how a particular social group is portrayed. For example, a more focused research question might read: 'How are stereotypes of Travellers reinforced by the documentary film *My Big Fat Gypsy Wedding*?'

A

B

EXTRA

Image A from Activity 1.26 depicts First Nation (indigenous) children attending 'residential schools' in Canada in the early 20th century. The Canadian government has apologised for this system of education, which led to the deaths of thousands of children. Before you present your mock individual oral on Image A, carry out research to find out more about residential schools and the suffering they caused among the native people.

Writing

1.27 In this unit you have read people's stories about their access to good education. But what facts do we have about (ethnic) minorities and education?

a Research a minority group in an English-speaking country and find out as much as you can about their access to education, their performance on assessment and their graduation levels. Keep track of your sources and make notes on any statistics, facts or figures that you find.

b Study Unit 6.8 on report writing. What stylistic and structural features are typical of an official report?

c Return to one of your sources and look for evidence of stylistic and structural features that are typical of an official report.

d Think of an institution or organisation that would benefit from a report on minorities and education, such as a ministry of education or even the IB.

e Write a report on your minority group and their access to education. Use the conventions of report writing that you have learned from Unit 6.8.

f Ask a classmate and your teacher to assess your report, using the assessment criteria for Paper 1.

g Re-write your report, taking your feedback into consideration and submit your final result to your teacher for assessment. Keep in mind that your teacher will not assess you on your final Paper 1, but this activity serves as good practice for your exams.

1.28 Throughout this unit, you have been encouraged to reflect on your learning experiences at your school. Write a review of your school, that could appear on a website for parents abroad seeking a good school for their children. Keep any criticism constructive and comment carefully on the curriculum and policies of your school. See Unit 6.2 for more help on how to write a review.

Higher level extension

1.29 Look at the image on the right showing a Maasai man with his cattle. Which of the following words apply to this man? Support your answers by referring to the photograph.

a proud

c pleased

e wealthy

g traditional

b leader

d simple

f kind

h backward

Text 4.3

Maasai schools

From Afghanistan to Arizona, schools are at the centre of nearly every struggle over cultural identity. Governments use schools to instil common values, to prepare young people to contribute economically, and to create citizens. Minority groups often see them as machines designed to strip their people of their language, their traditions, their beliefs.

Until recently, that was the prevailing view among the Maasai of Kenya and Tanzania. The Maasai (numbering about 400,000) are traditionally cattle herders who follow their animals on seasonal migrations. They are proud of their warriors, or ilmuran, and fiercely defensive of their independence. When the British ruled East Africa, the Maasai used passive resistance to ensure that their culture remained intact, refusing to take up agriculture, to settle in towns, to send their children to school.

Now the Maasai are finding that resistance isn't enough. Agriculture and urbanisation have eaten up much of their grazing land. Communications and roads have exposed young Maasai to the temptations and opportunities of the outside world. Many are now questioning traditional practices such as polygamy, early marriage and female circumcision (also known as female genital mutilation, or FGM).

Some Maasai worry that change is coming too fast. 'The foundation of our culture is respect and unity,' says Oloiboni Ole Pareiyo, a 65-year-old herder. 'What is happening with modernity is that it is undermining the very principle on which the culture is founded.' Others disagree. They say the only way to survive as a people is to adapt to changing realities. Education, they argue, need not be seen as a surrender to **mainstream** culture, but rather as a way to fix those aspects of their own culture that need fixing particularly in the treatment of women and girls.

Minority groups in many parts of the world have tried to reconcile these sorts of differences by establishing 'bicultural' models of education, where modern skills are taught alongside traditional concepts and practices. The idea is not to force young people to choose between two systems, but rather to help them see that western-style modernity and tradition can coexist, and even reinforce one another.

For Kenya, emerging from decades of authoritarian rule, modern education is a top priority. In 2003, incoming President Mwai Kibaki made primary education compulsory and free. Despite a range of problems (including teacher shortages and a lack of classroom space), that year saw a significant jump in the number of Maasai students attending rural schools. But primary education is only part of the picture, particularly when it comes to preparing students for a modernizing economy. Secondary schools (many of them residential) are still too costly and too distant for most Maasai families. When children are away at school, they cannot help with herding or other daily responsibilities. And for many parents, sending a daughter to secondary school is considered a poor investment, given that she will live with her husband's kin once she is married. As a result, the number of Maasais with secondary school or college diplomas is still very small.

www.homelands.org

1.30 The following sentences are based on your understanding of Text 4.3. Match the beginnings of the sentences on the left with the endings of the sentences on the right.

Beginnings	Endings
1 The author explains that governments see education as a way to shape …	a others criticise its treatment of women.
2 Minority groups, like the Maasai, often see education as …	b more Maasai parents sent their children to school.
3 The Maasai were difficult for the British to colonise, because of …	c a way to make them conform to mainstream culture.
4 While some Maasai members say their culture is about 'respect and unity', …	d model citizens who participate in the economy.
5 Some minority groups prefer a 'bicultural' form of education, where …	e they will be marrying young and moving away.
6 When attendance of primary school in Kenya became mandatory in 2003, …	f both traditional and modern teachings are given equal value.
7 It is difficult to convince parents that their children should attend school, because …	g children are needed to herd the cattle.
8 Many parents do not see the point in sending their daughters to secondary school, because …	h their unwillingness to settle, farm and go to school.

1.31 You might have stumbled upon several words in Text 4.3 that need explaining. Discuss the meaning and importance of the italicised words when answering the questions below.

a   How do governments *instil* common values in citizens?

b   How does education *strip* minorities of their culture?

c   What was the Maasai's *prevailing* view on education, until recently?

d   How did the Maasai use *passive resistance* against the British?

e   How have the Maasai been *exposed* to the *temptations* of the outside world?

f   Why is *polygamy* questioned as a cultural practice?

g   How is education a way for the Maasai to *adapt* to modern civilisation?

h   How did education in Kenya change after *authoritarian* rule?

i   Why do the Maasai consider secondary school a poor *investment*?

1.32 Here are three discussion questions that address points raised in Text 4.3:

a   Can you can 'fix' a culture, as the text suggests? If something needs 'fixing' then it must be broken. How do you feel about discussing Maasai culture in these terms?

b   Is national education good or bad for Maasai children?

c   In developing countries around the world, many nongovernmental organisations (NGOs) are encouraging more girls to go to school. Why do these NGOs see this as one of the solutions to poverty?

1.33 You have learned about several cultures and different people in this unit so far. What do you think the children of the Bronx, Australian Aboriginals, Sioux, and Maasai have in common, if anything?

Literature

1.34 You are about to read the opening lines of a short story by Anita Desai called 'Studies in the Park' (Text 4.4). Read the discussion questions below. Write your answers down before discussing them with your classmates.

a Many of the sentences are incomplete. Other phrases are repeated. What is the effect of the author's style on the reader?

b What does Suno think of his parents?

c How old is Suno, do you think? What evidence can you find to support this suggestion?

d Why do you think it is so important for Suno to study quietly?

Extended Essay

For a Category 3 extended essay, you might compare and contrast works that were originally written in English. They do not have to be works that you have read in class, but if they are, then you must use an original research question that was not explored as part of your coursework. Extended essays that compare and contrast two works, rather than focusing on one work, tend to have more depth and meaningful analysis.

Text 4.4

Studies in the Park

1   Turn it off, turn it off, turn it off! First he listens to the news in Hindi. Directly after, in English. Broom – broom – brroom – brrroom – the voice of doom roars. Next, in Tamil. Then in Punjabi. In Gujarati. What next, my God, what next? Turn it off before I smash it onto his head. Fling it out of the window. Do nothing of the sort. Of course, nothing of the sort.

2   And my mother. She cuts and fries, cuts and fries. All day I hear her chopping and slicing and the pan of oil hissing. What all does she find to fry and feed us on, for God's sake? Eggplants, potatoes, spinach, shoe soles, newspapers, finally she'll slice me and feed me to my brothers and sisters. Ah, now she's turned on the tap. It's roaring and pouring, pouring and roaring into a bucket without a bottom.

3   The bell rings. Voices clash, clatter and break. The tin-and-bottle man? The neighbours? The police? The Help-the-Blind man? Thieves and burglars? All of them, all of them, ten or twenty or a hundred of them, marching up the stairs, hammering at the door, breaking in and climbing over me: ten, twenty or a hundred of them.

4   Then, worst of all, the milk arrives. In the tallest glass in the house. 'Suno, drink your milk. Good for you, Suno. You need it. Now, before the exams. Must have it, Suno. Drink.' The voice wheedles its way into my ear like a worm. I shudder. The table tips over. The milk runs. The tumbler clangs on the floor. 'Suno, Suno, how will you do your exams?'

5   That is precisely what I ask myself. All very well to give me a room. Uncle's been pushed off on a pilgrimage to Hardwar to clear a room for me and to bring me milk and say, 'Study, Suno, study for your exam.' What about the uproar around me? These people don't know the meaning of the word 'quiet'. When my mother fills buckets, sloshes the kitchen floor, fries and sizzles things in the pan, she thinks she is being quiet. The children have never even heard the word. It amazes and puzzles them. On their way back from school they fling their satchels in at my door, then tear in to snatch them back before I tear them to bits. Bawl when I pull their ears, screech when mother whacks them. Stuff themselves with her fries and then smear grease on my books.

6   So I raced out of my room, with my fingers in my ears, to scream till the roof fell down about their ears. But the radio suddenly went off, the door to my parents' room suddenly opened and my father appeared, bathed and shaved, stuffed and set up with the news of the world in six different languages....

Extract from 'Studies in the Park' by Anita Desai

1.35 Below is a list of adjectives that describe the *atmosphere* of Text 4.4. Atmosphere describes the mood of a text, as created through the author's choice of words and use of tone. For each of the words below explain how the author establishes this atmosphere. Find words or phrases from the text to support your point. You might need to look up the definitions of some words.

Example: I find the atmosphere of the text quite 'explosive' because it seems like the main character might break out into violence at any point, such as in line 5 where he says he will smash his father's radio into his head or 'fling it out the window'.

a explosive   **b** anxious

c urgent   **d** frustrated

e volatile   **f** claustrophobic

REFLECT

Discuss your answers to the following questions with your classmates and teacher.

a How difficult or easy is it for you to find a quiet place to study? How important is quietness for you when studying?

b What other factors contribute to your success as a student?

c Do you feel that the International Baccalaureate Diploma is the key to a successful future for you? Why?

d To what degree is your upbringing and family background an indication of how successful you will be at your studies and in life?

e To what degree does the IB reflect your cultural values? Does the IB clash with some cultural values, norms and practices that you were raised with?

f Looking back on this unit, identify three things you have learned about educational systems and minorities.

Unit 4.2
Partners for life

Guiding questions	Learning objectives
• What does 'marriage' mean to you or your culture? • What constitutes a good marriage or partnership?	• Appreciate cultural differences with regards to marriage practices. • Acquire appropriate language for discussing the topic of marriage.

When two people get married, they take **vows**, that are promises that each partner makes to the other. Such a **commitment** is not taken lightly.

In this unit, you will explore a wide range of topics and issues about relationships, including **divorce**, gender roles in marriage, same-sex relationships and **arranged marriage**.

You will explore the question of what it means to be 'partners for life'. Before you start forming lasting relationships in your own life, it helps to learn from what others have to say on the matter.

Word bank

vows
commitment
divorce
arranged marriage
spouse
ceremony
split up
sacrament
sanctity
socialised
pledge
purity
taboo
intimacy
resolve
unconditional love
dependent
sympathise
duties
tone
courting
dating

Getting started

2.1 Complete the following sentence anonymously on a piece of paper:

'My ideal husband/wife/partner for life would be someone who …'

If you are working with a group of classmates, collect all pieces of paper and read them out. Can you guess who wrote each statement? How well do you know each other?

2.2 Look at the different pictures of weddings a–c below. How is each image similar to, or different from, the kind of wedding you might like to have one day? Do you imagine yourself getting married?

a b c

4

Social organisation

CAS

While CAS projects and experiences are often about 'growing the self', you do not have to do them by yourself. Find a classmate that you know and trust and brainstorm on how you can help each other fulfil the CAS requirement.

2.3 Can all of the words in the box below be used in all the following sentences? Why might some words work well in some sentences, while other words do not? How does context determine the words we use to describe the people we love? (Note: you might have to add an 's' to the ends of these words to make them fit the context of the sentence.)

husband/wife	**spouse**	partner	boyfriend/girlfriend	friend

a   My … and I are moving in together.

b   I can tell my … anything.

c   Have you met my … ? Let me introduce you.

d   On the application form, he gave the name of his … as his next of kin.

e   We can still be … .

f   Tom and Jim have been … for over 20 years.

TOK

There are many TOK questions related to love and emotion. Discussing these questions might make you more aware of how complex relationships can be:

- Is it possible to 'work on' a relationship, as the saying goes? To what extent do relationships require hard work?

- Can there be one true definition of 'love'?

- How far is our understanding of 'marriage' determined by the culture in which we live and grow up?

- Do you believe in love at first sight? To what degree is love a human instinct?

- Do we 'choose' our husband or wife? To what degree is marriage a rational decision?

2.4 To what extent do you agree or disagree with the following statements about marriage and relationships? If you do this activity with classmates, you might want to divide your classroom into five areas, as listed below. As you discuss each statement, stand in the area that shows your opinion. This way, others can see 'where you stand' on these issues. Explain to others why you have decided to stand where you have. There are no right or wrong answers to this activity.

Front of classroom
1   Strongly agree
2   Agree
3   Neither agree nor disagree
4   Disagree
5   Strongly disagree
Back of the classroom

a   Marriage is old-fashioned. Love and commitment do not require a ring and a **ceremony**.

b   Couples should try living together before getting married.

c   Marriage is a family decision. Parents should be involved in deciding whom you marry.

d   Marriage is religious. It is a promise to a higher being or it is witnessed by other deities.

e   Couples of the same gender should be allowed to marry.

f   Those who do not get married run the risk of living sad, lonely lives.

2.5 Many people say that love is a universal language. Divorce, on the other hand, is very different in every culture. How much do you know about divorce in various English-speaking cultures? Are the following statements true or false?

a   In the UK, 48 per cent of children are likely to see their parents **split up** or divorce before age 16.

b   One in every three marriages in Australia ends in divorce.

c   In the UK, the number of divorces increased as a result of the 2008–09 recession.

d   In India, only 1 per cent of all marriages end in divorce.

e   In America, the divorce rate of second and third marriages is higher than first marriages.

f   The average divorce in South Africa, and in many other countries, occurs after three years of marriage.

Watch and listen 🎥 🔊

2.6 You are going to watch a video of a New York State Senator, speaking about same-sex marriage. What arguments are often given to support and reject the case for same-sex marriage? Write arguments for both sides in the column of a table like the one below. You can use the phrases below

Arguments for same-sex marriage	Arguments against same-sex marriage

a   fairness

b   marriage is about procreation

c   eradicate inequality

d   threaten the institution of marriage

e   legally protect the ones you love

f   incompatible with beliefs

g   homosexuality is natural, homosexuals are 'sound of mind'

h   marriage is a holy **sacrament**

i   unfit for marriage

j   marriage is a privilege

k   homosexuality is immoral

l   government's role is not to determine the validity of a relationship.

m   Government cannot practice discrimination

n   marriage is not about procreation

o   marriage has already lost its sanctity anyways

p   changing the definition of marriage

> **TIP**
>
> In class you might be asked to explore both sides of an argument, as in Activity 2.6. There are websites, such as procon.org, that help you learn more about both the pros and cons of an issue. Use these to prepare a small debate or discussion. During the individual oral for standard level students, as you comment on a photograph, you might need to remember the arguments from a class debate.

NYS Senator Diane Savino speaks on the Marriage Equality bill

2.7 Do an online search for: 'NYS Senator Diane Savino speaks on the Marriage Equality bill' by the NYSenate (or TED.com). First listen to all of Diane Savino's speech. Listen carefully to how she uses the words and phrases a–p listed below. Then listen to the speech again. When you hear the words that appear in the same order as in the video, pause the video and discuss your answer to the question: 'Why has she decided to use that word or phrase?' You might have to look up the meanings of some words. The first phrase has been done for you as an example.

a *hanging in the balance – This phrase is used in the video to describe people who are eagerly waiting for the outcome of the vote for the equal marriage in the New York Senate.*

a	hanging in the balance	**b**	unbowed
c	sound mind	**d**	cavalierly
e	envy	**f**	protect
g	people on both sides	**h**	administer that contract
i	commitment	**j**	validity
k	to practise discrimination	**l**	divorce rate
m	devoted to	**n**	bachelorette
o	distasteful	**p**	**socialised**

2.8 Revisit your arguments for and against same-sex marriage from Activity 2.6. Are there words from Activity 2.7 that you could now use to add new arguments or better express previous arguments? Where do you personally stand on this debate? Write one sentence, using one word from Activity 2.6 or 2.7, that answers this question.

Listen

2.9 Listen to 🔊 Audio track 11, an interview with a psychologist about the topic of 'virginity **pledges**' also known as '**purity** pledges'. These are agreements that young people make, promising not to have sex before marriage. Before you listen to the recording, make a Know Want Learn (KWL) table, like the one below, together as a class. On a sticky note, write down one thing you know about this topic. On another sticky note, write down one question to which you would like an answer. Place your first sticky note in the first column and the second sticky note in the second column of your table, displayed on a large board.

A purity ring, given by a father to his daughter who promises to save her virginity for marriage.

What I already **know**	What I **want** to know	What I **learned**

2.10 The words in the box below have been taken from Audio track 11. Use them to fill in the blanks of the sentences below.

fantasy	deny	abstinence	shame	commitment
contract	ball	oath	nonchalantly	churches

a   The 'True Love Waits' pledge is organised through '…'

b   By taking a purity pledge, young people are making a '…' to God, their families and themselves.

c   Some young people who break the pledge might feel '…' and disappointment with themselves.

d   Pledgers may be asked to sign a '…' when they make their purity promise.

e   Some young people later '…' ever having taken the pledge.

f   To not have sex is to practise '…'

g   An '…' is a promise you often read aloud for others to hear.

h   A '…' is a formal dance or gathering, in which people dress elegantly and socialise.

i   A '…' is the opposite of reality.

j   To act '…' means to appear indifferent or to do something without much care.

2.11 Read out the first two columns from the KWL table from Activity 2.9.

a   Now listen to Audio track 11 for answers to your questions from the middle column of the table.

b   Take notes on what you hear by writing a few more sticky notes that describe what you have learned from listening to this recording.

c   Place these sticky notes in the right-hand column from the KWL table for all of your classmates to see and read.

2.12 Answer the following questions a–g. To help you, look at the sticky notes from the right-hand column of the KWL table from Activities 2.9 and 2.11. If you cannot answer all of the questions, listen to the recording again.

a   Why do the interviewer and the interviewee find it 'perfectly logicial' for young people to take a purity pledge?

b   According to the research, what percentage of those who take a purity pledge break it?

c   Why might believing in abstinence be considered a bit of a 'fantasy'?

d   Fill in the gap. Some youngsters take a purity pledge as young as '…' years old.

e   Why might an individual who has taken a pledge not take it seriously?

f   According to Professor Waters, how do some young people justify denying ever having taken a purity pledge?

g   Why is sex education in the United States 'abysmal' according to Professor Waters?

4

Social organisation

Photograph of a father and his daughters at a Purity Ball.

EXTRA

The information from Audio track 11 has been taken from several studies and papers on the topic of virginity pledges. Research this topic on your own and give a presentation on what you believe to be true about this topic. Refer to your sources and give your own opinion on the issue. You might want to show photographs by David Magnusson, taken in 2015, of Purity Balls to support your presentation.

Exploring texts

2.13 The paragraphs of Text 4.5 are not in the right order. Re-order the paragraphs so that the story makes sense. To do this, you will need to read each paragraph carefully first. List paragraphs 1–12 in the correct order, for example, Paragraph 1 = D.

Text 4.5

a I walked over and silently held her. She wept in my arms. After a few minutes, she thanked me for not leaving. She told me that she just needed to feel me holding her.

b At this point I exploded. My fuse was also very short that day. I was angry that she hadn't called me. I was furious that she was blaming me when I didn't even know she was in pain. After exchanging a few harsh words, I headed for the door. I was fired, irritable, and had heard enough. We had both reached our limits.

c How had I missed this? She just needed me to go over and hold her. Another woman would have instinctively known what Bonnie needed. But as a man, I didn't know that touching, holding, and listening were so important to her. By recognising these differences I began to learn a new way of relating to my wife. I would have never believed we could resolve conflict so easily.

d A week after our daughter Lauren was born, my wife Bonnie and I were completely exhausted. Each night Lauren kept waking us. Bonnie had been torn in the delivery and was taking painkillers. She could barely walk. After five days of staying home to help, I went back to work. She seemed to be getting better.

e I said defensively, 'Why didn't you call me?' She said, 'I asked your brother, but he forgot! I've been waiting for him to return all day. What am I supposed to do? I can barely walk. I feel so deserted!'

f I had no idea that her day had been so awful. When I returned home she was very upset. I misinterpreted the cause of her distress and thought she was blaming me. She said, 'I've been in pain all day ... I ran out of pills. I've been stranded in bed and nobody cares!'

g Then something started to happen that would change my life. Bonnie said, 'Stop, please don't leave. This is when I need you the most. I'm in pain. I haven't slept in days. Please listen to me.' I stopped for a moment to listen.

h While I was away she ran out of pain pills. Instead of calling me at the office, she asked one of my brothers, who was visiting, to purchase more. My brother, however, did not return with the pills. Consequently, she spent the whole day in pain, taking care of a newborn.

i She said, 'John Gray, you're a fair-weather friend! As long as I'm sweet, loving Bonnie you are here for me, but as soon as I'm not, you walk right out that door.'

j That day, for the first time, I didn't leave her. I stayed, and it felt great. I succeeded in giving to her when she really needed me. This felt like real love. Caring for another person. Trusting in our love. Being there at her hour of need. I marvelled at how easy it was for me to support her when I was shown the way.

k Then she paused, and her eyes filled up with tears. As her tone shifted she said, 'Right now I'm in pain. I have nothing to give, this is when I need you the most. Please, come over here and hold me. You don't have to say anything. I just need to feel your arms around me. Please don't go.'

l At that moment I started to realise the real meaning of **unconditional love**. I had always thought of myself as a loving person. But she was right. I had been a fair-weather friend. As long as she was happy and nice, I loved back. But if she was unhappy or upset, I would feel blamed and then argue or distance myself.

Extract from *Men Are from Mars, Women are from Venus* by John Gray

2.14 Answer the following questions with short answers. Check your answers with a classmate or your teacher.

a Why was John's wife taking painkillers?

b Why did John 'explode'?

c Why didn't John's wife call John at the office?

d 'Then something started to happen that would change my life.' What happened that would change John's life?

e What does John's wife mean when she calls him a 'fair-weather friend'?

f 'This felt like real love.' What is meant by 'this'?

2.15 Unscramble the words in the sentences below, from Text 4.6, so that they make sense. Then, as you read Text 4.6, look for the correct sentences. They appear below in the same order as they do in the text.

a people I that known to classification as wives. belong of

b recent fresh the mine long a of on scene too from friend a divorce. ago appeared Not male

c And I I a to care of am children. wife while want school my going take to

d properly are I sure a make children eat kept wife want to my clean. and

e written type I who for them. And a wife my me I want papers have will when

f while my Needless working. for wife and say pay arrange of the children wife care is to my the will,

g about wife complaints I a with rambling a who want bother wife's me will duties. not

TEXT AND CONTEXT

- Judy Syfers wrote this piece in 1970 and read it aloud at a gathering in San Francisco to celebrate the 50th anniversary of women's right to vote in the USA women's right to vote in the USA.

- This text has become famous and is discussed in literary classes and courses on Women's Studies.

Text 4.6
Why I Want a Wife

I belong to that classification of people known as wives. I am a Wife.

And, not altogether incidentally, I am a mother. Not too long ago a male friend of mine appeared on the scene fresh from a recent divorce. He had one child, who is, of course, with his ex-wife. He is looking for another wife. As I thought about him while I was ironing one evening, it suddenly occurred to me that I too, would like to have a wife. Why do I want a wife?

I would like to go back to school so that I can become economically independent, support myself, and if need be, support those **dependent** upon me. I want a wife who will work and send me to school. And while I am going to school I want a wife to take care of my children. I want a wife to keep track of the children's doctor and dentist appointments. And to keep track of mine, too. I want a wife to make sure my children eat properly and are kept clean. I want a wife who will wash the children's clothes and keep them mended. I want a wife who is a good nurturing attendant to my children, who arranges for their schooling, makes sure that they have an adequate social life with their peers, takes them to the park, the zoo, etc. I want a wife who takes care of the children when they are sick, a wife who arranges to be around when the children need special care, because, of course, I cannot miss classes at school. My wife must arrange to lose time at work and not lose the job. It might mean a small cut in my wife's income from time to time, but I guess I can tolerate that. Needless to say, my wife will arrange and pay for the care of the children while my wife is working.

I want a wife who will take care of my physical needs. I want a wife who will keep my house clean. A wife who will pick up after my children, a wife who will pick up after me. I want a wife who will keep my clothes clean, ironed, mended, replaced when need be, and who will see to it that my personal things are kept in their proper place so that I can find what I need the minute I need it. I want a wife who cooks the meals, a wife who is a good cook. I want a wife who will plan the menus, do the necessary grocery shopping, prepare the meals, serve them pleasantly, and then do

the cleaning up while I do my studying. I want a wife who will care for me when I am sick and **sympathise** with my pain and loss of time from school. I want a wife to go along when our family takes a vacation so that someone can continue to care for me and my children when I need a rest and change of scene. I want a wife who will not bother me with rambling complaints about a wife's **duties.** But I want a wife who will listen to me when I feel the need to explain a rather difficult point I have come across in my course of studies. And I want a wife who will type my papers for me when I have written them.[…]

If, by chance, I find another person more suitable as a wife than the wife I already have, I want the liberty to replace my present wife with another one. Naturally, I will expect a fresh, new life; my wife will take the children and be solely responsible for them so that I am left free.

When I am through with school and have a job, I want my wife to quit working and remain at home so that my wife can more fully and completely take care of a wife's duties.

My God, who wouldn't want a wife?

Abridged extract from *Why I Want a Wife* by Judy Syfers

2.16 When discussing texts, we often talk about **tone**. This describes the writer's attitude, as expressed through the language of the text. Look up the definitions of the words a-l below. After you have found and understood the meanings of these words, relate them to Text 4.6. Which words describe the tone of Text 4.6? Justify your answers by referring to examples from the text.

a	tongue-in-cheek	**b**	critical
c	biting	**d**	mocking
e	serious	**f**	sarcastic
g	cynical	**h**	humorous
i	subversive	**j**	ironic
k	passionate	**l**	begrudging

CONCEPTS

Meaning

What does Judy Syfers really mean when she says she wants 'a wife'? Quite frequently, writers do not mean what they write literally. When there is such a mismatch between what a writer states and what a reader interprets, then the writer is using a stylistic device known as irony. In fact the tone of Text 4.6 is very ironic. Since readers and audiences are always looking for *meaning* in a text, authors do not always have to communicate directly. 'Wife' in Text 4.6 carries symbolic *meaning*. Can you define it?

2.17 In Text 4.6, Judy Syfers explains that she wants a 'wife'. What does she really want? What other words could be substituted for 'wife'?

Form and meaning

2.18 Text 4.5 includes several expressions and phrases which use prepositions. Prepositions, as you might already have learned, are those small words, such as 'in', 'on' and 'of', that point to places, express relationships and combine ideas. In the box below are several examples of prepositions. Select the correct preposition to complete each of the sentences that follow. Look back at Text 4.5 for the answers. You will use each preposition once.

as	of	in	over	up	around	for	at	out

a Being there at her hour … need.

b Please, come … here and hold me.

c Caring … another person.

d I just need to feel your arms … me.

e I succeeded … giving to her when she really needed me.

f I had always thought of myself … a loving person.

g Then she paused, and her eyes filled … with tears.

h … this point I exploded.

i I ran … of pills.

2.19 When using quotations, you should also consider carefully the correct use of punctuation, such as commas, capital letters and full stops. Look at the sentences below and then answer the following questions about punctuation.

- Do you 'choose' your husband or wife?

- I said defensively, 'Why didn't you call me?'

- Bonnie said, 'Stop, please don't leave. This is when I need you the most. I'm in pain. I haven't slept in days. Please listen to me.'

- What other words could be substituted for 'wife'?

- 'What kind of wife do you want?' she asked.

- 'I just want you to hold me,' she explained.

- People speak of 'congressmen', 'firemen' and 'mankind'.

a When do you use single quotation marks? And when do you use double quotation marks?

b When do you use capital letters?

c How do you use commas to present a quotation?

d Do question marks, full stops and commas belong inside or outside *single* quotation marks?

e Do question marks, full stops and commas belong inside or outside *double* quotation marks?

2.20 The sentences below do not use any quotation marks or punctuation. Rewrite them correctly. Compare your answers to those of your classmates and teacher.

a Parents often ask me, when is the time right

b Technically she is not a pledger but has made a promise to herself

c Some people prefer the term same-sex marriage to gay marriage.

d Judy Syfers ends her speech by asking my God who wouldn't want a wife

e I had never been called a fair-weather friend before.

f Open-minded caring and reflective are a few useful traits for maintaining a healthy relationship

g Do you believe in love at first sight

Discussion

2.21 Text 4.5 describes a moment where a woman and man differ in their response to a situation. Look at the list of activities a–g below. How do men and women in your culture differ in the ways they do these things? Try not to base your answers on stereotypes, but on your experiences. You can discuss these points in relation to yourself, your friends or family. The following phrase might help you discuss each situation: 'My mother/girlfriend/sister/I tend(s) to …, while my father/boyfriend/brother/I tend(s) to …'.

a Shopping for shoes

b Talking to his/her mother on the phone

c Cleaning the house

d 'Hanging out' or spending free time with a friend of the same gender

e Reading maps and navigating

f Cooking

g Playing sports

Social organisation

2.22 Text 4.6 was written in the USA in 1971. Judy Syfers is commenting on what many men expected from their wives at that time. How is the role of women where you live similar to or different from the context of Text 4.6? Discuss the following statements and the images a–d with reference to the countries and cultures in your own experience. How likely are these situations in your culture? How true are these statements for your culture?

a Men and women have equal employment opportunities.

b Men and women have equal rights in society, such as the freedom to vote, drive, divorce or own property.

c Fathers and mothers share the responsibilities of raising children.

d Men and women share the responsibilities of housekeeping.

2.23 This unit has explored two topics that might not be discussed often in schools in the country where you live:

- same-sex marriage
- sex before marriage.

Discuss your answers to the following questions as a class. If you feel comfortable stating your position on these topics, share your opinions with your classmates. Remember to be respectful of other people's opinions and differences.

a Why do you think these topics are either taboo or open for discussion at your school or other schools in your area? What role should your school play in helping you to think about these topics?

b How safe is it for you to express your opinions on these issues in the country where you live? What makes you think this?

c How is the country where you live different from other countries on these matters?

d How is the culture where you live changing with regards to these topics? What is driving these changes?

2.24 Use the photograph below for a mock individual oral.

a Take 15 minutes to prepare a presentation on the following visual stimulus. During this time make notes that address questions such as: How do different cultures define marriage differently? How are cultural values on marriage changing? What would I value in a 'partner for life'?

b Speak for 3–4 minutes on your own about the photograph and your chosen caption before engaging in a 5–6-minute conversation with your teacher.

c Explore the ideas that you discussed in class. Use vocabulary that you have learned from this unit.

Communication skills

As you might know, the IB Diploma Programme aims to help you develop your *communication skills*. As you have seen in this unit so far, this skill includes the articulation of your arguments on issues such as same-sex marriage. What's more, *communication skills* include listening to and understanding counter arguments. Whether you write your speech (Activity 2.25) for or against same-sex marriage, it is important to consider all points of view.

Extended Essay

Is the English language inherently sexist? Many people speak of 'congressmen', 'firemen' and 'mankind', while it is often assumed that doctors are men and nurses are women. Sexism and the English language is a good topic for a Category 1 extended essay. Remember, however, that an extended essay on this topic would need to focus on a particular cultural context or a specific text. A good title might read 'How sexist was the language during the Hilary Clinton and Donald Trump US presidential campaigns in 2016?' Such an essay should define sexist language and include examples from various sources.

Writing

2.25 Imagine you are a politician making a speech about gay and lesbian rights and same-sex marriage. Write out the first 500 words of such a speech.

a To start, study Unit 6.4 on speech writing. Learn more about this text type and its conventions.

b Watch the video of NYS Senator Diane Savino speaking on the Marriage Equality bill again (see watch and listen section). Look for evidence of the stylistic and structural devices that are explained in Unit 6.4.

c Write your own speech about same-sex marriage. Include arguments that you have explored in this unit. Be sure to include the key features of speech writing, as you have learned from Unit 6.2.

d Ask a fellow classmate and your teacher to assess you speech, using the assessment criteria from Paper 1.

e Rewrite your speech, taking your classmate's and teacher's feedback into consideration.

f Read your speech in front of your class and submit it for assessment, using the assessment criteria for Paper 1.

2.26 Carry out your own research to find out more about virginity pledges and abstinence-only programmes taught in schools in the United States. Write an 'official report' that could be sent to a politician to explain the effects of these pledges and programmes. See Unit 6.8 for more help on how to write official reports.

2.27 Text 4.6 is about the kind of housewife that some men with traditional views might wish for. What kind of husband might a traditional wife desire? As a writing assignment, write a satire on Text 4.6, using the same ironic tone (see concept box) to write about the 'ideal' husband, titled 'Why I want a husband'.

Higher level extension

2.28 What is the difference in meaning between the two words in each pair below? Discuss these differences with classmates.

A	belief	opinion
B	feelings	commitment
C	to arrange	to force
D	**courting**	**dating**
E	marriage	relationship

2.29 Text 4.7 is about arranged marriages. As you read the text, identify any examples of bias. Use a scale of 1 to 5 to score each example, where 1 is very objective and non-biased, and 5 is extremely biased. Share the sentences that you have rated as extremely biased with your classmates and teacher. Discuss any differences in the examples you have selected.

TEXT AND CONTEXT

- While many marriages are still arranged in India, laws have changed to allow unmarried couples to live together. As the following points indicate, ideas on marriage are changing in India.

- The term 'love marriage' has sometimes been used in India to refer to relationships where the initial contact between two people does not involve parents or family.

- In many urban and modern areas of India, there are also 'self-arranged marriages' where couples start a relationship, but parents must approve of the relationship.

Text 4.7

The Culture of Arranged Marriages in India

Arranged marriages have always been a debatable subject. It is in the major outlook on relationships that Indians are vastly different, in the way they perceive the institution of marriage, to those beliefs of other countries especially in the west.

Many people have a pretty major misunderstanding of the topic of arranged marriages and, in fact, have a fairly negative attitude regarding arranged marriages. The best way to understand the reasoning behind such cultures is to put aside your own beliefs, opinions and preconceived ideas in order to see more clearly before dismissing it as wrong. While it might not be for all, and love marriages in India are not unheard of or a rare sighting by any means. Arranged marriages aren't necessarily a bad thing either!

Here are some points to better understand the Culture of Arranged Marriages in India:

Feelings vs Commitment

Many Indians say that marrying a person they don't know, gives one 'a lifetime to learn to love them', as opposed to the American ideal of learning a person inside and out before entering into marriage. It can be said that an arranged marriage in India is not based on feelings, but rather on commitment.

An Indian woman described it as, 'Here, we get married without having feelings for the person. We base our marriage on commitment, not on feelings. As our marriage progresses, the feelings develop. In America, you base your decision to marry on feelings, but what happens when the feelings wane? You have nothing left to keep the marriage together if you get married according to feelings and then the feelings go away.'

In India, a relationship between two people is something that is presumed to be fostered and created throughout a lifetime of marriage. Whereas in the west, people do not take the idea of marriage seriously until after they know a person for a number of years, or feel like they know everything about the person. One way of looking at this difference is that after marriage you tend to accept your spouse's differences and habits more easily than when you have a choice. A relationship not bound by marriage is more easily broken for the smaller nuances in life. After marriage, you tend to accept what you have rather than look for someone better, as people often do while courting or dating.

Arranged Marriages are Not Forced Marriages

When people think of arranged marriages, they often picture a boy or girl forced into a relationship in which they have absolutely no choice. However, in reality, this is simply not the case. Before the marriage becomes official, the potential bride and groom have the opportunity to meet each other and decide whether or not a relationship is something that they would wish to pursue. It's not like the couple see each other on the wedding day for the first time or just once before the wedding. Once approved they meet and get engaged.

There is usually a period of months or even a year or more after the couple are engaged and before the wedding, where the couple gets to know each other, meet, talk and discuss the future. This time after the engagement to the wedding day is sort of the dating period for the couple.

www.IndiaMarks.com

TOK

TOK is concerned with logic and reasoning. Reasoning, as you might have learned, is a process of coming to a conclusion based on two or more 'premises'. A 'premise' is a statement or claim that must be accepted in order for the conclusion to be 'valid'. Sometimes these premises are implied, meaning they are not stated clearly. They do not have to be true to be valid. For example, Text 4.7 states that 'arranged marriages aren't necessarily a bad thing either!', implying that someone does not approve of arranged marriages. What premises are implied by the following conclusion (hint: discuss the words printed in italics in the paragraph, which is taken from the text):

'The best way to understand the reasoning behind such cultures is to put aside *your own* beliefs, opinions, and preconceived ideas in order to see *more clearly* before dismissing it as wrong.'

2.30 The author of Text 4.7 often expresses the same idea twice, using synonyms. The words in the following list are taken from Text 4.7. For each word, find a synonym in the text that expresses the same idea. They are in the same order in which they appear in Text 4.7.

a attitude

b unheard of

c wane

d fostered

e courting

2.31 Do you agree or disagree with the following statements from Text 4.7? Discuss your opinions with fellow classmates.

a Arranged marriages aren't necessarily a bad thing.

b You have nothing left to keep the marriage together if you get married according to feelings and then the feelings go away.

c After marriage you tend to accept what you have rather than look for someone better as people often do while courting or dating.

d Marrying a person [you] don't know gives one 'a lifetime to learn to love them'.

2.32 Only 1.1 per cent of Indian marriages end in divorce. Discuss how this fact changes your understanding of arranged marriages, divorce, India or your own culture.

EXTRA

Get together with a group of classmates or friends and watch a Bollywood movie. Bollywood movies often involve singing, dancing, love and Indian culture. *Bride and Prejudice* or *Just Married* are two interesting Bollywood films about arranged marriage. Discuss how the depiction of marriage and family relationships in one of these films is different from how these things are in your own culture.

A scene from a Bollywood movie

Literature

2.33 Text 4.8 is a short story which contains the words listed below. Before you read the story, check your understanding of these words by using them to fill the gaps in the following sentences.

pivotal	smirk	possessed	cog	implode	elaborate
	beckoned	quest	improvised		

a   The word … means the opposite of explode. It describes a situation where something is crushed and collapses.

b   If something is … , then it is done without much care or planning.

c   A … is a kind of grin or smile, often used in a negative way.

d   When someone is … , they are consumed by an idea.

e   A … is part of a set of gears or the inner workings of a mechanism.

f   An … project is one that is fancy and time-consuming.

g   When going on a … , we search for something in an adventurous way.

h   If someone is … , then he or she is called or requested.

i   A … moment means a turning point.

Text 4.8

Defining Moments

1   'Where art thou, Lady Guinevere?' …

2   Oh no! I don't deserve this, do I? I sighed nervously, ragged breaths following, my second week of high school about to implode! As I turned, I saw Peter, missing his old knight costume, but beautifully improvised with a paper crown and branch sword. He was surrounded by a group of smirking teens, shooting names and sarcastic arrows. Peter didn't notice! Not really! He was too absorbed, possessed by his latest role.

3   King Arthur's face lit up. 'Guinevere! My lady, I have returned!' I twisted my neck as if on some jarring cog, scanning behind me, praying for escape! …

4   I was four. Peter and his parents moved into the flat above and straight away, young as I was, I knew something wasn't quite normal. Maybe it was the way his room was full of astronaut gear. Not your usual Buzz Lightyear plastic stuff; no, this was a collector's dream, real deal Nasa in the room above me! Maybe it was the way he spoke about space, a knowing far-off glimmer in his eye. When we weren't playing Moon Landings we were building teleporters: only his were always a bit more elaborate than mine, real wires connecting,

lighting up. My cereal boxes and three inches of Sellotape security never quite matched up! But we were little; it didn't matter! Peter was the most fun ever, knowing everything about everything: really!

5   He didn't like to be touched. He didn't like me to move things in his room, not from their places, their carefully catalogued places. But we were little; it didn't matter. Peter was still the most fun ever.

6   When we started school, it was fine, but as we got older, some of the kids thought Peter was a bit strange. They didn't understand him like I did; they didn't take the time. By Year 2 we had been champions of the Wild West, Leonardo da Vinci's apprentices and soldiers of the First World War. I closed my eyes and listened to him as he became my talking history book, transporting us to another time and place.

7   I could almost see the smoke of the teepees, smell the oil on the canvas, hear the guns in my ears. We were the champions of the playground, Peter and I.

8   Yet the summer marking the end of our primary years saw Peter off to relatives in Ireland. Peter's parents had set me the task of easing the change and so we had thrown ourselves into Camelot; Peter was to go on a quest across the water, leaving his kingdom and his Guinevere to wait anxiously for his safe return.

9   He caught chickenpox and was three weeks late!

10   Guinevere, meanwhile, met Katie and Alice and was on the way to 'populardom' before term began. They talked hair, boys, boys … boys … ! There was no escape. Smug faces beckoned, sneering, pitying!

11   Defining, pivotal moment … I knelt. 'My Lord!' I grinned! Peter was still the most fun, ever.

Defining Moments by Isobel Harwood

2.34 Answer the following questions to check your understanding of this story.

a   Who plays King Arthur and Lady Guinevere in this story?

b   How old is the narrator in this story?

c   Why did other children begin to find Peter a bit strange?

d   Why does the narrator want to 'escape'?

e   Why does Peter come to school three weeks late?

f   Why does the narrator kneel?

2.35 What do you think is meant by each of the following sentences and phrases, taken from Text 4.8? Discuss what is meant by the underlined words.

a   'Where <u>art thou</u>, Lady Guinevere?' (paragraph 1)

b   … shooting names and <u>sarcastic arrows</u> (paragraph 2)

c   He was <u>too</u> absorbed, possessed by his latest role. (paragraph 2)

d   Maybe <u>it</u> was the way he spoke about space, a knowing far-off glimmer in his eye. (<u>paragraph</u> 4)

e   But we were little; <u>it</u> didn't matter! (paragraphs 4 *and* 5)

f   … they didn't take <u>the time</u>. (paragraph 6)

g   Yet the summer marking the end of our primary years <u>saw</u> Peter <u>off</u> to relatives in Ireland. (paragraph 8)

h   Peter's parents had set me the task of easing the change and so we had <u>thrown ourselves into</u> Camelot… (paragraph 8)

2.36 What is the conflict of this story? When discussing conflict in literature, you might begin to recognise similarities between stories. There are several common types of conflict in fiction, and these are listed below.

a   Which descriptions best describe the type(s) of conflict in Text 4.8?

b   How are these types of conflict relevant to the two literary works that you're reading for IB English B?

- *Individual versus another individual:* many stories are about one main character who makes the action happen. This person, in literature, is known as the *protagonist*. Conflict arises when another person tries to stop the protagonist from achieving his or her goal. This person is known as the *antagonist*.
- *Individual versus society:* the protagonist is often pitted against society. The protagonist seems to be the only shining light in a dark world. Antagonists are often part of 'the system' that keeps people like the protagonist from achieving their goals.
- *Individual versus circumstances:* sometimes protagonists simply have bad luck. They happen to be caught in a natural disaster or epidemic. They are in the wrong place at the wrong time and have to deal with the consequences.
- *The individual versus themselves:* sometimes protagonists are their own worst enemy. As you read their thoughts, follow their actions and listen to them speak, you the reader can see that they have flawed personality traits. They have to solve their own problems by making a personal change.

2.37 Do you think *Defining Moments* is a fictional or a factual story? Is it an autobiographical work, meaning that it is based on the author's personal experience? Or do you think it is a work of complete fantasy? Give the reasons for your answer.

2.38 *Defining Moments* (Text 4.8) is about a friend who feels torn between her 'cool' girlfriends and her 'not-so-cool' childhood friend. Is this a conflict that you recognise? Has a similar situation ever occurred for you? With a classmate, exchange stories about choices that you have had to make with regards to friends.

2.39 Read the following sentence:

'If I had not been so embarrassed, I would have talked to him.'

This type of verb phrase is known as the *past conditional*. You can use past conditionals for writing or speaking about situations that did not actually happen in the past. Conjugate the missing verbs from the sentences below to turn them into the past conditional tense.

First part of sentence			Second part of sentence		
If I	had done	this,	then I	would have done	that.
	(past perfect)			(would + present perfect)	

a   If she … (not greet) Peter, then she … (regret) that.

b   If Peter … (not come down) with chickenpox, he … (start) school with the other pupils that year.

c   He … (play) with her more that summer, if his parents … (not take) him to Ireland on holiday.

REFLECT

The resources in this unit have introduced you to a range of ideas and topics about relationships and marriage:

- divorce
- same-sex marriage
- purity pledges
- gender differences
- expectations in marriage
- arranged marriages
- childhood sweethearts.

Have the ideas presented in this unit changed your views on any of these issues? How and why?

Unit 4.3
The future of jobs

Guiding questions	Learning objectives
• How has globalisation affected employment practices and opportunities? • How is technology changing the way people are employed?	• Develop an understanding of how globalisation and technology are affecting employment opportunities and practices. • Be able to speak proficiently and write coherently about globalisation, technology and job opportunities.

Word bank

job security

self-employment

knowledge economy

soft skills

freelance

outsourcing

collaborate

artificial intelligence

meritocracy

entrepreneur

innovative

creativity

emotional intelligence

flexible

resourcefulness

vocational

native worker

migrant

qualifications

In this course, you have explored how globalisation is changing the way we travel, socialise and work. While globalisation and technological advancements present exciting opportunities, they are also having negative impacts, such as threatening people's **job security**. Many people are worried that their jobs will be taken over by a robot or computer. Others fear that immigrants will take their jobs. Some people have seen their jobs moved to developing countries, where their work can be done at a lower cost.

In the past, the strength of a country's economy was measured by how much it could produce. Nowadays it is measured by access to, and use of, knowledge, information and education. In a world that is changing so quickly, the future for jobs and employment is uncertain. Some jobs might become obsolete; new jobs will be created. One day, you might find yourself doing a job that hasn't yet been thought of!

This unit asks you to consider how the world of employment is changing. You will see a video that will give you tips on preparing for a career in an ever-changing world. The audio track explores the future of **self-employment**.

Text 4.9 introduces nine career paths that might be futureproof. Text 4.10 focusses on the need for continuing education in an era when skills can quickly become outdated. Text 4.11 offers insight into the question of whether immigrants really pose a threat to job security in the UK. In the literature section, you will read the story of a famous literary character, Gregor Samsa, who wonders why he works where he does.

Through a study of the sources in this unit, you will hopefully gain a better understanding of your place in the future of the workplace.

Getting started

3.1 'What do you want to be when you grow up?' This is a question you might have heard before. It suggests that you will 'be' what you 'do'. Complete the three sentences below. Do not write your name on the paper. Give it to your teacher. They will read out the completed sentences on each piece of paper. Can you guess who wrote these answers? How well do you know your classmates?

a In the future, for my own financial gain, I see myself...

b I want to do this kind of work because...

c I think I possess these qualities, that will help me do this successfully: ...

3.2 What is the difference in meaning between the two words in each of the following pairs? Describe the difference in meaning for each pair. Discuss your answers with your classmates.

a job/career

b employer/boss

c education/learning

d unemployed/self-employed

e calling/profession

3.3 In the box below are several concepts that are explored in this unit. Match them with the definitions that follow. It is OK if you have never heard of these concepts before. Make an educated guess. Check your answers with those of your classmates.

knowledge economy	on demand mobile service	the gig economy
future-proof career	**soft skills**	automation	flattening of the world
race to the bottom	**freelance**	lifelong learning	**outsourcing**

a A system where free agents work on a project-by-project or event-by-event basis.

b A trend caused by globalisation, where services and products are constantly made cheaper because someone, somewhere is willing to do the job at a lower cost.

c The idea that people must continue with their education to keep up with changes in their industry or field of expertise.

d The skills to communicate effectively, interact with different kinds of people, **collaborate**, be open-minded, show empathy and perform well.

e The act of giving a task, which would normally be done within a company, to another person, free agent or company.

f The idea that, as a result of globalisation, the competition for products and services has become more level or fairer. It is an idea introduced by Thomas L. Friedman.

g The idea that a job or line of work will not disappear as a result of globalisation, migration or technological advancements.

h A system in which people's financial welfare is dependent on their ability to access quality information rather than their means of producing things.

i Another term for self-employment.

j A kind of job that can be requested quickly through an online platform or phone app.

k The process of letting computers or robots with **artificial intelligence** do the work of humans.

3.4 Do you agree or disagree with the following statements? A different person in your class reads out each statement. Move to one side of the room if you agree with the statement. Move to the other side if you disagree with the statement. After each statement, discuss why you agree or disagree.

a It will be more difficult for our generation to find jobs than it was for our parents' generation.

b What you contribute to society is more important than the amount of money you earn.

c I would much rather be self-employed than work for an organisation or company.

d Outsourcing jobs to low-wage countries is ethically acceptable.

e Technology creates more jobs for people than it takes away.

f Immigrants create more jobs than they take away from a country's native population.

Do you see yourself being self-employed in your own small business?
Or are you the kind of person who thrives in a large company?

EXTRA

There has been a fear of machines taking over human employment since the time of the Luddites. This was a group of people in England who protested about the introduction of machines in cotton and woollen mills in the early 19th century. Do some research on the term 'Luddite' and give a presentation on their history. Are there modern day Luddites?

Luddites destroying machines in mills in 1811

Watch and listen 📹 🔊

3.5 Before watching the Thomas L. Friedman video, write down your answers to the following questions and discuss them with a classmate.

a How do you imagine yourself applying for a good job in the future? What steps do you think you'll take?

b What kind of education will best prepare you for this job?

c What do you think employers usually look for in a good employee?

d How do you think your LinkedIn profile page will look in 10 years? Why would you want to develop a profile on this platform?

e What motivates people to work hard at any place of employment?

LinkedIn is an online platform for sharing your CV and increasing your 'visibility' in the employment market.

LEARNER PROFILE

After watching the video on the 'Next New World', describe which character traits from the IB's learner profile are useful in this Next New World, according to the people that Thomas Friedman interviews. Select one or more characteristics from the learner profile below and explain how they are relevant to the video.

- inquirers
- knowledgeable
- thinkers
- communicators
- principled
- open-minded
- caring
- risk-takers
- balanced
- reflective

3.6 Do an online search for a video called: 'Thomas L. Friedman's Next New World: Dispatches From the Front Lines' by The New York Times. Read the questions below, before watching the video. Take notes as you watch the video, writing key words and phrases to help you answer these questions. Then, write out your answers as complete sentences. Share your answers with a classmate and check them with your teacher.

a What question does Thomas L. Freidman aim to answer during his symposium on the 'Next New World'?

b Why does Andrew McAfee think that his Montessori education has helped prepare him for life?

c Why does he believe students should spend time on 'both sides of campus'?

d Why does Elli Sharef say that you should think of yourself as a 'product'?

e What does she mean by saying that you have to 'hustle' your way into a job?

f What kind of people is Ben Kaufman looking for in his business?

g According to Laszlo Bock what is 'cognitive ability', besides 'smarts'?

h How does he define 'emergent leadership'?

i What traits are useful for dealing with the culture of the workplace at Google?

j What suggestions does Jeff Weiner offer for people who are creating a LinkedIn profile?

k What kinds of opportunities can arise from keeping your LinkedIn profile 'fresh' and 'relevant'?

l According to Dov Seidman, what motivates people?

Thomas L. Friedman is a Pulitzer prize-winning columnist for the New York Times, who wrote *The World is Flat* about the effects of globalisation and technology

3.7 Return to your answers from Activity 3.5. After watching the video, how would you change your answers? Discuss any changes that you have made with your classmates.

Listen

3.8 Before you listen to Audio track 12, check if you already know some of the phrases that you will hear. In the box below is a list of nouns. Which of the following words (a–o) is each noun commonly used with? If you do not know the meaning of any phrases that you have created, look up their definition before you listen to the audio track.

| description | rights | progression | countries | equation | app | force | media |
| production | generation | trade | contractor | resources | plan | line | |

a	job...	b	pension...	c	human...	d	the bottom...
e	low-wage...	f	social...	g	baby-boomer...	h	work...
i	the power...	j	means of...	k	a natural...	l	mobile...
m	independent...	n	workers' ...	o	fair...		

3.9 Based on the noun phrases above, predict what you think Audio track 12 will be about.

3.10 You are going to listen to 🔊 Audio track 12, which is an imagined talk given at a conference on 'the future of jobs'. Before you listen to the talk, select one person from your class to leave the room or ask for a volunteer. You will listen to Audio track 12 without them in the room. After you have listened to the audio, they will come back into the classroom. You will then do a role-playing activity. Here are more details about the different roles in the activity:

The person who leaves the room: You are the owner of a large taxi company in a large city. In recent years, your company has been losing business due to competition from Uber, a global, on demand mobile app for taxi services. Some of your drivers have left your company, and you don't understand why. You wanted to attend the conference on 'the future of jobs', but you were unable to. You want to find out what you missed by talking to those who were there (your classmates). Ask them questions that are relevant to your role and business.

The rest of the class: You attended the conference and you learned a lot from the talk. Afterwards, you start a conversation with a person who owns a taxi company, and who was unable to attend the talk. He asks you what he missed. Summarise the talk for him, making use of the following words and phrases that have been taken from the talk. You can assign each person in your class one of these words.

a	shareholders	b	reorganisation
c	cutthroat	d	to strike out on your own
e	platform economy	f	**meritocracy**
g	disruptive technology	h	to use carrots and sticks
i	sense of ownership	j	middleman
k	**entrepreneur**	l	race to the bottom
m	collective bargaining	n	ratings
o	flexibility		

Remember: The point of this exercise is to have fun *and* demonstrate your understanding of the recording. You might want to listen to the recording twice before your classmate comes back into the room. You should select this person carefully. Finally, let that person listen to the recording after your role-playing conversation.

ATL

Communication skills

Activity 3.10 asks you to engage in a role-playing game. You do not have to be a skilled actor to understand the benefits of this method of learning. Simulating a situation is an excellent way to develop your communication skills. Not only are these skills part of the IB's approaches to learning, but they are also valuable for your future in the workplace.

Exploring texts

3.11 In small groups create a list of *five* jobs that you think are 'futureproof'. These are jobs in which job security will not be under threat from automation and artificial intelligence. Discuss this list as a group before presenting your group's list to the rest of the class. As a class discuss why you think these professions are least likely to be automated.

3.12 The following phrases a–k have similar meanings to phrases taken from Text 4.9. Read the text and identify the words and phrases that have a similar meaning. The phrases below appear in the same order as their corresponding phrases in Text 4.9. The first answer has been given as an example.

a *jobs could be made* **redundant** = *careers might become obsolete*

b jobs that are less susceptible to automation

c technologies could streamline the processes of factories and offices

d despite their efforts

e computers do not have an imagination, nor can they innovate

f qualities that computers do not currently posses

g retaining new knowledge from someone else is easier

h the title speaks for itself

i improbable that computers will replace such people in the near future

j computers are limited by systems and programs

k hiring individuals on this basis is controversial

Extended Essay
'How has the integration of technology in the workplace changed the way people use the English language?' This would be a good research question for a Category 2a extended essay. There are many books and articles about this phenomenon, that you should reference in your essay.

Text 4.9
Nine 'futureproof' careers, according to the world's largest job site

The automation of jobs has many advantages, like increased productivity. However, the main disadvantage is that people are concerned that their careers might become obsolete in the next few decades.

A recent study showed that millennials in general choose professions that are more 'future-proof,' and less likely to be taken over by machines, but that still leaves many unsure of whether a robot will steal their job or not.

The world's number one job site, Indeed, has over 200 million unique visitors per month, which gives them an insight into what kinds of jobs are available, and what skills are in demand.

Based on this data, Indeed's EMEA economist Mariano Mamertino has come up with a list of nine career paths that are the least likely to be taken over by machines, or will complement their work.

Mamertino said that the occupations which will be harder to automate 'often involve managing and developing people' and 'decision-making and strategic planning, or creative work.'

'Machines have the potential to make the workplace more efficient, by automating mechanical and routine processes, but humans will always play a key-role at the centre,' he said.

Scroll down to see if your career makes the list, which is ranked in ascending order by average salary, according to data from Indeed and job search site Glassdoor.

Chef: £18 730 per year

People will always enjoy the experience of going out for dinner and trying new flavours. Without a chef who is able to taste, new and **innovative** menus wouldn't be so readily available. A robot wouldn't be able to combine manual skills with **creativity** the way a chef does, no matter how hard they try. In the UK, chefs are in demand, with 22.4% of Head Chef, 22% of Sous Chef, and 21.3% of Executive Chef jobs remaining on the Indeed website for more than 60 days.

Marketing, communications, and design: Around £25 000 per year

Machines aren't great at critical thinking, or coming up with new and exciting ideas, so your creativity might well be future-proof. People who design for a living, or who work with ideas, words, and images will probably survive the increase in automation, because machines don't function like humans. Not yet, at least.

Healthcare professionals: £26 380 per year

Some roles are not going to be taken over by machines for a long time, if at all, because they require human interaction. Healthcare professionals are very much in this category. Nursing requires strong interpersonal and communication skills, that are things you probably won't get from any machine that exists now. At the moment, in the UK home care nursing jobs are the hardest to fill in the sector, so if you have this job you are still rare and in-demand.

Healthcare professionals are not likely to be replaced

Education and training: £28 664 per year

Teachers are always in high demand, according to Indeed. There's something about learning new things from a

While computers and the World Wide Web have changed education, teachers are still very much a part of the learning process

person that makes the information stick better than if you were learning everything remotely. Teachers are especially important when they have languages, because there are often children in classes who have migrated from other countries. Teaching vacancies in the UK rose by 5% in the past two years, according to Indeed.

Cyber security expert: Around £30 000 per year

A recent Indeed study shows that the UK had the third highest number of adverts for cyber security roles in the world. London alone is one of the biggest centres for cybersecurity firms. However, the employer demand for these jobs is three times higher than the candidate interest. Over the past 18 months, there has been an 18% increase in cyber security postings on the Indeed site, so it's unlikely robots will be taking these jobs away any time soon.

Human resources: Around £36 000 per year

The clue is in the name. While finding the right candidate is becoming increasingly reliant on data and automated screening in some professions, the soft skills that people bring to the table are still valuable. **Emotional intelligence** and the ability to read people will always be important in this sector, which robots probably won't be able to do any time soon.

Delivery or Logistics management: £43 435 per year

There's been a lot of talk in the past year or so about delivery drones, and how they will take over as a method of receiving your post. However, the logistics sector still requires humans to be involved in the oversight and management.

According to Indeed, delivery driver job postings are some of the hardest roles to fill, often being on the site for 60 days or longer.

Data scientist: £55 765 per year

According to Indeed, there has been a 54% increase in people searching for data science jobs in the UK over the last 12 months. Not only is there a lot of interest, the demand is keeping up with it. There's only so much a machine can do with algorithms and code. It's the people who combine their scientific expertise and the ability to find the stories hidden in masses of data who are especially useful.

Gig-worker: variable

The 'gig economy' includes short-term contracts or freelance work, like Deliveroo and Uber drivers. This way of working is on the rise, and it requires employees to be **flexible** and independent: two things robots aren't great at.

There is a lot of debate around the issue of employing people in this way, but overall there has been a sharp rise in users searching for flexible and part-time work in the UK.

www.businessinsider.com

3.13 After you have read Text 4.9, return to your top five 'futureproof' professions from Activity 3.11 and see how they compare to the nine professions listed in Text 4.9. Are they similar or different? What qualities or characteristics make your professions future-proof?

3.14 Text 4.10 contains some challenging vocabulary. Which of the following words a–t, taken from this text, do you know? Match the words from the text with their synonyms in the box below. Look up the meanings of any words that you do not already know.

list	concern	first	memorise	carry	keep	time	ease	
	add to	appear	strength	exact	financial	exceptional		
occupational	overstate	central	responsibility	inventiveness	change			

a exaggerate		**b** brawn		**c** anxiety	
d materialise		**e** unprecedented		**f** era	
g recall		**h** rank		**i** very	
j resourcefulness		**k** retain		**l** complement	
m pivotal		**n** onus		**o** bear	
p vocational		**q** adjust		**r** convenience	
s initial		**t** fiscal			

Form and meaning

3.15 How good are you at using *connectives* or 'linking words' in the English language? These small words (usually adverbs) help you communicate more effectively. In the box below are examples of linking words. What purpose do they serve? Copy the table and place each of the words from the box into one or more of the boxes.

whereas	if	since	but	rather	in fact	however	yet	
instead	only	even though	consequently	as much as	not only			
thankfully	which	nevertheless	that said	while	but also			

Words that connect ideas	Words that conclude	Words that indicate sequence of ideas

Words that express contrast	Words that compare	Words that explain

3.16 The linking words have been removed from Text 4.10. Fill the gaps using linking words from Activity 3.15. You must use some words more than once. Some gaps can be filled using more than one or more words.

Text 4.10

'Reports of the Death of Jobs Have Been Greatly Exaggerated'

We are living in a time of major change in the labour market. Recent studies have predicted that over the next 20 years, 15 million UK jobs, about half the total, are at risk of being lost to automation.

(a)...... previous job-replacing technological change was limited to tasks requiring human brawn, the next wave of technology looks like replacing human brains.

(b)...... managed well, this revolution is not necessarily a cause for concern. (c)...... the first Industrial Revolution, every new labour-saving technology has been met with anxiety about the impact on jobs, (d)...... concerns over mass unemployment have never materialised. (e)......, technology has been a net creator of employment. Efficiencies gained through new technologies reduce the cost of production, (f)......, when passed on to the consumer, increase spending power, stimulating demand and creating new jobs. (g)...... than making humans redundant, technology has simply shifted work to other areas.

The fact that 20m jobs disappeared in Britain between 1980 and 2000 shows that predictions of 15m automated jobs would not be unprecedented. The lesson from the 1980s, (h)......, is the importance of enabling those who have lost their job to re-skill in order to find alternative employment.

The UK education system began to take its present form with the establishment of our current exam system in 1858. At its core, this system is characterised by competition between classmates, with students learning and are being assessed as individuals. (i)......, as technology and globalisation progress, working with others is becoming increasingly important. In an era of skilled factory work, this mass public examinations system was designed to assess and rank school leavers on their ability to recall information and apply the standard methods required to satisfy the needs of 19th century employment. (j)...... today, method and recall are the very things that are easiest to automate.

(k)......, 'soft' skills such as **resourcefulness**, creativity, and emotional intelligence are the likely domains where humans will retain a comparative advantage because these are skills where computers complement our abilities (l)...... than substitute for them. (m)...... today online communication over vast distances is possible at almost zero cost, face-to-face interactions are still the key engine of collabouration and growth.

Many people today, particularly younger generations, will work in jobs that do not exist yet, in industries that haven't been created. Most will change jobs multiple times and brief periods of unemployment, for people at all levels, will become more common. (n)......, there is a need to ensure better career guidance.

A young person today begins to make choices in education that affect the skills for their career (o)...... a decade before entering the workforce, by which time, technology and consumer

preferences will have altered significantly. In the UK schools system, where learner choice is increasingly important, it is vital that students, teachers, and parents, can access quality and timely information on the likely skills needed by employers in the future. Big data will no doubt prove pivotal in this.

The onus will also be on employers, who bear responsibility for helping young people learn about employment. The UKCES employment and skills survey found that (p)...... 66% of employers think work experience is important, (q)...... 38% offer it. There needs to be much stronger links between schools and employers. There is also a need to support in-work progression. Government estimates show that around 30% of graduates are still in entry-level positions five years after graduating. Career guidance must develop a focus (r)...... on helping people into work, (s)...... on helping those already in work to progress.

Affordability is the biggest barrier to workers enrolling in part-time or further education. (t)......, this is one area where automation offers not a problem but a solution. The growth of MOOCs, Personalised Learning Algorithms, and computer-based collabourative and virtual reality tools are enabling people to access independent **vocational** learning 'anywhere, anytime' in a way that can be adjusted to meet the student's individual needs, interests, and abilities.

Computer based learning is not a perfect substitute for a traditional university education. (u)......, the cost savings, convenience, and flexibility it affords have the potential to revolutionise education and training.

(v)......, while on-the-job training and e-learning offer part of the solution, on their own they will not be enough. Government should also explore tax incentives to encourage continuous engagement in education for adults. A tax nudge would be simple to introduce but more importantly, it would represent an initial step in aligning the UK's fiscal policies with some of its most significant employment challenges.

(w)...... the UK is to build a competitive economy for the 21st century, a shift to lifelong learning will be crucial to ensuring workers have the skills they need to succeed in the new world of work.

By Seamus Nevin

3.17 When you have filled the gaps in Text 4.10, decide whether each of the following statements are true or false based on your understanding of the text. Give evidence from the text to support your answers.

a   The author does not feel that people should be worried about technology replacing human jobs.

b   Technology, according to the author, has increased unemployment.

c   The author feels that 'method' and 'recall' are useful skills in a digital environment.

d   The author thinks that people who develop offline communication skills will be successful in the future.

e   Because technology changes quickly and individuals change jobs quickly, there is no reason for educational organisations to consult businesses.

f   The author feels that face-to-face higher education is superior to online learning platforms.

g   The author suggests that the government pays adults to go continue to go to school, during their working career

Discussion

3.18 Text 4.10 comments critically on education in the UK. Do you think the system at your school is similar to the system described in the text? Is it 'characterised by competition between classmates, [...] designed to assess and rank school leavers on their ability to recall information and apply the standard methods required to satisfy the needs of 19th century employment?'

Many schools these days aim to develop '21st century skills'. These are set out in the diagram below.

a How similar are these skills to those in the IB learner profile?

b How are you developing these skills at school?

c How do you think they will help you face the challenges of the future?

Critical thinking
- Information handling and research
- Interpretation and analysis
- Reasoning
- Constructing clear and effective arguments
- Problem solving
- Systems thinking

Communication
- Effective listening
- Oral presentation
- Communication using digital media
- Effective contribution to conversation, debate and discussion
- Communication in different contexts and situations
- Writing to inform, argue or entertain

21st Century Skills

Collaboration
- Leadership and initiative
- Cooperation
- Flexibility
- Responsibility
- Productivity
- Collaboration using digital media
- Responsiveness and constructive feedback

Creativity
- Generation of ideas
- Organisation and refinement of ideas
- Openness to new ideas
- Working creatively with others
- Innovation and creative production

3.19 For a mock individual oral (Unit 7.3) at standard level, you can practise with the image on the left. Using the ideas that have been explored in this unit, give a 3–4 minute talk to your teacher based on the image. Then have a conversation for 5–6 minutes with your teacher about 'the future of jobs.' Even if you're taking this course at higher level, this activity will prove useful.

a Technology will never have that 'human touch'. Let robots take the jobs that are easily automated, and let people do jobs that require creativity and emotional intelligence.

b Technology should be regulated. Measures should be taken to protect people's jobs and careers.

Writing

3.20 Go to *Wired* magazine's website and look for a video called 'Could this Robot Chef Change the Future of Cooking?'. Write a blog post in response to this, in which you state your opinions about the future of robots in the kitchen or other places of work. Imagine that the blog is frequently read by readers of Wired Magazine or a similar platform that focuses on technology and life. See Unit 6.3 for help with how to write blog posts.

3.21 Imagine you have to give a speech to the graduating students of a university about the challenges and opportunities that await them in the working world. You can pretend to be someone like Daniel Pink or Thomas L. Friedman, who often write about technology and the economy. In your speech, refer to the ideas that have been expressed in this unit, such as 'soft skills', 'entrepreneurship' and 'innovation'. See Unit 6.4 for help with how to write speeches.

CONCEPTS

Audience

Do you find it difficult to write an imaginary speech (Activity 3.21)? You might find it easier once you imagine the *audience* for whom you are writing. Why did they come to hear you speak? Why are you an authority on a topic? Where are you speaking? Once you have envisioned an audience, a context and purpose, your speech should almost write itself.

Extended Essay

Jargon is an interesting phenomenon to explore in a category 1 extended essay for English B. Jargon is a specific use of language, that uses words and technical phrases that are rarely understood by 'outsiders' of a particular workplace or culture. A good research question might read: 'How has the automation of market trading threatened the unique language of Wall Street?' For such an essay it is important that you have access to the trading floor or a place where job-specific language is spoken.

Higher level extension

3.22 So far in this unit you have considered technology as a threat to job security. Many people regard immigration as a threat to job security as well. Much research has been done on this controversial issue. You are going to read an article that is based on research in this field of 'migration economics'.

Before you read the article, decide which of the following statements are 'fact' or 'myth' according to your understanding of this topic. Discuss these statements with your classmates and give reasons for your answers.

a Immigrants often help with labour shortages, taking jobs that **native workers** are not able to do.

b Most immigrants are unskilled and take jobs that most native workers do not want to do.

c Countries with a large immigrant population have weaker economies.

d More than 50 per cent of people in the US and UK believe that immigrants take jobs away from native workers.

e More than 50 per cent of people in the US and UK believe that immigrants create jobs that did not previously exist.

f Immigrants often live on social welfare or government handouts.

g Immigrants often take jobs below their skill level and ability level when they move to a new country.

h A higher immigrant population creates a higher demand for products and services in any given country.

i Immigrants are more likely to start a new business or create their own job than native people.

3.23 Before you read Text 4.11, check if you understand the concepts in the box below. Match each concept with one of the following definitions (a–g).

| economic migrant | labour shortages | technological adaptation | public opinion |
| human capital | specialisation | occupational mobility |

a the ability to try and use new devices and computer applications

b the ability to move up (or down) in status or position in the economy

c the value created by employees' skills

d when there are not enough people to filled the jobs that are needed

e the ability to master a unique skill

f what people think

g a person who travels to a new country in search of a better financial future

3.24 Read Text 4.11 to find out which statements from Activity 3.22 were 'fact' or 'myth'.

TEXT AND CONTEXT
Text 4.11 uses the terms migrant and immigrant interchangeably. Usually, the term 'migrant worker' is used to describe a 'seasonal worker' often in the agricultural industry. An 'immigrant', while also from a foreign country, usually looks for a less transient lifestyle in the host country.

Text 4.11

● ● ●

5 Reasons Why Immigrants Do Not Take Natives' Jobs

'Do migrants take the jobs of natives?' That is the perpetual question that all countries (politicians and natives) ask. Fortunately, migration economics has an answer based on research and international evidence.

In my World of Labour article 'Do migrants take the jobs of native workers?' I lay down the pros and cons of the impact of migration on natives and show that 'migrants rarely take native workers' jobs, and indeed they tend to boost employment effects in the long term.' The five reasons are: a) self-employed migrants directly create new jobs; b) migrant innovators indirectly create jobs; c) new migrants fill labour shortages and lubricate the labour markets; d) the high-skilled contribute to technological adaptation and the low-skilled to occupational mobility, specialisation, and human capital creation thus creating new jobs; e) by raising demand, immigrants cause firms to expand and hire more workers.

Public opinion research carried out in the U.S., France, Germany and the UK after the 2008-2009 recession also supports that finding. Accordingly, most people believe that immigrants fill job vacancies and many believe that they create jobs, rather than taking jobs away from native workers (see Figure 1).

Economic migrants are looking for economic opportunities, meaning jobs, and so they tend to choose locations where jobs are readily available. Whether they are high or low-skilled, migrants rarely substitute for native workers. Instead migrants often complement native workers or accept jobs that natives don't want or can't do. Immigrants create new jobs by increasing production, engaging in self-employment, and easing upward job mobility for native workers. The mere presence of immigrants increases demand in the economy and can spur new businesses to open, creating more jobs for both immigrant and native populations.

So where does this anxiety about migrant workers come from? The simple labour market model of demand and supply assumes that migrants are exactly the same workers as natives, with the same skills, education, and talents, and thus, their arrival increases the supply of labour. The irrefutable prediction of this model is that the wages of all workers go down and unemployment increases for all, as the market for labour becomes saturated in the short-run.

The reality is somewhat different: native workers and migrants differ in their country-specific human capital, such as language fluency, professional networks, and social and cultural knowledge. Initial skill differences make new immigrants imperfect substitutes for native labour. In addition, we all know that labour shortages and job vacancies can co-exist. Vacancies exist even under high unemployment because of mismatches between job opportunities and the ability (**qualifications**) or willingness of natives to fill those jobs.

Regarding repetitive low-skill jobs, and in countries with a strong welfare state, native workers often might choose to stay unemployed. However, while those same jobs might be below the skill levels of migrants as well, migrants are often willing to accept these jobs in order to seize the opportunity that a new country offers them. Besides, immigrants view low-skill jobs as temporary and a means to the end, usually do not qualify for welfare upon arrival, and often identify with their home country so their pride is not hurt.

At higher skill-level jobs, vacancies can also exist in the short-term because the native labour force might not be qualified as could be the case for example with opportunities arising from rapid technological advances. Here, hiring qualified immigrant workers can fill the gap. Immigrants are also more likely than natives to start a business and create their own jobs at the very least.

Immigrants as consumers increase the demand for goods and services. This higher demand in turn affects the labour market by boosting the demand for labour, leading to an increase in equilibrium employment.

In summary, the quantitative evidence shows that, overall, immigrants do not take native workers' jobs in the long term and that they stimulate job creation through increased production, self-employment, entrepreneurship and innovation. Evidence also shows that for the most part, these findings align with public opinion in developed countries.

By Amelie F. Constant

3.25 As a group, create a large information board with the opening question of this article at the top: 'Do migrants take the jobs of natives?' Find appropriate images, create drawings or include info-graphs. Include headings, key words and visuals to answer the question in detail. Reference any ideas that you take from Text 4.11 or other sources. Present your info-board to your classmates and display it somewhere in your school for others to learn from.

Literature

3.26 You are about to read the opening passage from a piece of classic literature: *The Metamorphosis*, by Franz Kafka. The first line of the novel reads:

> When Gregor Samsa awoke one morning from troubled dreams, he found himself changed into a monstrous cockroach in his bed.

Before you read the rest of the passage (Text 4.12), try some creative writing. Write roughly 500 words about Gregor Samsa's morning after waking up to discover his transformation into a cockroach or beetle. Share your piece of creative writing with your teacher and classmates. There are no right or wrong responses for this activity – just creative ones!

3.27 Now read Text 4.12 – the opening passage from *The Metamorphosis*. How does Kafka's version compare to your version?

Text 4.12

As Gregor Samsa awoke one morning from uneasy dreams he found himself transformed in his bed into a gigantic insect. He was lying on his hard, as it were armour-plated, back and when he lifted his head a little he could see his dome-like brown belly divided into stiff arched segments on top of which the bed quilt could hardly keep in position and was about to slide off completely. His numerous legs, which were pitifully thin compared to the rest of his bulk, waved helplessly before his eyes.

What has happened to me? he thought. It was no dream. His room, a regular human bedroom, only rather too small, lay quiet between the four familiar walls. Above the table on which a collection of cloth samples was unpacked and spread out (Samsa was a commercial traveller), hung the picture which he had recently cut out of an illustrated magazine and put into a pretty gilt frame. It showed a lady, with a fur cap on and a fur stole, sitting upright and holding out to the spectator a huge fur muff into which the whole of her forearm had vanished! Gregor's eyes turned next to the window, and the overcast sky-one could hear rain drops beating on the window gutter-made him quite melancholy. What about sleeping a little longer and forgetting all this nonsense, he thought, but it could not be done, for he was accustomed to sleep on his right side and in his present condition he could not turn himself over. However violently he forced himself towards his right side he always rolled on to his back again. He tried it at least a hundred times, shutting his eyes to keep from seeing his struggling legs, and only desisted when he began to feel in his side a faint dull ache he had never experienced before.

Oh God, he thought, what an exhausting job I've picked on! Travelling about day in, day out. It's much more irritating work than doing the actual business in the office, and on top of that there's the trouble of constant travelling, of worrying about train connections, the bed and irregular meals, casual acquaintances that are always new and never become intimate friends. The devil take it all! He felt a slight itching up on his belly; slowly pushed himself on his back nearer to the top of the bed so that he could lift his head more easily; identified the itching place which was surrounded by many small white spots the nature of which he could not understand and made to touch it with a leg, but drew the leg back immediately, for the contact made a cold shiver run through him.

He slid down again into his former position. This getting up early, he thought, makes one quite stupid. A man needs his sleep. Other commercials live like harem women. For instance, when I come back to the hotel of a morning to write up the orders I've got, these others are only sitting down to breakfast. Let me just try that with my chief; I'd be sacked on the spot. Anyhow, that might be quite a good thing for me, who can tell? If I didn't have to hold my hand because of my parents I'd have given notice long ago, I'd have gone to the chief and told him exactly what I think of him. That would knock him endways from his desk! It's a queer way of doing, too, this sitting on high at a desk and talking down to employees, especially when they have to come quite near because the chief is hard of hearing. Well, there's still hope; once I've saved enough money to pay back my parents' debts to him (that should take another five or six years) I'll do it without fail. I'll cut myself completely loose then. For the moment, though, I'd better get up, since my train goes at five.

Extract from *Metamorphosis* by Franz Kafka

TEXT AND CONTEXT

The Metamorphosis, by Franz Kafka, was originally written in German, so you cannot read it to meet your literature requirement for English B at higher level. Nevertheless, it is a classic piece of literature that you might enjoy reading in your own language or in an English translation.

3.28 Re-read the passage (Text 4.12) to answer the questions below. Discuss your answers with your classmates and teacher.

a   What seems to concern Gregor more than his deformation?

b   What does Gregor think caused his deformation?

c   Why does Gregor not like his job?

d   Why does Gregor not resign from his job?

e   Why is the last line of this passage so funny?

f   How does this passage describe typical human behaviour?

3.29 Besides focusing on technology and migration, this unit has touched on the question: 'What motivates people to do a job?' What kinds of things usually motivate you in your work or schoolwork? Make a list of motivational factors in your life. Share these with your classmates. Compare these to Gregor Samsa's motivation to go to work.

REFLECT

Below are the words from the word bank at the beginning of this unit. Assign each person in your class one or two words.

a Do you remember the context in which this word appeared in this unit?

b How is your word relevant to the title of this unit 'The future of jobs'?

c How have the ideas in this unit changed the way you think about future employment opportunities?

> job security   self-employment   knowledge economy   soft skills   freelance   outsourcing   collaborate   artificial intelligence   meritocracy   entrepreneur   innovative   creativity   emotional intelligence   flexible   resourcefulness   vocational   native worker   migrant   qualifications

Sharing the planet

Chapter

5

This chapter continues to explore of theme of living in a globalised world through the topic 'Sharing the planet'. It is becoming more and more apparent that the challenges of the modern world cannot be faced by countries working alone. International cooperation is required to tackle issues such as poverty, climate change and poor governance. This chapter encourages you to think about your role in making the world a better place.

In this Chapter

- In Unit 5.1, you will explore ways in which poverty can be eradicated.
- In Unit 5.2, you will learn about the causes and effects of climate change, thinking of ways in which you can help alleviate it.
- In Unit 5.3, you will be inspired by the stories of individuals who have fought for their rights.

Unit 5.1
Ending poverty

Word bank

basic universal income

fair trade

exploit

microcredit

aid

child mortality rate

scarcity mentality

philanthropist

sustainable

marginalise

capital

wages

debt cancellation

integrity

dignity

corruption

plague

Why is it so difficult to reduce the level of poverty in the world? In this chapter, you will be asked to consider 'absolute poverty' – a lack of basic human needs, such as clean water, proper nutrition, health care and education. How can these be improved?

The percentage of the world's population living below the World Bank's poverty line of $US1.90 a day has, in fact, reduced dramatically since 1990, from 35 per cent to 10 per cent in 2013. However, 80 per cent of those live in countries where the gap between rich and poor is growing. These statistics question the definition and nature of `poverty'.

There are many ways to reduce poverty, that you will explore in this unit. The 'watch and listen' section introduces you to **basic universal income**, the idea that everyone is entitled to a sufficient amount of money. The listening section explores a term called 'factivism' – the idea that activists, armed with facts, can bring about a positive change in the world. Text 5.1 introduces you to the **fair trade** label that you can find on various products such as coffee or tea. This label or 'mark' means that the product does not **exploit** the people who make it. Text 5.2 is the story of a woman who received **microcredit**: a small loan to help start her juice-making business in Kenya. These are in contrast to the traditional view that **aid** is the solution to poverty. In fact, as Text 5.3 argues, aid might even make the economic situation in developing nations worse.

If the world produces enough food to feed everyone, then no-one should have to go hungry. The question to ask is not *if* we can beat poverty, but *when* and *how*.

How do we define 'poverty'? Do the people shown in these images live in poverty?

Getting started

1.1 Before you discuss the solutions to poverty, it is important to ask: 'What are the *causes* of poverty?' You can brainstorm this question by creating a spider diagram as a class.

1.2 Using your spider diagram on the causes of poverty from the first activity, create a list of ways to relieve poverty.

1.3 Match the definitions and descriptions a–f below with the six correct words from the word bank.

a A means of doing business where the all parties divide the profits of a transaction equally.

b This word is used to describe countries that are poor but have a growing economy. It also means 'progressing' or 'changing' in a good sense.

c This word describes how many children die before they reach the age of five.

d This world describes a relationship in which one person's rights and welfare are abused for the sake of improving the welfare of another person.

e This is another word for financial support.

f This world describes a frame of mind where resources such as time, money and energy seem limited.

LEARNER PROFILE

Caring

You might be shocked to learn the answers to the questions in Activity 1.4. How much do you care about, and care for, those who are less fortunate than you? Even if you cannot directly help the starving children of the world, you can still ask yourself, 'Who do I care for, help and spend time with regularly?'

1.4 Here are some questions to make you think about poverty in the world. If you don't know the answers, just take a guess. Compare your answers with those of your classmates. Your teacher will provide the actual answers.

Did any of the answers surprise you? Is the world 'better 'or 'worse' off than you thought? Is the world becoming better or worse off than before? What accounts for these changes?

a In 2015, what percentage of the world's population lived on less than $10 a day?

b **Child mortality rate** measures the number of children who die before the age of five. It is a strong indicator of the wealth and health of a country. In 1990, 91 out of 1000 children died before the age of five. How did this figure change by 2015? How many out of 1000?

c In 2008 1.6 billion people lived on planet earth without electricity. How many people were living this way by 2015?

d 'Extreme poverty' is defined as living on less than $1.90 per day. How many people lived in extreme poverty in 2013?

e In 1820 only 12 per cent of the world could read and write. What percentage of the world is literate today?

f In 2006 1.1 billion people worldwide did not have access to clean water. How many people did not have access to clean water in 2015?

TOK

How do you feel about social inequality and the level of poverty in the world? Is it something you think about often? Or is it something you can easily ignore? In TOK, 'emotions' are discussed as a 'way of knowing' (WOK). Describe your 'gut feeling' or emotional response to each of the images on this page. Individually, try to make a 'knowledge claim' about the nature of poverty. Share your claim with your classmates and discuss everyone's claims. How 'emotional' are these claims? Or are they based on facts?

CAS

Looking at your class list of ideas to relieve poverty (Activity 1.2), find one that you can contribute to through a CAS project. One of the main ideas of CAS is service-based learning, meaning that you can learn through helping others.

5

Watch and listen

1.5 You are about to watch an online TED Talk. The speaker uses several two-word combinations that are common in the English language. Perhaps you know some of these already. For each word a–j below, select a word from the box that best follows it. You might need to check the definitions of any words you do not know.

	scan	line	capital	potential	quo
	sugar	analysis	assumptions	care	violence

a underlying   b blood

c brain   d poverty

e statistical   f domestic

g venture   h health

i human   j status

1.6 Based on the two-word phrases that you have created in Activity 1.5, what do you think the TED Talk will be about? Share your prediction with your classmates.

1.7 Do an online search for Rutger Bregman's TED Talk titled 'Poverty isn't a lack of character; it's a lack of cash.' Listen for answers to the following questions. Take notes as you watch and listen to the talk.

a Bregman asks the question: 'Why do the poor make poor decisions?' What is the answer that most people, including British Prime Minister Margaret Thatcher, offer in response to this question?

b What persuaded Bregman to change the way he thinks about poverty?

c What is meant by the phrase '**scarcity mentality**'? Explain how and why people behave in a certain way when they find themselves in a scarcity mentality.

d What does Bregman say about the effectiveness of investments in education for poor people?

e What kinds of solutions to poverty are popular with politicians these days? Why does Bregman not find these solutions effective?

f What is a 'basic income guarantee'?

Rutger Bregman, author of *Utopia for Realists*

g What happened in Dauphin, Canada between 1974 and 1978? Why is this important for Bregman's argument?

h What is a 'negative income tax' and how much would it cost the United States of America to implement it?

i What kind of future does Bregman believe in?

TOK

How do you know what you know? Language is one of the ways of knowing (WOKs) in TOK. In Rutger Bregman's TED Talk (Activity 1.7), he shares his knowledge of the nature of poverty through analogies. An analogy is the comparison of one idea, thing or relationship to another. How does Rutger Bregman use the following analogies to explain the points that he makes about the nature of poverty?

a A computer that is running ten heavy programmes at the same time.

b Swimming in a storm.

c The elephant in the room (a common expression).

Are there any typical analogies, metaphors or expressions in your first language? Explain them to your classmates and ask them if these uses of language change the way they see the world.

EXTRA

Quite a few famous people are active **philanthropists**, meaning they aim to make the world a better place for all. Research one of the following people (or another philanthropist of your choice) and find out what they have done to help relieve poverty. Present your findings to your classmates. Discuss how effective their efforts have been.

- Bono
- Bill and Melinda Gates
- George Clooney
- George Soros
- Li Ka-shing

Bono, frontman for the group U2 and philanthropist

1.8 Listen to 🔊 Audio track 13, that includes several verb phrases related to poverty. Below you see a list of the phrases with the verbs removed. As you listen, identify the missing verbs that complete these phrases.

a   to ... transparency

b   to ... against poverty

c   to ... the facts

d   to ... awareness

e   to ... corruption

f   to .... backroom deals

g   to ... citizens with facts

h   to ... money in offshore accounts

i   to ... evil acts

j   to ... dictators

k   to ... poverty

l   to ... to the cause

1.9 Read the comprehension questions below. Now that you have listened to Audio track 13 once, answer the questions to the best of your ability, then listen to the recording again to complete what you could not remember the first time around.

a   What is 'Factivism' according to the interviewer?

b   What term does the host use to describe the global campaigns that Max has previously fronted?

c   Max mentions three positive pieces of news. Can you name one of them?

d   What are the two aims of Max's campaign?

e   According to Max, why do some people refuse to give money?

f   What does Max say he will do in the event that poverty is eradicated by 2028?

1.10 Audio track 13 explores the notion of 'Factivism', an idea that Hans Rosling has been promoting through his Gapminder foundation.

- Do an online search for Hans Rosling and for videos of him talking. Divide your class into smaller groups, assigning each group a different video.
- Answer the three following questions and share your answers with your class.

a   How are the ideas in your video connected to what you already knew?

b   What ideas did you learn that extended your knowledge or pushed your knowledge in a new direction?

c   How were you challenged in your thinking? What was difficult to understand? What do you still question, wonder or think about?

Hans Rosling, founder of Gapminder, an organisation that spreads awareness about poverty and global development

Thinking skills

Activity 1.10 asks you to do three things when exploring a Hans Rosling video:

- connect new knowledge to existing knowledge
- extend your knowledge in new directions
- challenge what you know.

This 'thinking routine', designed by Harvard's Project Zero, is useful for helping you to make your thinking 'visible'. You can use different coloured sticky notes, or write on a whiteboard to share your ideas with classmates.

Exploring texts

1.11 What do you see when you look at the Fairtrade logo on the opposite page? Write down the first thing that comes to mind. Then share your answer with classmates. Does everyone have the same answer? Why might you see something different?

1.12 Text 5.1 contains some challenging vocabulary, which it might help you to study before you read the text. Which one of the four words in each of the sets 1–12 below does not have the same meaning as the other words in the set? Which is the 'odd one out'? You might need to look up the definitions of some of the words. Check your understanding of these words as you read the text.

1	**a** way	
	b approach	
	c strategy (paragraph 1)	
	d idea	

2	**a** reduction	
	b inflation	
	c improvement	
	d alleviation (paragraph 1)	

3   **a** manageable
     b sustainable (paragraph 1)
     c adjustable
     d workable

4   **a** marginalised (paragraph 1)
     b side-lined
     c included
     d excluded

5   **a** remarkable
     b normal
     c conventional (paragraph 1)
     d usual

6   **a** oppressed
     b disadvantaged (paragraph 2)
     c unfortunate
     d exploited

7   **a** warranty
     b promise
     c guarantee (paragraph 3)
     d code

8   **a** founded
     b started
     c produced
     d established (paragraph 3)

9   **a** standards (paragraph 5)
     b habits
     c values
     d principles

10   **a** consultation (paragraph 5)
     b agreement
     c discussion
     d rules

11   **a** interest
     b interpretation (paragraph 6)
     c understanding
     d analysis

12   **a** campaign
     b promotional (paragraph 7)
     c marketing
     d reporting

TEXT AND CONTEXT

- The term 'fairtrade' implies that there is unfair trade in the world. The aim of the Fairtrade organisation is to make sure that farmers and manufacturers are paid a fair price for the products they produce.

- In many developing nations, farmers and manufacturers are not paid fair wages and their working conditions are bad.

Text 5.1

The FAIRTRADE Mark

Background

'Fairtrade is a strategy for poverty alleviation and **sustainable** development. Its purpose is to create opportunities for producers and workers who have been economically disadvantaged or **marginalised** by the conventional trading system. If fair access to markets under better trade conditions would help them to overcome barriers to development, they can join Fairtrade.'

Fairtrade is a tool for development that ensures disadvantaged farmers and workers in developing countries get a better deal through the use of the international FAIRTRADE Marks we are introducing new 'Marks' this year to include the core Mark shown.

Fairtrade Labelling was created in the Netherlands in the late 1980s. The Max Havelaar Foundation launched the first Fairtrade consumer guarantee label in 1988 on coffee sourced from Mexico. Here in the UK, the Fairtrade Foundation was established in 1992, with the first products to carry the FAIRTRADE Mark launched in 1994.

The FAIRTRADE Mark

The FAIRTRADE Mark is a registered certification label for products sourced from producers in developing countries.

For a product to display the FAIRTRADE Mark it must meet international Fairtrade Standards which are set by Fairtrade International. These Standards are agreed through a process of research and consultation with key participants in the Fairtrade scheme, including producers themselves, traders, NGOs, academic institutions and organisations such as the Fairtrade Foundation who are the UK member of Fairtrade International.

What does the symbol represent?

The eye-catching blue, green, white and black FAIRTRADE Mark is used globally to show Fairtrade certified products. The symbol is open to interpretation – some see a parrot, others a green leaf, some see the black swirl at the centre as a road leading to a brighter future. The most popular interpretation is to imagine the blue as sky, the green as grass, and the black dot and swirl at the centre as a person holding one arm aloft. That figure represents the people at the heart of the Fairtrade system: it could be a farmer holding up their product, a shopper reaching to purchase, or a campaigner fighting for greater justice in international trade.

How can the Mark be used?

As a registered certification mark and trademark, there are strict rules for how the FAIRTRADE Mark can be used: both for product packaging, and for wider promotional and campaigning use packaging, and for wider promotional by shops and use in campaigns asking the government and the public to consider who makes our food and clothes.'

www.fairtrade.org.uk

READING STRATEGY

Spider diagrams or 'mind maps' can be an excellent tool for brainstorming or giving an overview of ideas. You can also use them to map out the contents of a text. In the middle of a large sheet of paper, write the title of Text 5.1 The FAIRTRADE Mark'. Make four branches that come from this title, using the four main headings. How would you branch out further? Spider diagrams can give you a visual representation of how information is organised.

1.13 Here are some comprehension questions based on Text 5.1. Answer them in complete sentences with reference to the text.

a   How does Fairtrade help farmers in developing countries?

b   What was the first Fairtrade product?

c   How does a product receive the FAIRTRADE Mark?

d   What do most people see in the FAIRTRADE Mark?

1.14 Imagine that images A and B accompany Text 5.1. Write a caption for each image that connects the image to the content of the text. Compare your captions to those of your classmates. Which captions would encourage people to buy Fairtrade products the most?

Fairtrade: producer and consumer

1.15 Imagine you are shopping with a friend or relative. They see the FAIRTRADE Mark on a chocolate bar, but do not know what it means. The chocolate bar is 10 per cent more expensive than a comparable chocolate bar. How would you explain the Fairtrade concept to them, the reason for the price difference, and persuade them to buy the Fairtrade bar? You can take on these two roles with a classmate and act out a discussion.

1.16 Imagine someone loaned you $30. Write a paragraph to explain how you would invest this money in a business idea. Write a second paragraph to explain how you would pay it back. You might consider ideas involving selling, working or collecting.

1.17 Some adjectives go well with certain nouns. Before you read Text 5.2, match the adjectives in the box below with the nouns a–h in the list below. Then write briefly what you think Text 5.2 will be about.

small	nutritious	increasing	living	basic
	food	juice-making	powdered	

a loans   **b** vendors

c profits   **d** drinks

e food   **f** standards

g needs   **h** equipment

1.18 As you read Text 5.2 identify any words that could be used to answer the following questions below. You may give one-word answers. After reading the article, check your answers with a classmate and your teacher.

a What do you call a sum of money used to start a business?

b What word is used to describe the money paid for schooling?

c When you have enough money to buy something, you can … it. (Fill in the blank.)

d What do you call the customers of a business?

e What word is used to describe the place that Saumu owns and rents out to others at the market.

f Saumu sells her juices to customers of other stalls near to her own. What is another word for 'near to'?

g What do we call people who rent space from someone else?

h What do we call the people who supply Saumu with fruit and other goods, so that she can make her juices?

i What is another word for the money paid to employees?

j This word is used to describe how the loans help Saumu go beyond basic needs and enjoy life. What word is used for 'go beyond'?

CONCEPTS

Purpose

What type of Text is 5.2? Why would someone be interested in Saumu's story? Why would FINCA want to tell it? Is the text like a testimonial, a text that tells about a consumer's experience in hopes of selling a product? Every text has a *purpose*. Most texts inform, entertain, persuade or do some combination of these three things. What is the purpose of Text 5.2?

Text 5.2

Saumu Eneza lives in Dar-es-Salaam, Tanzania, with her husband and four children. Before joining a FINCA Village Banking group, she operated a tiny business selling juice on the street to help support her family. But she had no **capital** to improve her business, so she contemplated closing it and finding another, better source of income, so the family could afford better food and the school fees for all the children.

Then one day, Saumu met a FINCA loan officer and learned about FINCA's financial services and how its small loans could help her transform her business and improve her family's living standards. She soon joined FINCA's Mchafukoge Village Banking group and received a first loan of $30, that she used to purchase fruit, sugar and other supplies for the juice business.

Within three FINCA loan cycles, Saumu's earnings had grown substantially, because she could afford to buy fruit in bulk at better prices and expand the variety of juices she offered for sale, including powdered drinks. Saumu was able to move to a permanent stall in the market, upgrade her juice-making equipment, and hire three neighbours to help her make her juices and sell them to her growing clientele.

With increasing profits and FINCA loans of $1,000, Saumu purchased her own place of business. Today she rents part of her premises to other food vendors, which allows

her to sell juice to the customers eating in the adjacent food stalls. Her success is contributing to the growth of other businesses in her community, not only her tenants, but also the wholesalers who supply her with fruit and other goods. Three families benefit from the **wages** she pays to her workers.

Saumu is very happy that her business has allowed her to buy better and more nutritious food for her family and to pay her children's school fees so they can continue their education. 'I love FINCA,' says Saumu, 'because I've been able to fulfil and exceed my basic needs. I am proud to own a stable business and to be an employer.'

www.finca.org

LEARNER PROFILE

Risk-takers

To what degree is FINCA taking a risk by investing in poor entrepreneurs? Which is the greater risk: lending money to those in poverty, or giving it to them? Why should an IB learner be a risk taker? Discuss your answers with classmates.

TEXT AND CONTEXT

- FINCA (Foundation for International Community Assistance) is an organisation that lends small amounts of money to lends small amounts of money to poor people in developing nations, often entrepreneurs in rural areas.

- The main idea illustrated in this story is that of microcredit.

1.19 Activity 1.16 asked you how you would invest $30 wisely. How did Saumu spend the $30 that FINCA loaned her to help her make more money? How was the way she spent her loan different from the way you would have spent yours? How is her context different from yours?

1.20 Where do you think Text 5.2 came from? What might be the purpose of telling Saumu's story? What might the article want to achieve?

1.21 If you were promised your money back, would you make a loan to someone in a developing country for little or no interest? Give reasons for your answer.

5

Microcredit in action

Form and meaning

1.22 When should you use a comma in English? There are different conventions for using commas in the English-speaking world. In this activity you will explore how commas are used in twelve sentences taken from Texts 5.1 and 5.2. Find pairs of sentences that use commas for similar purposes. Then make a list of six rules for how commas are used in these texts.

Example: *Commas are used to list items. This rule is used in sentences a and f.*

a It could be a farmer holding up their product, a shopper reaching to purchase, or a campaigner fighting for greater justice in international trade.

b Before joining a FINCA Village Banking group, she operated a tiny business selling juice on the street to help support her family.

c These standards are agreed through a process of research and consultation with key participants in the Fairtrade scheme, including producers themselves.

d Saumu's earning had grown substantially, because she could afford to buy fruit in bulk at better prices.

e She soon joined FINCA's Mchafukoge Village Banking group and received a first loan of $30, that she used to purchase fruit.

f Saumu was able to move to a permanent stall in the market, upgrade her juice-making equipment, and hire three neighbours to help her make her juices.

g She could afford to buy fruit in bulk at better prices and expand the variety of juices she offered for sale, including powdered drinks.

h She contemplated closing it and finding another, better source of income.

i Today she rents part of her premises to other food vendors, which allows her to sell juice to the customers eating in the adjacent food stalls.

j Within three FINCA loan cycles Saumu's earning had grown substantially, because she could afford to buy fruit in bulk at better prices.

k The eye-catching blue, green, white and black Fairtrade Mark was adopted by FLO International in 2002.

l Then one day, Saumu met a FINCA loan officer and learned about FINCA's financial services.

1.23 Could you find all six pairs of sentences in Activity 1.22? In the table below are six rules for how commas are used in Texts 5.1 and 5.2. Copy and complete the table to match each pair of sentences from Activity 1.22 to the relevant rule.

When commas are used	Sentence pair
to separate a list of ideas	
to separate multiple adjectives	
before the word 'which', if a non-essential clause follows	
after a time phrase at the beginning of a sentence	
if a non-essential clause follows the word 'because'	
before an '-ing' verb that starts a new clause	

1.24 Here are several sentences with the necessary commas missing. Using the six rules from Activity 1.23, write out each sentence, inserting commas where you think they should go.

a Recently there has been a promotion of responsible government because a report has connected poverty with corruption.

b Fundraising can be hard frustrating yet rewarding work.

c My grandmother left everything to charity which surprised my parents.

d Before coming to Australia they worked for a good cause in South America.

e Some people believe that charity causes more problems than it helps which is a strange but interesting idea.

f The interest on their loan was too high making it impossible for them to ever get out of poverty.

g Every year they organise an auction take part in a charity run and cook for the homeless shelter.

h After five loan cycles she was able to buy a piece of land.

i Because the government received so much money from charity organisations they did not tax the people heavily.

j The men returned to the village from work stopping at the shops on their way home.

5

Discussion

1.25 In this unit you have already learned about efforts to eradicate poverty. Do you agree or disagree with the following statements? Discuss each statement with a classmate and share your opinions with the class.

a We should stop sending shoes and teddy bears to the poor, and start giving them cash.

b Debt relief or **debt cancellation** is the best way break the cycle of poverty in developing countries.

c Initiatives like the Fairtrade label sound good, but they are not very effective.

d Poverty is the price of privilege. In other words, a wealthy class cannot exist without an impoverished class.

e Microcredit stimulates economic growth. Entrepreneurs in developing countries benefit, and lenders make a profit.

f One day, poverty will be eradicated.

1.26 One company that understands the power of microcredit is United Colors of Benetton. This clothing brand ran an ad campaign in 2008 called 'Africa Works', which showed pictures of entrepreneurs who had received small loans. Study the image below carefully and discuss your answers to the following questions.

a How does the ad make you feel?

b How does the ad use colour, fonts, body language, icons, lighting and general layout to make you feel this way?

c What do you think of the campaign title, 'Africa Works'? What different meanings do these two simple words have?

d The people in this ad are not wearing clothing from United Colors of Benetton. Nevertheless, how does the ad achieve its aim of selling more Benetton clothing?

e Imagine that all of these people were white, and were holding and carrying the same things: the brooms the instrument and the goat. If the title read 'Europe Works', would the advertisement still 'work'?

1.27 If you had enough money to spare, would you give it to the following causes? Which of these would you most like to be able to donate to? Explain why and discuss your answers with classmates.

a A blind man, who is begging on the streets.

b A young woman standing in a busy shopping street, signing up donors for Doctors Without Borders, asking for $5 every month through automatic bank transfer.

c   Your neighbour's daughter, asking you to sponsor her for a charity run.

d   A microcredit organisation that wants you to invest in a small business in a village in India, advertising on one of your favourite websites.

e   A vocabulary-building website (www.freerice.com/ricebowl) that donates ten grains of rice to the World Food Programme every time you answer a question correctly.

f   Your school, that wants to build a health centre in South Africa, asks you and your parents to donate something of value (a weekend trip, a piece of art, a set of dinnerware) for an auction.

g   The Ronald McDonald's House, that supports families of ill children all over the world, has placed a box next to the cash register at every McDonald's worldwide, for people to donate.

1.28   There are many different kinds of humour. Which of the following terms do you think apply to the cartoon below? Explain how and why they are relevant.

a   'Black' humour: where we are invited to laugh at things that might be sad or difficult, and not usually funny.

b   Irony: where there is a mismatch between what is done or said and what is expected.

c   Pun: a play on words.

d   Satire: critical humour, where we are invited to laugh at cultural norms.

e   Understatement: where a large idea is reduced to a few words

f   Repartee: a clever reply or response, usually an insult

g   Parody: when one style imitates another

P. BYRNES.

Writing

1.29   You have read about microcredit and its advantages. Now write a brochure that could be used to persuade people to participate in microcredit, either by giving a loan or by applying for a loan.

a   Read Unit 6.6 on brochure writing and learn more about the conventions of brochure writing.

b   Many websites allow you to download a brochure from their organisation. In fact, many websites function like brochures. Visit a website or download a brochure from a website to see if these texts include the main stylistic and structural elements of a brochure.

c   Write a brochure for a microcredit organisation, encouraging people to lend out and borrow money for projects in developing countries.

d   Ask a classmate and your teacher to assess your brochure, using the assessment criteria for Paper 1.

e   Taking your teacher's and classmate's feedback into consideration, rewrite your brochure and submit it one more time for assessment.

Extended Essay
Much controversy has surrounded United Colors of Benetton and its advertising campaigns. The company's ads could even be considered as interesting 'cultural artefacts'. The ads say a lot about taboo, target audience and advertising techniques. A good Category 2b essay might have a research question that reads, 'How and why have Benetton ads been controversial for the past thirty years?'

TIP
You might be asked to write a brochure on your Paper 1 exam. Under exam conditions you are not expected to spend a lot of time on graphics and formatting. If you want to break the page into three panels though, you can do so by drawing lines. You can draw stick figures where you think photographs should be. In brief, you do not have to be artistic in order to show that you have understood the conventions of the text type.

1.30 Fairtrade products are known to be slightly more expensive than 'regular' products. Write an essay on whether we should be expected to pay more for Fairtrade products, and the reasons why (see Unit 6.9 for more guidance on essay writing).

1.31 Imagine the year is 2008 and United Colors of Benetton has just launched its 'Africa Works' campaign. Write a short blog post with your response to the campaign (remember that Activity 1.26 presents only one of many ads from this campaign). Be sure to research the topic and show evidence of critical thinking.

Higher level extension

1.32 Text 5.3 starts with the following question: 'In the past fifty years, more than $1 trillion in development-related aid has been transferred from rich countries to Africa. Has this assistance improved the lives of Africans?' Discuss your answer to this question with classmates.

1.33 Text 5.3 contains some challenging vocabulary. Several words have been removed from the text. Decide which word from the list below belongs in each gap. You might need to look up their definitions first.

a	debunking	**b**	dependent	**c**	desperate
d	myths	**e**	optimistic	**f**	rejected
g	reduce	**h**	vicious	**i**	escalate
j	reliance				

Text 5.3

Why Aid Is Not Working and How There Is a Better Way for Africa

In the past fifty years, more than $1 trillion in development-related aid has been transferred from rich countries to Africa. Has this assistance improved the lives of Africans? No. In fact, across the continent, the recipients of this aid are not better off as a result of it, but worse: much worse.

In Dead Aid, Dambisa Moyo describes the state of post-war development policy in Africa today and unflinchingly confronts one of the greatest (1) … of our time: that billions of dollars in aid sent from wealthy countries to developing African nations has helped to (2) … poverty and increase growth.

In fact, poverty levels continue to (3) … and growth rates have steadily declined and millions continue to suffer. Provocatively drawing a sharp contrast between African countries that have (4) … the aid route and prospered and others that have become aid-(5) … and seen poverty increase, Moyo illuminates the way in which overreliance on aid has trapped developing nations in a (6) … circle of aid dependency, corruption, market distortion, and further poverty, leaving them with nothing but the 'need' for more aid.

(7) … the current model of international aid, Moyo offers a bold new road map for financing development of the world's poorest countries that guarantees economic growth and a significant decline in poverty – without (8) … on foreign aid or aid-related assistance.

Dead Aid is an unsettling yet (9) … work, a powerful challenge to the assumptions and arguments that support a profoundly misguided development policy in Africa. And it is a clarion call to a new, more hopeful vision of how to address the (10) … poverty that plagues millions.

www.dambisamoyo.com

1.34 What kind of text is Text 5.3? Where might you find this text (apart from on Dambisa Moyo's own website)? What clues made you think this? Support your answers with evidence from the text.

1.35 Together with classmates, do more research on Dambisa Moyo and find out her opinions on the following topics. Why do you agree or disagree with her opinions on these matters?

a The solutions to the economic crisis in the West

b China's investments in Africa

c The effectiveness of microcredit

d Debt relief or debt cancellation

e Paul Kagame and Uganda

f Celebrities who raise money for Africa

g The future of Zambia, her home country

h The book *Ending Poverty* by Jeffrey Sachs

Dambisa Moyo

TEXT AND CONTEXT

- Dambisa Moyo has written several books on the topic of aid and poverty.

- She is a writer who comes from Zambia but works as a columnist for the *New York Times*.

- A 'clarion call' (final paragraph) is a request for the public to take action.

Literature

1.36 Before you read Text 5.4, read the 'text and context' box on the next page. Based on these explanations, what do you think the text will be about?

1.37 Read Text 5.4 and then complete the sentences below in your own words, using your understanding of the text.

a Bakhu's father once said, 'You lover of your mother' because...

b 'But Bakhu was a child of modern India.' This line suggests...

c Bakhu had the chance to observe the British soldiers when...

d Bakhu wants to wear the clothing of British soldiers because...

e Bakhu does not go to the clothing shop because....

f Bakhu is called 'naïve' because...

Text 5.4

He shivered as he turned on his side. But he didn't mind the cold very much, suffering it willingly because he could sacrifice a good many comforts for the sake of what he called 'fashun,' by which he understood the art of wearing trousers, breeches, coat, puttees, boots, etc., as worn by the British and Indian soldiers in India. 'You lover of your mother,' his father had once abusively said to him, 'take a quilt, spread a bedding on a string bed, and throw away that blanket of the *gora* white men; you will die of cold in that thin cloth.' But Bakhu was a child of modern India. The clear-cut styles of European dress had impressed is naïve mind. Bakhu had looked at the Tommies, stared at them with wonder and amazement when he first went to live

TEXT AND CONTEXT

- 'Untouchable' is a reference to the Dalits, an ethnic minority group that is often excluded from socio-economic opportunities in India.

- By 'fashun' the narrator refers to 'fashion', using the character's Indian accent.

- 'Gora' means 'fair skinned' in Hindi, and has been used by Indians to refer to British people or Europeans.

- British soldiers were often known as 'Tommies'.

- Sepoy was a term given to Hindu or Muslim soldiers by the British Raj.

- Puttees are strips of cloth wrapped around the ankles and calves. They were commonly worn by British soldiers in the early twentieth century.

at the British regimental barracks with his uncle. He had had glimpses, during his sojourn there, of the life the Tommies lived, sleeping on strange, low canvas beds covered tightly with blankets, eating eggs, drinking tea and wine in tin mugs, going to parade and then walking down to the bazaar with cigarettes in their mouths and small silver-mounted canes in their hands. And he had soon become possessed with an overwhelming desire to live their life. He had been told they were sahibs, superior people. He had felt that to put on their clothes made one a sahib too. So he tried to copy them in everything, to copy them as well as he could in the exigencies of his peculiarly Indian circumstances. He had begged one Tommy for the gift of a pair of trousers. The man had given him a pair of breeches which he had to spare. A Hindu sepoy, for the good of his own soul, had been kind enough to make an endowment of a pair of boots and puttees. For the other items he had gone down to the rag-seller's shop in the town. He had long looked at that shop. Ever since he was a child he had walked past the wooden stall on which lay heaped the scarlet and khaki uniforms discarded or pawned by the Tommies, pith solar topees, peak caps, knives, forks, buttons, old books and other oddments of Anglo-Indian life. And he had hungered for the touch of them. But he had never mustered up courage enough to go up to the keep of the shop and to ask him the price of anything, lest it should be a price he could not pay and lest the man should find out from his talk that he was a sweeper-boy.

Extract from *Untouchable*, by Mulk Raj Anand

1.38 Discuss your answers to the questions below. There are no wrong or right answers, only informed opinions.

a   Bakhu is a sweeper-boy in India in 1935. In the time and place where you live, are there people with so few opportunities? Who are they and why are their opportunities so limited?

b   Bakhu lives in India during a time of Britain's colonial rule. In the place where you live, is there evidence of a colonial history? If so, what evidence do you see of this history in your day-to-day life or on the news?

c   Have you ever felt ashamed of your social class or background? Have you ever not gone into a shop out of a fear that you could not afford anything?

d   Bakhu is poor but seemingly happy. To what degree does one's happiness depend on wealth?

REFLECT

You started this unit by exploring the causes of, and solutions to, poverty. After reading the four texts in the unit, listening to the audio track and watching videos, return to Activities 1.1 and 1.2.

- Are there new causes and solutions that you have discovered in this unit?

- What have you learned about the nature of poverty in the world?

- What measures can *you* as an individual take to make the world a fairer and more prosperous place for everyone?

Unit 5.2
Climate change

Guiding questions	Learning objectives
• How and why is the climate changing? • What can you do to help prevent climate change?	• Become more aware of the causes of climate change and their effects on the world. • Be proficient in discussing climate change and ways to prevent it.

In Unit 5.1, you considered a global perspective on poverty, showing how individuals from around the world can help reduce poverty through Fairtrade, microcredit, debt relief or universal basic income. In this unit we will look at another issue that affects everyone in the world: climate change.

Unlike what the cartoon below might suggest, the air we breathe is not contained within any national boundary. The pollutants of one country often harm another, meaning that international cooperation is needed to solve environmental problems.

While there is clear evidence that climate change is caused by human activity, the subject is debated continuously. You will consider this debate and its coverage in the media in Text 5.5. In Text 5.6, you will explore ways to reduce the human impact on the environment. Text 5.7 reports on a village in Bangladesh, where water levels have risen and created more problems in an area already threatened by flooding, disease and poverty. Finally, in the higher level extension activities, you will discuss the effects of **global warming**.

Working through this unit will help to give you a better understanding of the causes and effects of global warming and to appreciate the kinds of solutions in which individuals around the world, including you, can play a part.

"They have very strict anti-pollution laws in this state"

Word bank

global warming
greenhouse effect
carbon dioxide (CO_2)
carbon footprint
livestock
methane
animal agriculture
species extinction
vegetarian
vegan
deforestation
desertification
dead zones
ice caps
pollution
fuel efficient
renewable energy
flooding

LEARNER PROFILE

Caring

The IB learner profile suggests that we should be caring, because 'we have a commitment to make a positive difference in the lives of others and in the world around us.' The 'world' certainly includes the environment. Caring about climate change is, in many ways, also caring for others.

5

Getting started

2.1 What human activities contribute to global warming? Sit in a circle with several classmates. Go around the circle, giving everyone a turn to briefly give one cause of global warming. No cause can be used more than once. Record all of the causes mentioned. How many could the group think of?

2.2 Once you have listed the causes of global warming, rank them in the order in which you think they contribute to the problem, from 'greatest' to 'least'. What are the challenges of ranking the items in this way?

2.3 In your own words, write a brief explanation of how you think the **greenhouse effect** is created. How would you explain this concept to someone who knows nothing about global warming? Use the diagram below to support your explanation. You may use some of the words from the word bank as well as the words listed below. You might need to look up the definitions of some of these words.

a the Sun's rays

b gases

c heat

d trap

e escape

f atmosphere

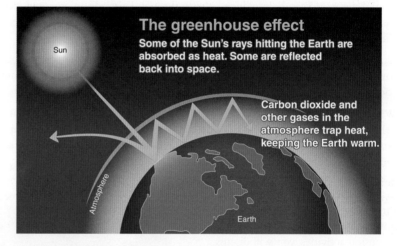

CONCEPTS

Meaning

Activity 2.4 asks you to guess how much CO_2, in tonnes is created by certain activities. It defines one tonne of CO_2 carefully so that there can be no doubt about its *meaning*. As you read more texts about global warming, it's important to note that *meaning*, sometimes, is not open to interpretation. With reports, facts, figures and other non-literary texts, authors aim to inform you of the truth. Some people do not believe in global warming, because they do not believe in the scientific reports. Numbers, however, do not lie.

2.4 The amount of **carbon dioxide (CO_2)** we emit by doing various activities is measured in tonnes. One tonne (1000 kilograms or approximately 2205 pounds) would be released into the atmosphere if you set fire to 545 litres (120 gallons) of benzene. It is helpful to compare the amount of CO_2 created by different human activities. This puts your **carbon footprint** into perspective. Below is a list of human activities. Decide how much carbon dioxide you think is emitted from each activity (in tonnes). Then place the letter for each activity in the appropriate column in a copy of the table below. Discuss your answers with classmates.

a Driving the average car non-stop for 2.5 days

b A 25-minute flight on a Boeing 747

c A 42-inch LCD TV used continuously for 374 days

d The energy used by an average house in 1 year

e A 13-watt low-energy bulb lit continuously for 61 years

f Energy used to produce 500 kg of beef

Amount of CO_2 emitted		
1.5 tonnes	7 tonnes	13 tonnes

Watch and listen 📹 🔊

2.5 You are going to watch an online video called, 'The Hidden Costs of Hamburgers' by Reveal. Before you watch the video, read the questions below and predict an answer for each question. Then watch the video online. After listening carefully for the answers in the video, compare them to your original predictions. How similar were your predictions?

a   On average, how much more meat do Americans eat than people from other countries?

b   According to the author's estimate, how many hamburgers do Americans eat per year?

c   What percentage of the world's landmass is used by **livestock** and agriculture that feeds those animals?

d   How many gallons (or litres) of water does it take to make a single pound (.454 kilograms) of grain-fed beef?

e   How many cows are there in the United States of America?

f   How much more manure do cows create than humans?

g   How much more does **methane** affect climate change than CO_2?

h   How much nitrogen fertiliser is needed to grow feed for cows in America?

i   How many different cows can end up in a single hamburger patty?

j   How many tonnes of greenhouse gases does hamburger consumption create in the United States every year?

k   How much more expensive should a hamburger be in order to compensate for costs to the environment and human health?

l   How many people live in China and why does the author think that this matters?

2.6 The presenter of the video, 'The Hidden Costs of Hamburgers' (by Reveal) uses language quite informally. What do you think she means by the following underlined phrases? Watch the video again and listen for these phrases. In your own words describe what she means. Discuss your answers with a classmate and your teacher. The phrases appear below in the same order as they do in the video.

a   [It] <u>turns out</u> that livestock are a major contributor to greenhouse gas pollution.

b   [It is] <u>right up there with</u> cars, planes and trains.

c   <u>Big time</u>.

d   But what we don't pay for <u>at the counter</u>, we <u>end up paying for</u> in other ways.

e   So, <u>voila</u>: Now corn is in everything.

f   <u>Anyway, back to</u> the feedlot.

g   Too many burgers <u>take a toll</u> on the environment.

h   Could our planet <u>keep up</u>?

2.7 You are going to listen to Audio track 14, a conversation that includes the following words. Place these words into groups with commonalities and label each group. There are many different ways of grouping the words. Share your way of grouping the words with your classmates. Based on this activity, what do you think the audio track will be about?

animal rights activists	animals	species extinction	meat industry	vegetarians
fossil fuels	non-profit organisations	polar bears	methane	climate change
animal agriculture	environmental groups	Carbon dioxide	global warming	
whales	factory farms	livestock	charity organisations	vegans	cows

Have you ever thought of hamburgers as contributors to climate change?

Sharing the planet

2.8 Listen to 🔊 Audio track 14 and answer the multiple-choice questions below.

1 Chuck likes David because...
   a he has made some people angry
   b he is a 'disrupter' who reports what he finds out
   c his book is critically acclaimed
   d he has heard so many good things about him.

2 Chuck has invited David to a meeting because...
   a he needs David's help in making a documentary
   b he needs a 'talking head' to comment on animal agriculture and climate change
   c he wants to interview David about charity organisations
   d he wants to learn more from David about the meat industry.

3 David has not been able to talk to charity groups because...
   a they disagree with his claims
   b they demonstrate hypocritical behaviour
   c they are afraid of being put in an embarrassing position
   d they haven't agreed to any interviews with him.

4 David disagrees with Chuck's comparison of the meat industry to the tobacco industry because...
   a David thinks that the tobacco industry causes more pollution than the meat industry
   b David thinks that the American Lung Cancer Association would never accept money from the tobacco industry
   c David thinks that Chuck's comparison should include the American Heart Attack Association instead of the American Lung Cancer Association
   d David does not think it is fair to compare industries that behave so differently.

5 Chuck uses the term 'bait and switch' in this context to suggest that...
   a while the meat industry is distracting people from environmental problems, they are making a lot of profits
   b while the meat industry is addressing the topic of species extinction and global warming, environmental groups are keeping quiet about methane gasses
   c while environmental groups are spreading awareness about the dangers of CO_2, they are taking money from the meat industry
   d while charity organisations talk about CO_2 and global warming, people overlook the environmental impact of animal agriculture.

6 Chuck and David think that people willingly ignore the problems of animal agriculture because...
   a they are scared of veganism
   b they do not want to be called '**vegetarian**' or '**vegan**'
   c they like to eat meat
   d they are afraid of change.

'**Cowspiracy: The Sustainability Secret' is bound to change your mind about animal agriculture and the environment**

EXTRA

How did you do on Activity 2.8? Practise multiple-choice questions by creating your own. Find a text or recording on which you can base your own multiple-choice questions. Try your questions on your classmates. How did they do? What strategies did you use to help you write the questions? How can these strategies help you answer multiple-choice questions in the future?

2.9 The ideas heard in Audio track 14 are similar to those found in the documentary 'Cowspiracy: The Sustainability Secret' by Kip Andersen and Keegan Kuhn.

- Individually, answer the following questions for yourself.
- Then, watch the documentary as a class. It is about an hour and a half long. Answer the questions again. Have your answers changed?
- Share your answers and the changes you have made to your answers with your classmates. What has made you change your mind?

a   What effect is animal agriculture having on climate change?

b   How is animal agriculture connected to **deforestation**, **desertification** and the creation of '**dead zones**' in oceans?

c   What are environmental organisations doing about the problems of animal agriculture?

d   What do you think of 'organic' beef and dairy compared to 'non-organic' in terms of contributing to a more sustainable earth?

e   Would you ever consider becoming vegetarian or vegan? Would you consider participating in 'meatless Mondays'?

Exploring texts

2.10 The title of Text 5.5 is 'Is Global Warming Real?' How can you know if global warming is real? Discuss this title with classmates, giving well-informed arguments, using reference to the TOK feature to the left.

2.11 As you read Text 5.5, find one word that matches each of the following definitions. (The words appear in the text in the same order as the definitions given below.)

a   to imagine or pretend to see

b   when something gets smaller and smaller

c   something that divides people into two groups

d   someone who receives something

e   a range of differences

f   exactness

g   to keep a record of

h   take someone's attention away from

i   related to, like, similar to

j   the measurable effects of a disease

k   raised, increased, heightened

l   directly, openly

m   pace, tempo, speed

n   debate, argument

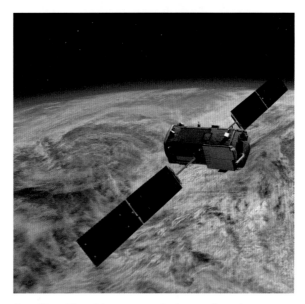

Satellites like this one regularly monitor the amounts of CO_2 in the atmosphere

READING STRATEGY
One useful reading strategy is called 'SQ3R': **Read, Recall, Review**. Try applying the following steps to Text 5.5:

- Survey: Take a very quick glance through the text without reading every word. This is also known as 'skimming' (see Chapter 3, Activity 3.12).

- Question: Before you read it, ask any questions that come to mind on the topic.

- Read: Now read the text carefully.

- Recall: Come back to the text after a short while and recall the main points.

- Review: What are you going to do with the text? Try telling a classmate or friend about the main points. If you can 'teach' it, it means you know it!

Text 5.5

Is Global Warming Real?

What do you think of when you hear the words 'global warming?' You might envision melting **ice caps,** drowning polar bears and shrinking coastlines. Or perhaps your mind turns to magazine covers, politicians and celebrity activists. Global warming has become a very divisive term, but is it real?

The short answer, according to environmental scientist David Keith, is yes.

'There is no disagreement among really anybody who is scientific in any way that the world is a lot warmer than it was 100 years ago,' Keith says. 'If there are interesting disagreements, the disagreements are about whether this is the warmest it's been since the ice ages 10 000 years ago.'

A recipient of honors that include MIT's prize for excellence in experimental physics, Keith has spoken to governments, corporations and media outlets about climate change. As he points out, scientists use various methods to measure global warming; they produce varying answers.

'If all the scientists in the world believed there was only one answer, it would be right for all the rest of us to be sceptical,' Keith said. 'There's nothing in the world that one ever measures with perfect accuracy.'

Those measurements include thermostatic records and satellite images that document temperature increases over the past century. Additionally, paleoclimate databases suggest the current rate of increase is substantially higher than normal.

Undercutting the Issue

While global warming is certainly an important aspect of climate change, the term's use in mass media may actually serve to distract people from the real issues. Keith uses the example of a human patient hooked up to a mercury drip to illustrate this point.

The hypothetical human will eventually die from mercury poisoning: it's the scientific reality of the situation. The media focus on year-by-year warming or cooling, he argues, is akin to focusing on the patient's symptoms instead of the proven underlying condition and the cause behind it. In the case of climate change, elevated carbon dioxide (CO_2) levels are the deadly mercury drip.

'The core theory says if you double or triple CO_2 in the atmosphere, it's going to get warmer,' Keith said. 'This is something we've known from pretty basic physics and proved with a lot of good science for more than 100 years. That's the reason to worry, not the warming over the last few decades.'

Scientists first raised concerns over the warming effects of CO_2 in the atmosphere in the 1960s, when the climate was actually cooling. While there's nothing overtly problematic about natural climate change, it's the rate of change that worries experts.

Approximately 55 million years ago, the climate was warm enough to support alligators in the high Arctic. It took 10 million years for those CO_2 levels to decrease to the current level. At humanity's current rate of CO_2 production, Keith said, levels will rise back up to that point in only 100 years: 100 000 times faster.

'There is no controversy among anybody, even the sceptics, that the amount of CO_2 in the atmosphere is going up – unless you pick ones that are just nutballs,' Keith said. 'We know that without any doubt.'

www.seeker.com

TEXT AND CONTEXT
MIT (paragraph 4) is an abbreviation for Massachusetts Institute of Technology.

2.12 Consider the following comprehension questions on Text 5.5. Write a short, complete answer to each question, with reference to the text.

a What do scientists disagree on?

b Why do scientists report different results on global warming?

c Analogy is the comparison of two ideas, things or events. How does David Keith use analogy to describe the media's reporting on global warming?

d Why are scientists alarmed and concerned?

e What can climate change sceptics and scientists agree on?

2.13 Imagine you have to convince a skeptical friend that global warming is real. After having read Text 5.5, how might you do this in less than two minutes? Write a list of key arguments that you could use as notes for your two-minute presentation.

2.14 Text 5.6 is characteristic of an information website. It has many bullet-point lists with hyperlinks to other webpages. Several links from this text have been removed and placed below in a random order. Where would you insert them in Text 5.6?

a Recycling at home

b Find a bus for your journey

c Calculate your carbon footprint

d How to offset CO_2 emissions

e Food labels

f Water: using less at home

g Pressures on the environment

h Re-using and recycling electrical waste

i Choose fuel-saving cars

j Cut your energy bills

k Food and drink: greener choices

l Energy labels

m Find a cycle route

CAS

Text 5.6 might give you some ideas for a CAS project. How could you help reduce CO_2 emissions? You could:

- produce a plan to have solar panels installed on a local building
- start an awareness campaign about the importance of recycling in your area
- help with the improvement of a local recycling facility.

Discuss possibilities with your CAS coordinator or advisor.

Text 5.6

Greener living: a quick guide

This article can help you start being greener, with links to more detailed information if you want it. You can cut your carbon footprint, help look after nature and save money with simple changes. Try making your home more energy efficient, using greener driving tips and wasting less food.

Environmental problems: where can you start?

The biggest effects most people hae on climate change come from:

- energy used at home
- travel
- the food they eat

LEARNER PROFILE

Principled

What is the main principle being explored in Text 5.6? It tells us how to reduce emissions and our impact on the environment, but for what reason? As an IB learner, it is good to think about the kinds of principles that drive your everyday decisions. What kinds of responsibilities do you have towards creating a better environment?

Most other environmental problems, like **pollution** or loss of rare animals, are also a result of everyday demands for food, products and energy.

Find out what your carbon footprint is, and how to reduce it, using the link below.

1 • _____

2 • _____

• Climate change: a quick guide

Greener home

Saving energy at home is one of the most important things you can do to fight climate change and can save you money.

Energy saving help

You could be eligible for money off insulation or other energy saving home improvements. Call the Energy Saving Trust's free helpline to find out more or complete their online home energy check. Their advice could save you around £300 a year.

Turn down your heating

Turn your thermostat down one degree to cut your heating bills by up to 10 per cent and reduce carbon emissions.

3 • _____

Buy energy saving products

Find the most energy efficient electrical products by looking for the Energy Saving Trust Recommended label and European energy label (rating of A or higher). The European energy label also gives information to help you choose items that use less water.

4 • _____

5 • _____

• Home and Shopping

Greener travel choices

A more fuel efficient car could save you three months' worth of fuel a year.

Personal travel causes around a quarter of all the damage individuals do to the environment and most of this is from cars.

6 • _____

If you're buying a car, use the fuel economy label to choose one that will use less fuel. The more **fuel efficient** your car, the less tax you pay.

• Buy a fuel efficient new or used car.

Drive less

Use your car less for short trips. Walking, cycling, or taking the bus will help reduce local air pollution and carbon emissions. Walking and cycling can also help keep you fit.

7 • _____

8 • _____

• Keeping fit for young people

Fly less and offset CO_2 emissions

Think about how you could get what you need without flying. For example, try holidaying closer to home and travelling by rail or sea. If you have to fly, think about offsetting your CO_2

emissions. This means paying money to projects that reduce CO_2 emissions in other ways, like setting up **renewable energy** projects.

- Greener travel and leisure

9 • _____

Greener food choices

Food counts for nearly a third of most people's effect on climate change.

Waste less food

The average UK household spends £420 a year on food that could have been eaten but is thrown away. Wasting food wastes all the energy needed to make it. Visit the 'Love Food, Hate Waste' website for recipes and tips to help you waste less food and save money.

- Love Food Hate Waste

Buy climate friendly foods

The following tips can help you choose food with a lower carbon footprint:

- meat and dairy foods have a much bigger effect on climate change and the environment than most grains, pulses, fruit and vegetables

- buying fresh and unprocessed foods can mean fewer carbon emissions, because processing food and freezing or refrigerating it uses a lot of energy

- buying food grown outdoors in season can help reduce CO_2 emissions, because it doesn't need heated greenhouses.

Buy wildlife friendly foods

Some food is made in ways that are more wildlife friendly, for example without using pesticides. Other food supports the countryside and local communities, for example by creating local jobs. Find these by looking for labels like LEAF, organic and the Marine Stewardship Council, or choosing retailers that are trying to stock greener food.

10 • _____

11 • _____

- Organic labels

Recycle and waste less

Reusing and recycling instead of throwing items away will mean less waste and less energy needed to make new items.

Reuse and repair

Avoid waste in the first place, by reusing, upgrading and repairing. Try saving money by upgrading computers and hanging on to mobile phones, rather than replacing them. Avoid disposable items and pass things on when you've finished with them.

12 • _____

- Reducing waste, reusing and repairing

Recycle more

Nearly two thirds of all household rubbish can be recycled and most councils run doorstep recycling collections for paper, glass and plastics. Waste and recycling centres often accept many other things, from wood to textiles and TVs.

13 • _____

www.direct.gov.uk

TEXT AND CONTEXT

- Carbon footprint (paragraph 1) refers to the impact a person or person's actions can have on the environment.

- Some products are required by law to have a label. They tell the consumer how energy efficient the product is. They look like this:

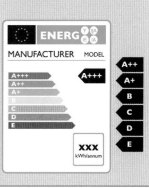

2.15 Here are several questions on Text 5.6. Answer them in short, complete sentences, with reference to the text.

a What are the three main ways in which individuals affect the environment?

b What are two ways of reducing your environmental impact in and around the home?

c Of all the damage individuals cause to the environment, how much of this is caused by travel?

d What does it mean to 'offset' CO_2 emissions?

e What kinds of food require a lot of energy to produce and keep?

f What should you do with an old mobile phone?

g How do many local authorities in the UK support recycling?

2.16 What kinds of measures do you take around the house, in your travels and at school, to help the environment? Use Text 5.6 and other sources to create a list of 5 habits that you would like to change. Compare your list with a classmate's. Decide on one habit that you are going to change for the next 31 days. Write out a short 'challenge' to yourself on a piece of paper. Post each student's challenge on a bulletin board for everyone to see. You can include the following phrases in your challenge:

a 'I believe that…'

b 'In order to make a difference, I have challenged myself to …'

c 'In the next 31 days I will …'

After 31 days see who accomplished their challenge. Reflect on the experiences you encountered and share your findings with your classmates.

Form and meaning

Text 5.5 is based on an interview with David Keith. Much of what he says is directly quoted. Other statements are indirectly reported by the writer. Depending on the context, you may also need to report what someone else has said. How should you do this? Compare the following two sentences:

Direct speech: David Keith said, 'There is no disagreement among scientists.'

Reported speech: David Keith said that there was no disagreement among scientists.

Notice that reported speech does not use quotation marks and the verbs are all in the past tense. The word 'that' now appears after 'said' (even though this is not necessary). Reported speech is useful for writing about past discussions. Note what happens to questions when reported speech is used:

Direct speech: She asked, 'What can I do to help?'

Reported speech: She asked what she could do to help.

2.17 Change the following sentences about environmental awareness from direct speech into reported speech.

a   Five years ago he predicted, 'The planet will be warmer in 100 years than it was 10 million years ago.'

b   'Why do I have to take the glass and paper out every week?', she asked.

c   David Keith said, 'There is no controversy among anybody.'

d   'The Earth does not belong to us. We belong to the Earth,' Chief Seattle once said.

e   'When will we run out of oil?', my four-year-old daughter asked.

f   'How do we know where 'green energy' comes from?', I asked at the meeting last night.

g   'Try using a carbon footprint calculator online,' he suggested.

Discussion

2.18 Here are three discussion questions that are often debated by politicians. What is your opinion on these issues? Research these topics before discussing them with your classmates.

a   As strange as it might sound, emissions can be traded. Governments often limit the amount a company may pollute. This is known as a 'cap'. If a company wants to break this limit or cap, they must buy a permit from another company that has not reached its limit or cap. Companies can buy and sell the right to pollute. What do you think of this 'cap and trade' idea?

b   Many politicians believe there would be less war if each country were less dependent on other countries for their energy. Do you think more solar, wind and thermal energy would lead to a more peaceful planet? How are current wars really all about non-renewable resources?

c   Nuclear power is sometimes seen as the 'lesser of two evils'. While nuclear power plants do not produce CO_2 like coal-fired power plants, they do present the problem of nuclear waste. Should countries build more nuclear power plants in order to reduce the amount of CO_2 that's being produced?

Climate change can be very political. There is often an assumption that protecting the environment comes at a cost to the economy. Do you agree with this assumption? Why or why not?

2.19 The purpose of the two advertisements below is to spread awareness about global warming.

a How do these advertisements manipulate photographs to make us more aware of reality?

b What is the underlying message of each image? What makes you say that?

c Are you persuaded by the advertisements to care more for the environment or make changes in your life?

d Which of the two ads do you find more effective in warning against the dangers of climate change? Why do you think this?

2.20 Drawing from the ideas in this unit, prepare an individual oral on one of the images below. You can select one of the two captions as a springboard for your individual oral. After a 3–4 minute presentation, be prepared to conduct a 4–5 minute conversation with your teacher about the ideas that you have presented. Unlike the actual individual oral, you will have time to research your presentation thoroughly, finding facts and supporting data. Keep in mind that the actual individual oral will not include captions. These are only meant to help you in your practice round.

ATL

Research skills

Activity 2.20 asks you to prepare an individual oral presentation on a photograph and a caption. You can think of these things as the tip of a very large iceberg called 'climate change'. In order to talk meaningfully about the entire iceberg, you will have to do research on this topic, gathering sources, finding data, learning about facts and studying charts. Before you make any claims in your presentation, make sure they are cross-referenced by multiple sources. It takes more time, but it makes your talk more valid.

A

a Every 60 seconds a species dies out due to human activity on planet earth. It's time to make changes.

b This cliché image has done more harm than good for environmental causes. Forget polar bears and focus on factory farms. Forget panda bears and feed people in a sustainable way.

B

a Los Angeles needs the Paris Climate Agreement. Global issues like climate change require international solutions.

b 'What goes around comes around.' Unfortunately, people only think about changing their ways once they've suffered the consequences of their behaviour.

C

a Desertification, deforestation and dead zones: meet our new planet. Is this what we want to give our grandchildren?

b Save the planet to save its people. The environment is not the cost of the economy. It is its reward.

Writing

2.21 Write a letter to your future child about the problems of climate change. To do this, take the following steps.

a Do an online search for 'open letter to my future child.' You will find many different examples. As a class explore three or four of these letters by breaking up into smaller groups and assigning one to each group of students.

b As a group, define the stylistic and structural features that typify this text type. How does the author of your text use language to create a certain effect from his audience? Discuss these defining characteristics as a class and make a list of them.

c Now turn your attention to what is going on in the news today as far as climate change is concerned. Are there frequent hurricanes and typhoons? Are climate agreements being made or broken? As a class, come up with a list of topics that are related to climate change that you can draw from for your writing assignment.

d Write a letter to your future child, taking into consideration the ways in which other people have done this before. In your letter, explore one or more of the topics that you discussed as a class.

e Ask a classmate and teacher to read your letter and give you advice, using the assessment criteria from Paper 1.

f Rewrite your letter for final submission. Keep a copy of this letter in a safe place, in case you ever want to give it to someone in the future.

2.22 Research one issue in the world today that is directly caused by global warming. It could be about flooding in Bangladesh (Text 5.7), hungry polar bears, or the frequency of hurricanes and typhoons. Write a news article in which you report on this issue. Support your article with evidence and facts. For help on writing news reports see Unit 6.5.

2.23 There are several films and documentaries about global warming and its effects. *An Inconvenient Truth* is often cited as a landmark film in the genre. *An Inconvenient Sequel* (2017) is even more up to date. Watch these films, or one of the following:

- *A Sea Change*
- *The 11th Hour*
- *The Age of Stupid*
- *Cowspiracy.*

After viewing one of these films, write a journalistic review for a popular magazine. For more support on review writing, see Unit 6.2.

Extended Essay
Your Category 1 extended essay should be a study of language related to its cultural context or a specific text. Language is used as a tool for persuading people to care more or less about global warming. Find a lengthy text that discusses global warming and analyse its use of language. Remember, a 'text' may be anything that conveys meaning, including film, graphic novels, advertising campaigns, or magazine articles. A good example might be the film An Inconvenient Truth by Al Gore. A good extended essay would explore how Al Gore uses language to convince people to care more about the environment.

5

Higher level extension

2.24 Carry out some research to find out what would happen if the oceans rose by 58 cm (23 inches). How might that directly affect your life and the place where you live? If possible, discuss this question with someone who comes from a different part of the world. Compare your answers to this question.

2.25 In the following sentences, the underlined words are synonyms for words used in Text 5.7. Substitute the underlined words with the appropriate words from the text. The words appear in the same order as the synonyms in the text.

a   After swimming he had a salty taste in his mouth.

b   Beads of sweat formed on his forehead.

c   Due to heavier rains, the sandbanks have disappeared.

d   The waves came rushing up our driveway.

e   After the spill, oil was soaking into the ground.

f   After the ship ran aground, it began to sink unavoidably.

g   He had a dreary outlook on the future.

h   The chemicals have spread, polluting the water supply.

i   The hedges form a wall between the two farms.

j   Opening the gates will set off an alarm.

k   They had lost all their possessions, and were now in a wretched situation.

TEXT AND CONTEXT

- Bangladesh is on the Ganges Delta, where the Ganges River and its many tributaries enter the Bay of Bengal.

- Seventy-five per cent of Bangladesh is less than 10 metres above sea level and 80 per cent is prone to flooding.

- Every year in Bangladesh, thousands of people are killed and millions of homes are destroyed because of flooding.

Text 5.7

BHAMIA, Bangladesh – Global warming has a taste in this village. It is the taste of salt

Only a few years ago, water from the local pond was fresh and sweet on Samit Biswas's tongue. It quenched his family's thirst and cleansed their bodies.

But drinking a cupful now leaves a briny flavour in his mouth. Tiny white crystals sprout on Biswas's skin after he bathes and in his clothes after his wife washes them.

The change, international scientists say, is the result of intensified **flooding** caused by shifting climate patterns. Warmer weather and rising oceans are sending seawater surging up Bangladesh's rivers in greater volume and frequency than ever before, specialists say, overflowing and seeping into the soil and the water supplies of thousands of people.

Their lives are being squeezed by distant lands they have seen only on television – the United States, China, and Russia at the top of the heap – whose carbon emissions are pushing temperatures and sea levels inexorably upward. Earlier this month, a long-awaited report by the United Nations said global warming fuelled by human activity could raise temperatures by 8 degrees and the ocean's surface by 23 inches by 2100.

In southwest Bangladesh, the bleak future forecast by the report is already becoming a reality, bringing misery along with it.

Heavier-than-usual floods have wiped out homes and paddies. They have increased the salinity of the water, which is contaminating wells, killing trees, and slowly poisoning the mighty mangrove jungle that forms a natural barrier against the Bay of Bengal.

If sea levels continue to rise at their present rate, by the time Biswas, 35, retires from his job as a teacher, the only home he has known will be swamped, overrun by the ocean with the force of an unstoppable army. That, in turn, will trigger another kind of flood: millions of displaced residents desperate for a place to live.

'It will be a disaster,' Biswas said.

Bangladesh, a densely crowded and painfully poor nation, contributes only a minuscule amount to the greenhouse gases slowly smothering the planet. But a combination of geography and demography puts it among the countries that specialists predict will be hardest hit as the Earth heats up.

LA Times

2.26 In order to check your understanding of the text, explain what is meant by the following phrases:

a 'their lives are being squeezed by distant lands'

b 'the United States, China, and Russia at the top of the heap'

c 'the bleak future forecast by the report is already becoming a reality'

d 'an unstoppable army'

e 'that, in turn, will trigger another kind of flood'.

2.27 How does Text 5.7 use language to make you care more about the threat of global warming? Find five adjectives, five verbs and five nouns from the text that encourage you to think about the threat of global warming. Complete a copy of the table below. Compare your table with a classmate's.

	Adjectives	Verbs	Nouns
1			
2			
3			
4			
5			

2.28 Activity 2.24 asked you how your life might be affected by rising sea levels. How was your answer similar or different to the story told in Text 5.7? Who is affected most by climate change and why?

Literature

2.29 Fiction can in fact teach us about reality, and Fantasy can help us understand facts. This is the case with 'The Lake', a poem by Roger McGough. Create a table like the one below. As you read through the poem, make a list of the fantastical ideas that you read. Explain why they are fantasy and how each idea or image comments on reality. An example has been done for you.

Things that are fantasy	Why these things are fantasy	How these things comment on reality
A lake that is so dirty that the moon's reflection cannot be seen on it.	Any lake, dirty or not, would create a reflection.	It suggests that something as beautiful as the moon refuses to be seen in something as ugly as a polluted lake.
Underwater pigs		
...		

TIP

Text 5.8 is very visual. As you read any text on an exam paper, you should try to visualise the setting, people, things and events. What do you <u>see</u> in your mind as you read it? What do these images make you <u>think</u> about? What do these thoughts make you <u>wonder</u>? Apply this 'see, think, wonder' (from the Harvard Project Zero) routine to your exam paper for more careful reading and better understanding.

Text 5.8

For years there have been no fish in the lake.
People hurrying through the park avoid it
like the plague. Birds steer clear
and the sedge of course has withered.
Trees lean away from it,
and at night it reflects, not the moon,
but the blackness of its own depths.
There are no fish in the lake.
But there is life there. There is life…

Underwater pigs glide between reefs of coral debris.
They love it here. They breed and multiply
in sties hollowed out of the mud
and lined with mattresses and bedsprings.
They live on dead fish and rotting things,
drowned pets, plastic and assorted excreta.

Rusty cans they like the best.
Holding them in webbed trotters
their teeth tear easily through the tin,
and poking in a snout, they noisily suck out
the putrid matter within.

There are no fish in the lake.
But there is life there. There is life…

For on certain evenings after dark
shoals of pigs surface
and look out at those houses near the park.
Where, in bathrooms,
children feed stale bread to plastic ducks,
and in attics,
toy yachts have long since run aground.
Where, in living rooms,
anglers dangle their lines on patterned carpets,
and bemoan the fate of the ones that got away.

Down on the lake, piggy eyes glisten.
They have acquired a taste for flesh.
They are licking their lips. Listen…

The Lake by Roger McGough

TEXT AND CONTEXT

- Sedge is a grass-like plant found in wet ground.

- Excreta is another word for waste product.

- 'Putrid' means 'rotting'.

- 'To bemoan' means 'to complain'.

2.30 Poetry, like any art form, makes use of style and structure. Here are few questions about the choices made by the author when writing this poem. Discuss your answers to these questions. There are no right or wrong answers, only more informed ones.

a   Why does the author repeat the phrases: 'But there is life. There is life…'?

b   Why does the author include a few rhyming words, such as 'glisten' and 'listen'?

c   Why does the poem list so many things, using commas and the word 'and' so often?

d   Why does the poem lack so much structure?

e   Why does the poem refer to so many physical spaces, such as 'bathrooms', 'attics' and 'livingrooms'?

f   How is the poem both scary and funny?

g   Why are the pigs 'licking their lips'?

h   Why did the author write this poem?

2.31 'The Lake' is full of images. Make an illustration that could accompany this poem. You do not have to be a talented artist to do this. Share your illustration with your classmates and describe your choices as an illustrator.

2.32 Try writing your own poem, in the spirit of 'The Lake', that spreads awareness about environmental concerns. Your poem can be as literary as you want to make it, but try to write something that is enlightening and meaningful.

REFLECT

In this unit you have learned about *how* global warming works, *what* the causes of climate change are and *where* the world is changing most. But the question that remains is: *Why* should you care? This is a possible easy question that you might like to answer!

Before you move on to another unit, consider your answer. Sit in a circle with your classmates and take turns giving short answers to this important question. How many unique answers can you come up with as a class?

Unit 5.3
Power to the people

Guiding questions	Learning objectives
• How are young individuals fighting for a safer and fairer world? • What is the importance of democracy in solving social injustices?	• Learn how young individuals are making a difference in the world. • Develop proficiency in speechmaking and argumentation techniques.

Word bank

democracy

activist

dictatorship

voting

republic

despotism

grassroots

protest

consensus

sovereignty

petition

election

campaign

rights

equality

voice

tolerant

revolution

donation

regulation

submission

'Sharing the planet' means sharing ideas about how people should be governed, sharing resources and power, and creating equal opportunities across cultures and regions.

This unit focuses on **democracy**, an idea that has been around for centuries but has gained ground rapidly in the age of globalisation. In the 'Listen and watch' section, you will learn how the Occupy movement has called for a fairer distribution of wealth. Text 5.9 is a speech by a young, political **activist** from Pakistan, who has spoken out against terrorism and fought for children's rights to education. Text 5.10 is about Tunisia, the first of many countries in North Africa and the Middle East to overthrow a **dictatorship** and move towards democracy – a geopolitical phenomenon known as the 'Arab Spring'.

In the Higher level extension, you will be introduced to Emma Gonzalez, a student who survived a school shooting in Florida and called on her government to change gun laws. In the literature section you will analyse the lyrics of a song that has been sung by protesters for decades.

Getting started

3.1 This unit contains some abstract vocabulary, as you can see from the word bank. Explaining the meaning of words like 'despotism', for example, is not easy. Which words from the word bank do you already know? Go through the list as a class and discuss the meanings of each word.

3.2 Below are several quotations about democracy. Select a quotation that you:

- *agree* with most
- *disagree* with most
- find confusing
- find funny.

For each quotation that you have chosen, explain to your classmates why you find it agreeable, disagreeable, confusing or funny.

a 'Democracy is the art and science of running the circus from the monkey cage.'
– H. L. Mencken

b 'Democracy is good. I say this because other systems are worse.' – Jawaharlal Nehru

c 'The best argument against democracy is a five-minute conversation with the average voter.'
– Winston Churchill

d 'Democracy cannot succeed unless those who express their choice are prepared to choose wisely. The real safeguard of democracy, therefore, is education.' – Franklin D. Roosevelt

e 'Democracy must be something more than two wolves and a sheep **voting** on what to have for dinner.' – James Bovard

f 'Democracy is the road to socialism.' – Karl Marx

g 'Democracy is a device that insures we shall be governed no better than we deserve.'
– George Bernard Shaw

h 'A mature society understands that at the heart of democracy is argument.' – Salman Rushdie

i 'Without God, democracy will not and cannot long endure.' – Ronald Reagan

j '**Republics** decline into democracies and democracies degenerate into **despotisms**.' – Aristotle

3.3 Look at the two photographs A and B. For each photograph think of sensible answers to the following questions. Discuss your answers with your classmates.

a Who are these people?

b What are they doing?

c Who is their audience?

d Why are they doing this?

e What do you think of their actions?

TOK
Activity 3.2 asks you to examine several famous quotations about democracy. Every quotation is an *assertion*. Your TOK course encourages you to formulate 'knowledge claims': statements about *how* we know what we claim to know.

Jawaharlal Nehru claims that democracy is good, because other systems are worse. While this is an interesting statement, it is not a knowledge claim. A knowledge claim answers a knowledge question. A good knowledge questions in this case would read: 'How can one know which form of governance is best, without having lived under several forms of governance in the course of a lifetime?'

Suggest a knowledge claim or question in response to another quotation from Activity 3.2.

B
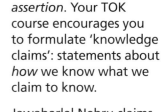

A

3.4 Look at the cartoon below. In one sentence, write down what you think is the cartoonist's main message. What does it say? Share your sentence with you classmates. Discuss your different interpretations of this cartoon as a class?

Watch and listen 🎦 🔊

3.5 You are about to listen to Audio track 15, about the Occupy movement, which started in 2011. Below is a list of items (a–m) that are important for understanding the context of the recording. Assign each person in your class a different item from the list. For the item you are assigned, do a quick online search, and explain to your classmates briefly why you think your item appears in this list of names, places and concepts.

a Zuccotti Park	**b** 'We are the 99%'
c to Balkanise	**d** 'Drain the swamp'
e **grassroots**	**f** Black Lives Matter
g Occupy Gezi Park	**h** Paris Climate Agreement
i Arab Spring	**j** Foreclosure
k 'too big to fail.'	**l** 'Get out of jail free' card
m Ferguson unrest	

The riots in Ferguson, Missouri in the United States were caused by the police's killing of 18 year-old Michael Brown. The incident raised concerns about the militarisation of the police and the profiling of African Americans.

3.6 Listen 🔊 for answers to the following questions in Audio track 15. See how well you can answer the questions after listening once. Then listen to the recording again to complete any answers you missed the first time round.

a   Where did the Occupy Wall Street movement start in 2011?

b   According to Mike, what makes the anniversary event taking place different to a typical march or protest?

c   What does the reporter refer to as a 'rather sombre message'?

d   What has Harrison done since 2011 to contribute to the Occupy movement?

e   Why doesn't Harrison think that Occupy can get a candidate elected to public office?

f   The reporter lists five issues that she observes being represented at the Occupy event. Name two of these issues.

g   What slogan does Susan use to sum up Occupy's core message?

h   In what way were the occupiers 'naïve', according to Susan?

3.7 In the box below are words taken from the video that you are about to watch. Use the words to fill in the blanks in the sentences below. Look up the definitions of words that you do not already know.

mayhem	**consensus**	underpinning	disruptive	**sovereignty**	**petition**
insidious	hack	evict	symptomatic	decentralise	nomination

a   The protesters created … downtown by blocking traffic.

b   Her political party gave her the … because she had the strongest best chance of winning the **election**.

c   The committee could not reach a … and so they could not pass the bill.

d   To … power means to take it away from one person or one institution and give it to several or many.

e   The squatters had no right to live there, and so the police could … them.

f   A country's … is its right to rule and govern itself.

g   The Anonymous group has been known to … the email accounts of corrupt politician.

h   Corruption is … of oligarchies and autocracies.

i   The … message of their **campaign** was one of unity and cooperation.

j   Some people consider backroom deals a typically … way of conducting politics.

k   … protesters prevented the politicians from entering the building.

l   After 10,000 people signed the … it was presented to congress as a proposed new law.

3.8 Do an online search for a video called: 'Micah White on The National with Wendy Mesley discussing The End of Protest'. As you watch the video, listen for answers to the following questions. Take notes and write our complete answers. Share your answers with your classmates and check your understanding by watching the video again.

a   Why is Micah White being interviewed by Wendy Mesley?

b   In what way is Micah White important to the Occupy movement?

c   Why, according to Micah White, was the one demand of Occupy not clearly articulated?

d   Why does Micah White call the Occupy movement a 'constructive failure'?

CAS
This unit is about politics and power. Getting involved in political organisations where you live is an excellent way to work on your CAS requirements. How can you think globally and act locally to make your world a better, fairer place?

e What, according to Micah White was the 'wrong lesson' that the Black Lives Matter campaign learned from the Occupy movement?

f What advice does he offer the Black Lives Matter campaign in order to make lasting change?

g What, according to Micah White, is wrong with online petitions?

h How can North Americans learn from what happened in Spain?

i What should Bernie Sanders have done which Donald Trump did well, according to Micah White?

j What is Micah White's grand vision for his lifetime?

Audio track 15 and the Micah White (left) video suggest that the rise of Donald Trump as US President marked the failure of the Occupy movement.

Exploring texts

3.9 Read Text 5.9 carefully once. Then complete the sentences below in a way that shows your understanding of Malala Yousafzai's speech. Do this without re-reading the text. Instead, write what you remember in your own words. Compare your answers to those of your classmates. How much did you retain and remember? Note: You may be able to find a recording of this speech online. Search for: 'Malala Yousafzai addresses United Nations Youth Assembly.'

a Despite being shot in the head by the Taliban, Malala...

b Thanks to the inspiration of great leaders like Nelson Mandela and Gandhi, Malala...

c Education scares the Taliban because...

d Of all the problems in her country, Malala says we should focus on... because...

e She calls on the developed countries of the world to...

Malala Yousafzai addressing the United Nations Youth Assembly

Text 5.9

There are hundreds of human rights activists and social workers who are not only speaking for human rights, but who are struggling to achieve their goals of education, peace and **equality**. Thousands of people have been killed by the terrorists and millions have been injured. I am just one of them.

So here I stand... one girl among many.

I speak: not for myself, but for all girls and boys.

I raise up my **voice**: not so that I can shout, but so that those without a voice can be heard.

Those who have fought for their rights:
Their right to live in peace.
Their right to be treated with dignity.
Their right to equality of opportunity.
Their right to be educated.

Dear Friends, on the 9th of October 2012, the Taliban shot me on the left side of my forehead. They shot my friends too. They thought that the bullets would silence us. But they failed. And then, out of that silence came, thousands of voices. The terrorists thought that they would change our aims and stop our ambitions but nothing changed in my life except this: Weakness, fear and hopelessness died. Strength, power and courage was born. I am the same Malala. My ambitions are the same. My hopes are the same. My dreams are the same.

Dear Sisters and Brothers, I am not against anyone. Neither am I here to speak in terms of personal revenge against the Taliban or any other terrorist's group. I am here to speak up for the right of education of every child. I want education for the sons and the daughters of all the extremists, especially the Taliban.

I do not even hate the Talib who shot me. Even if there is a gun in my hand and he stands in front of me. I would not shoot him. This is the compassion that I have learnt from Muhammad, the prophet of mercy, Jesus Christ and Lord Buddha. This is the legacy of change that I have inherited from Martin Luther King, Nelson Mandela and Muhammad Ali Jinnah. This is the philosophy of non-violence that I have learnt from Gandhi Jee, Bacha Khan and Mother Teresa. And this is the forgiveness that I have learnt from my mother and father. This is what my soul is telling me, be peaceful and love everyone.

Dear Sisters and Brothers, we realise the importance of light when we see darkness. We realise the importance of our voice when we are silenced. In the same way, when we were in Swat, the north of Pakistan, we realised the importance of pens and books when we saw the guns.

The wise saying, 'The pen is mightier than sword' was true. The extremists are afraid of books and pens. The power of education frightens them. They are afraid of women. The power of the voice of women frightens them. And that is why they killed 14 innocent medical students in the recent attack in Quetta. And that is why they killed many female teachers and polio workers in Khyber Pukhtoon Khwa and FATA. That is why they are blasting schools every day. Because they were and they are afraid of change, afraid of the equality that we will bring into our society.

I remember that there was a boy in our school who was asked by a journalist, 'Why are the Taliban against education?' He answered very simply. By pointing to his book he said, 'A Talib doesn't know what is written inside this book.' They think that God is a tiny, little conservative being who would send girls to hell just because of going to school. The terrorists are misusing the name of Islam and Pashtun society for their own personal benefits. Pakistan is a peace-loving democratic country. Pashtuns want education for their daughters and sons. And Islam is a religion of peace, humanity and brotherhood. Islam says that it is not only each child's right to get education, rather it is their duty and responsibility.

Honourable Secretary General, peace is necessary for education. In many parts of the world especially Pakistan and Afghanistan; terrorism, wars and conflicts stop children from going to their schools. We are really tired of these wars. Women and children are suffering in many parts of the world in many ways. In India, innocent and poor children are victims of child labour. Many schools have been destroyed in Nigeria. People

TEXT AND CONTEXT

Text 5.9 is a speech given by Malala Yousafzai. She is a Pakistani activist for human **rights**, and the youngest-ever Nobel Prize winner. She gave this speech in 2013, when she participated in the first Youth Takeover of the United Nations.

in Afghanistan have been affected by the hurdles of extremism for decades. Young girls have to do domestic child labour and are forced to get married at early age. Poverty, ignorance, injustice, racism and the deprivation of basic rights are the main problems faced by both men and women.

Dear Fellows, today I am focusing on women's rights and girls' education because they are suffering the most. There was a time when women social activists asked men to stand up for their rights. But, this time, we will do it by ourselves. I am not telling men to step away from speaking for women's rights rather I am focusing on women to be independent to fight for themselves.

Dear Sisters and Brothers, now it's time to speak up.

So today, we call upon the world leaders to change their strategic policies in favour of peace and prosperity.

We call upon the world leaders that all the peace deals must protect women and children's rights. A deal that goes against the dignity of women and their rights is unacceptable.

- We call upon all governments to ensure free compulsory education for every child all over the world.
- We call upon all governments to fight against terrorism and violence, to protect children from brutality and harm.
- We call upon the developed nations to support the expansion of educational opportunities for girls in the developing world.
- We call upon all communities to be **tolerant** – to reject prejudice based on

cast, creed, sect, religion or gender. To ensure freedom and equality for women so that they can flourish. We cannot all succeed when half of us are held back.

- We call upon our sisters around the world to be brave – to embrace the strength within themselves and realise their full potential.

Dear Brothers and Sisters, we want schools and education for every child's bright future. We will continue our journey to our destination of peace and education for everyone. No one can stop us. We will speak for our rights and we will bring change through our voice. We must believe in the power and the strength of our words. Our words can change the world.

Because we are all together, united for the cause of education. And if we want to achieve our goal, then let us empower ourselves with the weapon of knowledge and let us shield ourselves with unity and togetherness.

Dear Brothers and Sisters, we must not forget that millions of people are suffering from poverty, injustice and ignorance. We must not forget that millions of children are out of schools. We must not forget that our sisters and brothers are waiting for a bright peaceful future.

So let us wage a global struggle against illiteracy, poverty and terrorism and let us pick up our books and pens. They are our most powerful weapons.

One child, one teacher, one pen and one book can change the world.

Education is the only solution. Education First.

www.theirworld.org

CONCEPTS

Audience, Context, Purpose, Meaning, Variation

After you have read Malala Yousafzai's speech or watched it online, discuss how all five concepts for the English B course are relevant.

- How is her _language_ appropriate for her _audience_?
- How does Yousafzai's _context_ and personal background help shape the _meaning_ of her speech?
- What is the _purpose_ of her speech?

3.10 In the box below are several words that have been taken from Text 5.9. Read the text again and, in small groups, use some or all of the words to make a mind map, poster or other visual representation of the ideas in Malala's speech. If you are not familiar with one of the words, look up its meaning. You may also add words of your own. You can draw pictures to include if you want to. Present your group's visual depiction of the text to the rest of your class.

Malala	forgiveness	Prophet Mohammed	terrorism	pens	Taliban
poverty	Buddha	right to education	Afghanistan	peacefulness	
bullets	girls	injustice	schools	courage	Martin Luther King
extremism	Pakistan	child labour	education	books	boys
brotherhood	ignorance	fear	equality for women		

3.11 In the English language, many verbs have meaning once they take a preposition. Prepositions are words such as 'in', 'on' or 'after' that express a relation to another word, usually a noun or pronoun. How many of the verb phrases a–g from Text 5.10 do you already know? Fill in the blanks, using prepositions from the box. The meanings of the phrases are given to help you.

down	out	at	back	at	ahead	on

a to stand … = to be noticed

b to lie … = to loom

c to balk … = to hesitate

d to trace … = to have origins

e to come … = to fall

f to build … = to develop

g to keep … bay = to prevent

3.12 What associations can you think of for the words a–h below, taken from Text 5.10? Just quickly write the first thing that comes to mind after reading each word in the list. Share your list of associations with your classmates. Discuss why you think you associate these things with these words. Based on this list of words, what do you think Text 5.10 will be about?

a Arab Spring

b Tunisia

c Egypt

d Syria

e military coup

f dictator

g jihad

h democracy

3.13 You are about to read Text 5.10. Before you read the text, read questions a–g below. Then as you read, look for the answers to the questions. Write out your answers in complete sentences.

a Why has the author written this article?

b How did Tunisia's dictator come to an end?

c What started the Arab Spring?

d According to the author, how successful has the Arab Spring been? Why does he think this?

e Why are some people worried about the election of Beji Caid Essebsi?

f Why does the author think that Tunisia is more successful at transitioning to democracy than other countries in the Middle East and North Africa?

g What kinds of problems does Tunisia face at the time of the author writing this text?

EXTRA

Activity 3.10 asks you to create a 'visual representation' of Text 5.9. It suggests creating a mind map or poster. If you're artistic, you can try to illustrate this text (or any other speech) as 'live scribing' or 'whiteboard animation'. Do an online search for 'RSA Animate' and you will find many talks that have been illustrated using this technique. Creating a Prezi or a PowerPoint with stock images are other options that you can explore for this creative activity.

READING STRATEGY

Activity 3.10 and the 'Extra' box both encourage you to make visual representations of a speech. You do not have to be an artist to try this. The act of creating something in response to a text will always help you internalise and understand that text better.

Text 5.10

The Guardian view on Tunisia's transition: a success story

One nation stands as an exception in the Arab world for having peacefully completed a democratic electoral process, four years after the downfall of its dictator. It deserves support.

Four years ago, the death of a young street vendor sparked a popular uprising that led to the overthrow of the Tunisia's dictator, Zine al-Abidine Ben Ali. Today, although many challenges still lie ahead, Tunisia offers the closest thing to a success story in the aftermath of the 2011 Arab spring. Indeed, the country where those momentous changes all began remains the country that offers the greatest hopes of a stabilised democracy in the Arab Muslim world.

Tunisia stands out as an exception in the region. Its political evolution stands in stark contrast to many of the region's tragic turmoils: Egypt's return to military authoritarianism, Syria's civil-war slaughter-house, and Libya's utter chaos. For the first time in its history, Tunisia has freely elected its president, the 88-year-old former speaker of parliament, Beji Caid Essebsi. This vote completed an electoral cycle that has harnessed the peaceful emergence of a new post-revolutionary democratic order in this 11-million strong nation.

Some critics have balked at Mr Essebsi's profile: an old guard politician, associated with the fallen Ben Ali regime. But it is hard to deny that Tunisia offers a rare source of optimism in the post-2011 Arab world. For one thing, it has avoided the dreaded scenario of 'one man, one vote ... but just once'. Indeed, whatever their earlier mistakes, the Islamists of the Ennahda movement that came to power in 2011 accepted their defeat at the ballot, allowing genuine political alternation. In Egypt, by contrast, a violent military coup in 2013 ended the Islamists' rule.

Some of the reasons for Tunisia's democratic exceptionalism trace back deep into the nation's history: 19th-century reforms had introduced a constitutional order, and the notion of separation between the state and religion. Habib Bourguiba's post-independence presidency (from 1959 to 1987) left an important legacy of public education, social reform and female emancipation. In many ways, Tunisia's 2011 **revolution** carried the seeds of its own success: Islamist fundamentalists played no role, the army came down on the side of peaceful change, and there was a strong civil service and middle class to build on. The role of Tunisian women in keeping militant Islamism at bay has been essential. Being smaller and less strategically positioned than Egypt may also have protected it from disruption from external powers.

None of this is to deny that there are clouds on the horizon. Tunisia's new president may be a respected and experienced moderate, but he will need a government capable of solving deep economic problems, including a north-south regional divide. He will have to manage relations with neighbours in a volatile region where there is much anxiety about jihadi spillover from Libya and Syria.

But Tunisia's success so far confirms that democracy and Islam are in no way a contradiction. It is an example that should, with time, inspire others in the region. As such, Tunisia deserves strong financial assistance from those in the west that claim they favour democracy.

The Guardian

Form and meaning

3.14 The *–ing* verb ending can be very useful. Compare the following sentences and answer the question: 'when do we use the *–ing* verb ending?'

a   The Islamists of the Ennahda movement that came to power in 2011 accepted their defeat at the ballot, <u>allowing</u> genuine political alternation.

b   The role of Tunisian women in <u>keeping</u> militant Islamism at bay has been essential.

c   <u>Being</u> smaller and less strategically positioned than Egypt might also have protected it from disruption from external powers.

d   He will need a government capable of <u>solving</u> deep economic problems, <u>including</u> a north-south regional divide.

3.15 There are several ways of using the *–ing* verb ending. In Activity 3.14 however, you see two ways.

-ing as a subject or object of a sentence (like a large noun phrase)	*ing* as a clause, adding information to the words it succeeds.
For example: • <u>Fishing</u> from a pier isn't for me. (subject) • I look forward to <u>seeing</u> you. (object)	For example: • She stopped protesting, realising there was no point. (clause)

Questions a–k on the next page ask you to take two sentences and use the *–ing* verb form to make them into one. You might need to add commas and prepositions or leave out words entirely. The first one has been done for you as an example.

a   I like to swim. It is something I like to do on holiday. = *Swimming is something I like to do on holiday.*

b   Some people protest for over a week. This has been banned in many countries.

c   Voter turnout was good. There were people who lined up outside stations all over the country.

d   The UN was in the country. They monitored the election.

e   I like to read political science magazines. It makes me understand the news better.

f   The economy went down. He was disappointed by this.

g   They told people not to vote. This was a bad idea.

h   The government shut down access to social networks before the election. These included Twitter and Facebook

i   The Taliban shot her. She can forgive them for this.

j   Security prevented them. They wanted to disrupt the election.

k   She focuses on education. It is her way of reforming the country.

Discussion

3.16 Use one of the images and one of the captions below to practise for an individual oral. Even if you are a higher-level student, this exercise is a good way to practise your proficiency and express the ideas that you have studied in this unit. Keep in mind that you will not receive captions for visual stimuli during the actual individual oral and standard level.

a   The Occupy movement that started in 2011 has changed the world.

b   Protesting in the street, occupying a square and petitioning online are ineffective ways of creating political change.

a   As Malala Yousafzai has said: 'One child, one teacher, one pen and one book can change the world. Education is the only solution. Education First.' In other words, democracy can only work in a country where the citizens are educated and informed.

b   Democracy and Islam are in no way a contradiction. Tunisia has proven that democracy is possible in any country that is predominantly Muslim.

3.17 To what extent is democracy dependent on peace? To what extent is peace dependent on democracy? How does this cartoon show the difficulty of holding elections in a volatile region like the Ukraine?

Extended Essay
How have politicians changed the way we use the English language? This is an interesting topic for an extended essay. Consider, for example, how the election of Donald Trump in the United States introduced a series of new words such as: 'post-truth', 'alternative facts' and 'fake news'.

Before writing an essay of this nature, check the specifications for a 'category 2b' extended essay and the IB's definition of 'cultural artifacts'. In the case of the Donald Trump essay, you would want to include references to speeches that he delivered using these terms, and articles that comment on its impact on society, as cultural artifacts.

Writing

3.18 Write a blog entry for a news website about a recent development or news event in the world. To do so take the following steps:

a   Read Unit 6.3 on blog writing. Learn more about stylistic and structural elements that define this text type.

b   Re-read Text 5.10. Identify the stylistic and structural elements of a blog in this text, as you learned about them in Unit 6.3.

c   Research a topical topic that is related to the ideas of this unit. Read articles that include facts and opinions about this topic. Find one source that you would like to write for, if you were a blogger or columnist.

d   Write a blog post for this source in the style and structure that are commonly found on that source.

e   Ask a classmate and your teacher to assess your work using the assessment criteria for Paper 1.

3.19 Write a part of a political speech by taking the following steps:

a   Turn to Unit 6.4 to learn more about speech writing and the type of language that is characteristic of this text type.

b   Find an issue or recent event in the world that is relevant to the themes of this unit, such as democracy or human rights. Is there a group of people behind this 'movement'? Who are they? What have they done? Do they have a leader?

c   Pretend that you are involved in organising or leading this movement. Think of a context in which you could give a speech to an audience that cares about your movement or cause. Write the first part of your speech, considering the text type and your purpose.

d   Read your speech to your classmates and ask your teacher to assess you according to the criteria for Paper 1.

e   Rewrite and submit your speech, taking your teacher's feedback into consideration.

TIP

The writing activities in this course book help you prepare for the Paper 1 exam. By practicing with multiple writing assignments, you should become very familiar with the assessment criteria for this component. Study Unit 7.1 to learn more about these criteria. Committing them to memory before your exam is also useful.

Higher level extension

3.20 What do you know about guns in the United States? Select an item from the list below and do some quick online research on it. Tell your classmates what you found out.

a Number of gun-related deaths each year in the US

b The Second Amendment of the Constitution of the US

c The National Rifle Association (NRA)

d Annual number of deaths caused by school shootings in the US

e The Marjory Stoneman Douglas shooting

f President Trump's tweet in response to the Marjory Stoneman Douglas shooting.

g Background checks on people who wish to purchase assault rifles in the US

h Contributions to political campaigns in the US by special interest groups

i 'Conceal and carry' laws for teachers and coaches in the US

3.21 Do an online search for a speech given by Emma Gonzalez on the 17th of February 2018, by using the phrase: 'Florida student to NRA and Trump'. Search for both a transcript of her speech and a video of her delivering her speech. She was a survivor of a school shooting in the United States. Read her speech first, then watch her deliver it in the video. Discuss your answers to the following questions as a class.

a How does Emma Gonzalez' delivery of the speech in the online video make you react differently from when you read it quietly?

b What is Gonzalez arguing for? What arguments does she make for this cause? How are her arguments constructed?

c Focus on Gonzalez' use of pronouns. Who is 'we', 'you', 'he', 'they'? What are the effects of using these pronouns?

d How typical is her speech of good speeches? Read or re-read Unit 6.4 and discuss how the concepts of ethos, pathos and logos apply to her speech.

e What is the effect of repeating the phrase 'we call BS' on her audience? How do they respond? How effective is this phrase in helping her achieve her purpose?

f Gonzalez claims that her school's shootings will go into the textbooks as the last school shooting. Is this the case? Do some research to find out what has happened to her and her fight for gun-law reform in the US. Why has her fight been successful or unsuccessful do you think?

3.22 Watch the documentary *Bowling for Columbine* as a class and discuss your answers to the questions below:

a What is the movie's main message? How is the movie about more than gun violence?

b In what ways is the United States different from other countries in the world and what historical reasons account for these differences according to Michael Moore?

c Although this film is rather dated, how relevant is it to today's context?

d How biased is this movie? Give examples of bias from the movie.

e What do you think can be done to stop the cycle of fear and gun violence in the US?

f How likely is he to succeed in achieving his ends?

TEXT AND CONTEXT

- In her speech, Emma Gonzalez refers to PTSD. PTSD stands for post traumatic stress disorder, a psychological state experience by those who have suffered horrific, traumatising experiences.

- Tinker versus Des Moines was a Supreme Court case, which defended Mary Beth Tinker's right to express her opinion about the Vietnam War in 1965 by wearing a black arm band to school.

LEARNER PROFILE

To what degree is Emma Gonzalez a **risk-taker**? What other traits from the IB learner profile does she exemplify in her speech? Provide evidence from her speech to support your answer.

Literature

3.23 Do an online search for the lyrics to the song 'Blowin' in the Wind' by Bob Dylan. This song has been sung during demonstrations, rallies and protests for decades, (it was first released in 1962). Read the lyrics carefully. Do an online search for a video of Bob Dylan singing his song as well. After reading the lyrics and watching his performance, discuss your answers to the questions below:

a What do you think this song means? This question has been debated for years, but answers vary. What does it mean to you?

b Dylan begins each line of each verse with a question. Are these rhetorical questions, that don't have an answer? Or are they metaphorical questions, that seem to ask something else? What do the questions have in common?

c Why does Dylan answer each question with the same vague answer, which is 'blowin' in the wind?'

d Why do you think this song has been sung during peaceful marches and protests?

e Is this song relevant to the context of the world today? How might its message still be relevant?

3.24 Do an online search for interpretations and analyses that people have offered on 'Blowin' in the Wind'. Find one response that you find interesting. Summarise this response for your classmates and explain why you agree or disagree with the interpretation. How is this response similar to or different from your answers to Activity 3.23?

ATL

Self-management skills

As an IB learner you should develop *self-management skills*. One aspect of self-management is the ability to reflect and learn from reflection. The five chapters in this coursebook have addressed the five 'themes' of the English B syllabus. How has this book to expand your knowledge and understanding of the English-speaking world and the English language? What kinds of study habits have you developed to enable yourself to learn effectively?

Peter, Paul and Mary singing Bob Dylan's "Blowin' in the Wind" on the steps of the Lincoln Memorial, a few hours before Martin Luther King delivered his famous 'I have a dream' speech in 1963

Bob Dylan singing 'Blowin' in the Wind' in 1962

REFLECT

This unit has introduced you to a range of 'causes' worldwide, from the Occupy movement in New York to the Arab Spring.

*   Which causes were new to you?

*   Which causes did you find most interesting?

*   Which causes do you think might succeed in changing the world for the better? Give reasons for your answer.

You have reached the end of this chapter about 'Sharing the planet'. We have focused on poverty (Unit 5.1), environmental issues (Unit 5.2) and social movements (Unit 5.3). These topics all have a global dimension.

*   What do they suggest that people and nations will have to do in order to make the world a better place?

*   What other topics or issues come to mind when you think of the theme 'Sharing the planet'?

Brainstorm as a class on how you can explore this theme further.

Exploring text types

This chapter introduces different types of texts that you will read and write during your studies and in your exams.

By focusing on the key stylistic and structural features that define these text types, you will develop your text handling skills for your Paper 2 exam. An understanding of the key characteristics of different text types will help you in your writing assignment for Paper 1.

In this Chapter

- In Unit 6.1, you will explore the features of a formal e–mail.
- In Unit 6.2, you will study review writing.
- In Unit 6.3, you will define the conventions of blog writing.
- In Unit 6.4, you will learn about speech writing and rhetorical devices.
- In Unit 6.5, you will analyse news reports.
- In Unit 6.6, you will identify the defining features of a brochure.
- In Unit 6.7, you will discuss how to write guidelines.
- In Unit 6.8, you will read an official report.
- In Unit 6.9, you will concentrate on essays.

Unit 6.1
Formal letter

Guiding questions	Learning objectives
• How do you write a letter to the editor?	• Become familiar with the elements of letter writing. • Develop skills for writing letters of complaint or letters to the editor.

Word bank

greeting
salutation
synthesise
direct opening
concise argument
call to action

Writing an effective letter is not only a useful skill for your Paper 1 writing task, but also for life in general.

In this unit, you will practise writing a formal letter to the editor.

Paper 1-style writing tasks are also included in this unit to help you prepare for the exam.

Model text

Text 6.1

Your address — Melissa Davenport
123 Sunrise Dr.
Tulsa, Oklahoma

Their address — American Apparel
456 Sunset Rd.
Los Angeles, California

Date — 28 August 2020

Greeting — To whom it may concern,

Direct opening — I am writing to you to express my concern about your recent advertisement featuring Lauren Phoenix, which I find inappropriate and disturbing.

Concise argument — I fear that women who view this ad will think that they must look young, skinny and sexually available in order to be fashionable and attractive. By stating her weight
Reference to source text — ('150lbs of magic'), claiming she is famous and showing her sexually aroused, you create an unrealistic definition of 'beauty'. Such images encourage bulimic, depressed and loose behaviour. In fact studies by Martin Lindstrom suggest that sex in advertising only distracts from the product and brand being promoted.

Call to action — I kindly ask, for the sake of young American women, that you pull this ad from all media. Your company's image would benefit more by focusing on 'sweatshop free' instead of 'sexually discriminatory'.

Thank you for taking my opinion into consideration for future advertising campaigns.

Salutation — Kind regards,
Signature — Melissa Davenport

Key features explained

ATL

Communication skills

Learning how to write various types of letters for different purposes is a useful life skill. Writing a letter, especially in response to a passage or event, requires the ability to read, **synthesise**, formulate, argue and communicate. You can practice these skills throughout Chapter 6 by studying the 'model texts' and 'Key features explained' sections.

Key features	Examples from Text 6.1
Addresses: Write your own address first, followed by the address of the person to whom you are writing. These can be written top left or top right.	Melissa Davenport 123 Sunrise Dr. Tulsa, Oklahoma American Apparel 456 Sunset Rd. Los Angeles, California
Date: There are different formats for writing the date. Any of these can be used.	28 August 2020 28th of August 2020 August 28th 2020
Greeting: With a letter to the editor, it is important to remain formal. 'Hi' would not be appropriate.	Dear Mr. ...or Ms.... To whom it may concern, To the editor,
Direct opening: Explain why you are writing your letter. You should make the point clearly at the beginning. The reader might not want to read the rest of your letter, if you do not state your main point from the start.	'I am writing to you to express my concerns about...' 'I would like to bring to your attention...'
Concise argument: Letters to the editor tend to be short (200–300 words). Make an effective argument in the *second* paragraph, explaining why the editor should care about the complaint. Refer to the stimulus text.	'Stating [the model's] weight ('150lbs of magic'), claiming she is famous and literally showing her sexually aroused, leads to bulimic, depressed and innappropriate behaviour.'
Call to action: What should the editor do after reading your letter? Offer the editor a solution.	'I kindly ask that you pull the ad from all media.' '...focus on 'sweatshop free' instead of 'sexually discriminatory'.'
Salutation and signature: There is no need to be original or especially creative. 'Kind regards' is very business-like. Be sure to write your name in full below your signature.	'Kind regards,' Sincerely, (more personal) All the best, (less formal)

CONCEPT

Purpose

In some cultures it is not polite to be very direct when stating your *purpose*. With regards to formal letters in the English-speaking world, however, it is important to state very clearly why you are writing and what you want the reader to do in response (call to action).

THERE ARE NO
SILVER SPOONS
FOR CHILDREN BORN INTO
POVERTY

Baby Amy is two minutes old. Poverty has already mapped out her future. Poverty is waiting to destroy Amy's hope and joy and is likely to lead her to a future of alcoholism. We can't end poverty but we can provide the practical skills that Amy and thousands of others in the UK need to stop it predetermining their lives. Don't let poverty destroy a future. Call 0800 032 7222 or visit www.barnardos.org.uk now.

Barnardo's
GIVING CHILDREN BACK THEIR FUTURE

1.1 On the left is an advertisement for Barnardo's, a charity organisation for the support of children. This advertisement, that first appeared in 2003, was considered controversial and shocking. Text 6.2 is a letter to the editor, and is not very well written. Make a list of what you can identify is wrong with it and ways in which the letter could be improved. Use a copy of the table below.

What is wrong with Text 6.2?	How could you improve it?

Barnardo's ad on which Text 6.2 is based

CONCEPT

Context

Whenever you receive a letter or email, the first sentence that you read should give you a sense of *context*:

- Who is the writer?
- Why have they written this letter?
- Who is the reader?
- When was it written?

Answering simple 'who', 'what', 'when', 'where' and 'why' questions can help to give you a better sense of context.

Text 6.2

Dear Barnardo's,

I was travelling on the subway the other day with my two daughters, ages 4 and 10 months. My oldest girl saw your ad and completely flipped out. She asked me if something like that could happen to her or her little sister. I had to spend the rest of the day reassuring her that it wouldn't. But I think your poster gave her nightmares anyways.

I don't know why you would publish such disturbing images. You're only scaring people, like mothers and small children. The subway is a place for people to travel without having to think about dying babies and poverty. But your ad ruins that whole experience.

In fact, your ad is a disgrace.

Cheers,

Rachel Carmichael

1.2 Write an improved version of the letter to the editor (Text 6.2) complaining about the Barnardo's advertisement. Apply what you know about the key features of this text type. Before you write your letter, have a class discussion and make a list of the complaints that could be made about the Barnardo's ad.

1.3 Write your own letter to the editor in response to the Barnardo's ad. Take into consideration the class discussions that you had in Activities 1.1 and 1.2.

Standard Level Exam preparation

1.4 Write a 250–400 word letter in response to one of the following writing tasks. Include the key features of this text type. You have one hour and 15 minutes to write your letter.

a *Identities*: You have seen an advertisement that uses models to sell mobile phones. You are worried that the models' lack of clothing and unrealistic body size set false expectations for young readers. Write a letter to the mobile phone producer to express your concerns. (Look at Unit 1.3 on 'Beauty and self-esteem' for some ideas.)

b *Experiences*: You have just returned from an outdoor adventure holiday that did not go as you had expected. The travel agency's website promised better facilities and services than you received. Write a letter of complaint that describes your dissatisfaction. Feel free to use your imagination when describing this outdoor adventure and the services promised by the organisation. (See Unit 2.2 on 'Extreme sports' for some ideas and inspiration.)

c *Human ingenuity*: You have recently been to an exhibition at an art gallery. The featured artist explores themes that you find very interesting. He uses techniques that are very contemporary and materials that are very unconventional. Write a letter to the gallery, in which you offer your response to his artwork. (Go to Unit 3.3 for inspiration.)

Higher Level Exam preparation

1.5 Write a 450–600 word letter to the editor in response to one of the following writing tasks. Include the key features of this text type. You have one hour and 30 minutes to write this.

a *Human ingenuity*: You have just heard someone speak about the effect of technology on human relationships. She has made claims that younger generations are addicted to their devices, disappointed by their career choices and self-absorbed by social media. Write a letter to the speaker in which you agree or disagree with her point of view. Feel free to refer to examples from your own life experience, where relevant. (Go to Unit 3.2 on 'Technology and human interaction' for ideas.)

b *Social organisation*: A local university wants to stop its affirmative action/positive programme, where ethnic minorities are given scholarships and grants to attend the university. Write a letter to the university, giving them your opinion on the matter. (Turn to Besides focusing on technology and migration for ideas and inspiration.)

c *Sharing the planet*: There is a politician in your state or country, running for an elected position. He has promised to re-open coalmines and stop investments in renewable sources of energy. What's more, he does not believe in global warming. Write him a letter expressing your opinion on this matter. (Look at Unit 5.2 for inspiration.)

> **TIP**
>
> When tackling a Paper 1 writing task, be flexible when considering the different text types that you have learned about.
>
> Letters to the editor are similar to letters of complaint or other types of letters.
>
> However, you might be asked to write a letter of praise or a letter or application. Rather than sticking to a rigid template for a text type, keep key concepts in mind such as 'audience' and 'purpose'. If you know *why* and *to whom* you're writing, the letter will be easier to write!

Unit 6.2
Review

Guiding question	Learning objectives
• How do you write a review?	• Understand the key features of review writing. • Develop skills for writing a review about a movie, novel, text or experience.

Word bank

newsworthy

hook

thesis

credits

Thanks to the Internet, visitors, readers and consumers are reviewing everything from gadgets to restaurants. Reviews are perfect text types for offering your opinion in a constructive way to inform other people.

In this unit you will learn the key features of review writing. You will read a film review and a book review. At higher level, you will assess a piece of student writing, using the criteria for Paper 1.

Model text

CONCEPT

Purpose

Readers read with *purpose*. When readers read reviews, they want to know: 'Should I see this movie?' 'Should I visit this exhibition?' When writing reviews be sure that the readers' questions are answered. Note: They will not read a novel because you write 'I think it is good.' Your arguments must be stronger than this. It is not recommended to use the phrase 'I think'.

Text 6.3

Shaken, not stirred: Skyfall brings Bond into the 21st century

Newsworthy — Last week *Skyfall* became the highest-grossing film of all time in the UK. For the few who haven't seen it yet, you might wonder: How could a 007 film receive such praise and popularity in this age of political **Hook** — correctness? Aren't 007 films only for gadget-loving, misogynists? Aren't the days of British spies over? For those who have seen *Skyfall*, you know: **Thesis** — It's the first Bond film of its kind, with stronger female characters, a more humble British intelligence agency and a softer James Bond. It's a long overdue but welcomed change.

Perhaps nothing indicates this change better than Judi Dench's character, M, the head of MI6. She is the ideal Commander in Chief, both firm and fair, strong and feminine. She is the antithesis of all the weak female roles that have come before her. Remember Kissy Suzuki, Pussy Galore and Xenia Onatopp? They provided Bond with sex, information or both. In *Skyfall*, Eve Moneypenny proves she can outrace Bond in a daring car chase. Yes, she accidentally almost kills Bond with a high-powered rifle, but this only seems to deepen their relationship. You might say that Moneypenny and M are the first women Bond truly respects.

— **Interpretation**

Indeed, Bond is a changed man. He appears softer and more loveable; his character is richer and more human. In the film, he returns to his childhood home. He has traded his vodka Martinis for Heinekens. He has ditched his gadgets for hunting rifles and pistols. In fact, the newest Aston Martin has taken a back seat to the vintage DB5. And while the villain makes the usual sexual advances on our beloved Bond, this villain happens to be a man. Director Sam Mendes has here introduced something that has never been seen in a Bond film before, challenging audiences on their views of masculinity and power.

— **Present tense**
— **Limited summary**

— **Credits**

Not only has 007 changed its depiction of gender roles, it also recognizes that the British Empire no longer rules the world. This is perhaps the most striking departure from Ian Fleming's novels, where MI6 regularly unravels the sadistic plots of Russian spies. In *Skyfall*, however, the British secret intelligence agency is under attack by none other than itself. Politicians question the agency's ability to function properly. A British secret agent has gone rogue. And James is tempted to pack it all up and retire to a tropical island. In brief, the Brits' mandate to rule the world, which was implicit in so many previous 007 films, has also gone up in smoke.

Despite these crucial changes, the whole film still feels true to its heritage. You could say it's only shaken, not stirred. After all, weapons, sex and intrigue remain the driving forces of the film. But putting the 'sexist, misogynist dinosaur' to rest (as M calls Bond) was a smart move by the brand. By respecting women, 007 has doubled its target audience and consequently its box office sales. So ladies, if you're looking for a good date-night film, Daniel Craig awaits.

— **Humour**

Key features explained

Key features	Examples from Text 6.3
Newsworthy: A review of anything is more relevant and meaningful if it is about something new.	'Last week...' Include facts or quotations.
Hook: Start your review with something that grabs the audience's attention.	'Aren't the days of British Spies over?' Questions or claims are good hooks.
Thesis: As in an essay, a review should have an argument. Every good review focuses on why the reader should or should not see the movie or read the book. The thesis also outlines the *scope* of the review. In other words what will the review be about.	'It's the first Bond film of its kind, with stronger female characters, a more humble British intelligence agency and a softer James Bond. It's a long overdue but welcomed change.' (Note: The word 'change' appears in the first sentence of every paragraph. This links each paragraph back to the thesis.)
Interpretation: The reviewer's interpretation should be clear. Adjectives work best to express opinion.	'[M] is both firm and fair, strong and feminine.' '[Bond] is a changed man.'
Present tense: Always write about novels, films or exhibitions in the present tense.	'[Bond] appears softer...' 'James is tempted to pack it all up.'
Limited summary: The audience is curious to know more about the plot and characters. Good reviews limit the amount of summary information, to keep audiences curious, and to avoid a 'spoiler'.	'[Bond] returns to his childhood home.' '... hunting rifles and pistols.'
Credits: The name of the director, author or artist should always be mentioned. Review comment on the creator's intentions.	'Sam Mendes [challenges] audiences on their views of masculinity and power.'
Humour: Good reviews are fun to read. Humour can lighten criticism.	'You could say it's only shaken, not stirred.' (Note: this is a reference to how James Bond orders his vodka Martinis!)

2.1 How are journalistic book reviews different from academic essays or study notes on a work of literature? Below are several statements that describe either essays, study notes or reviews. On a copy of the table below, write each statement in one *or more* of the columns. Discuss your answers with classmates and your teacher.

Book review	Study notes	Academic essay

a   A summary of the events that happened in a story

b   A brief description of the general subject matter of a work

c   A critical analysis of a literary work

d   An answer to the question: 'Would you recommend this book?'

e   A comment on the popularity or poor reception of a new work

f   An exploration of the author's intentions

g   An interpretation of the novel or literary work

h   A comment on the story's plot, including its ending

i   A comment on the work's significance to the world of literature

j   A comment on how the book makes its intended audience feel

2.2

a   As you read Text 6.4, annotate a copy of the passage, using the letters from Activity 2.1. For example, if you read a line that summarises the events of the story, write the letter 'a' alongside in the margin.

b   Annotation is a useful strategy for understanding text types. Is there a letter that appears more often than others?

c   Show your annotations to a classmate and discuss any differences.

Text 6.4
Room by Emma Donoghue

Much hyped on acquisition and by its publisher since (and longlisted for the Booker prize last week), *Room* is set to be one of the big literary hits of the year. Certainly it is Emma Donoghue's breakout novel, but, seemingly 'inspired' by Josef Fritzl's incarceration of his daughter Elisabeth, and the cases of Natascha Kampusch and Sabine Dardenne, it's hard not to feel wary: what is such potentially lurid and voyeuristic material doing in the hands of a novelist known for quirky, stylish literary fiction?

It is a brave act for a writer, but happily one that Donoghue, still only 40 but on her seventh novel, has the talent to pull off. For *Room* is in many ways what its publisher claims it to be: a novel like no other. The first half takes place entirely within the 12-foot-square room in which a young woman has spent her last seven years since being abducted aged 19. Raped repeatedly, she now has a five-year-old boy, Jack, and it is with his voice that Donoghue tells their story.

And what a voice it is. 'Ma' has clearly spent her five years devoting every scrap of mental energy to teaching, nurturing and entertaining her boy, preserving her own sanity in the process. To read this book is to stumble on a completely private world. Every family unit has its own language of codes and in-jokes, and Donoghue captures this exquisitely. Ma has created characters out of all aspects of their room – Wardrobe, Rug, Plant, Meltedy Spoon. They have a TV and Jack loves *Dora the Explorer*, but Ma limits the time they are allowed to watch it

LOVE KNOWS NO BOUNDARIES

ROOM

for fear of turning their brains to mush. They do 'phys ed' every morning, keep to strict mealtimes, make up poems, sing Lady Gaga and Kylie, and most importantly, Ma has a seemingly endless supply of stories – from the Berlin Wall and Princess Di ('Should have worn her seatbelt,' says Jack) to fairytales like *Hansel and Gretel* to hybrids in which Jack becomes Prince Jackerjack, Gullijack in Lilliput: his mother's own fairytale hero. And really, what is a story of a kidnapped girl locked in a shed with her long-haired innocently precocious boy if not the realisation of the most macabre fairytale?

Donoghue has not been so crass as to make light of their plight: at times it's almost impossible not to turn away in horror. [...] Ma has days where she is 'gone' to blank-eyed depression and Jack, left to his own devices, reveals: 'Mostly I just sit.' But the grotesque is consistently balanced with the uplifting and there is a moment, halfway through the novel, where you feel you would fight anyone who tried to wrestle it from your grasp with the same ferocity that Ma fights for Jack, such is the author's power to make out of the most vile circumstances something absorbing, truthful and beautiful.

Thereafter, the setting moved to 'Outside', the relationship diluted by alternative voices, by the number of new things with which Jack has to deal, the novel loses some of its intensity and has the more familiar feel of the naive child narratives of Roddy Doyle and Mark Haddon. Jack's introduction to the confusing world of freedom is handled with incredible skill and delicacy – as is his first separation from Ma. But the novel, like Jack, now has to follow a more logical and straightforward path.

For me, the rhythm of Ma and Jack's speech bears traces of the author's native Irish brogue, though the second half reveals the setting to be America (Donoghue now lives in Canada). But this only adds to the strange, dislocating appeal of *Room*. In the hands of this audacious novelist, Jack's tale is more than a victim-and-survivor story: it works as a study of child development, shows the power of language and story-telling, and is a kind of sustained poem in praise of motherhood and parental love.

The Guardian

ATL

Thinking skills

In order to write a review, you will need to apply several *thinking skills*.

- As you read a novel or watch a film, you might want to take notes and think about what will go into your review.

- You will want to 'analyse' the stimulus material, meaning you will have to think about how meaning is constructed.

- You might 'evaluate' the book or film, meaning you can compare its qualities to other works before you 'critique' it, or comment on its value.

In short, it is time to put on your thinking cap!

2.3 In order to write your own review, you will need to use appropriate vocabulary, including a strong set of adjectives. Some of the vocabulary in Text 6.4 is challenging. Below is a list of words taken from the extract, in the same order as they appear in the text. For each word select the correct synonym from the four options a–d.

1	acquisition:	**a** learning,	**b** purchase,	**c** tale,	**d** sale
2	incarceration:	**a** imprisonment,	**b** trial,	**c** story,	**d** freedom
3	lurid:	**a** carefree,	**b** shocking,	**c** fancy,	**d** pure
4	voyeuristic:	**a** nosey,	**b** picturesque,	**c** appropriate,	**d** cool
5	quirky:	**a** gross,	**b** lost,	**c** average,	**d** strange
6	abducted:	**a** injured,	**b** killed,	**c** captured,	**d** tortured
7	exquisitely:	**a** bluntly,	**b** skillfully,	**c** plainly,	**d** creatively
8	precocious:	**a** clever,	**b** stubborn,	**c** simple,	**d** playful
9	macabre:	**a** awful,	**b** interesting,	**c** horrific,	**d** complicated
10	crass:	**a** informal,	**b** insensitive,	**c** disinterested,	**d** silly
11	plight:	**a** dilemma,	**b** flight,	**c** journey,	**d** circumstances
12	grotesque:	**a** gratitude,	**b** perfectness,	**c** difficulty,	**d** weirdness
13	ferocity:	**a** passion,	**b** anger,	**c** fierceness,	**d** looseness
14	vile:	**a** awkward,	**b** disgusting,	**c** strange,	**d** ideal
15	audacious:	**a** daring,	**b** blunt,	**c** carefree,	**d** superb

2.4 Would the author of Text 6.4 recommend the novel, *Room*? After reading this review, complete a copy of the table below with arguments for why the novel may or may not be worth reading.

Reasons why this novel might be worth reading:	Reasons why this novel might *not* be worth reading:

TIP

Higher level students will find it useful to do Activity 2.5 before Activity 2.6, as you should practise applying the assessment criteria before writing a task. Standard level students will also benefit from trying the Higher Level exam preparation activities throughout Chapter 6.

Standard Level Exam preparation

2.5 Read Text 6.5, a book review of the novel *The Road* by Cormac McCarthy, which was written by a student.

a Mark the text as if it were a Paper 1 writing task, using the assessment criteria for Paper 1 at the beginning of this coursebook.

b Compare your marks to a classmate's. Give reasons and arguments to support your marks.

c Discuss the candidate's results as a class.

Text 6.5

The Road (not taken)
Cormac McCarthy asks big questions about life

The long-awaited novel, *The Road*, by Cormac McCarthy, came out this week, and readers will have a lot to talk about. You could say that McCarthy has nearly written a masterpiece.

This novel borrows themes and topics from his other novels such as mystery, lonely journeys and the Wild West. It's about a boy and his father travelling through an empty country, where civilisation has almost been wiped out entirely. The reader wants to find out why the world is covered in ash. Why are there only a few cannibals walking the earth in search of fresh 'meat' and canned food? 'The boy' and 'the man' seem to be the only 'good guys' around. It

is not easy for the father to keep his promise to his son to remain 'good', because everyone – including himself – is so desperate for food and water. They have a gun with one bullet, a shopping cart and a plan: Follow 'the road' to the coast. What will they do when they reach the coast? No one really knows.

Like most adventure novels, the reader learns that the journey is more important than the destination. The question on the mind of the reader is 'What destroyed this civilisation?' Once you realise that this question will never be answered, you start to wonder: 'What is civilisation?' That is what this book is really all about. We are supposed to look to the

relationship between the father and his son to answer this philosophical question, but it is not easy to do when these characters do not have names and their conversations are so short and simple. Readers are probably supposed to cry at the end (and I'm sure many will). But for some reason, I couldn't shed a tear. I think it is because the characters do not feel very real.

Critics will probably praise this book for leaving so much detail out instead of including a lot of detail. The style of this novel is minimalistic. But you have to wonder: Is this 'man' supposed to be the universal man? And is this 'boy' the universal boy? A novel like this can only go so far with such a simple understanding of people and relationships. Early in the novel, 'the man' has flashbacks of life before the world came to an end, which makes the novel and the character more believable. But after a while, McCarthy stops writing these flashbacks and the story becomes kind of flat, which is a real shame. Maybe that's why I couldn't cry at the end.

Nevertheless, it is fair to say that McCarthy has given everyone a lot to think about with his new novel, The Road. These days everyone is on edge, waiting for banks to fall apart and the environment to go up in smoke. So a novel like this makes us stop and think about what we are doing here. Are we supposed to be working together to save the human species?

Or are we going to eat each other to survive for a few more weeks? Are we supposed to travel on the road that everyone takes? Or is that road dangerous because everyone takes it?

It's great when a novel can make you ask such deep questions. McCarthy has definitely taken the road that other authors don't usually take. This is what makes it such a unique novel.

Higher Level Exam preparation

2.6 Try writing a review under exam conditions. Choose one of the three writing tasks below. Write a 450–600 word review and include the key features of this text type. You have one hour and 30 minutes to write this.

a   *Identities*: Write a review of a biography or film documentary that you have recently read or seen. Why would you recommend or not recommend this to someone?

b   *Experiences*: Write a review of a novel that you have recently read. How is the main character's 'journey' meaningful or relevant to the reader of your review? Write your review as if it would appear in a popular newspaper.

c   *Human ingenuity*: Write a review of the latest application (app), gadget or piece of technology that interests you or your peers. Why should others care about this? Write a review for a magazine that specialises in technology and current trends.

Unit 6.3
Blog

Guiding questions

- What is a blog?
- What kinds of blogs are there?
- How do you write a blog?

Learning objectives

- Become familiar with various forms of blog writing.
- Develop the skills for writing a blog post that others might find interesting to read.

Have you ever written a blog or a blog post? It is remarkably easy to start an online blog and publish your ideas instantly. A 'blog' as a text type is difficult to define because so many people write them for many different reasons. So what is a blog?

The term 'blog' comes from the words 'web' and 'log'. A log is an account of what happens, as it happens. In the past, the captains of sailing ships kept a logbook of all the events on board, such as a sailor becoming ill or the wind changing direction. A log is written for future reference. It allows you to keep a record, look back and reflect on something that has happened. Most blogs allow you to search through their archives, using a tagging and dating system.

The content of blogs can be about almost anything. In this unit you will explore two blog posts, one about transgender rights and the other about marriage. Take some time to explore the world of blogs and perhaps write a blog post of your own!

Word bank

diary
opinion column
journal
press release
topical
voice

EXTRA

As a long-term project for your English B course, you might want to write a blog. Be sure that your blog has focus and is relevant for a particular audience. Ask yourself a very important question: 'Why would anybody want to read my blog?' Keep it interesting, relevant and up to date. If writing a blog is part of your coursework, then be sure you understand what your teacher expects of you.

Model text

3.1 Here is a list of text types that are similar to, but different from, blogs. Based on what you know, explain how blogs might be similar or different to each of these text types.

a	**diary**	b	essay
c	**opinion column**	d	news report
e	review	f	**journal**
g	website	h	**press release**
i	tweet	j	Facebook post

3.2 Read Text 6.6 and say which text type from the list a–j in Activity 3.1 it is most similar to. Give your reasons for your answer.

Text 6.6

● ○ ○ ○

Blog by Hadley Freeman, 18 March 2017

Identity is the issue of our age: so why can't we talk more honestly about trans women?

As Adichie said, acknowledging differences and being supportive are not mutually exclusive

Hadley Freeman, columnist for *The Guardian*

Tip —

Personal — experience

1 Should you be struggling with a gift idea for that special person in your life, here's a suggestion: how about a home DNA kit? These are all the rage in America, I recently read in the New York Times, with 3m sold by ancestry.com alone in the past five years. At last, Americans can find out how Irish they actually are.

[...]

Topical —

2 Nowhere is the discussion about identity more passionately felt than within the transgender movement. If you feel you are a woman, you are a woman is the rule, although some women are querying this. Last week, the novelist Chimamanda Ngozi Adichie was asked by Channel 4's Cathy Newman whether trans women are 'real women'. 'My feeling is trans women are trans women,' Adichie replied, a response not so much tautological as almost palindromic. 'I don't think it's a good thing to conflate everything into one.'

[...]

Chimamanda Ngozi Adichie

Voice —

3 This kumbaya approach is an increasingly popular one. Why can't we ladies all just get along? Hakuna matata! Yet no one is asking why more women than men are raising objections here. Perhaps people think this is just what women are like: uniquely catty. [...] But there are real ethical issues here, and they overwhelmingly affect women.

Examples —

4 Sport is one obvious example. Male-born bodies have had different testosterone levels and muscle distribution from female ones. No one knows what the solution is but pretending there isn't a difference is ridiculous. Then there are prisons. It's easy to cheer on Chelsea Manning, but Ian Huntley – who now reportedly wishes to be known as Lian Huntley and be transferred to a women's prison – is a tougher sell. Should a man with a history of crimes against women and girls really be in a female prison?

[...]

Opinion —

5 Just as the fringe elements of the political world have taken centre stage, so the more extreme end of the trans movement – which insists there are no differences between trans and cis women – has moved to the frontline. Some will call this progress; to me, it seems more a case of throwing out the commonsensical baby with the transphobic bath water. [...]

6 That trans people have long suffered from hideous prejudice and violence, and continue to do so, is without question. But as Adichie said, acknowledging differences and being supportive are not mutually exclusive. If anything, they go hand in hand, because they allow women, trans and non-trans, to talk honestly and see each other as people, instead of reducing themselves to manicures and menstruation.

The Guardian

CONCEPT

Context

Text 6.6 is very much relevant to the context in which the author, Hadley Freeman, writes. Several people are mentioned, including a BBC journalist (Cathy Newman), a novelist (Chimamanda Ngozi Adichie), a famous prisoner (Chelsea Manning), all of whom had been in the news at time of Freeman's piece. If you write a blog make sure that it makes sense in a certain *context*. Writing about something newsworthy will ensure that this is the case.

LEARNER PROFILE

Open minded

Text 6.6 raises an interesting question about transgender people. Should men who want to be treated as women be treated as women or as men who want to be treated as women? The author suggests that the latter can be respectable. Do you agree? Part of being an open-minded, IB learner is about acknowledging and respecting people's differences.

Key features explained

Key features	Examples from Text 6.6
Tip: Blogs often offer advice or help, especially 'how to' blogs. Use imperative verbs for this.	'Here's a suggestion: …'
Personal experience: Blogs can be like public diaries or journals. Anecdotes are common.	'I recently read...'
Topical: Popular blogs are often topical, about current affairs that are important to people.	'Last week...' 'In recent news ...'
Voice: Popular bloggers have a style that followers recognise and like. It may be informal and personal.	'Why can't we ladies just get along?' 'Hakuna matata!'
Opinion: Many blogs clearly state the writer's opinion.	'Some will call this progress; to me it seems like throwing out the baby with the bathwater.'
Examples: For any opinions, arguments or suggestions, blog readers will expect to be given real-life, supporting examples.	'Sport is one obvious example.' 'For example ...'

3.3 Does the cartoon below reveal the truth about blogging? Do you agree or disagree with this interpretation of what blogging is? Why *do* people blog?

3.4 Read Text 6.7, a post from a blog called Rachel's Ruminations. Identify examples of the six key features of a blog:

- tip
- topical
- opinion
- personal experience
- voice
- examples.

You could use different colour highlighter pens and a copy of the text, or you might prefer to complete a table.

Compare your answers to a classmate's.

Text 6.7

Five Keys to a Successful Marriage

As of today, my husband and I have been married for 25 years. When people hear how long we've been married, I get one of two possible responses:

1. 'Congratulations! We're coming up on (fill in a number of years).'
2. 'Wow! How do you do it?'

This post is directed at the second group, who wonder how we've stayed together so long.

I realize that personalities vary, and that my husband and I are both fairly even-tempered people who avoid conflict in our lives. That might be a large part of the secret to the longevity of our marriage. So, in other words, your mileage may vary (no pun intended), but if you're curious how we do it, it comes down to these five points:

I Stay independent

The number one most important 'secret' to an enduring relationship, in my view, is to remain independent people. That may sound contradictory if you see marriage as implying that you have to do everything together. It shouldn't.

My husband and I have always been independent people. It's one of the things that attracted us to each other: that we were both people who could manage ourselves, being able to make independent decisions and act on them with little drama.

We have separate interests and do separate things. He loves both playing and watching soccer. His Sunday morning soccer game is absolutely sacred; I wouldn't expect him to do anything else on Sunday morning.

I do none of those things: I like to write and play on social media.

We both enjoy reading and watching good dramas on TV. We both love to travel, though he prefers active travel that includes things like long-distance hikes, while I'm happier exploring cities and villages.

2 Maintain a balance

Being independent doesn't mean being alone all of the time, though, just as marriage shouldn't mean being together all of the time. We've found a balance that works for both of us. We pursue our own interests but spend quality time together as well.

For us, that quality time tends to involve travel, but it could be anything you both enjoy: gardening, or attending a ball game or a carnival or going out to dinner together. Many couples have regular 'date nights'. When our kids were little, we went away without them for a long weekend about once a year. We felt it was important to prevent us from losing sight of each other.

3 Make deals

In order to accommodate each other's needs and wishes in this way, we often make deals. This can be small things like, when our kids were little, when one of us would say 'Can you stay home with the kids tonight so I can go to my club meeting? I'll watch them tomorrow when you go to your game.'

But it can also be big things. We first met in Malawi when I was on a two-year Peace Corps assignment and he worked for Memisa Medicus Mundi on a four-year contract. I went home to the US when my contract ended and we carried on a long-distance relationship. He decided he wanted to study public health and planned to apply to schools in the UK, but since we were not married and I had US citizenship, I wouldn't be able to move to the UK and find work. So we made a deal: he agreed to apply to schools in the US. I agreed to move to wherever in the US he decided to study. It meant higher costs for him, and, for me, it meant giving up a good job in New York.

I think it's important to make sure you can live with your end of the bargain. Negotiate respectfully and make sure that you're okay with what you are agreeing to, so you don't have feelings of resentment later.

4 Keep money separate

One of the best pieces of advice we got when we married was to have separate accounts. Many couples end up fighting about money, and often that has to do with overdrawing because they're both using the same account. Instead, we have separate accounts and separate payments that we're each responsible for. My husband earns more, so he pays the mortgage, for example. I do the bigger grocery shopping trip each week, and I pay for that. And so on.

For safety's sake, in case something happens to one of us, some of the accounts are actually joint accounts, but we don't treat them that way. My husband's daily account, for example, has my name on it too, but I don't use it unless it's an emergency, and in that case I call him to let him know.

5 Respect each other

You might have noticed that all of the above rules come down to respect. Respect is something I think a lot of people pay lip service to, but don't actually feel. If you truly respect the other person, you don't see him or her as a possession or a force to be controlled, but honor the person as he or she is. So that also means not trying to change the person, or expressing negativity if that person doesn't live up to your expectations.

As an example, despite the fluctuations in my weight over the years, my husband has never once made a negative comment about my appearance.

Another example: when I announced that I wanted to quit one of my jobs and take a sabbatical, his response was 'Do what you need to do.' That shows an automatic respect for my feelings and my decisions.

So respect means a) viewing the other person as a valuable, independent individual. It means b) balancing your needs and wishes. It means c) give and take: making deals. And it means d) avoiding conflict over money. All of these together, at least in our case, have added up to a long, happy marriage.

Marriage is easy

I often hear people say that 'marriage is hard work.' It isn't for us. This may just be because of our personalities. But in our experience, any little disagreements become insignificant and hardly worth arguing about, since we feel valued for who we are.

Are you in a long-term relationship? Is there anything you'd add to this list?

www.rachelsruminations.com

ATL

Research skills

As you conduct research for your extended essay or any form of IB assessment, you might come across blogs as source texts. It is important to carefully judge the value of blog posts as sources, by using questions such as those from Activity 3.6. Remember an IB learner is critical, and anyone can publish a blog about anything without peer review or any sort of checks or approval.

CAS

Where can parents, teachers and friends read about your school's CAS activities? If your school does not already have one, you might consider starting and maintaining a CAS blog, posting information and stories about your school's latest activities and projects. In fact, maintaining a CAS blog could count as a CAS activity in itself! Discuss possibilities with your CAS coordinator.

3.5 Read through Text 6.7 again. Comment on how the following uses of language add meaning to the text. What is the effect of these language forms on the reader? Find examples to support your points.

a   imperative verbs ('Negotiate respectfully')

b   second person pronoun (you)

c   contractions ('you'd')

d   quotation marks

e   questions

f   very short sentences

g   expressions ('to pay lip service')

3.6 Can you find evidence of the same forms of language a–g from Activity 3.5 in Text 6.6 by Hadley Freeman? Do you think these forms of language are typical of blog writing in general? What makes you say this?

3.7 The following are currently some of the world's most popular blogs.

Huffington Post	TMZ	Business Insider	Mashable	Gizmodo	LifeHacker
The Verge	Tech Crunch	Perez Hilton	Engadget	Cheezburger	Deadspin	Kotaku

Assign each classmate a different blog from the list. Each person should find one blog post on their blog and answer the following questions. For each question explain your answer, referring to the blog that you have researched.

a   Who is the target audience of this blog?

b   How does this blog contribute to a greater conversation on a particular topic?

c   What are the opinions of the author(s) of the blog?

d   What can you learn from this blog?

e   Why do you think this blog so popular?

CONCEPTS

All of the key concepts for the English B course are relevant as you read (and write) blog posts. Use these points for Activities 3.6–3.8.

Audience: The most meaningful blogs target a specific audience.

Context: Good blogs are topical and relevant to the audience's context.

Purpose: The clearer the purpose, the more likely it is to be read.

Meaning: Blogs are most meaningful when they contribute to the conversation on a particular topic.

Variation: No two blogs are alike, because each writer is unique. And the individual 'voice' usually carries a blog.

Standard Level Exam preparation

3.8 Choose one of the two writing tasks below. Write a 250–400 word blog post and include the key features of this text type. You have one hour and 15 minutes to write this.

a *Identities*: Imagine you frequently blog about physical or mental health (whichever you prefer). Write a blog post about a recent trend or development in this field, sharing tips and ideas with your readers. Be sure to relate your blog post to the central theme of identities.

b *Human ingenuity*: In the form of a blog post for a mainstream newspaper, introduce and explore a recent scientific breakthrough. Explain to your audience why they should care about this development and its likely impact on society.

Higher Level Exam preparation

3.9 Choose one of the two writing tasks below. Write a 450–600 word blog post and include the key features of this text type. You have one hour and 30 minutes to write this.

a *Social organisation*: Imagine you are the writer of a regular blog about education, from your perspective as a student! Write a blog post that explores a recent development in learning that has affected your school or another school. Make it interesting for anyone who might be interested in education, such as teachers.

b *Sharing the planet*: Imagine you manage a blog called 'Doing more with less', in which you share your tips and ideas on how to downsize and live a more 'minimalist' lifestyle. Write a blog entry in which you explain how to do this and why it is important and relevant for the sustainability of planet earth.

TIP

For all of the exam preparation exercises in Chapter 6, apply the assessment criteria from Paper 1 to anything that you or a classmate have written. Peer assessment can be very valuable way to learn. You can also learn a lot by revising your writing tasks, taking your teacher's or classmates' feedback into consideration.

TIP

If you do not feel ready to write a blog entry under exam conditions (as suggested in Activities 3.8–3.9) you might want to try writing a Paper 1-style task as a group project. Discuss your decisions with one or two classmates and try writing it together.

Unit 6.4
Speech

Word bank

argumentation fallacies

rhetorical devices

ethos

logos

pathos

anecdote

imagery

allusion

parallelism

antithesis

anaphora

The power of language can be at its strongest in speeches. What is it about good speeches that make people excited, scared or motivated?

In this unit you will learn more about speeches and their key features. Understanding how speeches work is a useful skill; not only for learning how politicians inform and persuade, but also for learning how you too can persuade others to accept your own arguments. Careful study of how others use words can help you to become a stronger speaker.

Model text

4.1 Text 6.8 is a speech by Barack Obama from 2004, when he was a Senator, supporting John Kerry's candidacy for President of the United States.

Before reading Text 6.8, say whether the following statements are true or false. Then read the text and see if you have changed your mind about any of them. Justify your answers with evidence from the text.

a Effective speeches avoid starting a sentence with 'And' or 'But'.

b Good speeches are not about the speaker, but a topic.

c It is common to start a speech by explaining why you are speaking.

d Speeches are like essays read out loud.

e A good speech refers to the past, present and future.

f Persuasive speeches quote others and refer to facts or real events.

g Effective speeches paint images in the minds of their audience.

h Good speeches must have very difficult vocabulary to show the audience how smart the speaker is.

Text 6.8

On behalf of the great state of Illinois, crossroads of a nation, land of Lincoln, let me express my deep gratitude for the privilege of addressing this convention. Tonight is a particular honour for me because, let's face it, my presence on this stage is pretty unlikely.

Imagery — My father was a foreign student, born and raised in a small village in Kenya. He grew up herding goats, went to school in a tin-roof shack. His father, my grandfather, was a cook, a domestic servant to the British.

But my grandfather had larger dreams for his son. Through hard work and perseverance my father got a scholarship to study in a magical place, America, that's shown as a beacon of freedom and opportunity to so many who had come before him.

While studying here my father met my mother. She was born in a town on the other side of the world, in Kansas.

Her father worked on oil rigs and farms through most of the Depression. The day after Pearl Harbor, my grandfather signed up for duty, joined Patton's army, marched across Europe. Back home my grandmother raised a baby and went to work on a bomber assembly line. After the war, they studied on the GI Bill, bought a house through FHA and later moved west, all the way to Hawaii, in search of opportunity.

And they too had big dreams for their daughter, a common dream born of two continents.

Anecdote — My parents shared not only an improbable love; they shared an abiding faith in the possibilities of this nation. They would give me an African name, Barack, or 'blessed,' believing that in a tolerant America, your name is no barrier to success.

They imagined me going to the best schools in the land, even though they weren't rich, because in a generous America you don't have to be rich to achieve your potential.

Pathos — They're both passed away now. And yet I know that, on this night, they look down on me with great pride.

And I stand here today grateful for the diversity of my heritage, aware that my parents' dreams live on in my two precious daughters. I stand here knowing that my story is part of the larger American story, that I owe a debt to all of those who came before me, and that in no other country on Earth is my story even possible.

Tonight, we gather to affirm the greatness of our nation not because of the height of our skyscrapers, or the power of our military, or the size of our economy; our pride is based on a very simple premise, summed up in a declaration made over two hundred years ago: 'We hold these truths to be self-evident, that all men are created equal, that they are endowed by their Creator with certain inalienable rights, that among these are life, liberty and the pursuit of happiness.'

[...]

Anaphora — If there's a child on the south side of Chicago who can't read, that matters to me, even if it's not my child.

If there's a senior citizen somewhere who can't pay for their prescription and having to choose between medicine and the rent, that makes my life poorer, even if it's not my grandparent.

TEXT AND CONTEXT

The ex-US President Barack Obama is famous for his speeches. Many people think that this speech at the Democratic National Convention (Text 6.8) was the speech that launched his own candidacy for President. Do an online search and watch his delivery to feel the effect of his words as he speaks them. How does he look and sound 'presidential'?

Barack Obama as a boy

6

Principled

Perhaps what makes Obama's speech (Text 6.8) so strong is its emphasis on principles. By telling his family history to the audience, he explains the principle of equal opportunity. As you write your own speech, think of the principles that you want to articulate. How can you persuade your audience to share your principles?

TOK

Rhetorical devices can also be used to present poor arguments and bad logic. We call these **'argumentation fallacies'**. For example, one type of argumentation fallacy is the 'false dilemma', where an audience is presented with two choices and forced to choose. Obama presents his audience with a false dilemma, when he says: 'Do we participate in a politics of cynicism, or do we participate in a politics of hope?' Be aware of such fallacies when extending your knowledge.

Ethos ——

If there's an Arab-American family being rounded up without benefit of an attorney or due process, that threatens my civil liberties.

It is that fundamental belief – I am my brother's keeper, I am my sisters' keeper – that makes this country work.

It's what allows us to pursue our individual dreams, yet still come together as a single American family: 'E pluribus unum,' out of many, one.

Now even as we speak, there are those who are preparing to divide us, the spin masters and negative ad peddlers who embrace the politics of anything goes.

Antithesis ——

Well, I say to them tonight, there's not a liberal America and a conservative America; there's the United States of America.

There's not a black America and white America and Latino America and Asian America; there's the United States of America.

The pundits like to slice and dice our country into red States and blue States: red States for Republicans, blue States for Democrats.

Problem/ solution ——

But I've got news for them, too. We worship an awesome God in the blue States, and we don't like federal agents poking around our libraries in the red states.

We coach little league in the blue States and, yes, we've got some gay friends in the red States.

Parallelism ——

There are patriots who opposed the war in Iraq, and there are patriots who supported the war in Iraq.

We are one people, all of us pledging allegiance to the stars and stripes, all of us defending the United States of America.

In the end, that's what this election is about. Do we participate in a politics of cynicism, or do we participate in a politics of hope?

[...]

Allusion ——

It's the hope of slaves sitting around a fire singing freedom songs; the hope of immigrants setting out for distant shores; the hope of a young naval lieutenant bravely patrolling the Mekong Delta; the hope of a millworker's son who dares to defy the odds; the hope of a skinny kid with a funny name who believes that America has a place for him, too.

Hope in the face of difficulty, hope in the face of uncertainty, the audacity of hope: In the end, that is God's greatest gift to us, the bedrock of this nation, a belief in things not seen, a belief that there are better days ahead.

[...]

Logos ——

America, tonight, if you feel the same energy that I do, if you feel the same urgency that I do, if you feel the same passion that I do, if you feel the same hopefulness that I do, if we do what we must do, then I have no doubt that all across the country, from Florida to Oregon, from Washington to Maine, the people will rise up in November, and John Kerry will be sworn in as president. And John Edwards will be sworn in as vice president. And this country will reclaim its promise. And out of this long political darkness a brighter day will come.

Thank you very much, everybody.

God bless you.

Barack Obama 2004

Key features explained

Key features	Examples from Text 6.8
Imagery: Good speeches appeal to the audiences' senses of sight and sound.	'He grew up herding goats, went to school in a tin- roof shack.'
Anecdote: Small stories that explain a bigger idea are called anecdotes.	Obama's story about his parents serves as an illustration of the 'American Dream'
Pathos: Speakers appeal to emotion. Why should the audience *care* about the speech's message?	'[My parents] look down on me with great pride.'
Anaphora: Audiences are more likely to remember and follow a speech if there is repetition, also known as 'anaphora'.	'If there's a child...' 'If there's a senior citizen...' 'If there's an Arab-American...'
Ethos: Good speeches appeal to a sense of ethics. The speaker shows that he or she embodies these ethics.	'It is that fundamental belief – I am my brother's keeper, I am my sisters' keeper – that makes this country work'
Antithesis: Showing a contrast between two things helps the speaker make a point.	'There's not a liberal America and a conservative America; there's the United States of America.'
Problem/solution: Persuasive speeches often present a problem which the speaker aims to solve.	'Now even as we speak, there are those who are preparing to divide us. [...]But I've got news for them.'
Parallelism: Good speeches often use sentence structures that have parallel forms.	'There are patriots who opposed the war in Iraq, and there are patriots who supported the war in Iraq.'
Allusion: Allusion is a subtle reference to something that people know and value.	Obama alludes to the Declaration of Independence. He alludes to himself when he says 'skinny kid with a funny name.'
Logos: Good speeches appeal to logic. They include words such as 'if', 'then' and 'because' to persuade the audience.	'If we do what we must do, then I have no doubt that [...] John Kerry will be sworn in as president.'

ATL

Communication skills

This unit on speeches is based on **rhetorical devices**. Rhetoric is the art of effective or persuasive speaking or writing. As you develop your communication skills, find out about rhetorical devices and how to use them. The 10 devices listed here are only a starting a point for learning about rhetoric.

EXTRA

Look up the definitions of the other rhetorical devices listed below, if they are not familiar to you. Try to find examples in Text 6.8 or Activity 4.3.

- alliteration
- analogy
- expletive
- hypophora
- tricolon

4.2 Below are several quotations taken from Obama's 2004 speech (Text 6.8). For each one, discuss your answers to the question: 'Why does he say that?' Compare your answers to those of your classmates and teacher.

a Tonight is a particular honour for me because, let's face it, my presence on this stage is pretty unlikely.

b Back home my grandmother raised a baby and went to work on a bomber assembly line.

c It's what allows us to pursue our individual dreams, yet still come together as a single American family: 'E pluribus unum,' out of many, one.

d We coach little league in the blue States and, yes, we've got some gay friends in the red States.

e Do we participate in a politics of cynicism, or do we participate in a politics of hope?

4.3 The quotations a–i below are taken from famous speeches in the English language. For each one, state which key feature or features from the list above are relevant. Explain why.

Winston Churchill's oratory skills were famous for rallying the people of Great Britain during WWII

Nelson Mandela's Inaugural address in 1994 marked the end of apartheid in South Africa

Martin Luther King marched for civil liberties to the Lincoln Memorial in 1963, where he delivered his famous 'I Have a Dream' speech

a 'Never, never and never again shall it be that this beautiful land will again experience the oppression of one by another and suffer the indignity of being the skunk of the world.' Inaugural address, Nelson Mandela, 1994.

b 'We shall fight on the beaches, we shall fight on the landing grounds, we shall fight in the fields and in the streets, we shall fight in the hills; we shall never surrender...' *We Shall Fight on the Beaches*, Winston Churchill, 1940.

c 'I am honoured to be with you today at your commencement from one of the finest universities in the world. I never graduated from college. Truth be told, this is the closest I've ever gotten to a college graduation.' Stanford Commencement, Steve Jobs, 2005

d 'And so, my fellow Americans, ask not what your country can do for you, ask what you can do for your country.' Inaugural address, John F. Kennedy, 1961

e 'Government of the people, by the people, for the people, shall not perish from the Earth.' *Gettysburg Address*, Abraham Lincoln 1863

CONCEPTS

Audience

When writing a speech for Paper 1 or for any other purpose, it is important to keep your audience in mind. Who are they and what are their beliefs? How can you appeal to their beliefs to convey your message?

f My fellow citizens: I stand here today humbled by the task before us, grateful for the trust you have bestowed, mindful of the sacrifices borne by our ancestors.' Inaugural address, Barack Obama, 2008

g 'We dedicate this day to all the heroes and heroines in this country and the rest of the world who sacrificed in many ways and surrendered their lives so that we could be free. Their dreams have become reality.' Inaugural address Nelson Mandela, 1994.

h 'I have a dream that one day this nation will rise up and live out the true meaning of its creed: 'We hold these truths to be self-evident, that all men are created equal.' *I Have a Dream*, Martin Luther King, 1963

i 'One child, one teacher, one book, one pen can change the world.' Malala Yousafzai, 2013

Standard Level Exam preparation

4.4 Choose one of the two following writing tasks. Write a 250–400 word speech and include the key features of this text type. You have one hour and 15 minutes to write this.

a *Identities*: Imagine you are a politician running in an election in a country that is absorbing a lot of immigrants. Write the opening lines to a speech that addresses your country's concerns and convinces them of your principles. (See Unit 2.3 for inspiration.)

b *Sharing the planet*: Imagine you were asked to speak at a school meeting for students and parents about the future policies of your school. Make a case for including environmental awareness as a topic in your school's curriculum. (See Unit 5.2 for inspiration.)

Higher Level Exam preparation

4.5 Choose one of the two writing tasks below. Write a 450–600 word blog post and include the key features of this text type. You have one hour and 30 minutes to write this.

a *Human ingenuity*: Imagine you had to speak at an IB conference about the importance of art in learning. Convince your audience that a Group 6 subject on the arts should become a requirement for attaining the full IB Diploma. Write the opening lines or an extract from your speech. (See Unit 3.3 for inspiration.)

b *Sharing the planet*: Imagine you are a politician running for an important public office in a region where poverty is a problem. Write the opening lines or an extract from a speech in which you convince your audience to vote for you because of your awareness of poverty, and your proposed solutions. (See Unit 5.1 for inspiration.)

TIP

Here are some useful phrases that you might want to include in your speech:

- 'I stand here today to …'
- 'And so we must ask ourselves …'
- 'Others have claimed that … But …'
- 'The choice is clear: …'
- 'In order to meet these challenges, we will have to …'

TIP

If you do not feel you are ready to write a writing task under exam conditions, you might want to take more time both in and out of class time to:

- research and gather ideas
- organise these, using spider diagrams or outlines
- consider some of the language elements from the text type that you intend to write, by reading more examples of the text type
- write a smaller part of the text, such as an introduction
- draft multiple versions
- apply the assessment criteria for Paper 1
- rewrite your draft, taking your teacher's comments into consideration.

Guiding questions

- What are the defining elements of news reports?
- How should a news report be written?

Learning objectives

- Become familiar with the defining features of news reports.
- Develop skills for writing your own news reports.

Word bank

newsworthy

source

bias

weasel word

glittering generality

euphemism

dysphemism

loaded word

Journalism is an engaging and exciting profession, as it requires thorough investigation and unbiased reporting. Journalists, like IB learners, must be inquirers, constantly asking questions and showing curiosity.

For your writing task for Paper 1, you might decide to write a news article. Writing a news report does not have to be difficult. Once you are familiar with the main features of this text type, you can write a news report about anything.

Model text

5.1 News reports are written by journalists. Who are journalists? Write a list of qualities that you think a good journalist should have (for example: inquirer).

As you analyse news reports, you might find it helpful to annotate them using the 'five Ws and one H', writing 'who?', 'what?', 'when?', 'where?' 'why?' and 'how' next to the relevant words in the text. Or, as Activity 5.2 suggests, you can create a table and write the key words of the article in the appropriate boxes.

LEARNER PROFILE

Inquirer

As you list the qualities that make a good journalist (Activity 5.1), you can start with 'inquirer' from the IB's learner profile. What does it mean to be an inquirer? It means you are curious; it means you ask questions. It means that you want to figure out how the world works. In this sense, if you go through life like an investigative journalist, you will become knowledgeable and wise!

What qualities must a good journalist have?

The typical questions that any good journalist asks

5.2 As you read Text 6.9, a news report, make a note of the 'five Ws and one H' (see the 'Reading strategy' feature). Write your notes in a copy of the table below.

What has happened?	Who is involved?	When did it happen?	Where did it happen?	Why did it happen?	How did it happen?

READING STRATEGY

When reading news reports, you should look out for the 'five Ws and one H':

- *Who* is involved?
- *What* has happened?
- *When* did it happen?
- *Where* did it happen?
- *Why* did it happen?
- *How* did it happen?

Text 6.9

18-Year-Old Student From Tamil Nadu Designs World's Lightest Satellite Weighing Just 64 Grams
— **Headline**

Eighteen-year-old Rifath Sharook, belonging to a comparatively unknown town of Pallapatti in Tamil Nadu, is all set to break a global space record by launching the lightest satellite in the world, weighing a mere 64 grams.
— **Newsworthiness**

The satellite, called KalamSat, will be launched by a NASA sounding rocket on June 21 from Wallops Island, a NASA facility. This will be the first time an Indian student's experiment will be flown by NASA.

Speaking to Times of India from Pallapatti, Rifath said it will be a sub-orbital flight and post-launch, the mission span will be 240 minutes and the tiny satellite will operate for 12 minutes in a micro-gravity environment of space.
— **Source**

'The main role of the satellite will be to demonstrate the performance of 3-D printed carbon fibre,' he explained. He said the satellite was selected through a competition called 'Cubes in Space', jointly organised by NASA and a organisation called 'I Doodle Learning'.
— **Quotations**
— **Context**

The main challenge was to design an experiment to be flown to space which will fit into a four-centimetre cube weighing exactly 64 grams. 'We did a lot of research on different cube satellites all over the world and found ours was the lightest,' he said. Rifath said the satellite is made mainly of reinforced carbon fibre polymer. 'We obtained some of the components from abroad and some are indigenous,' he said.
— **Facts**

— **Photograph**

Times of India, by Srinivas Laxman

6

Key features explained

Key features	Examples from Text 6.9
Headline: Headlines grab the readers' attention and capture the essence of the news story.	'18-Year-Old Student From Tamil Nadu Designs World's Lightest Satellite Weighing Just 64 Grams'
Newsworthiness: Any good news story answers the question: 'Why should the reader care about this piece of information or event?' (See Activity 5.4)	'Rifath Sharook [...] is set to break a global space record by launching the lightest satellite in the world.'
Source: News reports draw on reliable sources in order to be credible. Otherwise it is hearsay.	'Speaking to *Times of India* Pallapatti, Rifath said...'
Quotations: It is very common to quote sources directly in news articles. This adds to the credibility.	"The main role of the satellite will be to demonstrate the performance of 3-D printed carbon fibre,' he explained.'
Context: Readers might not know the background story of the news event. Good articles briefly describe what happened before the events outlined in the report.	'He said the satellite was selected through a competition called 'Cubes in Space', jointly organised by NASA and a organisation called 'I Doodle Learning'.'
Facts: Numbers, dates, people's names, statistics and any facts add credibility to news.	'64 grams.' '21 June' '12 minutes'
Photograph: Many news articles are accompanied by a photograph that illustrates the news story.	Photograph of Sharook's small satellite

5.3 Read Text 6.10 and identify the five features of a news article as outlined above: newsworthiness, context, source, facts, and quotations. Use five different coloured highlighter pens, one for each key feature, and a photocopy of the article.

5.4 Below are several questions that help you to consider the writing style of a news article and Text 6.10. Discuss your answers with classmates and your teacher.

a Why does the headline use the present simple verb tense? '...skull painting sells for record $110.5m.'

b Why does the first line of the article use the present perfect verb tense? 'An artwork by Jean-Michel Basquiat has sold for a record $110.5m'

c Why does the author use the passive voice? 'The piece was purchased by noted Japanese collector and entrepreneur Yusaku Maezawa...'

d Why is the present simple verb tense used to describe the paining? 'The 1982 painting depicts a face in the shape of a skull.'

Use coloured highlighter pens to highlight the key features of a news article or any type of text.

e   Why does the article include information about the previous auction? 'The previous auction record for the artist was set last May when Untitled, 1982 sold for $57.3m, also to Maezawa.'

f   Why does the article end with a fact about the artist? 'Basquiat died of a drug overdose in 1988 at age 27.'

Text 6.10

Jean-Michel Basquiat skull painting sells for record $110.5m at auction

Sale in New York of painting that depicts a face in the shape of a skull sets a record price for an American artist at auction

An artwork by Jean-Michel Basquiat has sold for a record $110.5m at auction in New York.

Sotheby's said the sale of Untitled on Thursday night in Manhattan was an auction record for the artist. It also set a record price for an American artist at auction. The 1982 painting depicts a face in the shape of a skull.

The piece was purchased by noted Japanese collector and entrepreneur Yusaku Maezawa after a 10-minute bidding war. He said he plans to display the painting in his museum in Chiba, Japan, after loaning it to institutions and exhibitions around the world.

'When I saw this painting, I was struck with so much excitement and gratitude for my love of art,' said Maezawa.

The previous auction record for the artist was set last May when Untitled, 1982 sold for $57.3m, also to Maezawa.

Basquiat died of a drug overdose in 1988 at age 27.

The Guardian

5.5 Which image (A–C) would best accompany Text 6.10? Discuss why you think one image is more appropriate for this article than the others.

A   B   C

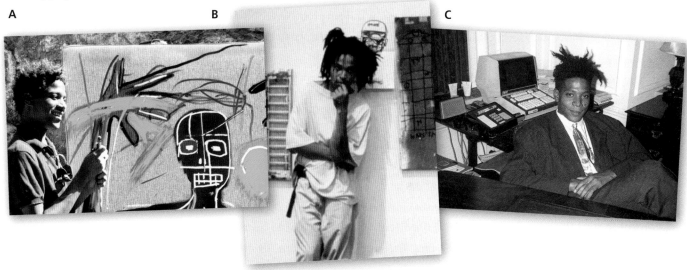

5.6 As you study news reports, you should ask yourself what makes a report or article 'newsworthy'. Newsworthiness refers to the value or interest that the story of the report may have to its audience. There are three main reasons why readers are interested in news stories:

- *Negativity:* Many people are drawn to bad news. 'If it bleeds it leads' is an expression in the media world, meaning that if the story is about something negative, it will come before (lead) all the other stories in the newspaper.

- *Relevance:* A story is newsworthy if it affects the daily lives of the audience. For example, if taxes increase, people will care, because it is relevant to their own lives.

- *Extraordinary:* If something unexpected or unique happens, it is often considered newsworthy. Even seemingly unimportant news will sometimes be published in national newspapers, for example if a little boy catches a very big fish. Newspapers sometimes include such extraordinary 'feel good' stories to counterbalance the bad news.

Here are several news headlines. For each headline, explain which aspects of newsworthiness (negativity, relevance, extraordinary) are relevant. Make a copy of the table to do this activity. An example, based on Text 6.9, has been done for you. As the source of each headline is unknown, you might speculate on their relevance to different audiences.

Heading	Negativity	Relevance	Extraordinary
a '18-Year-Old Student From Tamil Nadu Designs World's Lightest Satellite Weighing Just 64 Grams'	There is nothing negative about this story. In fact it is rather positive!	The news that a young Indian invented this satellite is relevant to the readership of the Times of India	A satellite that weighs only 64 grams is rather extraordinary. The fact that the inventor is so young and from a small village is also extraordinary.

a '18-Year-Old Student From Tamil Nadu Designs World's Lightest Satellite Weighing Just 64 Grams' (see example)

b 'Dutch King secretly piloted passenger flights for 21 years with KLM'

c '84 confirmed dead after lorry crashes into crowd during Bastille Day celebration'

d 'FCC (Federal Communications Commission) ends net neutrality, critics cry 'war on open internet''

e 'Trump denies collusion with Russia, calls investigation a 'witch hunt''

f 'Global warming opens shipping routes over North Pole'

g 'FA (Football Association) includes women on governing council'

5.7 A news report should be unbiased, which means that it does not express opinions when reporting. It does not take sides on arguments or debates. Rather it states the facts. Where, in the following headlines, do you detect **bias**? See the TOK box for tips on how to detect biased language.

a 'Tragic death of Cornell honoured by blacked-out Seattle Space Needle.'

b 'Times Square attacker almost flees scene before heroic bystander pins him down.'

c 'Assange off the hook for rape, other charges loom'

d 'US air strikes pound pro-Assad forces'

e 'May risks Brexiteers wrath by agreeing to insane Brussels payout deal'

f 'Find this thug: Erdogan's bodyguard brutally chokes peaceful, female protester'

g 'Man City topples Liverpool in bout of the year'

EXTRA

Look at three or four different newspapers that each target a different audience. Compare and contrast their way of reporting a current story or event. Alternatively, visit three different news sites to do a comparative study of a particular story.

You can find multiple versions of the same stories at newsstands

Standard Level Exam preparation

5.8 Write a 250–400 word news report based on one of the stimulus images A–C below. Although your report should be a work of fiction, use your understanding of news report writing from this unit to make your story sound as real as possible.

A

B

C

Higher Level Exam preparation

5.9 Choose one of the two writing tasks below. Write a 450–600 word news report and include the key features of this text type. For the sake of this assessment, you can make up any facts, figure or interviews to help you write this report. You have one hour and 30 minutes to write this.

a *Human ingenuity*: Write a news report on the latest piece of technology that is being used to improve human life. (See Unit 3.1 for inspiration.)

b *Sharing the planet*: Find a new piece of information about global warming and write a news report that informs the public in a nonbiased way. Use the key features of this text type. (See Unit 5.2 for inspiration.)

Literature

5.10

a Read Text 6.11, which is a news report, based on the events of the novel *The Great Gatsby* by F. Scott Fitzgerald. You do not have to know the novel to appreciate the writing style and structure.

b As you read the text, look for the key features of this text type, as outlined earlier in this unit.

c How does this text exemplify the language and structure of a typical news report?

5.11 Although you are not assessed on your understanding of your literary works through a writing task, writing about one of these works will help you understand it better.

After reading a literary work for your English B class, write a news report, like Text 6.11, which reports on the events and characters of the work. Share your news report with your classmates and teacher and discuss its merits as a news report. Make sure it demonstrates your knowledge and understanding of the literary work you are writing about.

Text 6.11

'Mystery shrouds the death of Jay Gatsby':
Businessman and socialite gunned down in his own swimming pool

NEW YORK - Police have confirmed the identity of the body found earlier today in the swimming pool of the Gatsby estate in West Egg to be that of entrepreneur and socialite Jay Gatsby. Authorities are operating on the theory that he was murdered by auto-mechanic George Wilson, whose body was found in the woods near the estate. Wilson is thought to have murdered Gatsby out of revenge before turning the same revolver on himself.

The murder-suicide comes after Myrtle Wilson, George Wilson's wife, was killed in a hit-and-run incident on the previous evening outside her husband's gas station near Flushing in the 'Valley of Ashes'. Witnesses claim that the perpetrator drove a yellow Rolls Royce.

During the investigation of the Gatsby murder, police discovered a yellow Rolls Royce with bloodstains and a broken headlight on the premises of the Gatsby estate. It is unclear, however, if Mr. Gatsby was personally involved in the hit-and-run incident, as witnesses claim to have seen a woman driving the automobile. The identity of the woman remains unknown, and the investigation is ongoing.

Jay Gatsby was last seen leaving the Plaza Hotel in Manhattan on 25 October around 7 p.m. He had rented a suite there for the afternoon. From his suite, a heated argument was heard by guests. Receptionists confirm that he left the suite with a woman in a fit of rage.

Persons with information on the murder of Mr. Gatsby and Mrs. Wilson are asked to come forward and provide local authorities with this information to assist investigations further.

Little is known about Jay Gatsby, despite the lavish parties that were hosted at his West Egg mansion. It is believed that his extravagant lifestyle was financed by a flourishing business in the illegal distribution of alcohol. One acquaintance of Gatsby's, who wishes to remain anonymous, claims to have seen Gatsby with New York crime kingpin Meyer Wolfsheim, though this cannot be confirmed.

To some, Jay Gatsby was known as an 'Oxford Man', though there is no record of him attending any college in Oxford, England. Sources within the US Army, however, confirm that he received a scholarship to attend schooling in Oxford after his valiant efforts in the Great War. Drafted into the Army, Gatsby quickly rose to the rank of Major. Rumors that Gatsby was a German spy appear to be ill-founded.

Gatsby's neighbor, Nick Carraway, had this to say about him: 'Gatsby was misunderstood by many, but he was a good man with a clear focus.' When asked what captured the focus of this aloof, though well-known man, Carraway, answered vaguely. 'His focus was on the past, and regaining what he had lost years ago. But it was in vain. He was like a boat rowing against the tide. And the world of Old Money will never give an inch to people like Jay Gatsby, people with New Money. They have to row their own boat. And for Gatsby, he simply wasn't strong enough.'

It is thought that Jay Gatsby is survived by none. Any family members or relatives are asked to make themselves known to the County of Great Neck.

An estate-sale will be organized by Nick Carraway and friend Jordan Baker on the 1st of November. Proceeds from this sale will benefit the Golf for Youth Foundation, of which Ms. Baker is the founder.

An open funeral will be held at Great Neck Memorial on October 31st at 3 p.m.

Unit 6.6
Brochure

Word bank

panel
negative space
logo
slogan
mission statement
testimonial

You will find brochures around you in your daily life. A brochure (or leaflet) is a succinct way to communicate a message, as it does not include much text.

Brochures come in many shapes and sizes. While this unit will focus on one type – the tri-fold brochure – the key features are standard for all types of brochures. These features are the tools that organisations and businesses use to persuade and inform readers about products and services.

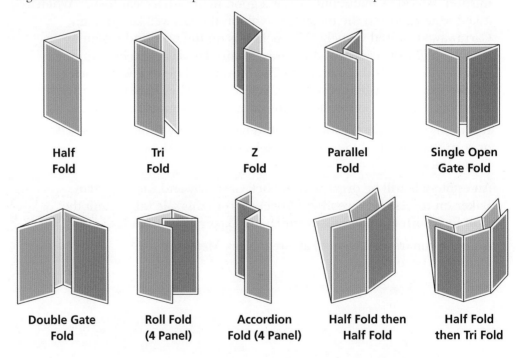

Brochures come in different shapes and sizes. The different ways in which they are folded can determine how they are read and how they are written

Model text

6.1 You are about to read a brochure for a yoga centre. Before you read Text 6.12, make a list of what you would expect to see in such a brochure. After listing your ideas, check the text to see if some or all of them are included in it.

Text 6.12

Call to action

Back panel

Slogan

Cover panel

Bullet points

Mission statement

Logo

Negative space

Contact details

Testimonials

Try a free trial session this week!

"My Thursday morning 'stress relief' session keeps me grounded, balanced and mindful."
–Myrna Olthof

"I understand myself in a very profound way now."
– Karla Tolak

Contact
Yoga Dreams
Churchillplein 6
2517JW The Hague
31 77 567- 8906
www.yogadreams.edu

Yoga Dreams
stands for

- physical vitality
- mental strength
- positivity

At Yoga Dreams we believe in the continuous development of the mind, body and soul. You too can find your way to physical vitality, mental strength and positivity through our range of yoga classes. Our teachers have the expertise and experience to help you on your personal journey.

Yoga Dreams

Find yourself

Yoga Dreams

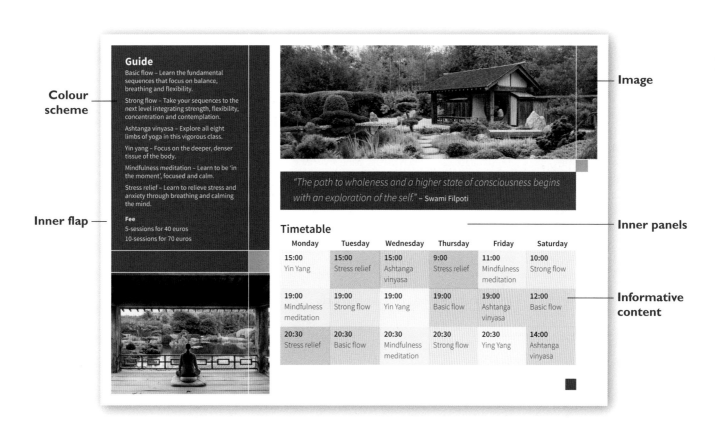

Image

Colour scheme

Inner flap

Inner panels

Informative content

Guide
Basic flow – Learn the fundamental sequences that focus on balance, breathing and flexibility.

Strong flow – Take your sequences to the next level integrating strength, flexibility, concentration and contemplation.

Ashtanga vinyasa – Explore all eight limbs of yoga in this vigorous class.

Yin yang – Focus on the deeper, denser tissue of the body.

Mindfulness meditation – Learn to be 'in the moment', focused and calm.

Stress relief – Learn to relieve stress and anxiety through breathing and calming the mind.

Fee
5-sessions for 40 euros
10-sessions for 70 euros

"The path to wholeness and a higher state of consciousness begins with an exploration of the self." – Swami Filpoti

Timetable

Monday	Tuesday	Wednesday	Thursday	Friday	Saturday
15:00 Yin Yang	**15:00** Stress relief	**15:00** Ashtanga vinyasa	**9:00** Stress relief	**11:00** Mindfulness meditation	**10:00** Strong flow
19:00 Mindfulness meditation	**19:00** Strong flow	**19:00** Yin Yang	**19:00** Basic flow	**19:00** Ashtanga vinyasa	**12:00** Basic flow
20:30 Stress relief	**20:30** Basic flow	**20:30** Mindfulness meditation	**20:30** Strong flow	**20:30** Ying Yang	**14:00** Ashtanga vinyasa

6.2 Find several brochures from places in your community. These might be brochures from a doctor's surgery, a recreation centre, church or a town hall. The brochures do not have to be in English. After collecting these brochures, bring them into class and compare them to the model brochure (Text 6.12). What similarities or differences to you see? Create a table like the one below to record your findings. Discuss these as a class.

	Similarities to Text 6.12	Differences from Text 6.12
Brochure X		
Brochure Y		
Brochure Z		

CONCEPTS

Variation

Activity 6.2 asks you to find several brochures so that you can compare and contrast their differences. A text type can be explored by considering all of its varieties. You might discover that the variations you see between texts is related to the different purposes of the brochures and the different audiences they target.

Key features explained

Key features	Examples from Text 6.12
Panels: - The tri-fold brochure is folded twice. Readers read the cover panel before opening to read the inner flap and the inside panels. - Images can stretch across panels. Writing tends to be in columns.	The mission statement appears on the inner flap. Contact details and testimonials are on the back. The timetable and image on the inner panels stretch across two columns.
Style: - Use one or two fonts. - Colour schemes should be consistent throughout the brochure. - Bullet points are common for communicating a message succinctly.	'Yoga Dreams stands for: - physical vitality - mental strength - positivity'

Negative space: In design terms, 'negative space' refers to white space or unused space. It keeps the layout uncluttered and allows the reader to focus on the main points of the brochure.	Notice the white space around the timetable and testimonials.
Logo: The company's logo should be visible on the front and back cover panels. The colour scheme of the brochure may use elements of the logo.	The Yoga Dreams logo appears on the cover panel. Its design is in tune with the philosophy of the business.
Slogan: A slogan is a catchy phrase that captures both the essence of the business and the reader's attention.	'Find yourself' helps the reader to feel they are on a 'personal journey'.
Mission statement: A mission statement articulates why the business does what it does.	'At Yoga Dreams we believe in the continuous development of the mind, body and soul.'
Informative content: Basic information that answers questions about 'what', 'where', 'when' and 'how much' should appear on the inner panels of the brochure.	'Guide' 'Fee' 'Timetable'
Testimonials: Testimonials are positive reviews of a product or service, given by customers.	'My Thursday morning 'stress relief' session keeps me grounded, balanced and mindful.'
Contact details: These usually appear on the back panel, and include the business's address, web address, e-mail and phone number.	'Contact Yoga Dreams Churchillplein 6 2517 JW The Hague'
Call to action: What should the reader *do* with the information? A call to action can be an imperative verb that tells the reader how to respond.	'Try a free trial session this week!'

TIP

Notice from the model text (Text 6.12 and Activity 6.3) that the language of brochures should be short and punchy. When writing text for a brochure remember to:

- start lines with an imperative verb (like this sentence here)
- use headings effectively (like the word 'tip' above)
- keep sentence structures simple (like these points)
- include bullet points (like these four points).

6.3 On the next page are six panels a–f from a trifold brochure. For each panel indicate:

- Where would this panel appear, physically on the brochure? In which order would they be read? Use the terminology from the model text above.
- Where do you see evidence of the key features of this text type? Identify the logo, slogan, mission statement, contact details, call to action and informative content.
- What do you think of the style and use of negative space? How effective is this in meeting the brochure's aims?

a

Why jump with Bungee Fix?

Charity bungee jumping is an excellent way of raising funds for your charity.

✓ Having raised millions for good causes and having worked with 200 charities we know what works!

✓ We can accommodate from 1 to 240 jumpers for weekend events.

✓ We can provide you with your own event or just send sponsored jumpers along on to our selected locations on our scheduled dates.

b

How to organise your Charity Bungee Jump

✓ Choose your charity. Get in touch with your chosen charity in the first instance. Check they are happy for you to hold the event.

✓ Contact your chosen charity. Ask your charity for a fundraising pack and sponsorship forms.

✓ Book your jump. Choose your jump location and book and pay for your Bungee Jump via our website.

✓ Confirm the details. Upon receipt of your booking you will be sent the date and time of your jump, with instructions.

✓ Start collecting your sponsorship money

✓ Complete your jump

✓ Collect all of your sponsorship money and send it to your charity.

> If you would like more information about organising your charity bungee jump with Bungee Fix, please contact us.

c

Benefits of Charity Bungee Jumping with Bungee Fix

✓ No limits to the amount of money you can raise.

✓ We can accommodate individual jumpers or groups.

✓ A safe and professional organisation that you can trust.

✓ Support from experienced and qualified staff.

✓ Online booking facility.

✓ Venues throughout the country, including bridge bungee and indoor bungee jumps.

✓ Wide choice of dates and locations.

d

Bungee Jumping for Charity with **Bungee Fix**

Information for fundraisers

e

Some comments from charity fundraisers:

'Jumping with Bungee Fix was awesome! We had a great day, and our charity were delighted with how much we raised for them!'

'Thank you to everyone at Bungee Fix for all your help to make it such a great day! We loved it!'

'A thrilling jump and helping our favourite charity too! What more could we ask? Thanks Bungee Fix !'

For further information on charity fundraising, please contact us.

bungeefix@fastmail.com

f

There are two ways you can raise funds for your charity:

✓ **Fundraiser pays**
The cost of the jump is paid for upfront by you the fundraiser, with all sponsorship money raised going directly to the charity – so you can raise more money for your charity!

✓ **Jump free**
The cost of the jump is taken from your sponsorship money – it won't cost you a thing to complete your charity bungee jump!

6.4 Text 6.12 includes a mission statement. Mission statements can be fun to write. Below are several mission statements a–h from well-known global brands. In the box below are the names of these brands. Match each mission to its corresponding brand.

Toyota	Chanel	Nike	Ikea	Facebook	Amazon
	Starbucks	Coca-Cola		Chanel	

a   To refresh the world in mind, body and spirit. To inspire moments of optimism and happiness through our brands and actions. To create value and make a difference.

b   To give people the power to share and make the world more open and connected.

c   To create a better everyday life for the many people.

d   To be the Ultimate House of Luxury, defining style and creating desire, now and forever.

e   It's our goal to be Earth's most customer-centric company, where customers can find and discover anything they might want to buy online.

f   To bring inspiration and innovation to every athlete★ in the world. ★If you have a body, you are an athlete.

g   To inspire and nurture the human spirit – one person, one cup and one neighborhood at a time.

h   To lead the way to the future of mobility, enriching lives around the world with the safest and most responsible ways of moving people.

Standard Level Exam preparation

6.5   Choose one of the two writing tasks below. Write a 250–400 word brochure and include the key features of this text type. You have one hour and 15 minutes to do this.

a   *Experiences*: You are organising a trip abroad which offers students an opportunity to learn a language, experience a culture and discover the history of a country. Write a brochure that persuades students to come on this trip. You can make up some information, but write about a real country. (See Unit 2.1 for inspiration.)

b   *Sharing the planet*: You are organising a recycling day at your school, in which you invite students and parents to bring old electric goods, textiles, books and toys. You have arranged for the local municipality to collect the items and give information on the value of reusing and recycling. Write a brochure that informs your school members and persuades them to participate. (See Unit 5.3 for inspiration.)

Higher Level Exam preparation

6.6   Choose one of the two writing tasks below. Write a 450–600 word brochure and include the key features of this text type. You have one hour and 30 minutes to do this.

a   *Experiences*: Imagine you operate an outdoor adventure school, where you organise team-building activities, camps, retreats and more. Write a brochure that encourages people to come to your school. (See Unit 2.2 for inspiration.)

b   *Human ingenuity*: Imagine you are organising an art exhibition in a gallery. Write a brochure that encourages art-lovers to come to the exhibition. You can make up information about the exhibition, the artist and the museum. Or you can write about an existing exhibition that you have seen.

TIP

Not all brochures include mission statements, but you might find them useful to include. Notice that they start with infinitive verbs 'To give ...' or 'To create ...' This is because businesses and organisations aim to do these things. You can start with an infinitive verb or the phrases: 'Our aim is to ...' or 'Our mission is to ...'

ATL

Thinking

Before you write your own brochure (Activities 6.5–6.6), brainstorm the kind of information and text that you would include, using a mind map. Extending out from your core topic, write 'Why', 'What', 'Who', 'When' 'Where' and 'How'. Answering questions that start with these words will help you generate ideas.

Unit 6.7
Guidelines

Word bank

instructions

policy

rationale

obligation

consequences

code of conduct

ATL

Thinking skills

Activity 7.1 asks you to compare different types of texts. When asked to compare or contrast, it might be helpful to record your thoughts using graphic organisers. Venn diagrams are particularly useful for brainstorming or making your ideas visible. Using the Venn diagram on the right, you can write the qualities that the text types share in the area where the circles overlap. You can write their unique qualities in the parts that do not overlap. Use this technique for recording differences and similarities.

We read guidelines, instructions and policy documents daily in different contexts – at bus stops, stores or at school. In Assessment 1/Paper 1, you may be asked to write a set of guidelines. In this unit you will do several exercises that prepare you for guideline writing.

7.1 First of all, it is important to define the term 'guidelines'. How are guidelines different from or similar to the following text types? Discuss these similarities and differences as a class.

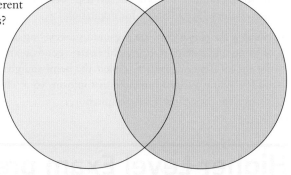

a **instructions**

b tips

c rules

d **policy** statements

e handbooks

7.2 Which of the sentences below do you think were taken from guidelines? What use of language indicates that these sentences belong to guideline writing? For the sentences that do not belong to guidelines, from which other text types do you think they were they taken?

a At the Blane Company, we have a commitment to quality jewellery.

b Jewellery should be worn in good taste, with limited visible body piercing.

c Cream blush is particularly suited for dry skin because of its rich, moisturising ingredients.

d Jelly shoes are so 1980.

e Her earrings did a dance that made my hips swing.

f A professional appearance is encouraged and excessive make-up is unprofessional.

g She was the only one I knew who could match blue eyes with green eyeliner.

h Flip-flops, Hawaiian slippers, and any casual shoe with an open toe are not acceptable.

7.3 As you read Text 6.13, make a list of sentences from the text that are used to give orders. Underline the verbs in these sentences, as in the example below. Do you notice any patterns?

List of 'telling someone what to do' verbs:

• Clothing <u>should</u> be pressed and never wrinkled.

Text 6.13

POLICY ON DRESS CODE

Valid for all employees

The Company's objective in establishing a formal dress code is to enable our employees to project the professional image that is in keeping with the needs of our clients and customers to trust us. Because our industry requires the appearance of trusted business professionals and we serve clients at our site on a daily basis, a formal dress code is necessary for our employees. You must project the image of a trustworthy, knowledgeable business professional for the clients who seek our guidance, input, and professional services.

Rationale

Formal Dress Code Guidelines

Headings

In a formal business environment, the standard of dressing for men is a smart trouser with shirt that has the company logo or a suit if the occasion demands and for women, a dress that has the company logo paired with appropriate accessories. In our work environment, clothing should be pressed and never wrinkled.

Obligation verbs

Dress Down Days

Passive verb tense

Saturday is declared as a dress down day. On these days, business casual clothing, although never clothing potentially offensive to others, is allowed. Clothing that has the company logo is encouraged. Clothing that reveals your back, your chest, your feet, your stomach or your underwear is not appropriate for a place of business. Torn, dirty, or frayed clothing is unacceptable. All seams must be finished. Any clothing that has words, terms, or pictures that may be offensive to other employees is unacceptable.

Formal Business Attire Recommendations

This is an overview of appropriate formal business attire. The lists tell you what is generally acceptable as formal business attire and what is generally not acceptable as formal business attire.

Shoes and Footwear

Conservative walking shoes, dress shoes, Oxfords, loafers, boots, flats, dress heels, and backless shoes are acceptable for work. Not wearing stockings or socks is inappropriate. Athletic shoes, tennis shoes, thongs, flip-flops, Hawaiian slippers, and any casual shoe with an open toe are not acceptable in the office.

Accessories and Jewellery

Tasteful, professional ties, scarves, belts, and jewellery are encouraged. Jewellery should be worn in good taste, with limited visible body piercing.

Makeup, Perfume, and Cologne

Avoid pronouns

A professional appearance is encouraged and excessive makeup is unprofessional. Remember that some employees are allergic to the chemicals in perfumes and makeup, so wear these substances with restraint.

Hats and Head Covering

Present tense

Hats are not appropriate in the office. Head covers that are required for religious purposes or to honour cultural tradition are allowed.

Conclusion

Consequences

If an employee fails to meet these standards, as determined by the employee's supervisor and Human Resources staff, the employee will be asked not to wear the inappropriate item to work again. If the problem persists, the employee may be sent home to change clothes and will receive a verbal warning for the first offense. All other policies about personal time use will apply. Progressive disciplinary action will be applied if dress code violations continue.

AKS Group website

TEXT AND CONTEXT
- The AKS Group, among many activities, sells real estate in central India.
- 'Trousers' (paragraph 2) are sometimes referred to as 'a trouser' in India.
- Oxfords (paragraph 5) are formal shoes with laces. Loafers (also for men) and flats (for women) do not have laces.

Key features explained

Key features	Examples from Text 6.13
Rationale: The opening paragraph of a set of guidelines usually explains why they are needed and how they relate to a wider philosophy.	'Because our industry requires the appearance of trusted business professionals and we serve clients at our site on a daily basis, a formal dress code is necessary for our employees.'
Passive and 'obligation' verbs: Guidelines should tell someone what to do, but in a polite way, and without sounding too forceful.	'Saturday is declared…' 'Clothing should be pressed.'
Headings: Guidelines should not take long to read. Headings, numbered points and short sentences help make the text clear and easy to understand.	'Formal Business Attire Recommendations'
Avoid pronouns: • 'I', 'we' or 'you' are not generally used in policy documents such as guidelines. • The use of 'he', 'she' and 'they' is rare. Instead it is common to write about things, roles and abstractions.	'A <u>professional appearance</u> is encouraged.' '<u>Saturday</u> is declared…' '<u>Not wearing stockings</u> is considered inappropriate.'
Present tense: Notice that guidelines are written in the present tense.	'Hats are not appropriate in the office.'
Consequences: • Guidelines may read like rules. 'If X does not happen, Y will.' • Consequences are usually communicated without sounding confrontational. Guidelines focus more on the *action* than the person.	'If an employee fails to meet these standards, the employee will be asked not to wear the inappropriate item to work again.'

7.4 While it is not recommended to use pronouns in guidelines, there are a few examples in Text 6.13 where these are used. Can you find them? Comment on the use of each pronoun and why it might or might not be appropriate for this type of text.

7.5 How do you kindly but firmly tell someone what to do? You are about to read a school policy statement (Text 6.14), in which students are told to wear uniforms. Some of the words have been left out. These words all relate to rules and obligations. For each of the gaps 1–8, decide which one of the four words or phrases *does not* fit into the context of the sentences. You may need to look up the definitions of words or phrases that you are not familiar with.

1	a	being a part of	2	a	starting point	3	a	needed	4	a	adhere to
	c	contributing to		b	corner stone		b	desired		b	violate
	b	belonging to		c	advantage		c	required		c	break
	d	following		d	prerequisite		d	necessary		d	infringe

5	a	maintain	6	a	permitted	7	a	dealt with	8	a	discharging
	b	uphold		b	allowed		b	admonished		b	removal of
	c	enact		c	all right		c	reprimanded		c	confiscating
	d	reinforce		d	tolerated		d	taken care of		d	taking away

Text 6.14

School Uniform Policy Statement

Vision Statement

'We expect all our pupils to wear a reasonable standard of dress, appropriate to the school situation.'

Aims

- School uniform enhances the appearance of the pupils and helps us create a business-like, purposeful atmosphere.

- School uniform assists us in our efforts to create a cohesive, corporate identity amongst our pupils - the idea of (1) … a positive, caring organisation.

- School dress is considerably cheaper than most 'fashion' garments currently available, and this helps to counteract the effects of hardship on those pupils whose parents are experiencing financial problems.

Guidelines

- Attached is the official uniform agreed by the Governors of the School in February 2002 for new pupils after August 2002.

- Parental support for school uniform is an essential (2) … for this policy, and they are informed each year of the details of specific items of uniform (3) … .

- Where specific pupils are suffering hardship, financial assistance is available at the discretion of the Headteacher in complete confidence.

- Pupils, who (4) … the code of dress agreed for the school, will be dealt with by procedures appropriate for the situation.

Procedures Concerning School Uniform

- All staff should read the policy on School Uniform and the sheets outlining details of the items required.

- Form tutors should regularly remind pupils of the code of dress agreed in the school policy, which should be displayed in every room.

- All staff, wherever they are in the school, will be expected to (5) … the school's policy on uniform.

- Unauthorised jewellery should not be brought into school.

- Make-up is not necessary in a school situation, though Year 10 and Year 11 girls may wear discreet make-up.

- Outdoor coats may be worn between lessons, but must not be worn in classrooms during lessons, or in the dining room whilst eating. Hooded sweatshirts and non-school sweatshirts are not (6) … in school.

- All pupils must change back into their school uniform after P.E. lessons, and should not be permitted to join other lessons or go home in their PE. kit.

- Pupils, who infringe the School Code of Dress on subsequent occasions should be (7) … as appropriate:

- further admonition - recording the incident.

- (8) … items until the end of the day.

- providing a tie or other item where appropriate.

- sending pupils home to get uniform, safeguards having been made (only by Head of Year).

- withdrawal from normal timetabled lessons in short term until matter is resolved.

- letter to parents.

- parental meeting.

7.6 As you read Text 6.14, you might have noticed that many sentences are in the passive form. Passive phrases involve the verb 'to be' and the past participle of another verb. For example:

Passive	Active
'The house was built (by me).'	'I built the house.'

Notice that passive phrases do not require an agent. In 'The house was built', the addition of 'by me' is not necessary. Passive phrases are very typical of policy documents. Take the active sentences below and make them passive by removing the agent. The first has been done for you as an example.

a Pupils may wear outdoor coats between lessons. (Active, 'pupils' = the agent)
Outdoor coats may be worn between lessons. (Passive, no agent)

b Guests may not hold the restaurant responsible for any lost items.

c Golfers must wear their caps with the peaks facing forward.

d Passengers must keep their arms and legs inside the vehicle at all times.

e We will remove any bicycles that are parked outside the designated area.

f Dogs must wear a leash at all times.

g Please remove your antenna before going through the carwash.

Many public signs like this one use the passive voice

7.7 Based on your understanding of Texts 6.13 and 6.14, write a set of guidelines that could accompany the image below. Assume there is a school philosophy or **code of conduct** to support your guidelines.

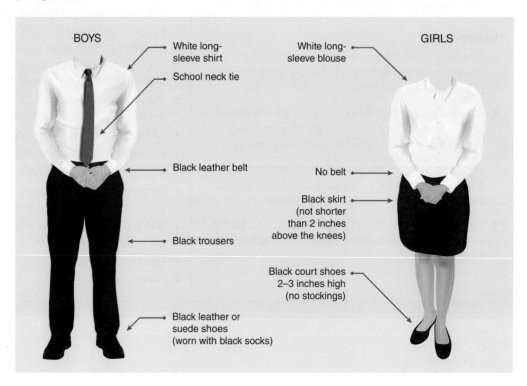

Standard Level Exam preparation

7.8 Choose one of the two writing tasks below. Write a 250–400 word set of guidelines and include the key features of this text type. You have one hour and 15 minutes to write this.

a *Human ingenuity*: Imagine your school is writing its policy on lab work and animal testing. Write a set of guidelines that encourages safe and ethical practice in the lab.

b *Social organisation*: Imagine you have been asked to write a set of guidelines on the use of mobile devices at school. Readers will want to know when and where it is appropriate to use devices and what consequences there will be for misuse. Write this set of guidelines so that parents, staff and students understand your school's expectations.

Higher Level Exam preparation

7.9 Choose one of the two writing tasks below. Write a 450–600 word set of guidelines and include the key features of this text type. You have one hour and 30 minutes to write this.

a *Social organisation*: Imagine you are rewriting your school's language policy. This policy explains the reasons for offering various languages as part of the school curriculum. It comments on the role of each language in different contexts and for different purposes in and around the school campus. Write this set of guidelines so that parents, staff and students can easily understand your school's expectations.

b *Sharing the planet*: Imagine your school is writing a new policy document on its recycling practices. What should be done? Write a set of guidelines that tell students and staff how and where to recycle and reuse items at school. (See Unit 5.2 for inspiration.)

CONCEPTS

Context

For Paper 1 you will be asked to complete a writing task. Before you write your response to the task, it is helpful to consider the context in which your text would appear. Your language should be appropriate to the situation for which you are communicating. In Activities 7.8 and 7.9, you are asked to write about the context of your own school. Using what you know from real life can help you make up a fictional text.

Unit 6.8
Official report

Guiding questions	Learning objectives
• What does an official report look like? • How should you write a report?	• Become familiar with the stylistic and structural conventions of reports. • Develop the skills to write your own official report.

Word bank

data

sponsor

abstract

methodology

survey

synthesis

findings

labelling

caption

appendix

In your studies, you may be asked to report on findings from an experiment you have carried out. For a school presentation, you may have to summarise and interpret facts or data that you have researched. While preparing your extended essay, you are likely to come across reports. Learning more about official reports is therefore likely to be useful to you both at school, in your future studies and in the world of work.

In this unit, you will do several activities to help you to understand this type of text. An extract from a report has been included for you to explore.

8.1 Read Text 6.15 and then answer the following questions about it. These will help you understand what is meant by an 'official report'. You may answer the questions with 'yes', 'no' or even 'possibly'. Give reasons to support your answers.

a   Should a report express an opinion?

b   Should a report be newsworthy?

c   Should a report tell a story?

d   Should a report summarise data?

e   Should a report use a lot of adjectives?

e   Should a report compare and contrast?

f   Should a report make interpretations of **data**?

g   Should a report use the first or second person, 'I' or 'you'?

8.2 Look at the list of report types below. Are there any structural and stylistic features that they might all have in common? What might these be? List them together as a class.

a   A lab report

b   A book review

c   A progress report

d   A police report

e   A weather report

f   A financial report

g   A yearly report

8.3 Read and scan Text 6.15. Look for the stylistic and structural features of report that you listed in Activity 8.2.

Text 6.15

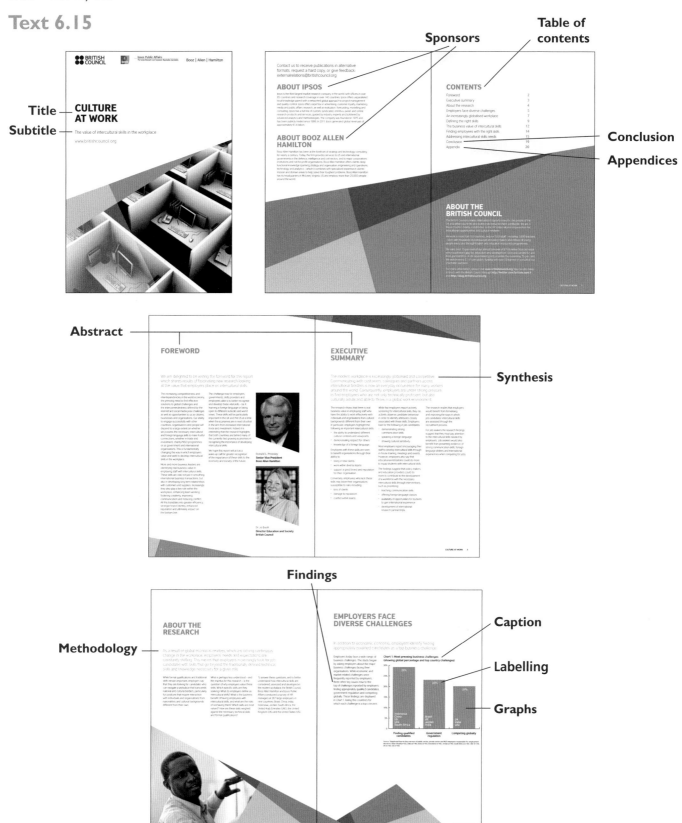

6

Key features explained

Key features	Examples from Text 6.15
Title and subtitle: Every report needs a title and subtitle. Simple/ 'boring' titles are fine, as they often cover the scope of the report best.	'Culture at Work: The value of intercultural skills at the workplace'
Sponsors: Who has commissioned the report? Readers will want to know who is responsible for funding and carrying out the research.	'Ipsos is the third largest market research company in the world...' 'Booz Allen Hamilton has been at the forefront of strategy and technology consulting for nearly a century.'
Table of contents: A table of contents is necessary for readers who wish to quickly scan the report.	List of contents Foreword (2) Executive summary (3) etc.
Conclusion: Good conclusions reiterate previous points. In some reports it is appropriate to suggest areas for further study.	'This research suggests that there is significant opportunity for employers, policy makers and education providers to work together to strengthen the development of intercultural skills to meet the needs of an increasingly global workforce.'
Appendices: An appendix is an addition to a report, and it may include raw data, survey questions, articles, or primary sources.	While the appendix of Text 6.15 is not shown here, this includes an overview of the number of participants surveyed in each country.
Abstract: The abstract summarises the key findings of the research and it describes the context in which the research was conducted.	The 'foreword' and 'executive summary' act as an 'abstract' in Text 6.15 'The modern workplace is increasingly globalised and competitive.' 'For job seekers the research findings suggest that they must pay attention to the intercultural skills needed by employers.'
Synthesis: Synthesis is act of processing multiple sources and basing claims on them.	The first paragraph of each page of this report is in a blue font. These paragraphs offer a synthesis of the ideas for quick reading.
Methodology: Readers of reports want to know how research was conducted. A section on the methodology comes toward the beginning of the report.	'To answer these questions, [...] Ipsos PublicAffairs conducted a **survey** of HR managers at 367 large employers in nine countries.'
Findings: Research aims to acquire results and report on its findings. The term 'findings' is broad and includes both the data or evidence that have been gathered and the conclusions that are based on them.	' of challenges reported by employers: finding appropriately qualified candidates, government regulation and competing globally.'

Labelling and captions: These are useful for in-text referencing and an easier reading experience. Readers should be able to understand what they are looking at.	'Chart 1: Most pressing business challenges (showing global percentage and top country challenges)'
Graphs, charts, tables, diagrams or figures: Readers like visual representations of data. Graphs, tables, diagrams and figures allow readers to reach conclusions more easily.	See 'Chart 1' in Text 6.15

8.4 Below are some detailed extracts from Text 6.15. For each extract, state which 'key features' are relevant. You might find that multiple terms are relevant for each statement.

a 'This survey was conducted with large private, public and NGO/charity sector employers in Brazil, China, India, Indonesia, Jordan, South Africa, the UAE, the UK and the US. In total, 198 private sector, 86 public sector and 83 NGO/charity sector employers took part.'

b 'More and more business leaders are identifying real business value in employing staff with intercultural skills.'

c 'Organisations in India, Jordan and Indonesia have the highest levels of interaction with business partners and suppliers overseas.'

d 'The research implies that employers would benefit from formalizing and improving the ways in which job candidates' intercultural skills are assessed through the recruitment process.'

e 'Chart 11: Percentage of employers that encourage the development of intercultural skills (by country, ranked by 'great deal')'

f 'Education has a role to play in providing students with opportunities to develop intercultural skills.'

g 'The British Council creates international opportunities for the people of the UK and other countries and builds trust between them worldwide.'

Standard Level Exam preparation

The following activity is similar to one that you could find on Paper 2.

8.5 Read Text 6.16. State whether each statement is true, false or unknown. Justify your answers with evidence from the text.

a The Earth's climate changed, as a result of the planet getting closer to and further from the sun.

b Scientists are absolutely certain that global warming is caused by human activity.

c The pace of global warming today is comparable to that of previous decades and millennia.

d Scientists have known about the effects of greenhouse gasses for over 150 years.

e Scientists have been documenting climate change for hundreds of years.

f There is evidence to suggest that planet Earth will be able to heal itself in the future as it has done in the past.

Extended Essay
You will notice that much of this unit is relevant to your extended essay writing, especially if you are writing an investigative essay in a science subject. While official reports are different from extended essays, they have similar structures. In fact some terms, such as 'methodology' and 'findings' may also be used in your essay.

TOK
Reports are characteristic of the natural sciences, which is considered an Area of Knowledge in your TOK course. Knowledge is acquired in the sciences through the scientific method – a process of hypothesising, experimenting, observing, analysing and reporting. Before you trust the findings of a report, ask yourself if the methods used are reliable and repeatable.

Text 6.16

The Earth's climate has changed throughout history. Just in the last 650,000 years there have been seven cycles of glacial advance and retreat, with the abrupt end of the last ice age about 7,000 years ago marking the beginning of the modern climate era, and of human civilisation. Most of these climate changes are attributed to very small variations in Earth's orbit that change the amount of solar energy our planet receives.

The current warming trend is of particular significance because most of it is extremely likely (greater than 95 percent probability) to be the result of human activity since the mid-20th century and proceeding at a rate that is unprecedented over decades to millennia.

Earth-orbiting satellites and other technological advances have enabled scientists to see the big picture, collecting many different types of information about our planet and its climate on a global scale. This body of data, collected over many years, reveals the signals of a changing climate.

The heat-trapping nature of carbon dioxide and other gases was demonstrated in the mid-19th century. Their ability to affect the transfer of infrared energy through the atmosphere is the scientific basis of many instruments flown by NASA. There is no question that increased levels of greenhouse gases must cause the Earth to warm in response.

Ice cores drawn from Greenland, Antarctica, and tropical mountain glaciers show that the Earth's climate responds to changes in greenhouse gas levels. Ancient evidence can also be found in tree rings, ocean sediments, coral reefs, and layers of sedimentary rocks. This ancient, or paleoclimate, evidence reveals that current warming is occurring roughly ten times faster than the average rate of ice-age-recovery warming.

www.climate.nasa.gov

Higher Level Exam preparation

8.6

a   Why has Text 6.17 included a quotation from John F. Kennedy?

b   Whom does this report target?

c   Why has this report been commissioned?

d   How does the report define two types of millennials?

e   How has an uncertain future affected millennials' behavior toward work?

f   What kinds of expectations do millennials have of their employers?

8.7 Complete the following table, about phrases from Text 6.17.

In the phrase...		the word...	refers to...
a	'For businesses seeking to attract, develop, and retain millennial talent, this report offers a guide to their concerns and motivations.'	'their'	....

b	'It reinforces the connection made between purpose and retention while outlining how increased use of exible working arrangements and automation are likely to impact millennials' attitudes and performance.'	'It'	....
c – d	'Business is viewed positively and to be behaving in an increasingly responsible manner; but, millennials believe <u>it</u> is not fully realizing <u>its</u> potential to alleviate society's biggest challenges.'	'it' 'its'	....
e	'For some, it encourages creative thinking and provides opportunities to develop new skills.'	'it'	....

Text 6.17
The 2017 Deloitte Millennial Survey
Apprehensive millennials: seeking stability and opportunities in an uncertain world.

Introduction

'The future promise of any nation can be directly measured by the present prospects of its youth.' John F. Kennedy

Deloitte's latest millennials study looks at their world view and finds many, especially in developed economies, are anxious about their future. They are concerned about a world that presents numerous threats and question their personal prospects. By JFK's measure, at least, many millennials are not sure they can trust the promises of their respective countries. However, there are strong reasons for optimism. And, as our millennials series has consistently found, the activities of businesses and the opportunities provided to their workforces represent a platform for positive change.

For businesses seeking to attract, develop, and retain millennial talent, this report offers a guide to their concerns and motivations. It reinforces the connection made between purpose and retention while outlining how increased use of flexible working arrangements and automation are likely to impact millennials' attitudes and performance. Key findings include:

- Millennials in developed countries feel pessimistic, while optimism reigns in emerging markets. There are distinct differences as to what concerns millennials in each group.

- In the current environment, millennials appear more loyal to employers than a year ago. In a period of great uncertainty, stability is appealing and they would be inclined to turn down offers for freelance work or as consultants.

- Business is viewed positively and to be behaving in an increasingly responsible manner; but, millennials believe it is not fully realizing its potential to alleviate society's biggest challenges.

- Businesses frequently provide opportunities for millennials to engage with 'good causes,' helping young professionals to feel empowered while reinforcing positive associations between businesses' activities and social impact.

- Built upon a solid, two-way exchange of trust, flexible working continues to encourage loyalty and make a significant contribution to business performance.

- Automation is rapidly becoming a feature of working environments. For some, it encourages creative thinking and provides opportunities to develop new skills. For others, automation poses a threat to jobs and is creating sterile workplaces.

Research scope

Figure 1.

EMERGING MARKETS	DEVELOPED MARKETS
Interviews achieved: 4,000	Interviews achieved: 3,900
Argentina | 300	Australia | 300
Brazil | 300	Belgium | 200
Chile | 300	Canada | 300
China | 300	France | 300
Colombia | 300	Germany | 300
India | 300	Ireland | 200
Indonesia | 300	Italy | 300
Mexico | 300	Japan | 300
Malaysia, Thailand and	South Korea | 300
Singapore (MTS) | 300	Spain | 300
Peru | 200	Switzerland | 200
Russia | 300	The Netherlands | 300
South Africa | 200	UK | 300
The Philippines | 300	US | 300
Turkey | 300	

Total number of interviews: 7,900

3   The 2017 Deloitte Millennial Survey

Unit 6.9
Essays

Guiding questions	Learning objectives
• What makes a good essay?	• Learn the features and characteristics of a good essay. • Develop the skills to become a better essay writer.

Word bank

deductive reasoning

hook

topic

thesis statement

topic sentence

evidence

explanation

conclusion

Throughout your IB Diploma Programme you will be writing essays. Your Paper 1 exam for English B might ask you to write an essay. Your Language A course will require you to write essays. There is the Extended Essay, a core requirement for your Diploma. Beyond the world of learning, essay writing is a useful life skill. Essays are a very concise and coherent way of presenting an argument and persuading readers.

In this unit you will learn to identify the key features and skills for writing effective and successful essays. Essay writing, like any skill, requires practice. It is recommended that you give yourself the opportunity to practice essay writing in class whenever you can. It is also useful to have a critical reader, like a teacher or classmate, who can give you feedback on your essay writing skills.

Model text

9.1 How have you been taught to write essays? As a class, discuss what you know about good essay writing.

• What are some of the key features that you would expect to see in a good essay?

• What structure should a good essay follow?

Record your class' answers to these questions. After reading Text 6.18, assess how well this text fits your class' definition of good essay writing. Discuss any differences you have identified.

9.2 Before you read the model essay (Text 6.18), you should know that it is about 'affirmative action'. This is a policy of favouring members of a disadvantaged social group who have suffered from discrimination within a culture. The type of affirmative action explored in Text 6.18 relates to university admissions in the United States and how universities give scholarships to ethnic minorities. Do you think this is a fair and just policy? Before you read Text 6.18, answer this question using a copy of the table below.

Affirmative action and university admission	
Before reading Text 6.18, I think …	After reading Text 6.18, I think …

Text 6.18

Affirmative action: Racist by nature

Abigail Fisher, making her case at the Supreme Court in 2015 again, after it had upheld University of Texas' decision to enforce affirmative action policies for admission in 2013.

Hook — In view of our nation's tragic history of segregation and discrimination, law makers realised that action was necessary to correct the many wrongs done to blacks and other minorities during this period. **Topic** — Their solution, called "affirmative action," includes giving minority citizens preferential treatment for college admission and scholarship purposes. At the time, this reverse-discrimination was exactly what the nation needed, and it served as an apology to those citizens whose lives were hurt by prior **Thesis statement** — policies. However, the continuance of affirmative action into modern society has become more of a plague than a benefit. Abigail Fisher v. University of Texas, a new discrimination case against UT, is going to the Supreme Court, and for the good **Thesis statement** — of Fisher, the University and the nation, the court should take Fisher's side and abolish affirmative action in college admissions once and for all.

Topic sentence — The biggest problem with affirmative action is simple. Using discrimination to combat discrimination encourages racial hatred in our **Evidence** — society. By being discriminated against, whites and Asian-Americans might feel resentment toward those races that have been selected as the most elite of the disadvantaged. In turn, African-Americans and Hispanics could feel inferior because the government is essentially telling them that – for no reason other than the color of their skin – they need special assistance to put them on par with their peers.

Ideally, we would like to reach a state where society does not judge its members based on the color of their skin but rather on the content of their character, as Martin Luther King Jr. said. If he could only see how his speeches are being interpreted and where the direction of racial equality is going in our nation today, he would surely be rolling in his grave. Reversing the direction of inequality **Explanation** does not bring anyone closer to equality.

Perhaps what is most foolish about affirmative action is that it doesn't even directly target the problem it is trying to solve. It makes the assumption that since blacks and Hispanics are typically more economically disadvantaged than whites and Asians, blacks and Hispanics should be given extra support. However, it would seem to make monumentally more sense to give the economically disadvantaged more support, regardless of race. For example, who needs a scholarship more: a black child from a family of doctors and lawyers or a white child living in a slum with a single parent working as a janitor? Financial data does a much better job of predicting financial need than does the color of one's skin. If scholarships and admission procedures aim to help the disadvantaged, they should target the disadvantaged. It makes no sense to simply target a race and assume that race will be disadvantaged.

Supporters of affirmative action point to the racial gap in socioeconomic equality. While they point to valid statistics, they have somehow come to flawed conclusions in their goal to help level the playing field. It is true that blacks and Hispanics represent the impoverished at higher rates than the general population, but by taking a socioeconomic approach to the problem, the government does not have to use racist policies to fix it.

Good arguments can be made for factoring financial need into scholarships. And while more of a stretch, factoring socioeconomic position into college admission criteria could have positive benefits. However, race has no place in either criterion. Though this may seem to be a complicated issue, it all boils down to a **Conclusion** single underlying question: Should it be legal to discriminate against people based on the color of their skin? Answer that, and you've answered whether we should continue affirmative action.

Daily Texan

TOK

Text 6.18, like any good essay, uses language to persuade the reader to think differently. Persuasive language usually takes the form of arguments. Good arguments are built on two or more premises before drawing conclusions. For example:

- Premise 1: all forms of discrimination are bad (general).
- Premise 2: affirmative action is a form of discrimination (general).
- Conclusion: therefore the affirmative action policy against Abigail Fisher is wrong (specific).

This form of reasoning, where we go from general premises to a specific conclusion, is known as **deductive reasoning**. Study any persuasive text found in this coursebook or elsewhere and write out the premises and conclusion. This will help you to understand how arguments are constructed.

TEXT AND CONTEXT

- Abigail Fisher applied to the University of Texas (UT) at Austin, USA, in 2008 and was not accepted. Other students with test scores lower than hers, who were not white, were accepted.

- At the time, The University of Texas at Austin accepted the top 10 per cent of high school graduates regardless of race. She did not fall into this bracket, however.

- In 2013 and 2016, The Supreme Court, which is the highest court in the USA, upheld UT's affirmative action policies as constitutional.

- To 'level the playing field' means that everyone is given an equal opportunity to participate, regardless of race, gender or sexual orientation.

Key features explained

Key features	Examples from Text 6.16
Hook: Good essays usually start with a generally accepted truth or interesting question; something to grab the reader's attention.	'In view of our nation's tragic history of segregation and discrimination, lawmakers realised that action was necessary...'.
Topic: What topic will the essay explore. This needs to be introduced and defined in the introduction.	'Affirmative action' includes giving minority citizens preferential treatment for college admission and scholarship purposes.
Thesis statement: This is the main argument or message, which is introduced at the end of the introduction.	'The continuance of affirmative action into modern society has become more of a plague than a benefit.' '...the court should [...] abolish affirmative action in college admissions once and for all.'
Topic sentence: This indicates what the paragraph will be about. It makes a claim that connects to the thesis.	'The biggest problem with affirmative action is simple. Using discrimination to combat discrimination encourages racial hatred in our society.'
Evidence: This is used to prove the point of the topic sentence and thesis statement.	'By being discriminated against, whites and Asian-Americans may feel resentment toward those races that have been selected as the most elite of the disadvantaged.'
Explanation: How does the evidence prove the point? Explanation, evaluation and analysis.	'Reversing the direction of inequality does not bring anyone closer to equality.'
Conclusion: This should echo the thesis statement and restate the main arguments.	'...it all boils down to a single underlying question: Should it be legal to discriminate against people based on the color of their skin? Answer that, and you've answered whether we should continue affirmative action.'

9.3 Revisit your answers to Activities 9.1 and 9.2.

a   Think about your answers to Activity 9.1. Consider how Text 6.18 was typical or atypical of the essays that you have been taught to write.

b   Complete Activity 9.2. How far has the essay changed your opinion on affirmative action, if at all?

Discuss your answers with the rest of the class.

9.4 As you can see from the table of key features, essays use different kinds of sentences, including questions, explanations and quotations. For the following activity you will use three kinds of sentences:

1   *Points*: these sentences state your argument clearly. They make claims. Topic sentences are points.

2   *Evidence*: these sentences provide evidence, examples or quotes to support the claims. They usually include words and phrases such as 'for example', 'to illustrate' or 'such as'.

3   *Explanations*: these sentences connect the illustrations to the points, explaining why they are relevant to the reader. They usually include words and phrases such as 'if x, then y', 'therefore', 'on account of' or 'because'.

Think of these sentences as the 'building blocks' of an essay. You can easily remember them using the acronym PEE (Point, Evidence, Explain). Body paragraphs in good essays tend to contain the PEE structure, with the three types of sentence appearing in the order shown above.

The following sentences are taken from Text 6.18. For each sentence, decide whether you think each is a point, evidence or explanation.

a   'Financial data does a much better job of predicting financial need than does the color of one's skin.'

b   'If scholarships and admission procedures aim to help the disadvantaged, they should target the disadvantaged.'

c   'Perhaps what is most foolish about affirmative action is that it doesn't even directly target the problem it is trying to solve.'

d   'For example, who needs a scholarship more: a black child from a family of doctors and lawyers or a white child living in a slum with a single parent working as a janitor?'

e   'It is true that blacks and Hispanics represent the impoverished at higher rates than the general population.'

f   'Though this may seem to be a complicated issue, it all boils down to a single underlying question: Should it be legal to discriminate against people based on the colour of their skin? Answer that, and you've answered whether we should continue affirmative action.'

9.5 You can identify the PEE structure in Text 6.18 or any good essay. Take three different colour highlighter pens. Use the three colours to highlight the different sentence types (points, evidence and explanations) in an essay. Do you notice any patterns?

9.6 Text 6.18 makes use of several 'cohesive devices', which are words and phrases that describe the relationship between ideas. Examples a–j are taken from the text. In a copy of the table below, write the letter of each example in one or more of the appropriate boxes, to explain its purpose.

Words that illustrate	Words that point to time and place	Words that show contrast	Words that show consequence

Extended Essay

Are you writing your extended essay in English B? Connective phrases, like those in Activity 9.6, will help your essay 'flow', and your examiner will find the essay easier to read. What's more, Criterion B of the extended essay specifically assesses your ability to write coherent sentences. Connectives will help you with this as well!

a At the time, this reverse-discrimination … (paragraph 1)

b However, the continuance of affirmative action … (paragraph 1)

c In turn, African-Americans and … (paragraph 2)

d However, it would seem … (paragraph 3)

e For example, who needs a scholarship more … (paragraph 4)

f While they point … (paragraph 5)

g but by taking a socioeconomic approach … (paragraph 5)

h And while more of a stretch … (paragraph 6)

i Though this may seem to be … (paragraph 6)

j Answer that, and you've answered whether … (paragraph 6)

9.7 After completing Activity 9.5, have you noticed a certain pattern to good writing? Such patterns are useful as guidance for writing your own essays. While there are different styles and traditions of essay writing, several defining characteristics can be found in most good essays. The '5-paragraph essay', a common way of organising an essay, uses the 'Point, Evidence, Explain' pattern in addition to the other 'key features' introduced earlier in this unit.

Return to Activity 9.1. How is this '5-paragraph essay' similar to or different from the way you have been taught to structure essays before? Discuss this suggested structure below with your teacher and ask him or her for further advice on how to organise your ideas in a coherent way.

The structure for a '5-paragraph essay'

Introductory paragraph

- a hook to grab the reader's attention
- the basics information about the topic
- thesis statement which will be proved

Three body paragraphs, each following this pattern:

- Topic sentence that introduces a main point
- Evidence that supports this point
- Explanation of how that evidence is relevant to that point
- Link back to topic sentence and thesis statement

Concluding paragraph

- Restate how the ideas of the essay were developed.
- Final sentence that reflects the wisdom gained through the essay.

TIP

You might find this '5-paragraph essay' structure useful for your individual oral exam as well. The structure of 'Point, Evidence, Explain' helps make any argument coherent and logical.

You might also find it helpful to use a form of 'thesis statement' in response to a literary passage (HL) or visual stimulus (SL). See Chapter 9 for more about the individual oral exam.

SL Exam Preparation

9.8 Choose one of the two following writing tasks. Write a 250–400 word essay and include the key features of this text type as outlined in this unit. Discuss with your teacher whether you will do this task under exam conditions or in your own time, writing with text-editing software or by hand.

a *Social organisation*: There has been another incident of gun violence in the United States, and there has been much debate about introducing stricter gun laws. Write an essay in which you present and argue your position on this matter.

b *Human ingenuity*: There has been much debate at your school about the use of mobile phones on school campus. Some teachers and parents want them banned all together. Other teachers rely on them as part of their teaching methods. Some students feel entitled to having them at all times. Write an essay for your school newspaper which presents your arguments and persuades others to agree with you.

HL Exam Preparation

9.9 Assess Text 6.18 as if it were the response to a Paper 1 writing task, using the assessment criteria for Paper 1 HL found in the introduction. What skills are assessed on Paper 1 and how are these demonstrated in Text 6.18?

9.10 Choose one of the two following writing tasks. Write a 450–600 word essay and include the key features of this text type as outlined in this unit. Discuss with your teacher whether you will do this task under exam conditions or on your own time, writing with text-editing software or by hand.

a *Identities*: Imagine you attend school in the United Kingdom, where school uniforms are customary. A growing number of students has challenged this tradition, questioned its purpose and argued for more freedoms to wear what they want. Articulate your position on this matter in an essay that could be published in the school paper.

b *Social organisation*: All-girls schools are growing in popularity because it is believed that girls learn better when they are not competing with or intimidated by boys, who statistically get more attention in the classroom. Write an essay in which you argue for single-sex or mixed schools.

ATL

Research skills

If you are not writing Activities 9.8 and 9.10 under exam conditions, you should research the topics carefully. What are the key facts that you would need to know to make a clear argument? For your Paper 1 exam it is useful to know a lot about a few topics. Research facts and ideas that are easy to remember, so that you are knowledgeable about several topics, and able to understand and discuss them clearly.

REFLECT

In this chapter you have learned about the conventions of nine different text types. You have learned to identify the key features for each text, and to label and categorise different forms of communication.

- How has this chapter helped you prepare for your Paper 1 exams?

- How has it helped you to understand different forms of communication?

- What other types of texts do you need to study before feeling confident taking your Paper 1 exams? Look back at the list of text types in the Introduction, and search for examples of any that you need to find out about.

Paper 1

At both higher and standard level, your understanding of a theme from the English B course and a text type will be tested on a Paper 1 exam. In this form of assessment you will be presented with three writing tasks, each taken from a different theme, each focusing on a different text type. To be successful in this exam, you will need to demonstrate:

- the ability to communicate a message effectively

- the ability to write using a style and structure appropriate to the audience and purpose of the text type you have selected.

This chapter provides you with exam preparation guidance. Unit 7.1 includes activities and practice for standard level students and Unit 7.2 includes material and practice for higher level students.

An overview of the differences between higher and standard level in Paper 1 are shown below.

Paper 1 SL	Paper 1 HL
1 hour 15 minutes	1 hour 30 minutes
25% of final course grade	25% of final course grade
250–400-word writing task	450–600-word writing task
Choice of three tasks, each taken from a different theme. For each task you choose one from three optional text types for your response.	Choice of three tasks, each taken from a different theme. For each task you choose one from three optional text types for your response.

Your school may ask you to take the Paper 1 exam online, in which case it is called 'Assessment 1'. In this coursebook, the term 'Paper 1' will be used.

Unit 7.1
Paper 1 Standard level

Guiding questions	Learning objectives
• What is required in the Paper 1 exam at standard level? • How can you write your Paper 1 effectively?	• A greater awareness of the expectations for Paper 1. • An understanding of the assessment criteria. • Be able to write good answers to Paper 1 questions.

1.1 Read the specimen exam Paper 1 for standard level below, in which you are presented with three writing tasks. Which task and text type would you select? Explain your reasons for selecting this task and text type to your classmates. Which reasons sound most reasonable to you?

TIP

Some text types are more appropriate for your response than others. For example, the first prompt in this Paper 1 specimen says that you are a 'popular' travel writer. For this reason a blog makes more sense than an e-mail. The IB exam will also contain a less appropriate and more appropriate text type for each prompt. Learn how to identify these for success on Paper 1.

English B – Standard level – Paper 1

Specimen paper   1 hour 15 minutes

Instructions to candidates

• Do not start this examination paper until instructed to do so.

• The maximum mark for this examination paper is **30 marks**.

• Complete **one** task. Use an appropriate text type from the options given below the task you choose. Write 250-400 words.

1   Imagine that you are an active and popular travel writer. You have just returned from an adventure trip that has changed your outlook on life. Write about your experience and its effects on you.

E-mail	Blog	Essay

2   You have noticed that your school's catering services do not offer very healthy options. Write a text in which you spread awareness about the importance of a healthy diet and request that changes be made to your school's canteen.

Proposal	Speech	Essay

3   Imagine that a new device has been introduced as the 'next big thing' at a recent technology fair. You can decide what this new device is and how it will improve people's lives. Write a text that communicates these ideas to a wider audience.

Review	Editorial	Brochure

1.2 After selecting one of the writing tasks, create a mind map around the task, to activate your imagination and make your thoughts visible. This should be similar to the example below, based on writing task 3 from the specimen Paper 1.

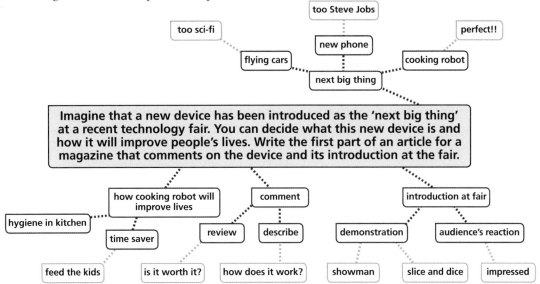

1.3 After you have created your mind map, organise your ideas into a *linear* outline, with your ideas in the order in which you intend to write them. Your outline does not have to be detailed. It may ask a series of questions. See the example below, which is based on the third writing task from the specimen Paper 1 and relates to the example mind map above.

Introduction	• Philip Dekker's robot is popular at 'Design and Technology Week' fair • Why it's useful: It'll make dinner for 'the kids'.
Body paragraph 1	• What happened at the conference? • Who demonstrated it? • What did audiences think?
Body paragraph 2	• How does the cooking robot work?
Conclusion	• Return to the question of why audiences should buy it. • How much does it cost?

TIP

Notice that the sample outline to the student's writing task asks a series of questions. It does not yet have all of the answers! But the writer knows the order in which they are going to answer these questions. It is also organised around the concept of 'purpose', or *why* someone should want to read this review.

1.4 Read the sample student response to Paper 1 below. It responds to the third writing task from specimen Paper 1. As you read this response, look for answers to the questions below, that are related to the assessment criteria for this paper.

Criteria	Questions
Criterion A: Language	• How successfully does the candidate command written language?
Criterion B: Message	• To what extent does the candidate fulfil the task?

Criterion C: Conceptual awareness	• To what extent does the candidate demonstrate conceptual understanding?
	  • audience • context • purpose
	  • meaning • variation

Sample student response

Philip Dekker's cooking robot captures audiences at the Design and Tech Week.

Perhaps the biggest conversation piece at this year's Design and Technology Week was Philip Dekker's new cooking robot. Whilst top chefs have every reason to turn up their nose at the sight of this invention, the rest of us now have a solution for preparing that spaghetti dinner for the kids. And yes, it will garnish that plate with fresh Parmesan and basil, plucking the leaves right off the plant.

Philip Dekker himself was demonstrating the robot, and his performance was like a beautiful dance between man and machine. In case you're wondering how a robot can know how to chop tomatoes or press garlic, the answer is quite simple: You have to teach it. Mr. Dekker dazzled audiences as he taught his robot how to grate cheese and stir sauce. The robot's 360 camera, which hung like a small disco ball above a sink, recorded Mr. Dekker's every move as he bounced around the sleek kitchen like Jamie Oliver talking to his mates. Then he casually served up his plate of pasta, wiped off the counter top and took off his apron. And that was when the real show started.

The kitchen took over. Two human-like arms with hands and fingers and joints came down from the ceiling and the rails on which they were attached. The audience cheered when an arm opened the refrigerator door and pulled out all the ingredients. And then it began to cook, which was even more amazing. Everything that Dekker did, it could do better. It was a kind of shadow of his every move, but without all the bouncing and babbling. It was effective and efficient. Yes, it could slice and sizzle and serve. And it could do it all over again and again and again, in different portions and quantities, if you asked it to.

Of course, Dekker's new toy is more than a pair of robot arms hanging from curtain rails. The whole kitchen is smart, with sensors on just about every surface, which means we're talking about a major home installation. Pricewise, we're talking about something comparable to a top-of-the-line Ferrari, which might be more tempting to buy, considering all that installation. But you have to ask yourself: Will a Ferrari feed your kids?

CONCEPTS

Notice that Criterion C for Paper 1 makes explicit reference to the concepts that you have explored in this course. As you look for evidence of each of the concepts in the sample response, ask yourself the following questions:

- Audience: Who would read a review like this?
- Context: When was this review written?
- Purpose: What is the writer's purpose in writing this review?
- Meaning: What message is the review communicating?
- Variation: How are various words (synonyms) used to articulate this message?

1.5

a What are the strengths and weaknesses of the sample response?

b What suggestions would you give the student for how to improve?

c What marks would you give the sample student response? Use the assessment criteria for Paper 1 standard level given at the beginning of this coursebook. Share your marks with a classmate. How similar or different are they? Discuss your marks with your teacher who can share comments and marks with you that you might expect from the examiner.

1.6 Besides using the assessment criteria for Paper 1, examiners are also given 'marking notes'. These are a list of points that are specific to each task, and indicate what a good task should include. Below is an example of marking notes for the first two tasks of the specimen Paper 1. Write the marking notes as you think they would have been written for the third task, which the student has responded to in the sample answer. Share your bullet-point list of notes with your teacher and classmates. Identify any points your lists have in common.

Marking notes

1 Travel writing

A good answer will:

- adopt a persona that speaks to an audience who care about travel and adventure
- adopt a 'voice' or use of language that sounds popular
- deliver a message about the author's new outlook on life
- explain how events have led to this new outlook on life

2 Healthier food in the canteen

A good answer will:

- comment on the current offering in the school's canteen
- raise awareness about the dangers of unhealthy food
- make recommendations for healthier foods in the canteen

3 Cooking robot

A good answer will:

- ...
- ...
- ...

TIP

If you are taking your Paper 1 exam offline, on paper, it is recommended that you practise writing the task *by hand* within the allocated time. You might find that this is a skill that you are not used to using. Build up the muscles in your hands in the weeks before the exam!

1.7 Imagine you are an examiner, setting the writing tasks for Paper 1. Write *three* writing tasks for your classmates. Study the specimen Paper 1 in this unit as a model. Consider the topics you have studied in this coursebook and the text types the IB recommends, as shown in the table below. Creating a writing task means writing a prompt in which three text types are suggested for a particular topic.

Topics	Text types
I Identities: • citizens of the world • belief and identity • beauty and self-esteem **2 Experiences:** • pilgrimages • extreme sports • migration **3 Human ingenuity:** • future humans • technology and human interaction • redefining art **4 Social organisation:** • minorities and education • partners for life • the future of jobs **5 Sharing the planet:** • ending poverty • climate change • human rights	• advertisement • article • blog • brochure • diary • e-mail • essay • invitation • interview • letter of recommendation • letter to the editor • news report • opinion column • personal letter • review • report • set of instructions • travel guide • web page

1.8 It is time for you to practise writing your own Paper 1 response. You should write a response to *one* of the three tasks in the specimen Paper 1 in this unit. Alternatively, you can use one of the stimulus writing tasks that you or a classmate wrote in Activity 1.7.

You can also look through this coursebook and find a writing task that interests you in the 'Writing' sections of Units 1.1–5.3.

Practise for exam conditions by writing your task in one hour and fifteen minutes.

Ask your teacher to assess you according to the assessment criteria for Paper 1. After you have received feedback from your teacher, rewrite your work so that you learn from your mistakes.

It is recommended that you practise this form of assessment as often as possible before the actual exam.

Unit 7.2
Paper 1 Higher level

Guiding questions	Learning objectives
• What is required in the Paper 1 exam at higher level? • How can you write your Paper 1 effectively?	• A greater awareness of the expectations for Paper 1. • An understanding of the assessment criteria. • Be able to write good answers to Paper 1 questions.

At both levels you are required to write a text in response to *one* of three tasks. If you are taking this course at higher level, you are encouraged to also read Unit 7.1 for standard level. The activities in this unit will help you to develop your skills for the Paper 1 exam.

2.1 Here is a specimen Paper 1 exam. Read the three writing tasks and discuss the 'pitfalls' and 'opportunities' of writing each task and text type, by completing a table like the one at the top of the next page. As you consider the possible advantages and disadvantages of each task, think about the coursework that you have studied and how it relates to each task.

English B – Higher level – Paper 1

Specimen paper   1 hour 30 minutes

Instructions to candidates

- Do not start this examination paper until instructed to do so.
- The maximum mark for this examination paper is **30 marks**.
- Complete one task. Use an appropriate text type from the options given below the task you choose. Write 450–600 words.

1   Imagine that a family member or good friend has recently died. Write a text that explains how this person has helped shape your identity. Be sure your text is appropriate for the context for which it is written.

Speech	Letter	Article

2   Imagine that you have had the opportunity to talk to a famous sports star. Write a text, in which you explain how the person's experiences have helped him or her rise to stardom. What lessons can you or others learn from his or her success?

Article	Blog	Interview

3   You have noticed that your school could do more for the environment. Write a text that comments on current situation and suggest how your school could reduce, reuse and recycle in more effective ways. Explain the importance of saving the environment.

E-mail	Report	Article

TIP

Notice that two of the three writing tasks in the specimen paper start with the word 'imagine'. While you are encouraged to use your imagination in the exam, you should also draw inspiration from your coursework. For the second task you could write a transcribed interview that you had with a sports star. The video that you watched in Unit 2.2 on the explorer Mike Horn could serve as a good starting point. In other words, you can prepare for the exam by reviewing the texts and videos that you read and watched in class.

		Possible pitfalls	Possible opportunities
1	Identities: memorial speech		
2	Experiences: interview for sports magazine		
3	Sharing the planet: letter to school board		

2.2 Below are the marking notes for the specimen Paper 1 exam. Marking notes are written for IB examiners to assist them in their marking. The notes for the third task have been completed for you. Write three or four bullet points that would assist an examiner who is marking a student's response to the first and second task. Share your bullet points with a classmate and your teacher and discuss their merits.

Marking notes

1 A friend or family member has died

A good answer will:

- ...

- ...

- ...

2 Famous sports star

A good answer will:

- ...

- ...

- ...

3 More environmentally-friendly school

A good answer will:

- describe the current practices at school which are not environmentally friendly,

- explain why saving the environment is important,

- explore improvements to the school's environmental policies, recommending ways to reduce, reuse and recycle more

---

2.3 On the following pages you can read two student responses to the third task on the specimen Paper 1 exam. The first response is very poor and the second one is very good. Read both responses and discuss the kinds of differences you see with a group of classmates. Then, as a group, create two lists to present to your class:

- a list of five things that students *should not do* on the Paper 1 exam,

- and a list of five things that students *should do* on the Paper 1 exam.

You can call these the 'do's' and 'don'ts' of Paper 1.

	Do this on Paper 1	Don't do this on Paper 1
1		
2		
3		
4		
5		

Poor student response to specimen Paper 1

Dear Steering Council,

I think that our school could do more for the environment. We should reduce, reuse and recycle more. I hope that you take this letter seriously, so that we can improve the school and help the environment.

First of all, a lot of heat leaks out of the windows, which are very old and only single-paned. In class we looked at our school's energy bills, which were given to us by your administrative department. Thank you for passing those on to us. We could save a lot of money by putting in double-paned windows. They keep in the heat better, and so it doesn't cost so much to heat the place.

Have you ever thought about solar panels? I visited a friend's school and they had these there. You could see how many kilowatts they were generating every day. We think that the panels, combined with the double-paned glass, would cut the heating bill by two thirds! Of course, it will take about nine years before you have saved more money than you spent on the panels and windows in the first place. But it's an investment.

Then there's the problem with bottled water at our school, which I think is really wasteful. I have seen a lot of students buying bottled water from the canteen, and I wonder why we even sell this. The tap water is just fine and it's free. I always bring my own bottle and fill it up in the bathroom. I know that I am not like other students, but we could teach other students to do this too. If we had school bottles that everyone could reuse, then we would not throw away all those plastic bottles, which just end up in a landfill. If you think about it, the bottling and transporting of all these bottles has a big carbon footprint.

When I was at my friend's school I also notice three-way rubbish bins: one for plastic, one for paper and one for other waste. We could do this at our school too. Our ESS teacher also showed us a video about a school that had a school garden, where they grew vegetables. If we take all the uneaten food from the canteen, we could make a lot of compost, and we could use that as fertiliser for the garden. So it is a win-win situation. I would be willing to organise this after-school club that manages this garden, because I like gardening a lot.

To conclude, we can reduce our energy costs, reuse water bottles and recycle our rubbish. The world is warming up and every little bit helps. Our school can make a difference. If you would like to talk to me about this letter and other ways of saving the environment, we could meet. Thank you for reading this.

Kind regards,

Student Y

TIP

As you compare the poor and good student responses (Activity 2.3), you will notice that their content is very similar. While both students have expressed similar ideas, the second response would be awarded higher marks. Its style and structure are very appropriate for the type of text, a formal letter. While your response should show understanding of the relevant course theme, you will also gain marks by choosing the appropriate text type and writing style.

Good student response to specimen Paper 1

Dear Steering Council,

I am writing as both an active student at our school and a concerned citizen. I feel that our school could do more to reduce its impact on the environment. With this letter, I would like to propose several measures that we can take to achieve this goal. Furthermore, I feel that by taking these measures, the Steering Council would demonstrate its commitment to education for a better world.

In our IB Environmental Systems and Societies (ESS) course, we have learned about the three pillars of environmentalism: reduce, reuse and recycle. Firstly, I believe that we can reduce our energy consumption and our energy bills greatly by investing in double-paned glass and solar panels. In class we have studied the school's energy bills and the costs of better glazing and solar panels. In brief, these two investments would cut energy costs by two thirds and pay for themselves within nine years. Furthermore these measures would send a message to the community that we are committed to a cleaner environment and cost efficiency.

Secondly, our school's current view on drinking water is very wasteful, as we sell bottled water in the canteen. Students pay for something that is essentially free, as our tap water in this country is some of the finest in the world. The carbon footprint caused by bottling and transporting this water is not necessary. What's more the plastic bottles are not recycled, meaning they end up in a landfill, seeping poisons into the soil. If we were to install free water fountains throughout the school and distribute reusable water bottles to every student, we would greatly reduce our carbon footprint. Naturally, the hardest part of this project would be to change people's minds about drinking water and tap water. An awareness campaign is necessary, which would go hand in hand with the distribution of reusable, refillable water bottles. These bottles could be branded with the school logo, which would contribute to school spirit and marketing.

Finally, our school can take a more forward approach to recycling. Currently there are only a few teachers who separate paper from waste. Throughout the school there is only one type of rubbish bin, which is used for all types of waste. I have been in contact with the municipality, which is able to pick up plastic, paper, compost and other, general waste for free on a weekly basis if we use their containers. I would like to suggest that we make use of their offer and install three-way rubbish bins for plastic, paper and waste throughout the school. Compost could be separated and collected at the canteen area and used to fertilise a school garden, which can be managed by ESS students or an after-school club. Again, a garden and three-way rubbish bins would show our school community how committed we are to the environment, acting as both an educational and marketing tool for the school.

I hope that with this letter I have informed and persuaded you to invest in a more environmentally friendly school. Furthermore, I hope that you can see how an investment in recycling bins, school garden, drinking fountains, double glazing and solar panels is also an investment in students, their education and their future. Thank you for considering the proposals mentioned in this letter. I am keen on discussing them with you in person, when you are available.

Kind regards,

Student Y

2.4 In Activity 2.3 you generated a list of 'do's and don'ts' for the Paper 1 exam, based on what you have learned in your course and comparison of a good and poor student response. Below are some questions relating to each of the criteria for Paper 1. Return to your lists. Beside each item on your list, write a letter ('A', 'B' or 'C') that corresponds to the assessment criteria below.

For example, if you wrote, "Don't use language that's too informal for the text type," then write an 'A' next to this item. You could also write the letter 'C' and argue that the student has not understood the concept of language variation. See the criteria at the beginning of this coursebook for detailed descriptors of Paper 1.

Criteria	Questions
Criterion A: Language	• How successfully does the candidate command written language?
Criterion B: Message	• To what extent does the candidate fulfil the task?
Criterion C: Conceptual awareness	• To what extent does the candidate demonstrate conceptual understanding? 　　• audience 　　• context 　　• purpose 　　• meaning 　　• variation

CONCEPTS

The assessment criterion C for Paper 1 asks you to demonstrate awareness of the five' key concepts' for the English B course. Remind yourself about these before you write your response in the exam:

- Audience: Whom does your text target?
- Context: When and were would it be written and read?
- Purpose: Why are you writing it?
- Meaning: What is your text's main message?
- Variation: How do you use language to construct this meaning?

2.5 Your success on Paper 1 will depend very much on your ability to write in the appropriate style for a particular text type. The introduction to this coursebook includes a list of text types on page v that you may be asked to use. Of the texts on this list, which ones do you think the exam paper is most likely to ask you to write? Why do you think some text types may not appear on the exam? Discuss your answers with your classmates.

2.6 There are nine units in Chapter 6, each of which explores the features and characteristics of a particular text type. Can you find a text on the list in Activity 2.5 which may be on the exam but is not explored in this coursebook? Find examples of this text type and present them to your classmates. What are some of the key characteristics of this text type?

ATL

The English B course encourages you to develop your communication skills. Learning how to write different types of texts for different purposes is a very useful skill, not only for your Paper 1 exam, but for life and work in general. Can you imagine a real-life situation where you are required to write one of the texts from the list of text types?

2.7 Based on your understanding of the assessment criteria and your lists of 'do's' and 'don'ts for Paper 1 (Activity 2.3), write your own 450 to 600-word response to one of the three tasks on the specimen Paper 1. Write your text within the time limit of one hour and 30 minutes under exam conditions.

2.8 When you have finished writing your own Paper 1 response (Activity 2.7) try assessing your work using the assessment criteria for Paper 1 at higher level given at the beginning of this coursebook. Ask your teacher to use these criteria when they mark your work. Then discuss any similarities and differences between your marks and your teacher's marks.

LEARNER PROFILE

Thinker

Remember that an IB learner is also a *thinker*. Remember to think *before* you write your response. Make mind maps and outlines (see Unit 7.1) to stimulate the thinking process. Thinking and planning can take up to 15 minutes of your exam time. You will find the writing process quicker, once your ideas are already organised.

REFLECT

In this chapter you have been introduced to the requirements for Paper 1. You have seen both a standard level and a higher level specimen Paper 1. You have read sample student responses for each paper and practiced writing responses of your own.

Make a list of five skills that you feel you need to improve in order to score well in this examination. Share your list with your classmates and teacher. Talk about how you plan to develop these skills further.

Paper 2

> Paper 2 tests your listening and reading comprehension skills. In this exam you will find several types of questions including, but not limited to:
>
> - multiple choice
>
> - fill-in-the-blank
>
> - open answer
>
> - matching exercises.

The questions cover a range of topics, all of which are related to the five themes of the course.

Here is an overview of the similarities and differences between the standard and higher level exams. Can you spot the difference?

	Paper 2 SL	Paper 2 HL
Listening comprehension	45 minutes	1 hour
	25 marks	25 marks
Reading comprehension	1 hour	1 hour
	40 marks	40 marks
Weighting	50%	50%

There are no assessment criteria for Paper 2. Using exam-specific grade boundaries, an external examiner will award you a grade from 1 to 7. The grade counts for 50% of your final grade for the English B course.

Listening comprehension (Section A)

The first section of the Paper 2 exam includes three listening texts. Here are a few points to remember about your listening exam, whether you are taking it at standard or higher level:

- These texts are based on the five prescribed themes: identities, experiences, human ingenuity, social organisation and sharing the planet
- The texts are recorded by actors who read from a script in a variety of accents.
- Each audio text will be introduced with a 15-second description of the text.
- The higher level audio texts will be slightly longer than the standard level texts.
- Audio text C at standard level will be the same text as audio text A at higher level.

Your school may conduct your Paper 2 exam offline or online. Either way, the exam is not self-paced. You will be asked to listen either on headphones or through speakers, writing your answers by hand or typing on a computer. Find out how your school will conduct this exam and practise the appropriate skills.

Whether taken on or offline, the listening part of the exam is not self-paced. You will be introduced to the listening section of the exam with a brief recording that says the following:

'These are the instructions for the Paper 2 listening comprehension examination paper. Write your session number on the boxes on the examination paper. Do not open the examination paper until instructed to do so. Answer all questions. Answers must be written within the answer boxes provided. Answers may be written at any time during the examination. There will be three audio texts. All answers must be based on the appropriate audio texts. There will be four minutes of reading time at the start of each audio text. Each audio text will be played twice. There will be a two-minute pause before each audio text is repeated. The maximum mark for this examination paper is 25 marks. The start and end of each audio text will be indicated by this sound [beep]. The end of this examination will be indicated by this sound [beep, beep, beep].'

Reading comprehension (Section B)

At both higher and standard level you will be allowed one hour for the reading comprehension section of the Paper 2 exam. In this section you will find *three* texts, Texts D, E and F. Like the audio texts, these texts relate to the five prescribed themes of the course. Text F on the higher level paper will be a literary text. Generally speaking, the higher-level texts are longer and more challenging than the standard-level texts. The questions at higher level may be more open-ended and require longer responses than the questions on the standard-level exam paper, which could include more multiple-choice, matching or fill-in-the-blank questions.

Preparing for Paper 2

The listening and reading activities in Chapters 1–5 will help prepare you for your Paper 2 exam. Further, you are encouraged to practise for this exam by attempting the 'specimen' Paper 2 exam papers in Units 8.1 and 8.2. These 'specimen' papers are not actual exam papers, but they will give you a good idea of what the exams could be like. Unit 8.1 includes a standard level Paper 2 and Unit 8.2 includes a higher level Paper 2. Whether you are taking this course at standard or higher level, it is recommended that you practise by attempting both papers.

The following points provide tips and guidance for approaching and preparing for Paper 2. Remember to read them as a helpful reminder before taking a Paper 2 exam.

- Before you answer any question, underline one or two of the most important words in the question, so you are clear about what it is asking.

- Generally speaking, easy questions come before difficult questions. Make sure you leave yourself more time for the last few, more difficult, questions.

- When answering open questions, try to use as much language from the recording or text as possible, even if the instructions do not tell you to do so.

- Always read the questions for a particular text, *before* listening to the recording or reading the text. If you have finished answering the listening comprehension questions for a particular recording, use the time to read the next questions before the next recording is played.

- You can take notes during the listening section. Do this while keeping the questions in mind. Note key phrases and words. Do not try to answer questions while listening to the recordings, as your brain can only do so much at once.

- You can also take notes as you read. In fact, you can annotate the text booklet. You are allowed different coloured pens and highlighter pens in the exam room. Use these to highlight key words, phrases and lines, keeping the exam questions in mind.

- Beware of true or false questions. If only *part* of the statement is true, you must still consider it false. If an answer makes a true claim about the real world, it is not necessarily the correct answer in your exam. The questions ask about your understanding of the text, not about reality!

- Never guess an answer. Skip answers that you do not know, or are unsure about, and come back to them later. As you find answers to later questions, you might come across clues that help you answer previous questions.

- In matching questions, cross out words or answers that you have already used, so that you do not use the same word or answer twice.

- With fill-in-the-blank questions, write your answer in the gap in the text to see how it reads.

- Multiple choice questions usually have one 'throw away' answer, meaning that it is incorrect or the opposite of the correct answer. This can be a helpful clue for finding the right answer.

- Open questions are not a test of your writing skills. You do not need to write long and elegant sentences. But you do need to communicate your ideas clearly!

- Do not leave the exam room early! If you finish early, go back and re-read the texts to double check that you have understood everything and given complete answers.

Unit 8.1
Paper 2 Standard level

Guiding questions	Learning objectives
• What does a Paper 2 exam at standard level look like? • How should you approach this listening and reading comprehension test?	• Become more familiar with Paper 2-style questions. • Become more confident in answering the text handling questions and exercises on Paper 2 effectively.

This unit consists of a specimen Paper 2 at standard level. You can attempt it under exam conditions, or work through it question-by-question as a class, discussing your reasons for each answer. You might want to attempt the higher level Paper 2 in Unit 8.2, for further practice.

English B – Standard level – Paper 2 – Listening comprehension

Specimen paper   45 minutes

Instructions to candidates

Write your session number in the boxes above.

- Do not open this examination paper until instructed to do so.
- Answer all questions.
- Answers must be written within the answer boxes provided.
- Answers may be written at any time during the examination.
- There will be three audio texts. All answers must be based on the appropriate audio texts.
- There will be four minutes of reading time at the start of each audio text.
- Each audio text will be played twice. There will be a two-minute pause before each audio text is repeated.
- The maximum mark for this examination paper is [25 marks]

Text A – Wingsuit jumping 🔊 Audio track 16

You are about to hear a conversation between a father and his son about wingsuit jumping.

For questions 1–5, choose the best answer (a, b, c, or d)

1   In this conversation, the son:

    a   asks his father what he thinks of wingsuit jumping

    b   questions his father's understanding of wingsuit jumping

    c   expresses interest in wingsuit jumping

    d   is concerned about the safety of wingsuit jumpers

2 In this conversation, the father:

    a explains that sponsors of wingsuit jumping are involved in a cover up

    b tells his son that he cannot go wingsuit jumping

    c expresses disapproval of people who practise this sport

    d questions the role of the sponsors in the sport of wingsuit jumping

3 Which of the following statements is true:

    a people are killed in wingsuit accidents

    b the sponsors publish videos of wingsuit jumping on their channel

    c wingsuit jumpers are professionally trained

    d the man in the video was flying at 200 miles per hour

4 According to the father, wingsuit jumpers:

    a are not good role models

    b are encouraged to take unnecessary risks by their sponsors

    c are not well informed about the risks of their sport

    d are only interested in collecting sponsor money

5 According to the newspapers:

    a sponsors underpay their wingsuit jumpers

    b videos posted by the sponsors on their channel are not truthful

    c reporters are not writing about the deaths of the jumpers

    d sponsor money depends on the level of risk that jumpers are willing to take

    Write a meaningful ending to the following sentence, which reflects the ideas suggested by the father in Text A.

6 "By sponsoring wingsuit jumping, filming it and posting it on their channel, the sponsor intends to…"

Text B – Cornrows 🔊 Audio track 17

You are going to listen to a radio show in which the host interviews a school principal about her school's dress code.

The sentences below are either true or false. Tick the correct response then justify your answer in your own words or those from the recording. Both a tick and a justification are required for one mark.

		True	False
7	The radio show host claims they have made calls to represent both sides of the debate on the matter being discussed on the show.	☐	☐

Justification: ....

		True	False
8	The principal claims that ethnic differences cannot be concealed by the school's dress code.	☐	☐

Justification: ....

		True	False
9	The principal's response suggests that there are no African models in the school's illustrated dress code for students.	☐	☐

Justification: ....

	True	False

10 The principal fears that the South Sudanese girl's hairstyle will
   have an adverse effect on the reputation of the school.

   Justification: ....

Give short but complete answers to questions 11–14 below.

11 Why does the principal call the girls 'recalcitrant'?

   ....

12 Why does the host ask the principal if the girls at her school wear their ties loosely?

   ....

13 Does the radio host express his own opinion in this debate? Explain.

   ....

14 How is the Principal's 'broken window theory' relevant to the two girls in question?

   ....

Text C – Cyber bullying 🔊 Audio track 18

You are going to listen to a phone conversation about cyber bullying.
Give short but complete answers to questions 15–21 below.

15 Why does the interviewer call Dr. Cass?

   ....

16 What is Dr. Cass' aim in his research on cyber bullying?

   ....

17 Why does the interviewer doubt the significance of Dr. Cass' research?

   ....

18 What are Dr. Cass' suggested three main points for the reporter's article? [3 marks]

   Point 1) ....

   Point 2) ....

   Point 3) ....

19 Describe three types of 'discrepancies' between what teenagers' say and what parents'
   think, with regards to cyber bullying. [3 marks]

   Discrepancy 1) ....

   Discrepancy 2) ....

   Discrepancy 3) ....

20 Why is it disturbing that three quarters of teenagers are silent bystanders of cyber
   bullying, according to Dr. Cass?

   ....

21 Why does the interviewer say that teenagers are naïve to the dangers of cyber bullying?

   ....

English B – Standard level – Paper 2 – Reading comprehension

Specimen paper   1 hour

Question and answer booklet – Instructions to candidates

Write your session number in the boxes above.

- Do not open this examination paper until instructed to do so.
- Answer all questions.
- Answers must be written within the answer boxes provided.
- All answers must be based on the appropriate texts in the accompanying text booklet.
- The maximum mark for this examination paper is [40 marks]

Text D – Underwater Wonder

Answer questions 22–25 in complete sentences.

22 Why is the word 'totally' in single quotations?

....

23 Why according to Pet-Soede, are people less concerned about the coral reef than deforestation?

....

24 How will Pet-Soede's underwater rap help save the Coral Triangle?

....

25 What do you think that Pet-Soede means when she says that people have to 'make the right choices'?

....

The sentences below are either true or false. Tick the correct response then justify it with a relevant brief quotation from the text. Both a tick and a quotation are required for one mark.

	True	False
26 Many people depend on the welfare of the coral reef.	☐	☐

Justification: ....

	True	False
27 The Coral Triangle Initiative aims to turn the reef into a Marine Protected Area.	☐	☐

Justification: ....

	True	False
28 Pet-Soede's children will be proud of their mother's underwater rap.	☐	☐

Justification: ....

The words in the left column are taken from the text. Find the word in the right column that is closest in meaning to one of the words on the left. Write the letter in the appropriate box.
Note: *there are more words on the right than needed.*

29 Rare (line 2)	☐	**a** be grateful for
30 Disown (line 5)	☐	**b** renounce
31 Appreciate (line 9)	☐	**c** unique
32 Iridescent (line 10)	☐	**d** belittle
33 Deplete (line 19)	☐	**e** wonderful
34 Slog (line 33)	☐	**f** shimmering
		g journey
		h struggle
		i diminish

Text E – How Cell Phone Behavior Affects Other People

Match the headings with the paragraphs in the text. Write the appropriate letter in the boxes provided.

35 (1) _____	☐	**a** Others Feel Unimportant When Interrupted by a Cell Call
36 (2) _____	☐	**b** Others Often Think Cell Phones are Being Used as Ego-Builders
37 (3) _____	☐	**c** Friends, Observers and Bystanders are Affected in Negative Ways
38 (4) _____	☐	**d** Others are Confused by Cell Phone Conversations in Public
39 (5) _____	☐	**e** Others Become Insecure
40 (6) _____	☐	**f** Private Conversations in Public Places Irritate Others
		g Four Tips on Using Your Cell Phone in Public
		h What to Do About Pesky Cell Phones
		i Others Feel Trapped and Controlled by Cell Phone Conversations

Complete the following sentence based on information as it appears in the text.

41 There used to be telephone booths in public spaces in order to

....

Choose the correct answer from a, b, c, d. Write the letter in the box provided.

42 According to Lisa Kleinman, 'absence presence' refers to … ☐

    a a feeling of being trapped in an unwanted social situation.

    b an unclear situation where cell phone callers are distanced from a social group.

    c a feeling of rejection, when a social group excludes a person for calling on the phone.

    d a behavioural problem caused by a virtual world.

43 Dr. Robbie Blinkoff believes that mobile phones …

    a must be used by people who have important calls.

    b are for people who like to hear themselves talk.

    c create a nuisance for everyone.

    d are used by people who want to let everyone know how important they are.

44 When people talk on their cell phone, they make others …

    a feel insignificant.

    b feel insecure.

    c feel rejected.

    d all of the above.

45 Answering the phone while with others creates a problem because …

    a one's brain cannot do two things properly at the same time.

    b both the telephone conversation and the social interaction are equally disturbed.

    c everyone becomes distressed.

    d none of the above.

46 Most people who call in social situations …

    a don't realise they are being rude.

    b feel they have the right to be rude.

    c are unaware of other people.

    d don't care about handicapped people.

Text F – The Challenge of Modern Parenting

Which words go in the gaps in Text F? Choose the words from the list and write them in the spaces below (questions 47–57). Note: there are more words than needed.

OPPORTUNITY	TERRITORY	NOTIONS	PROGRESS
GUARDIANS	COMPASSION	ADULTS	LEEWAY	SITUATIONS
INPUT	ERROR	CONCEPTS	GUILT	PROCESS	MISTAKES

Example: X guardians

47 ……………………………

48 ……………………………

49 ……………………………

50 ……………………………

51 ……………………………

52 ……………………………

53 ……………………………

54 ……………………………

55 ……………………………

56 ……………………………

57 ……………………………

Answer questions 58–60

58 According to the author, what is the challenge of raising children in modern times?

....

59 What are two things parents should keep in mind in order to face this challenge? (2 marks)

1) ....

2) ....

60 How does the author view this evolution of parenting strategies? Give evidence to support your answer.

....

English B – Standard level – Paper 2 – Reading comprehension

Specimen paper   1 hour

Text booklet – Instructions to candidates

• Do not open this booklet until instructed to do so.
• This booklet accompanies paper 2 reading comprehension.

Text D

Underwater Wonder

WWF's Lida Pet-Soede on the flight to protect the Coral Triangle, an area of sparkling and rare marine diversity

When a middle-aged mum offers to do an underwater rap in front of thousands, two things are certain. One: her pre-teen daughters will 'totally' disown her. Two: she must have a very good reason.

Step forward, or perhaps wade this way, Netherlands-born Lida Pet-Soede. As head of the World Wide Fund for Nature (WWF) Coral Triangle Initiative, Pet-Soede is on a mission to get us to "stick our heads in the water" to appreciate what lies under the sea's surface.

In the Coral Triangle: that's iridescent corals, psychedelically-hued fish, magical molluscs, turtles, sharks, mantas and countless plants. Spanning Malaysia, Indonesia, the Philippines, Papa New Guinea, the Solomon Islands and Timor Leste, the Coral Triangle generates an estimated $12 a year from nature-based tourism, much of which comes to the region's coral-encrusted 132,800 km of tropical coastline.

This six million sq kilometre area holds one third of the world's coral reefs and reef fish. It covers just 1% of the earth's surface, but contains more species in two football pitches-worth of its waters than the entire Caribbean.

But researchers warn that over-fishing, climate change, pollution and coastal development will so seriously deplete the reefs (which provide coral fish with food and breeding grounds) that by 2050, they will provide half the fish protein they do today.

With 125 million people relying on these reefs for their food and income, the threat to human health and wellbeing, as well as marine species, is very real.

Pet-Soede says the plight of the area is overlooked because of its 'invisibility'.

"My tree-hugger friends have it a bit easier in that respect. Within the last 20 years, the deforestation on the island of Sumatra has been shocking – you can see that. But when the problem is under the surface of the ocean, it's not so visible."

Though progress is being made, Pet-Soede argues: "There are just too many people taking too many fish. It's pretty straightforward. We cannot keep meeting the demand for tuna and shrimp from the USA, China and Japan.

"The Indonesian government and others in the Triangle have agreed to protect at least 10% of their oceans by setting up Marine Protected Areas (MPAs). We are on the way to achieving that," she explains, "but it has been a hard slog to secure the current 2% made up of MPAs."

And what of the underwater rap? "I am trying to get a former Miss Indonesia to do that with me. If 5,000 people buy a $5 spot in the Coral Triangle through the WWF website, I have committed to attempt the challenge. It's a bit of fun, and hopefully my kids will not be completely mortified, but I'm also doing it to get the message out there, and for people to take notice. These issues are not so far removed from your daily life, even if you do not dive or ever expect to. You don't have to be a conservationist to make the right choices," says Pet-Soede.

"I personally think you should eat seafood. I think you should eat it and enjoy it, but just don't waste it and when you buy it, make the right choice."

Holland Herald

Text E

How Cell Phone Behavior Affects Other People

[1]   Compulsive cell phone users leave others feeling confused, trapped, disrespected, and angry. These users are often feeding their own ego at the expense of others.

Telephone booths were invented for a reason. The first ones were made of beautiful hardwoods and often had plush carpet on the floor. They were placed in railroad stations, fancy hotels and banks for the sole purpose of providing privacy for the user. There was a door to keep others away during the conversation and a window to let others know the booth was occupied. It was a wonderful way to have a private transaction in a public place without involving a third person in a two-way call.

[2]   The days of phone booths are long gone, of course, but people haven't stopped having the need to talk privately in public. Cell phones have become pervasive in our society and have many social implications. There are four main reasons why bystanders and observers have a negative response to these kinds of conversations.

[3] One of the most disturbing elements of cell phone use is the "absent presence" described by Lisa Kleinman of the University of Texas School of Information. She writes "When technology use occurs, the individual can become an *absent presence* to the group, removing themselves from the context of shared group behaviors to become involved in a virtual world that is not available to those around them. Depending on group norms, this individual use of technology signals a particular social message and has implications …"

Observers, listeners and bystanders often get confused and wonder "Is he talking to me?" It is disconcerting to say the least.

[4] To some observers, people who carry on loud phone conversations in public are just showing off. They seem to project a "baffling sense of entitlement", according to anthropologist Dr. Robbie Blinkoff, and offer the public appearance of emotional fulfillment. They come across as self-important jerks who are advertising their own worth, status and/or desirability, depending on the portion of the conversation the observer can hear.

Alternately, some people perceive rude cell phone users as overgrown babies who are attached to their phones like a security blanket or pacifier. In any case, when someone disengages from reality to talk on the phone, he violates an everyday sense of normal behavior, which leaves everybody around him feeling violated.

[5] Disembodied talk by someone else on a cell phone makes almost anybody feel trapped and controlled by a passive-aggressive person. If the private conversation they are forced to listen to then turns into the ego-building sort of social transaction mentioned above, they are likely to suffer emotional damage as a result. The unwilling listener usually has limited options for escaping from or shielding himself from the conversation. He feels like an interloper in a private sphere and often looks around for an alternate activity or conversation.

[6] Observers generally feel suspended, ignored or dismissed when someone's phone rings. They feel disrespected and worthless. They feel that they have been invaded and disengaged from the public sphere through no fault of their own. Having been given a technological cold shoulder, the person who was relegated to the bottom of the social importance scale now feels worthless and will react with either anger or shame, depending on a number of factors. Since there is usually no escape from this kind of situation, his self-esteem plummets and the "flight or fight" reflex is triggered.

Talking on a cell phone while in the presence of others involves juggling two parallel social contexts. This often causes cognitive overload as well as social consequences for the user. The cell phone conversation disturbs the real-life situation more than the situation disturbs the conversation. Musical ringtones, loud voices, distracted talkers, inattention blindness and compulsive checking for text messages are all distressing to those in the real-life situation.

Cell phone users are not interacting with the world around them and often believe that the world around them isn't really there. This leads to the passive-aggressive stance that the real world shouldn't intrude on their right to disengage from it. Many cell-yellers and other rude cell phone users are actually oblivious to the reactions of others and blind to their own faults. What the rest of us can do about it is the topic of another article.

Suite 101

Text F

The Challenge of Modern Parenting

Over the last few decades, our culture has become less and less clear about its messages to parents and other **[47]** … and educators of its children. Parents often experience doubts or **[48]** … regarding the decisions they make for their children's sake because they receive so much conflicting advice from various "experts" in the field of child rearing.

Much of this confusion is a result of the rapid changes our society as a whole has been going through. We've discarded a lot of old **[49]** … about what the roles for men and women should be, but we haven't always been able to replace the models that we've done away with. Basically we have embarked upon an age of experimentation. We're working mostly with both helpful and not-so-helpful **[50]** … from other parents and teachers who are in the same boat as we are.

We're likely to have an easier time throughout this period of trial and **[51]** … if we can shed the belief that we must be perfect parents the first time around. The life of the family is a learning experience not only for children, but also for their guardians. If we are gentle with ourselves then our lessons will likewise be gentler. We're going to be venturing into a lot of unexplored areas with our children, and we'll need to trust our gut feelings and intuition. We may have firm notions about doing everything contrary to the ways that our parents did them, or we may encounter **[52]** … where their tried and true approaches seem to work best. What is most important is that our love and **[53]** … for our children be the forces that govern our decisions. If we are to do without role models and scripts throughout our lives as parents, then our hearts must be our guides.

Dispensing with the old blueprints for how mothers and fathers should raise their children can be seen as a fruitful phase in the growth of humanity. We have a(n) **[54]** … to try new approaches that could potentially work better than the methods that previous generations have used. This **[55]** … will go a lot smoother for us if we can let go of the expectation that we will be completely enlightened parents. Redefining our identities as men and women is a task that requires **[56]** … and a little room for error. Journeys into unknown **[57]** … often involve taking two steps forward and one step back.

We swell with pride in seeing our young ones make their first baby steps. Why not, then, take a little pride in our own?

www.FamilyLobby.com

Unit 8.2
Paper 2 higher level

Guiding questions	Learning objectives
• What does a Paper 2 exam at higher level look like? • How should you approach this listening and reading comprehension test?	• Become more familiar with Paper 2-style questions. • Become more confident in answering the text handling questions and exercises on Paper 2 effectively.

The Paper 2 exam at higher level, like the Paper 2 standard level exam, tests your reading and listening comprehension skills. If you have not already attempted the standard level Paper 2 in Unit 8.1, it is recommended that you do so. This unit offers you a specimen Paper 2 with the kinds of questions you can expect on your actual exam.

You might want to attempt this specimen paper under exam conditions, or you might want to attempt it collectively as a class. You should also revisit the Paper 2 'tips' section at the start of this chapter before you practise with the specimen paper in this unit.

English B – Higher level – Paper 2 – Listening comprehension

Specimen paper   1 hour

___

Instructions to candidates

Write your session number in the boxes above.

• Do not open this examination paper until instructed to do so.

• Answer all questions.

• Answers must be written within the answer boxes provided.

• Answers may be written at any time during the examination.

• There will be three audio texts. All answers must be based on the appropriate audio texts.

• There will be four minutes of reading time at the start of each audio text.

• Each audio text will be played twice. There will be a two-minute pause before each audio text is repeated.

• The maximum mark for this examination paper is [25 marks]

Text A: PISA Report 🔊 Audio track 19

You are going to listen to a conversation between two teachers at an international school.

For questions 1–5, choose the best answer (a, b, c, or d)

1   According to these teachers, the PISA report is controversial because …
    a   it ranks countries by students' test results for maths, reading and science
    b   it contributes to income inequality among teachers
    c   it is impossible to compare students' results from so many different countries
    d   none of the above

2   Martin believes that schools in Singapore are so successful because …
    a   students take school more seriously
    b   Singapore is an emerging country that values education and educators highly
    c   students do what they're told
    d   income inequality is low among its citizens

3   On Jack's trip to Poland …
    a   he was disappointed by students' lack of creativity
    b   he saw how they were hard-working and obedient
    c   he could see they were winning the education race against Russia
    d   he noticed very little critical thinking

4   Martin …
    a   believes that students cannot perform creative tasks without knowledge of basic facts
    b   finds the differences between education in Singapore and Holland paradoxical
    c   agrees with psychologists who say that creative thinkers are often good at memorization and arithmetic
    d   sees many similarities between students in Singapore and Poland.

5   According to Martin, teacher autonomy …
    a   accounts for the successful results of students in Finland
    b   is what he likes about his job
    c   both a and b
    d   neither a nor b

Give short but complete answers to questions 6 and 7.

6   What do all the high-ranking countries on the PISA list have in common?

    ....

7   Why is Martin reluctant to say that the smartest students are only from certain countries?

    ....

8

Text B: Cameron Rouge 🔊 Audio track 20

You are going to listen to an interview with Cameron Rouge, a fictional, famous model.

The sentences below are either true or false. Tick the correct response then justify in your own words or using those from the recording. Both a tick and a justification are required for one mark.

	True	False

8 Cameron Rouge is worried about what people will think of her ideas.   True ☐   False ☐

Justification: ....

9 Cameron Rouge is still doing modelling work despite speaking out in her new book.   True ☐   False ☐

Justification: ....

10 Cameron Rouge's new book includes photographs that have not been digitally retouched.   True ☐   False ☐

Justification: ....

11 Shows like *America's Next Top Model* and people like Tyra Banks offer an accurate representation of models in the modelling industry, according to Cameron Rouge.   True ☐   False ☐

Justification: ....

12 Cameron Rouge has been affected directly by racial profiling.   True ☐   False ☐

Justification: ....

Give short but complete answers to questions 13–15

13 Why does Cameron believe that she, of all people, has a right to speak out against racial discrimination?

....

14 Give two reasons why Cameron's life is not as great as people think. [2 marks]

Reason 1: ....

Reason 2: ....

15 Why does the interviewer accuse Cameron of being hypocritical?

....

Text C: Online gambling 🔊 **Audio track 21**

You are going to listen to an interview with Dr. Gurken, a professor of social and cultural anthropology. Answer questions 16–22 in complete sentences.

16 Why does the interviewer believe that the title of Dr. Gurken's article is paradoxical?

....

17 In Western Europe, what kinds of economic activities coincided with the rise of gambling?

....

18 According to Dr. Gurken, why could colonialism be seen as a kind of gamble?

....

19 What, according to Dr. Gurken, are three factors that lead to gambling in a society? [3 marks]

Factor 1: ....

Factor 2: ....

Factor 3: ....

20 Why did places like Papua New Guinea not have experiences with gambling as late as the 1950s?

....

21 Why have rates of addiction to gambling increased around the world in recent years?

....

22 What is Dr. Gurken's response to the interviewer's argument that gamblers will find a way to gamble, even if you block sites, pop-ups and IP addresses?

....

English B – Higher level – Paper 2 – Reading comprehension

Specimen paper   1 hour

Question and answer booklet – Instructions to candidates

- Write your session number in the boxes above.
- Do not open this examination paper until instructed to do so.
- Answer all questions.
- Answers must be written within the answer boxes provided.
- All answers must be based on the appropriate texts in the accompanying text booklet.
- The maximum mark for this examination paper is [40 marks]

8

Text D: We Need To Ensure That More African Girls Get An Education

Which words go in the gaps 23–31 in Text D? Choose the words from the list and write them in the spaces below. Note: there are more words than needed.

drive	accommodate for	gather	provide for	Harm
reinforce	resort to fetch	Face	optimise	strengthen
adjust	Confront	threaten	transition	offer

23 ....   28 ....

24 ....   29 ....

25 ....   30 ....

26 ....   31 ....

27 ....

Answer questions 32–35 in complete sentences.

32 Why has the author included the phrase: "It is the young trees that make up a forest and a wise farmer knows to invest in planting them while he can?"

    ....

33 Why does the author's heart sink when she sees the pots and food warmers in the computer laboratory of the school?

    ....

34 Why are families bigger than they used to be in many sub-Saharan African homes?

    ....

35 What hardships are often endured by teenage girls living outside urban areas? [2 marks]

    ....

    ....

Text E: Dramatic rise in plastic seabed litter around UK

The sentences below are either true or false. Tick the correct response then justify it with a relevant brief quotation from the text. Both a tick and a quotation are required for one mark.

	True	False
36 The amount of litter in the seabed around Britian had increased steadily in the years before 2016, according to the Department for Environment, Food and Rural Affairs (Defra).	☐	☐

Justification: ....

	True	False
37 Because of delays, Defra has not been able to publish their findings on the environment.	☐	☐

Justification: ....

38 Hugo Tagholm says that people have seen a steady increase of single-use plastic materials washing up in the tideline around the UK.

True ☐   False ☐

Justification: ....

39 Hugo Tagholm thinks that the government should regulate businesses and supermarkets with regards to their impact on the environment.

True ☐   False ☐

Justification: ....

Answer questions 40–43 in complete sentences.

40 How, according to Hugo Tagholm, is the plastic problem different from the problem of climate change?

....

41 How does Natalie Fee feel about the role of supermarkets and the government in changing people's habits?

....

42 Why might the problem of plastic waste become worse in the near future?

....

43 Besides polluting the sea, how else has plastic had an adverse effect on human activity?

....

Text F: A Stranger's Eye

Answer the following questions with complete answers.

44 To whom does the word 'they' refer in the last line of the opening paragraph?

....

45 Why do Gwylithin congregate around the old range in the kitchen?

....

46 Why are Gwylithin and Arwen reluctant to talk about their relationship with their landlord?

....

47 What does the phrase 'fail to make ends meet' mean in the context of this story?

....

48 With an oversupply of sheep, why has the price of mutton not gone down in the supermarkets across Wales?

....

49 Why does Arwen Jones feel that he is being made a fool of?

....

8

50 What has changed in the 10 years since Arwen and Gwylithin began sheep farming?

....

51 Why does Arwen feel like a failure?

....

52 Why is Gwylithin not consoled by the idea that other farmers are in the same position across Britain?

....

53 Why does Gwylithin think that her husband will not manage well in the future?

....

54 What reasons does Gwylithin give for not getting a job? [2 marks]

Reason 1: ....

Reason 2: ....

55 Why has Gwylithin signed up for a computer course?

....

English B – Higher level – Paper 2 – Reading comprehension

Specimen paper   1 hour

Text booklet – Instructions to candidates
- Do not open this booklet until instructed to do so.
- This booklet accompanies Paper 2 reading comprehension.

Text D

We Need To Ensure That More African Girls Get An Education

It is the young trees that make up a forest and a wise farmer knows to invest in planting them while he can.

Huge silver pots, large food warmers, shiny wooden mortars and pestles are some of the gifts a bride gets on her wedding day. They ____(23)____ her role as a homemaker and all belong in the kitchen. However, when I stumbled upon these same items in the computer laboratory of a public girls' secondary school in my community, my heart literally sank. The only computer in sight was a huge IBM computer covered in dust and just outside the school was a very busy market where more girls sold vegetables and young ladies served as porters.

According to the UNICEF Next Gen 2030 Report, as of 2015, the population of children under 18 in Africa totalled 560 million with girls representing the majority. If a girl has not started primary school by age 10, chances are she never will go to school in countries like Burkina Faso, Nigeria and Senegal.

These girls then become youths likely to ___(24)___ exclusion in addition to the discrimination based on their gender. One-third of girls in Africa are married off before their 18th birthday and in sub-Saharan Africa, there are over 29 million young women between the ages of 15 and 24 who are unable to read or write, let alone understand a medical prescription or help their children with homework.

This reinforces poverty as many of these youths have little or no skill set for employment and most often resort to becoming full-time housewives. With the fertility rate higher in poor homes and generally lower infant mortality rates (Generation 2030 Africa 2.0 Child Demographics in Africa), these women birth many children and their husbands find it difficult to ____(25)____ their large families.

This has contributed to an increased rate of domestic violence which many men ____ (26)____ as a means of letting out their frustrations. The situation is worse for girls and young women in conflict zones who are easily sucked into terrorism.

Girls who are privileged to go to school are not totally barrier-free. Adolescent girls from poor homes and rural communities often have to deal with economic and social demands which ___(27)___ their education – from walking long distances to ____(28)____ water every morning or selling wares in the market before they go to school, to adverse cultural practices like female genital mutilation or even the lack of access to menstrual hygiene products.

[...]

Governments need to do more than signing the dotted lines of charters and other international instruments. We need to spend more on educating girls and creating more avenues to harness the female youth population. This should also be supported by institutional structures and real-life workable policies that would enable these girls and women to ___(29)____ their potentials and make best use of opportunities afforded them.

By doing so, we would help an ever-increasing generation to ___(30)____ properly into a future that would be inclusive in all spheres and on all levels while exploring a large human capital that can ____(31)____ sustainable development across a rich continent.

It is the young trees that make up a forest and a wise farmer knows to invest in planting them while he can.

www.huffingtonpost.co.za

Text E

Dramatic rise in plastic seabed litter around UK

There has been a dramatic rise in the amount of litter found on the seabed around Britain, according to new government data.

An average of 358 litter items were found per square kilometre of seabed in 2016, a 158% rise on the previous year, and 222% higher than the average for 1992–94.

Almost 78% of the litter is plastic, 6.3% rubber and 2.7% metal, according to the data published by the Department for Environment, Food & Rural Affairs.

The amount of seabed litter has fluctuated over the years, but has been in long-term decline since a peak of 1,300 items per square kilometre in 2003. Statisticians link the fluctuations to weather changes, but the rise in 2016 was the first after three years of reductions.

Tim Farron, the Lib Dem spokesman on the environment, said: "It is particularly worrying to see such a sharp rise in plastic litter polluting our seas. Unless we take action, in a few years Blue Planet will have to be renamed Plastic Planet.

"The government needs to get its act together and take urgent action to clean up our seas and countryside. The long promised 25-year plan to protect our environment needs to be published now, not simply kicked into the long grass."

The publication of Defra's 25-year plan was originally scheduled for the summer of 2016 but has repeatedly been delayed.

Hugo Tagholm, the chief executive of Surfers Against Sewage, said the increase in seabed plastic reflected what tens of thousands of volunteers were finding along the UK coastline.

"They are seeing more and more plastic in the tideline, particularly single-use plastic, which has grown exponentially in the last two decades," he said.

Tagholm called for taxes and policy changes to increase recycling and reduce business and supermarket use of single-use plastics. He said Defra's current consultation on deposit-return systems for plastic bottles was crucial.

"The upstream thinking is what's vital to protect the seabed, the water column and our beaches," he said. "Without weaning the public off their plastic addiction we're not going to stop this increase. We really are at a crisis point, but unlike climate change we're at the early stages. We can stop this and reverse this trend."

Natalie Fee, the founder of the City to Sea campaign group, said: "This is sadly yet more evidence that the tide has yet to turn against plastic pollution and all the more of an incentive to really get the solutions embedded in mainstream culture.

"Joining the Refill movement and carrying a reusable water bottle or coffee cup in public, carrying a metal straw in your bag, switching to reusable menstrual products – these things spread a powerful message, we can choose to reuse.

"We don't have to rely on supermarkets or government to make these simple choices for us, although it would help if they were more proactive in tackling this environmental disaster."

The production of plastics is forecast to double in the next 20 years. A million plastic bottles are bought around the world every minute, and 38.5 million are used every day in the UK. Only half are recycled.

Sewage plants also contribute to plastic pollution in the oceans, because they use plastic pellets known as Bio-Beads in wastewater treatment that spill into the UK's coastal waters.

Academic studies have estimated that the damage to fishing equipment caused by anthropogenic sea litter costs UK fisheries £10m each year.

The Guardian

Text F

A Stranger's Eye

The house in which they lived dated back to 1560. They knew this because a group of local historians had turned up one day to look around the farm. People had been farming on the mountain for at least four centuries, they said.

It was a cold house that had never known central heating. Gwylithin lit big wood fires in the sitting room, but the cold lay in perpetual ambush beyond the narrow radius of the fire. There were three small bedrooms, a living room and a kitchen. Part of the upstairs ceilings and walls were mottled with damp. Most of the time Gwylithin and her children congregated in the kitchen around an old range they'd bought from a neighbour. At school she'd won lot of prizes for her cooking, and the kitchen invariably smelled of baking. Whenever there was a party or an eisteddfod at the chapel down in the valley, Gwylithin would be called into action.

The farmhouse and land were rented from an English landlord. They never said much about the landlord; they were dependent on his goodwill and understandably reluctant to talk about the relationship publicly. They saw him rarely, only when he came up during the season to shoot grouse. On the first day I met her, Gwylithin had just finished doing the accounts. It was a weekly ritual, the taking down of the big ledger and the realisation that yet again they had failed to make ends meet. The family owed £30,000 to the bank, all of it borrowed to pay for the livestock and machinery. Now the livestock was virtually worthless. Across Wales farmers were dumping sheep in public places in symbolic protest; there was an oversupply of sheep and the large supermarkets were essentially able to pay what they liked. And so the ewe that Arwen sold at 56 pence a kilo ended up costing the consumer £12.60 a kilo. It was a mark-up of over 2,000 per cent. The supermarkets could argue costs, but they would never convince the likes of Arwen Jones that he wasn't being made a fool of. It was the law of supply and demand all right, and the big chains held all the power.

Ten years ago when Arwen and Gwylithin had come to the farm, prices were relatively stable. They knew they would have to work hard, but there was a fair chance of a living wage. Now Arwen earned less than £80 a week. This was his return for a winter working day that began at seven in the morning and ended at nine in the evening; in summer he didn't get back to the farmhouse until half past midnight. It was his life seven days a week, fifty-two weeks a year. The couple were now receiving family credit of £104 a week. Arwen was ashamed of that, said Gwylithin. It made him feel like a failure. There were tens of thousands of tenant farmers in the same position across Britain, but that was scant consolation to Gwylithin as she waited for her husband night after night. 'He's like a robot. He's a workaholic. It's not fair what life is doing to him. He just works, works, works and you can't do that. He's OK now 'cos he's young, but give him ten, fifteen years and I don't think he'll manage.'

Arwen wanted Gwylithin to a get a job. But she wanted to be at home for the children. 'What would they do on their own up here in the school holidays? Who would meet them off the bus, at the end of the school day? It's not fair on them. they want to see their mum wen they get home from school. It's hard to say this in the modern age, you know. But I feel I need to be here for them. I get their meals and do their homework with them. And I work here at home on the farm. If he is working on another farm or away at his other fields, I need to watch for the cow that is calving, and do all the other jobs around the farm.' Still, she'd signed up for a computer course just in case.

Stranger's Eye by Fergal Keane

REFLECT

In this chapter you have studied the requirements for the standard and higher level Paper 2 exam. You have seen specimens of both exam papers and you have attempted one or both of these specimen papers.

As you reflect on what you have learned in this chapter, write a short list of exam tips to help you and your classmates to prepare for Paper 2.

Could you have improved your marks on these Paper 2 specimen exams? How? What can you learn from your mistakes?

The individual oral

In your final year of the IB English B course, your teacher will assess you on what you have learned through an individual oral. This is your opportunity to speak fluently and proficiently in the English language, showing that you have engaged with the coursework. This chapter provides you with sample individual orals for standard and higher level and tips on how to prepare for this form of examination.

The individual oral is your only form of internal assessment for the English B course and is worth 25 percent of your final grade. Your oral exam will be recorded and might be sent to an IB moderator, who will confirm or adjust the mark your teacher has awarded you, applying the assessment criteria. If a recording of your individual oral is not sent to an IB moderator, your marks might still be adjusted, as a moderation factor is applied to your entire class, based on the samples submitted.

The individual oral has a similar format at higher and standard level, but there are differences.

- At standard level you will comment on two of the prescribed themes of the course, starting with a visual stimulus.

- At higher level you will comment both on a literary work and one prescribed course theme.

Standard and higher level oral exams are explored separately in the two units of this chapter. The table below summarises the main differences for you.

	SL	HL
Percent of final grade	**25%**	**25%**
Choice	1 of 2 visual stimuli	1 of 2 extracts from a literary work studied in class
Preparation time	15 minutes	20 minutes
Part 1: Presentation	4 minutes about how the stimulus and culture relates to a course theme*	4 minutes about the extract
Part 2: Follow-up questions	5-6-minute discussion on this theme*	5-6-minute discussion on the literary work in its entirety
Part 3: General discussion	3-5-minute discussion on a second prescribed theme*	3-5-minute discussion on a prescribed theme*
Assessment criteria:	A: Language	A: Language
	B1: Message: Visual stimulus	B1: Message: Literary extract
	B2: Message: Conversation	B2: Message: Conversation
	C: Communication	C: Communication

*The five prescribed themes for the English B course are: identities, experiences, human ingenuity, social organisation and sharing the planet.

Unit 9.1
Standard level individual oral

Guiding questions	**Learning objectives**
• What is expected of you during your standard level individual oral exam? • How can you best prepare for and perform in your individual oral?	• Develop a good understanding of the assessment criteria for the individual oral. • Become more confident speaking about visual stimuli and the prescribed themes of this course.

TIP

If you are a higher level student, you might find it useful to practise your English proficiency by doing a mock standard level individual oral exam. Exploring the themes of your course through a presentation and a conversation will help you prepare for Paper 1, as you will be referring back to course work and articulating ideas from previous classroom discussions.

At standard level, the individual oral assesses your understanding of *two* of the prescribed themes from this course. You will choose one of *two* visual stimuli. A visual stimulus might be a photograph, political cartoon, advertisement, or any other image with little or no text. Each visual stimulus is labelled with a prescribed theme. After a three to four-minute individual presentation on one photograph, your teacher will have a four to five-minute conversation with you about the theme on which the photograph is based. Then your teacher will change the topic for the final five to six minutes of the oral exam to explore a second, prescribed theme from your English B course. The format of the standard level individual oral is summarised in the table below.

Supervised preparation time	Select one of two visual stimuli	15 minutes
Part 1: Presentation	Describe how the visual stimulus relates to the theme and Anglophone culture	3-4 minutes
Part 2: Follow-up discussion	Discuss this theme further with your teacher	4-5 minutes
Part 3: General discussion	Discuss a second, prescribed theme	5-6 minutes

The following activities will help you develop skills that are needed for the oral exam. You will also learn several strategies to help you prepare. You will listen to a sample student response and become familiar with the assessment criteria for the individual oral.

1.1 The visual stimuli used for the final individual oral will:

- provide you with a clear connection to one of the prescribed themes for the course
- be relevant to an Anglophone culture
- encourage you to speak about international-mindedness
- be intriguing and thought provoking, perhaps by telling a story
- be open to interpretation
- lend themselves well to a discussion in which you are able to formulate an argument

Study images a–f.

a Label each image with one of the prescribed themes: identities, experiences, human ingenuity, social organisation and sharing the planet.

b For each image, explain how they meet one or more of the criteria listed above.

1.2 During your 15 minutes of preparation time, it will help to develop a 'thesis'. This is the main point that you will argue, the claim you will make or the viewpoint you will take. It is the starting point for your 3 to 4-minute presentation. You will have to support your argument, claim or viewpoint with evidence from classroom discussion or source texts you have used in class. Below is a list of thesis statements that could be used in relation to images a–f. Match each of these statements with an image. (More than one statement might be relevant for each image).

a We rarely see our true selves. Instead we see lesser versions of TV models.

b Where you have been defines who you are. So go to interesting places!

c Future-proof careers embrace technology. They do not fear it. The skills that we teach younger generations should enable them to embrace technology.

d The increasing number of large hurricanes is a clear sign that people should take climate change seriously.

e Global warming is a new reality, which will displace more people than ever.

f Advances in science will make people's lives easier and more comfortable.

g Your identity is defined by what you would fight for, what you value and what you believe.

h One cannot find oneself without going on a spiritual journey.

i Social injustices do not just go away silently. Dissident voices must be heard.

1.3 Write two captions for image 'f'. Review the purpose of the captions from the previous activity. Think back to the previous units that you have explored in this coursebook to find connections to a topic from one of the five themes. Share your captions with your classmates. Have a vote to decide which captions were the best in your class.

1.4 If you could select one visual stimulus from images a–f for your individual oral, which would you select? Why would you select this one? Explain your reasons to your classmates and teacher. Listen to your classmates' reasons. How are these the same as, or different to, yours?

> **TIP**
>
> When your teacher presents you with the two visual stimuli at the beginning of your individual oral, how should you decide which one to select? You might want to select the most interesting stimulus. But you should consider which image gives you the most opportunity to talk about a theme that you have discussed in class and its relation to an Anglophone culture. Remember, the image is a *stimulus* for discussion about a theme and not for a *description* of the image.

ATL

Communication skills

Notice that you are assessed on your ability to communicate effectively. Communication skills are an important part of the IB's approaches to learning. What does it mean to 'communicate effectively' during the individual oral? During your individual oral you should aim to:

- express your ideas clearly
- listen carefully to your teacher's questions
- demonstrate your understanding of the questions
- respond according to the expectations of the questions asked by your teacher.

1.5 In this coursebook you have worked with various Visible Thinking Routines (from Harvard Project Zero). The 'see, think, wonder' routine is useful for preparing the individual oral at standard level. Using the image (a–f) that you selected for Activity 1.4, discuss your answers to the following questions with a classmate.

a   What do you *see*? Describe what is going on in the image.

b   What do the people, setting and symbols in the image make you *think* about? Explain their connection to ideas and themes.

c   What does the image make you 'wonder'? What questions remain unanswered about the people, places and things in the image?

1.6 Before you take your individual oral exam, you will have 15 minutes to prepare. How will you spend your time most effectively? What is your plan? You might want to start by 'unpacking' the visual stimulus, using a mind map like the one shown below for image a. Create a mind map in response to the visual stimulus you selected from images a–f in Activity 1.4.

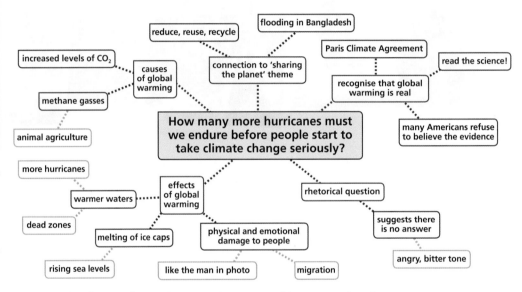

An example of a mind map that a student created in preparation for an individual oral on image a.

1.7 During your 15 minutes of preparation time, you are allowed to make notes. Based on your mind map from Activity 1.6, reduce your ideas to 10 note cards using key words that you'd like to mention in your presentation.

a   Use bullet points on each card to clarify your ideas.

b   Place the note cards in an order that is coherent and meaningful.

c   Compare your note cards with those of a classmate. How are your note cards similar or different?

d   What kinds of tips can you give each other for making effective notes?

1.8 You are going to listen to 🔊 Audio track 22, a standard level student's individual oral exam. It is in response to image a.

As you listen to the student's performance, try to find evidence that she has met the IB's criteria for the individual oral. The following table asks questions that relate to each criterion. Discuss how well the student performs on each criterion. Find examples from student's performance to justify your answers. For the full descriptors for each criterion look back to the beginning of this coursebook. Your teacher can provide you with a transcript of Audio track 22.

Criterion A: Language	• To what extent is the vocabulary appropriate and varied?
	• To what extent are the grammatical structures varied?
	• To what extent does the accuracy of the language contribute to effective communication?
	• To what extent do pronunciation and intonation affect communication?
Criterion B1: Message: Visual stimulus	• How well does the candidate engage with the stimulus?
	• How are the ideas linked to the target culture?
Criterion B2: Message: Conversation	• How appropriately and thoroughly does the candidate respond to the questions in the conversation?
	• To what depth are the questions answered?
Criterion C: Communication	• How well can the candidate express ideas?
	• How well can the candidate maintain a conversation?

1.9 As you prepare your own individual oral, you should ask yourself: "What questions should I aim to answer during the first four minutes of my individual oral?" How much do you remember from Audio track 22, the standard level student's individual oral? What were his answers to the questions below?

a Why did you choose this photograph?

b What features of the photograph capture your attention?

c How does it make you feel? How might it make other viewers feel?

d What does it make you wonder?

e How do the people, places and items in the photograph connect to a larger theme and topic?

f Why is this topic significant? In other words, why should anyone care about this topic?

g How is the image relevant to a particular Anglophone culture?

h How does the image lend itself to a discussion? Is it biased toward a particular position or argument?

i What is your position on this argument? What are other people's arguments on this topic?

1.10 In Activity 1.4 you were asked to select a visual stimulus. Using that stimulus, answer the questions from Activity 1.9 in the form of a four-minute presentation. Give your presentation to your classmates and teacher, as a kind of informal individual oral. What tips can you give your classmates on how to improve their presentations?

1.11 After the first 3–4 minutes of your individual oral exam, your teacher will begin a 4 to 5-minute conversation with you. The point of this conversation is to:

• expand on ideas that you have previously mentioned

• allow you to explore one or more topics within the same theme

• show interactive communication skills.

During this part of your exam your teacher will ask you questions like a–g on the next page. You can prepare yourself for this section of the exam by having a conversation with a classmate. After you have done your four-minute presentation (Activity 1.10) ask a classmate to have a discussion with you, as if he or she were your teacher. After 4–5 minutes, switch roles and take the role of the teacher, using the questions below.

TIP

Activity 1.10 asks you to listen to a classmate deliver the first four minutes of an individual oral. You can also record yourself speaking for four minutes in response to a photograph. Play it back and listen to yourself. Apply assessment criteria A and B1 (from Activity 1.8) to your performance. What can you learn from this process? How can you make improvements?

TIP

Notice in the sample individual oral (Audio track 22) that the teacher asks the student to explain how global warming works. In everyday conversation, people might not usually ask you to explain things that are considered common knowledge. But in an exam, it is an opportunity for you to show your communication skills. During your individual oral, be prepared to:

• remember classroom discussions

• refer to texts that you read in class

• explain key concepts

• present arguments

• evaluate sources

• be analytical and critical.

The individual oral

a   Can you explain/clarify/expand on what you said earlier?

b   What made you say that?

c   What (other) sources did you explore in class and how do they connect to the topic that you have presented?

d   What is your personal connection to this topic or theme?

e   How does this visual stimulus connect to an Anglophone culture?

f   Within this theme, is there another topic that you would like to discuss? Why does this topic interest you?

g   What are some of the key concepts that help you understand this topic better?

h   What evidence supports your position on this topic?

1.12   In the final 5–6 minutes of the individual oral, your teacher will change the topic and theme. Your teacher may give you a new prescribed theme from your English B course. In order to prepare for this conversation, you should be able to answer the following questions.

a   What are the five prescribed themes of this course?

b   What topics have you studied within each theme of this course? For example, you might have studied 'extreme sports' as part of the 'experiences' theme.

c   What texts, videos and activities have you explored in relation to these topics? (You might want to look back to Chapters 1–5 for ideas and reminders).

d   What connections did you make to Anglophone cultures and values?

e   What key concepts have you explored in class?

f   Can you remember some of your classroom discussions on each topic? What were the main arguments?

g   Which topics did you find most interesting? For what reasons?

1.13   The last part of your individual oral can be practised with a teacher, friend or family member. You can practise discussing each of the five prescribed themes with different people, referring to the materials that you explored in and out of class. Here are several phrases that you can use during these discussions:

a   I used to think... Now I think...

b   After reading more about... I discovered...

c   Some of the challenges of globalisation include...Some of the opportunities include...

d   There could be an increase/decrease of... in the future, due to...

e   Examples of ... can be seen in our local area where.... is happening.

f   In this English speaking country, people value...

1.14   Search for a visual stimulus that would lend itself well to a 4-minute talk on *one* of the themes you studied in class. Look back to Activity 1.1 to see the criteria for a good visual stimulus. Place your stimulus on a large table, together with the photographs that your classmates have found. Discuss answers to the following questions:

a   Which photographs are most interesting?

b   How do these photographs connect to the coursework?

c   What kinds of captions can you think of for these photographs?

d   What 'messages' are contained in these photographs?

TIP

Even though the final individual oral is conducted in final year of the Diploma Programme, your teacher may hold mock oral exams in the first year. It is recommended that you practise each form of assessment *at least once* in your first year. During practice orals your teacher will try to simulate the real exam conditions. There should be two rooms (one for preparation and one for the examination), recording equipment and an exam schedule.

Taking a practice exam seriously and carefully reviewing your performance is excellent preparation.

Unit 9.2
Higher level individual oral

Guiding questions	Learning objectives
• What is expected of you during your higher level individual oral exam? • How can you best prepare for and perform in your individual oral?	• Develop a good understanding of the assessment criteria for the individual oral. • Become more confident speaking about extracts from your two literary works and the prescribed themes of this course.

For your higher level individual oral exam, your teacher will present you with two extracts of about 300 words; one from each of the literary works you have read. From these two, you can choose the extract that you will prepare for your individual oral. You then have 20 minutes to prepare a 3 to 4-minute presentation on this extract.

Following your presentation, your teacher will engage you in a 4 to 5-minute discussion about the extract and the literary work from which it was taken.

After you have discussed this extract and the literary work as a whole, your teacher will initiate a further 5 to 6-minute discussion about one of the prescribed themes from your English B course. You will discuss one or more of the topics that you have explored in class, referring to any texts, videos, activities or concepts that you found relevant. The format of the higher level individual oral is summarised in the table below:

TIP

When your teacher presents you with the two literary extracts, select one carefully. Remember that you will have to speak about the extract for four minutes. An extract that is rich in stylistic and structural features has more to explore than an extract that is simplistic.

Supervised preparation time	Select one of two literary extracts	20 minutes
Part 1: Presentation	Place the extract in the context of the literary work as a whole. Discuss the events, characters, symbols, dialogue ideas and messages in the extract.	3-4 minutes
Part 2: Follow-up discussion	Discuss the content of the extract with your teacher, in the context of the work as a whole, and expand on the observations made in your presentation.	4-5 minutes
Part 3: General discussion	Discuss one of the prescribed themes.	5-6 minutes

2.1 Below is an extract from *The Collector*, a novel by John Fowles. Read the text and discuss your answers to the following questions with a classmate or the whole class. If you have not read the novel, then you will not know the answers. In this case, just try to answer the questions based on your understanding of the extract.

a Who are characters in this extract?

b Where are they?

c What do they aim to achieve?

d Where does this scene this appear in the novel?

e As the reader, how does this extract make you feel?

f Why do you feel this way?

g What do you think are the author's intentions?

TIP

When speaking about an extract from a literary text, do not forget to mention the basics. Simple 'who', 'what', 'when', 'where', 'why' and 'how' questions can lead to a deeper analysis. Apply the questions from Activity 2.1 to an extract from a novel that you are reading, and you will be surprised how effective they are in prompting a good response.

Text 9.1

'Where is this, who are you, and why have you brought me here?' she said it very coldly, not at all violent.

I can't tell you.

She said, 'I demand to be released at once. This is monstrous.'

We just stood staring at each other.

'Get out of the way. I'm going to leave.' And she came straight towards me, towards the door. But I didn't budge. I thought for a minute she was going to attack me, but she must have seen it was silly. I was determined, she couldn't have won. She stopped right up close to me and said, 'Get out of the way.'

I said, you can't go yet. Please don't oblige me to use force again.

She gave me a fierce cold look, then she turned away. 'I don't know who you think I am. If you think I'm somebody rich's daughter and you're going to get a huge ransom, you've got a shock coming.'

I know who you are, I said. It's not money.

I didn't know what to say, I was so excited, her there at last in the flesh. So nervous. I wanted to look at her face, at her lovely hair, all of her all small and pretty, but I couldn't, she stared so at me. There was a funny pause.

Suddenly she said accusing like, 'And don't I know who you are?'

I began to go red, I couldn't help it, I never planned for that, I never thought she would know me.

She said slowly, 'Town Hall Annexe.'

I said I don't know what you mean.

'You've got a moustache,' she said.

I still don't know how she knew. She saw me a few times in the town I suppose, perhaps she saw me out of the windows of the house sometimes, I hadn't thought of that, my mind was all in a whirl.

Extract from *The Collector* by John Fowles

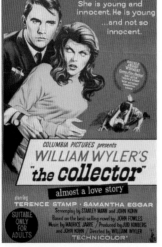

A poster for the 1965 movie based on the novel *The Collector*.

2.2 After answering the questions from Activity 2.1, think about ways in which the first four minutes of a good individual oral on the extract from *The Collector* would be organised. Make a bullet-point or numbered outline for this oral, keeping the following points in mind:

a Good orals usually start with some background information, such as the name of the novel, the author, the year of publication, and the names of the characters in the extract.

b In your introduction, you should place the extract in the context of the novel as a whole, explaining where it appears in the storyline or plot. Don't spend more than one minute doing this.

c Comment on the main idea or 'message' of the extract. This can be a statement about the author's intentions and how they are achieved through his or her use of storytelling techniques (for example, characterisation, narration, setting, imagery).

d Break up your presentation into sections. You can structure each section around a character, a symbol, an event, a conflict or anything else that contributes to the message of the extract.

e Be sure to comment on the five concepts listed on the following page.

f Include a conclusion, in which you restate your main ideas and the main message of the extract.

CONCEPTS

Activity 2.2 gives you the main points for an individual oral. As you organise your presentation on an extract of literature, you might find the following five 'key concepts' helpful:

- Audience: Who would read this work of literature?
- Context: When was the work published? How does this help you understand it?
- Purpose: What do you think are the author's intentions for writing the work?
- Meaning: How is language used to communicate a message?
- Variation: What devices or techniques does the author use to construct this meaning?

2.3 Listen to ◀)) Audio track 23, an individual oral from a higher level student on Text 9.1, an extract from *The Collector*. Pause the recording after the student has finished her initial presentation, when the teacher asks her questions. As you listen to the student's performance, listen for the way in which she organises her oral. Try to write an outline for the first four minutes of her oral, as she might have written it during her 20 minutes of preparation. How does this outline compare to what you wrote for Activity 2.2?

2.4 Remember to refer to the extract frequently during your 4-minute presentation. Listen to the first four minutes of Audio track 23 again, and answer the questions below. (Note, your teacher will have a transcript of Audio track 23 to help you with this activity).

a What quotations has the student used from the text?

b How do her quotations support the arguments that she is making?

c How does she integrate the quotations into her talk, so that they sound like they are part of her message?

2.5 Find an extract from a literary work that you have read for your English B course. Prepare the first four minutes of an individual oral on this extract. Return to the questions from Activity 2.1. Can you answer all of these questions in relation to your text? Here are some tips on preparing and practising this 4-minute presentation:

- Write an outline plan for your presentation (see Activity 2.2) as a list of bullet points. This should fit on one page and have no more than *ten* points.

- Have a main point or message that you want to communicate about the extract, the author's intentions or the way the language makes the reader feel. Return to this main point frequently.

- Practise by recording yourself on a device or phone and listen to yourself critically. Apply the assessment criteria for the individual oral (given in the Introduction) to your own performance.

- Listen to a classmate's 4-minute talk on the extract and assess him or her using the assessment criteria (A, B1 and C) for the individual oral at the beginning of this coursebook.

2.6 After the first four minutes of your individual oral, your teacher will ask you a few questions, to engage you in a 4 to 5-minute conversation about the literary work from which the extract was taken. You should be prepared to answer the following questions:

a Can you elaborate on what you said earlier?

b What makes you say that?

c How does this extract connect to the main message of the novel?

> **TIP**
>
> Notice in Audio track 23, the student does not *summarise* the novel. Instead, her comments are mostly *analytical*. She offers her *interpretation* of the events and characters. Orals that simply describe, summarise and retell the story will not score well. Orals that analyse, evaluate and interpret, will attract higher marks.

d What are your interpretations of this extract?

e How do these interpretations contribute to your understanding of the author's message?

f Why did you select this extract (over the other extract)?

g What connections can you make between this extract and the culture it is about?

2.7 Now listen to the second part of Audio track 23, in which the student and teacher discuss the literary work. After listening to this part, answer the following questions. (Note: your teacher can provide a transcript of Audio track 23 to help you with this activity).

a How fluent does the student sound? What examples of the student's language demonstrate that she is proficient using the English language?

b Find examples of the teacher using open and closed questions. (Closed questions can usually be answered with short answers such as yes or no; open questions require longer answers). Which are more effective in eliciting conversation?

c How complete are the student's responses to the teacher's questions? Where does she use language to demonstrate that she is answering the teacher's questions?

2.8 Listen to the complete sample individual oral (Audio track 23). You will notice that the last 5–6 minutes include a discussion about one of the themes from the English B course. As you listen to this part of the recording, look for answers to the following questions:

a What was the student's main 'message' during this section of the oral?

b How does she convey this message? What kinds of phrases and words does she use?

c What kinds of references are made to coursework? How do these examples support the message she is conveying?

2.9 For the final discussion, on a theme from the English B course, you should be prepared to answer the following questions. You might want to go back to Chapters 1–5 of this coursebook for reference.

a What are the themes of this course?

b What topics have you studied within each theme of this course?

c What texts, videos and activities have you explored in relation to these topics?

d What key concepts have you explored in class?

e Can you remember some of the classroom discussions you have had on each topic? What were the main arguments?

2.10 Listen to the sample higher level individual oral again (Audio track 23). Answer the questions in the table below, which address each of the criteria. Then discuss the marks that you would give this student, using the assessment criteria for the higher level individual oral given at the beginning of this book. How could the student improve their performance?

Criterion A: Language	• To what extent is the vocabulary appropriate and varied?
	• To what extent are the grammatical structures varied?
	• To what extent does the accuracy of the language contribute to effective communication?
	• To what extent do pronunciation and intonation affect communication?

ATL

Communication skills

In the individual oral you are assessed on your ability to communicate effectively. Communication skills are an important part of the IB's approaches to learning. What does it mean to 'communicate effectively' during the individual oral? During your individual oral you should aim to:

- express your ideas clearly

- listen carefully to your teacher's questions

- demonstrate your understanding of the questions

- respond according to the expectations of the questions asked by your teacher.

Criterion B1: Message: Literary extract	• How well does the candidate engage with the literary extract in the presentation?
Criterion B2: Message: Conversation	• How appropriately and thoroughly does the candidate respond to the questions in the conversation? • To what depth are the questions answered?
Criterion C: Communication	• How well can the candidate express ideas? • How well can the candidate maintain a conversation?

2.11 Now that you have studied a sample student response to the individual oral, you will now have the opportunity to prepare your own. Which two literary works are you reading or have you read for your English B course?

a Divide your class in half, with one half working on one literary work and the other half working on the other literary work.

b In pairs, and with help from your teacher, choose an extract from the literary work that your half of the class is focusing on. Make sure that every pair is working on a different extract.

c In your pairs, present your extract to the whole class, exploring the theme, message, setting, characters, storyline or any other concepts that are relevant to your extract. Keep your presentation under four minutes and make sure everyone in your class has ready a copy of your chosen extract before you give your presentation.

d Listen to the other presentations, and take notes on what they say. Then hold a 4 to 5-minute discussion about each passage with your classmates.

e Review your notes before having a round of 'mock' oral exams.

REFLECT

In this chapter you have explored the requirements for the standard and higher level individual oral component of your exam. You have listened to sample students' responses, and you have prepared and delivered your own individual 'mock' oral exam.

If you have not already done a mock oral exam, try to record yourself doing one with your teacher or someone else. Listen to the recording critically. What do you need to improve before your final exam?

> **TIP**
>
> Notice in the sample individual oral (Audio track 23) that the teacher asks the student to define the term 'citizen of the world'. In everyday conversation, people might not usually ask you to define things that are considered common knowledge. But in an exam, it is an opportunity for you to show your communication skills. During your individual oral, be prepared to:
>
> • remember classroom discussion
>
> • refer to texts that you read in class
>
> • explain key concepts
>
> • present arguments
>
> • evaluate sources
>
> • be analytical and critical.

Glossary

abroad in or to a foreign country or countries 3

abstract relating to ideas and not real things 318

accomplishment something that is successful, or that is achieved after a lot of work or effort 60

activist someone who tries to cause social or political change 258

adrenaline /adrenalin (English spelling) a hormone produced by the body when you are frightened, angry or excited, which makes the heart beat faster and prepares the body to react to danger 77

adventure an unusual, exciting and possibly dangerous activity such as a journey or experience, or the excitement produced by such an activity 60

aesthetic the study of beauty and artistic taste 168

agonistic someone who believes that we cannot know if God exists or not 21

aid help in the form of food, money, medical supplies or weapons that is given by a richer country to a poorer country 226

airbrushed describes a photograph which has been improved, having had faults removed 37

allusion a statement in which you refer to someone or something, but not directly 292

anaphora the use of a word that refers to a word used earlier in a sentence and replaces it, for example the use of "it" in the sentence "Joe dropped a glass and it broke." 292

anecdote a short, often funny story, especially about something someone has done 292

animal agriculture the business of raising and keeping animals for food 241

anorexia (nervosa) a serious illness often resulting in dangerous weight loss, in which a person, especially a girl or woman, does not eat, or eats too little, because they fear becoming fat 37

antithesis the exact opposite 292

appearance the way a person or thing looks to other people 3

appendix a separate part at the end of a book or magazine that gives extra information 318

application an official request for something, usually in writing 168

appreciate to recognise the value of something 168

argumentation fallacies arguments which fail to use valid logic, where the truth of the conclusion is not based on the truth of its premises 292

arranged marriage a marriage in which the parents choose who their son or daughter will marry 187

artificial intelligence the study and development of computer systems that do jobs that previously needed human intelligence 208

assimilation the process of becoming a part, or making someone become a part, of a group, country, society, etc. 96

association a connection or relationship between two things or people 3

asylum protection or safety, especially that given by a government to foreigners who have been forced to leave their own countries for political reasons 96

atheist (n) someone who believes that God does not exist (adj) believing that God does not exist 21

athlete a person who is very good at sports or physical exercise, especially one who competes in organised events 77

attendance when you go somewhere such as a church, school, etc. regularly 168

authorship being the creator a work of art 168

awareness the mental state of knowing about something 37

basic universal income a kind of welfare programme where every citizen is guaranteed a minimum sum of money, unconditionally 226

beauty a combination of quality that pleases the senses 168

bias a situation in which you support or oppose someone or something in an unfair way because you are influenced by your personal opinions 298

boredom the feeling of being tired and unhappy because something is not interesting or because you have nothing to do 134

bulimia a mental illness in which someone eats in an uncontrolled way and in large amounts, then vomits to remove the food from their body 21

call to action something such as a speech, piece of writing, or act that encourages people to take action about a problem 274

campaign a series of organised activities or events intended to achieve a result 258

capital money and possessions, especially a large amount of money used for producing more wealth or for starting a new business 226

caption words written under a picture to explain it 318

carbon dioxide (CO₂) a gas that is produced when people and animals breathe out, or when carbon is burned (formula CO_2) 208

carbon footprint a measurement of the amount of carbon dioxide produced by the activities of a person, company, organisation, etc. 241

celebrity someone who is famous, especially in the entertainment business 21

ceremony a formal event that is performed on important social or religious occasions 187

chat (v) to talk with someone in a friendly and informal way (n) a friendly, informal conversation 134

child mortality rate the number of deaths of children under 1 year of age per 1,000 226

citizen a person who is a member of a particular country and who has rights because of being born there or because of being given rights, or a person who lives in a particular town or city 168

clinic a building, often part of a hospital, to which people can go for medical care or advice relating to a particular condition. 116

clone to create a plant or animal which has the same genes as the original from which it was produced 116

collect to get and keep things of one type such as stamps or coins as a hobby 168

collaborate When two or more people collaborate, they work together to create or achieve the same thing 208

collaboration the activity of working together to create or achieve the same thing, or a product of this 134

commemorate to remember officially and give respect to a great person or event, especially by a public ceremony or by making a statue or special building 60

commitment a promise or firm decision to do something 187

communication the act of sharing information with other people by speaking, writing, etc. 3

competition when someone is trying to win something or be more successful than someone else 77

compulsory If something is compulsory, you must do it because of a rule or law 168

concise argument an argument which is very concise and to the point, where the truth of the conclusion clearly rests on its premises 274

conclusion the opinion you have after considering all the information about something 324

connected if people or things are connected, there is a relationship between them 134

consensus a situation in which all the people in a group agree about something 258

contender someone who competes with other people to try to win something 77

context the circumstances that form the setting for a text or idea 168

controversial causing disagreement or discussion 116

conversation a talk between two or more people, usually an informal one 134

convert to change the appearance, form, or purpose of something 21

corruption dishonest or immoral behaviour, usually by people in positions of power 208

courting (old-fashioned) regularly spending time with someone you are having a romantic relationship with and hoping to marry 187

creative good at thinking of new ideas or using imagination to create new and unusual things 134

creativity the ability to produce new ideas or things using skill and imagination 208

credits the list of the names of people and organisations who helped to make a movie, television program or book 278

criticism an analysis or judgement of the merits of a work or idea. 168

cult a system of religion directed toward a particular figure or object 21

culture clash arguments and difficulties caused by people from different cultural backgrounds coming together 3

curate select, organise and look after a collection, using expert knowledge 168

custom a way of behaving or a belief which has been established for a long time 3, 60

data information or facts about something 318

dating regularly spending time with someone you are having a romantic relationship with 187

dead zones a large place in open waters where little or no life grows 241

debt cancellation or debt relief is the partial or total forgiveness of debt 226

dedication when you give a lot of time and energy to something because it is important 60

deductive reasoning the process of reaching an answer or a decision by thinking carefully about the known facts 324

deforestation the cutting down of trees in a large area, or the destruction of forests by people 241

democracy a system of government in which people elect their leaders, or a country with this system 258

dependent needing the help of someone or something in order to exist or continue as before 187

desertification the process by which land changes into desert, for example because there has been too much farming activity on it or because a lot of trees have been cut down 241

despotism the government of a country by a leader who has unlimited power, in a way that is unfair and cruel 258

destination the place where someone is going or where something is being sent or taken 60

device a method that is used to produce a particular effect 134

devout have or showing deep religious feeling or commitment 21

diary a book in which you record your thoughts or feelings or what has happened each day 285

dictatorship a country ruled by a dictator (= a leader with complete power, who has not been elected by the people) 258

diet when someone eats less food, or only particular types of food, because they want to become thinner or for medical reasons 21

differentiate to identify and take into consideration people's differences 168

dignity one's honour or respect 226

diploma a document given by a college or university to show that you have passed a particular examination or finished a course 168

direct opening in a letter or speech, an opening line which clearly states the purpose of the text 274

disciple someone who follows the ideas and teaching of someone, especially of a religious leader 21

distracted driving the practice of driving while doing something else, for example using a mobile phone 134

diverse including many different types 3

divorce an official or legal process to end a marriage 187

dogmas religious principles laid down by an authority 21

donation money or goods that are given to help a person or organisation, or the act of giving them 258

dropout If a student drops out, they stop going to classes before they have finished their course 168

duty something you do as part of your job or because of your position 187

dysphemism an offensive or unpleasant word or phrase used instead of one with no negative meaning 298

election a time when people vote in order to choose someone for a political or official job 258

emigrant someone who leaves their own country to go and live in another one 96

emotional intelligence the ability to understand the way people feel and react and to use this skill to make good judgments and to avoid or solve problems 208

employment when someone is paid to work for a company or organisation 96

empathy the ability to imagine what it must be like to be in someone's situation 134

enroll to put yourself or someone else onto the official list of members of a course, college or group 168

entrepreneur someone who starts their own business, especially when this involves risks 208

entry requirements something that you must do, or something you need, in order to gain entry to, for example, a course of study 168

epiphany a moment of sudden and great realisation or understanding 21

equality the situation when everyone is equal and has the same opportunities, rights, etc 258

eradicate to get rid of completely or destroy something bad 116

ethos the ideas and beliefs of a particular person or group 292

euphemism a polite word or phrase that is used to avoid saying something embarrassing or offensive 298

evangelism the practice of trying to persuade people to become Christians, often by travelling around and organising religious meetings 21

evidence information that is given or objects that are shown in a court of law to help to prove if someone has committed a crime 324

exhibit a public display or show 168

expat (expatriate) someone who does not live in their own country 96

expectation when you expect good things to happen in the future 21

experience something that happens to you that affects how you feel 60

explanation the details or reasons that someone gives to make something clear or easy to understand 324

exploit to use someone or something unfairly for your own advantage 226

fair trade a way of buying and selling products that makes certain that the original producer receives a fair price 226

faith complete trust or confidence in someone or something 21

family balancing the practice of choosing the sex of an unborn baby on the basis of the sex of the children a family already has 116

fashion a style that is popular at a particular time, especially in clothes, hair, make-up, etc. 37

fatal A fatal illness or accident, etc. causes death 77

fate a power that some people believe decides what will happen 21

fertility (of animals and plants) the quality of being able to produce young or fruit 116

finding a piece of information that is discovered during an official examination of a problem, situation, or object 318

flexible able to change or be changed easily according to the situation 208

flooding when a place becomes covered in water 241

foreign belonging to or coming from another country, not your own 3

foreigner someone from another country 116

freelance working for several different organisations, and paid according to the hours you work 208

fuel efficient working in a way that does not waste fuel (= a substance burned to provide heat or power) 241

gadget a small machine or piece of electronic equipment that has a particular purpose 132

gear the equipment, clothes etc. that you use to do a particular activity 77

gene a part of the DNA in a cell which contains information in a special pattern received by each animal or plant from its parents, and which controls its physical development, behaviour, etc. 116

genetically modified (GM) describes a plant or animal that has had some of its genes changed **scientifically** 116

glittering generally sweeping statements which appeal to a very large audience because they state popular and positive ideas 298

global warming an increase in the temperature of the air around the world because of pollution 241

globalisation the process and trend of increasing interaction between people or companies on a world-wide scale due to advances in transportation and communication technology 3

goal an aim or purpose 60

grace the quality of moving in a smooth, relaxed, and attractive way 21

graduation when you receive your degree for finishing your education or a course of study 168

grassroots the ordinary people in a society or an organisation, especially a political party 258

greenhouse effect the gradual warming of the Earth's surface caused by an increase in pollution and gases in the air 208

greeting something friendly or polite that you say or do when you meet or welcome someone 274

habits something that you do regularly, almost without thinking about it 3

hazard something that is dangerous and likely to cause damage 77

heritage features belonging to the culture of a particular society, such as traditions, languages or buildings, which still exist from the past and which have a historical importance 3

holy relating to a religion or a god 21

hook a curved piece of metal or plastic used for hanging something on, or a similar object used for catching fish 278

humanitarian (adj) connected with improving people's lives and reducing suffering (n) a person who is involved in improving people's lives and reducing suffering 96

hymn a song of praise that Christians sing to God 21

ice caps a thick layer of ice that permanently covers an area of land 241

iconic easily recognisable as a standard 3, 168

identity who a person is, or the qualities of a person or group which make them different from others 3

illiterate unable to read and write 168

imagery the use of words or pictures in books, films, paintings, etc to describe ideas or situations 292

imagination the ability to form pictures in the mind 168

imitate to take or follow as a model 168

immigrant someone who comes to live in a different country 96

inclusive to be accepting of all different kinds 168

innovative using new methods or ideas 208

integration the process of combining two or more things into one 96

intelligent able to learn and understand things easily 134

intention one's purpose 168

internet the system that connects computers all over the world and allows people who use computers to look at websites (= electronic documents) 314

interpretation an explanation or opinion of what something means 168

intimacy a very special friendship or sexual relationship with someone 187

intuition one's gut feeling or innate sense of judgement 21

in vitro fertilisation (IVF) a treatment for a woman who cannot become pregnant with her partner naturally in which an egg is fertilised outside her body and the resulting embryo is put into her womb to develop into a baby 116

injury physical harm or damage to someone's body caused by an accident or an attack 77

integrity the quality of being honest or having strong moral principles 226

job security If you have job security, your job is likely to be permanent 208

journal a serious magazine or newspaper that is published regularly about a particular subject 258

journey the act of travelling from one place to another, especially in a vehicle 60

knowledge economy an economy based on creating and trading ideas and information 208

labelling the act of putting a label (a small piece of paper, etc. giving information) on something, or labels that are put on something 318

livestock animals that are kept on a farm 241

loaded word a word that is intended to cause a particular negative or positive response 298

logo a design or symbol used by a company to advertise its products 292

mainstream considered normal, and having or using ideas, beliefs, etc. which are accepted by most people 168

marginalise to treat someone or something as if they are not important 226

(the) media newspapers, magazines, radio and television considered as a group 21

memorial A memorial event or object is a way of remembering a person or people who have died 60

meritocracy the process by which the people who hold power have earned their power through skill and ability 168

methane a gas that has no colour or smell, used for cooking and heating (formula CH_4) 241

methodology the system of methods used for doing, teaching, or studying something 318

microcredit a very small loan to individual people or families, for example in developing countries, especially in order to start a business 44

migrant someone who goes to live in a different place in order to find work 208

Millennial a person who was born in the 1980s and early 1990s 134

mission statement a short written description of the aims of a business, charity, government department, or public organisation 306

model a person who wears clothes so that they can be photographed or shown to possible buyers, or a person who is employed to be photographed or painted 37

momento an object that you keep to remember a person, place, or event 60

mortality rates the number of people who die in a particular group or area in a particular period of time 77

motivation enthusiasm for doing something 168

multicultural including people of different races and religions 3

mysticism the belief that there is hidden meaning in life or that each human being can unite with God 21

nanorobots an extremely small robot (= a machine controlled by a computer that can do things automatically) 116

narcissism too much interest in and admiration for your own physical appearance and/or your own abilities 314

native worker Someone who comes from the place in which they work 208

negative space the space that is around an object in a picture 306

newsworthy interesting or important enough to be included in the news 274

nomad a member of a group of people who move from one place to another instead of living in the same place all the time 3

novelty the property of being new 168

obstacle something that blocks you so that movement, going forward or action are prevented or made more difficult 77

opinion column a piece of writing on a particular subject in a newspaper, giving the opinion of the author 285

outsourcing a situation in which a company employs another organisation to do some of its work, rather than using its own employees to do it 208

panel a group of people who are chosen to discuss something or make a decision about something 306

parallelism in a sentence, the repetition of grammatically similar phrases 292

past conditional the tense used for writing or speaking about situations in the past that did not actually happen 317

pathos a quality in a situation that makes you feel sympathy and sadness 292

petition (n) a document signed by a large number of people demanding or asking for some action from the government or another authority (v) to officially ask someone in authority to do something 258

persecution unfair or cruel treatment over a long period of time because of race, religion, or political beliefs 96

philanthropist a person who seeks to promote the welfare of others 226

phubbing ignoring someone you are with and giving attention to your mobile phone instead 134

plague a serious disease that spreads quickly and kills a lot of people 208

pledge (n) a serious promise (v) to promise seriously to do something or give something 187

pollution damage caused to water, air, etc by harmful substances or waste 241

press release an official piece of information that is given to newspapers, television, etc 258

principles one's set of guiding rules in life 21

protest (n) an occasion when people show that they disagree with something by standing somewhere, shouting, carrying signs, etc 258

public school in England, an expensive type of private school (= school paid for by parents not by the government); in Scotland, Australia and the US, a free school provided by the government 168

purity the fact of being clean or free from harmful substances 187

qualification the skills, qualities, or experience that you need in order to do something 208

race one of the groups that people are divided into according to their physical characteristics, such as skin colour 3

republic a country with no king or queen but with an elected government 258

reconcile if you are reconciled with someone, you become friendly with someone after you have argued with them 21

reflect to think in a serious and careful way 60

refugee a person who has escaped from their own country for political, religious or economic reasons or because of a war 96

regulation an official rule that controls how something is done 258

religion an organised system of belief 21

renewable energy energy that is produced using the sun, wind, etc., or from crops, rather than using fuels such as oil or coal 241

repatriate to send or bring someone, or sometimes money or other property, back to their own country 158

reproduction the process of producing babies or young animals and plants 116

resettlement when people are helped or forced to move to another place to live 96

rescue when someone in a dangerous situation is helped and made safe 77

resolve to solve or end a problem or difficulty 187

resourcefulness the quality of being good at finding ways to solve problems 208

retreat a period of time used to pray and study quietly, or to think carefully, away from normal activities and duties 60

revolution 1 a change in the way a country is governed, usually to a different political system and often using violence or war 2 a very important change in the way people think or do things 258

rhetorical devices in speech or writing, a technique used to create a particular effect, for example by making what is said or written more powerful or persuasive 292

rights something that the law allows you to do 258

risk to do something although there is a chance of a bad result 77

rite (a usually religious ceremony with) a set of fixed words and actions 60

ritual an activity or a set of actions that are always done in the same way or at the same time, sometimes as part of a religion 3, 21

roots one's origins or personal history 32

sacrament an important religious ceremony in the Christian Church 187

salutation a greeting in words or actions, or the words used at the beginning of a letter or speech 274

sanctity the quality of being important and deserving respect 87

scarcity mentality a frame of mind where one is afraid that there is not enough of a particular thing 226

sceptical not easily convinced, to question the certainty of something 21

screen a flat surface in a cinema, on a television, or as part of a computer, on which pictures or words are shown 134

secular not religious or not controlled by a religious group 21

self-determination the process by which a person controls their own life 21

self-employment work that you do for yourself and not for a company or other organisation 208

self-esteem belief and confidence in your own ability and value 21

self-image one's perception of one's self 21

sex selection the attempt to control the sex of an unborn child or offspring to achieve the desired gender 116

skill an ability to do an activity or job well, especially because you have practised it 168

slogan a short phrase that is easy to remember and is used to make people notice something 306

socialised used to being with others and able to behave suitably in company 187

soft skills people's abilities to communicate with each other and work well together 208

source where something comes from 298

sovereignty the power of a country to control its own government 258

species a set of animals or plants in which the members have similar characteristics to each other and can breed with each other 116

species extinction a situation in which one particular type of animal no longer exists 241

spirituality being concerned with one's soul as opposed to material or physical things 21

split up if two people split up, they end their relationship 187

sponsor to give money to someone to support an activity, event, or organisation, sometimes as a way to advertise your company or product 318

spouse your husband or wife 187

stereotype a fixed idea that people have about what someone or something is like, especially an idea that is wrong 3

submission the act of sending a document, plan, etc to someone so that they can consider it, or the document, plan, etc that you send 258

surfing the sport of riding on a wave on a special board 132

survey an examination of people's opinions or behaviour made by asking people question 318

sustainable causing little or no damage to the environment and therefore able to continue for a long time 226

sympathise to understand and care about someone's problems 187

synthesis the mixing of several things to make another whole new thing 318

synthesise to mix several things in order to make something else 274

taboo (an action or word) avoided for religious or social reasons 116

technique the method or way in which one achieves something 168

technological singularity the idea that the invention of artificial intelligence will lead to an incredibly fast growth of technology 116

technology knowledge, equipment, and methods that are used in science and industry 134

testimonial a statement about the character or qualities of someone or something 306

thesis a long piece of writing on a particular subject, especially one that is done for a higher college or university degree 278

thesis statement in an academic paper, a sentence in the introductory paragraph that describes the main ideas in the paper 324

third culture kid a child raised in a culture that is different to that of his or her parents 3

thrill a feeling of extreme excitement, usually caused by something pleasant 77

tolerant allowing people to do what they want especially when you do not agree with it 258

tone the general feeling or style that something has 187

topic a subject that you talk or write about 324

topic sentence in an essay, a sentence that gives the main idea of a paragraph 324

topical relating to things that are happening now 285

traditional following or belonging to the customs or ways of behaving that have continued in a group of people or society for a long time without changing 60

tweeting communicating on Twitter using short messages 134

unconditional love love that you give without any limits and without asking for anything for yourself 187

value the amount of worth or usefulness attached to something 3, 168

vegan (n) a person who does not eat or use any animal products, such as meat, fish, eggs, cheese, or leather 241

vegetarian (n) a person who does not eat meat for health or religious reasons or because they want to avoid being cruel to animals 241

vision the ability to make plans for the future that are imaginative and wise 243

vocational Vocational education and skills prepare you for a particular type of work 208

voice (n) the sounds that you make when you speak or sing (v) to say what you think about a particular subject 258

voting when people show their choice or opinion in an election or meeting by writing a cross on an official piece of paper or putting their hand up 258

vow(s) (v) to make a serious promise or decision 187

wages a fixed amount of money that is paid, usually every week, to an employee, especially one who does work that needs physical skills or strength, rather than a job needing a college education 226

weasel word something that someone says either to avoid answering a question clearly or to make someone believe something that is not true 298

whitening making or becoming whiter 37

winner someone who wins a game, competition or election 77

worldly a frame of mind where one is conscious of his or place in the world 3

xenophobia extreme dislike or fear of foreigners, their customs, their religions, etc. 96

Acknowledgements

The authors and publishers acknowledge the following sources of copyright material and are grateful for the permissions granted. While every effort has been made, it has not always been possible to identify the sources of all the material used, or to trace all copyright holders. If any omissions are brought to our notice, we will be happy to include the appropriate acknowledgements on reprinting.

Assessment criteria and IB syllabus themes chart are copyright of the IB Organization; Text 1.1 '10 years of living abroad: how moving to Australia changed by life' by Radhika for Digital Nomad Lifestyle, www.fulltimenomad.com; Text 1.2 Blog extract by Michelle Lai–Saun Guo from http://mybeijingsurvivaldiary.wordpress.com, copyright 2012; Activity 1.23 Headline A from Mail Online © Solo Syndication; Headline B adapted and used with the permission of The Corus Entertainment Inc. © Corus Entertainment; Headline C © The Times/News Licensing; Headline D Metro © Solo Syndication; Text 1.3 from *THE SUBTLE ART OF NOT GIVING A F*CK* by Mark Manson, reprinted by permission of HarperCollins Publishers and Macmillan Australia © 2016 by Mark Manson; Text 1.4 *Black Boy* by Richard Wright, adapted and used with the permission of HarperCollins Publishers and Random House UK © Richard Wright; Text 1.5 'What Twins Reveal About The Science Of Faith' by Tim Spector, reprinted by permission of The Overlook Press and Orion Books UK © Tim Spector; Text 1.6 'How Apple, Others Have Cultivated Religious Followings' by Martin Lindstrom, December 2008 www.adage.com; Text 1.7 from *A River Runs through It and Other Stories* by Norman Maclean, reproduced with permission from The University of Chicago Press; Text 1.8 'Expert Susie Orbach answers questions about the negative effects of culture on self-esteem and body image' from http://www.dove.co.uk/dsep/support-tools/articles/todays-beauty-pressures.html (l) by Susie Orbach reproduced by permission of Peters Fraser & Dunlop (www.petersfraserdunlop.com) on behalf of Susie Orbach; Text 1.9 'Addicted to fairness creams?' by Arunima Svirastava, Time of India, August 2011; Text 1.10 'Isabelle Caro, Anorexic Model, Dies at 28' by William Grimes from, New York Times, Dec. 30, 2010 © PARS International; Text 1.11 'The Diet' from *FEMININE GOSPELS* by Carol Ann Duffy, adapted and used by permission of Farrar, Straus and Giroux Copyright © Carol Ann Duffy, 2002. Text 2.1 Anzac Gallipoli from Topdeck Anzac tours website; Text 2.2 'In the footsteps of a thousand years of pilgrims' by Alison Gardener, Travel with a Challenge web magazine; Text 2.3 © Elvis Presley Enterprises, Inc.; Text 2.4 from IslamiCity.com; Text 2.5 from *Wild: From Lost to Found on the Pacific Crest Trail* by Cheryl Strayed, used with kind permission of Cheryl Strayed; Text 2.6 Top 10 Incredibly Dangerous Sports from listverse, adapted from listverse.com; Text 2.7 'The extreme future of Olympic sports' by Alex Layman, Huffington Post, 2012; Text 2.8 'Fear factor: success and risk in extreme sports' by Brian Handwerk, National Geographic Creative; Text 2.9 from *Karoo Boy* by Troy Blacklaws, published 2004 by Juta (Cape Town) and 2005 by Harcourt (New York); Text 2.10 'Why people are finding notes in London with messages from Syrian refugees' by Amy Willis, Metro © Solo Syndication; Text 2.11 by Cynthia Chitongo from www.xenophobia.org.za; Text 2.12 from Immigration Watch Canada website © Immigration Watch Canada; Text 2.13 'Irish emigration worse than 1980s' by Lisa O'Carroll © Guardian News & Media Ltd 2018; Text 2.12 from *House of Sand and Fog* by Andre Dubus III, published by W. W. Norton & Company Inc. and Random House UK; Text 3.1 'Fertility expert: I can clone a human being' by Steve Connor, Science Editor, 22nd April 2009, adapted, ©The Independent; Text 3.2 Article from www.geneticallymodifiedfood.co.uk © Genetically Modified Foods; Text 3.3 'IVF parents travel overseas to pick baby's sex' by Amy Corderoy, published in The Sydney Morning Herald 08/03/2011 © The Sydney Morning Herald; Text 3.4 from *Ender's Game* by Orson Scott Card, reprinted by permission of Macmillan Children Publishing Group and Little Brown © Orson Scott Card; Text 3.5 'Society is Dead: We have retreated into the iWorld' by Andrew Sullivan, (adapted) Sunday Times 2005 © The Times/News Licensing; Text 3.6 Excerpt(s) from *RECLAIMING CONVERSATION: THE POWER OF TALK IN A DIGITAL AGE* by Sherry Turkle, copyright © 2015 by Sherry Turkle, used by permission of Penguin Press, an imprint of Penguin Publishing Group, a division of Penguin Random House LLC, all rights reserved; Text 3.7 'Offline: day one of life without internet' by Paul Miller Reprinted by permission of Vox Media for The Verge; Text 3.8 'Google effect: is technology making us stupid?' by Genevieve Roberts, reprinted by permission of ESiMedia; Text 3.9 from 'Us and Them' by David Sedaris, from *Dress Your Family in Corduroy and Denim*, first published by the New Yorker and reprinted by permission of Don Congdon Associates and Little Brown USA, Inc. © 2003 by David Sedaris; Text 3.10 'Sorry, MOMA, video games are not art' by Jonathan Jones, The Guardian, 30 November 2012 © Guardian News & Media Ltd 2018; Text 3.11 'Stunning Portraits of Crying Children That Brought the Photographer Hate Mail' By Jordan G. Teicher, Slate.com August 2013, © PARS International; Text 3.12 'Banksy and fellow street artists are refusing to fuel the market for paintings taken from the streets' by Alexxa Gotthardt, adapted and used by the permission of Artsy © by Alexxa Gotthardt; Text 3.13 Billy Collins, "Introduction to Poetry" from *The Apple That Astonished Paris*, Copyright © 1988, 1996 by Billy Collins, reprinted with the permission of The Permissions Company, Inc., on behalf of the University of Arkansas Press, www.uapress.com; Text 4.1 'The fleeting promise of education' by Steve Young, © Steve

Young; Text 4.2 'My gypsy childhood' by Roxy Freeman, Copyright ©Guardian News & Media Ltd 2018; Text 4.3 Maasai schools article, 2004, by permission of Homlands.org; Text 4.4 from 'Studies in the Park' in *Games at Twilight* by Anita Desai, reprinted by permission of HarperCollins Publishers and Rogers Coleridge & White Literary Agency; Text 4.5 Introduction from *Men are from Mars, Women are from Venus* by John Gray, reprinted by permission of HarperCollins Publishers; Text 4.6 'Why I Want a Wife' by Judy Brady (Syfers), first published in Ms Magazine 1971, used with kind permission; Text 4.7 'The culture of arranged marriages' from IndiaMarks.com; Text 4.8 'Defining Moments' by Isobel Harwood, winner (10-13 category) of the BBC Radio 2 500-Word Writing Competition 2012, © Isobel Harwood; Text 4.9 '9 futureproof careers according to the world's largest job site' by Lindsay Dodgson for Business Insider UK, reprinted with the permission of Wright's Media, LLC as agent for Business Insider Inc.; Text 4.10 'Reports of the Death of Jobs Have Been Greatly Exaggerated' by Seamus Nevin, Huffington Post April 2017, adapted and used with the permission of author; Text 4.11 '5 reasons why immigrants do not take natives' by Amelie F. Constant, Huffington Post August 2016, reproduced by permission Prof. Amelie F Constant; Text 4.12 from *THE METAMORPHOSIS AND OTHER STORIES* by Franz Kafka, translated by Michael Hofmann, translation copyright © 2007 by Michael Hofmann, used by permission of Penguin Books, an imprint of Penguin Publishing Group, a division of Penguin Random House LLC and Penguin UK, all rights reserved; Text 5.1 text and the FAIRTRADE Mark are © of Fairtrade International and used with permission of The Fairtrade Foundation; Text 5.2 article contributed by FINCA International Inc. © FINCA International, Inc. 2013; Text 5.3 *DEAD AID: WHY AID IS NOT WORKING AND HOW THERE IS A BETTER WAY FOR AFRICA* by Dambisa Moyo, reprinted by permission of Farrar, Straus and Giroux Copyright © 2009 Moyo Dambiso; Text 5.4 from *Untouchable* by Mulk Raj Anand, 1935; Text 5.5 'Is global warming real?' by Robert Lamb, courtesy of Seeker Media Inc.; Text 5.6 Greener living: a quick guide from Directgov.uk website © Crown copyright; Text 5.7 from 'Where warming hits home' by Henry Chu, February 2007 Los Angeles Times © Los Angeles Times, reprinted with permission; Text 5.8 'The Lake' by Roger McGough from *Holiday on Death Row* (© Roger McGough, 1979) is printed by permission of United Agents (www.unitedagents.co.uk) on behalf of Roger McGough; Text 5.9 speech by Malala Yousafzai to the UN Youth Assembly is reprinted by permission of Curtis Brown; Text 5.10 'Tunisia's transition: a success story', 26 December 2014 © Guardian News & Media Ltd 2018; Text 6.4 review of *Room* by Emma Donoghue, 1 August 2010 © Guardian News & Media Ltd 2018; Text 6.6 'Identity is the issue of our age: so why can't we talk more honestly about trans women?' by Hadley Freeman, 18 March 2017 © Guardian News & Media Ltd 2018; Text 6.7 '5 Keys to a Successful Marriage' by Rachel Heller, reproduce with the permission of author © Rachel's Ruminations; Text 6.9 '18-Year-Old Student From Tamil Nadu Designs World's Lightest Satellite Weighing Just 64 Grams' from Times of India, Srinivas Laxman © India Times; Text 6.10 'Jean-Michel Basquiat skull painting sells for record $110.5m at auction' is reprinted by permission of Wright's Media, LLC as agent for Associated Press; Text 6.15 Culture at Work © British Council 2013, https://www.britishcouncil.org/organisation/policy-insight-research/research/culture-workintercultural-skills-workplace. Reprinted with the kind permission of the British Council. The British Council is the UK's international organisation for cultural relations and educational opportunities. Using the cultural resources of the UK, the British Council creates friendly knowledge and understanding between the people of the UK and other countries; Text 6.17 The 2017 Deloitte Millennial Survey © Deloitte; Text 6.18 'Affirmative action – racist by nature' by Stephen McGarvey, Daily Texan Online, March 2012; Unit 8.1 SL Text D 'Underwater wonder' by Angela Tweedie, Holland Herald, KLM's in-flight magazine by permission of MediaPartners Group; Unit 8.1 SL Text E 'How cell phone behaviour affects other people' by Marie Brannon, published on Suite101, used by permission of the author; Unit 8.1 SL Text F 'The challenge of modern parenting' by Seth Mullins from FamilyLobby; Unit 8.1 HL Text D 'We Need To Ensure That More African Girls Get An Education' by AnuOluwapo Adelakun, October 2017 from HuffPost, Copyright © HuffPost South Africa; Unit 8.1 HL Text E 'Dramatic rise in plastic seabed litter around UK' by Patrick Barkham © Guardian News & Media Ltd 2018; Unit 8.1 HL Text D from *A stranger's Eye* by Fergal Keane, adapted,© David Godwin Associates; Text 9.1 from *The Collector* by John Fowles, Vintage Classics, Penguin Random House

Thanks to the following for permission to reproduce images (GI = Getty Images, ASP = Alamy Stock Photo)
Cover SolStock/GI; *Inside* franckreporter/GI; Tim Graham/Corbis/GI; Fred Stein Archive/Archive Photos/GI; Isa Foltin/WireImage/GI; Thomas Imo/Photothek/GI; Splash News/ASP; LeoPatrizi/GI; Karen Kasmauski/Corbis Documentary/GI; Yasuyoshi Chiba/AFP/GI; Bettmann/GI (x2); Olga Maltseva/AFP/GI; Massimo Valicchia/NurPhoto via GI; peshkov/GI; Chip Somodevilla/GI; KristinaJovanovic/GI; chris-mueller/GI; Kevin Mazur/GI for J/P Haitian Relief Organization; FatCamera/GI; Yuri Nunes/EyeEm/GI; Chris Whitehead/GI; Calvin and Hobbes by Bill Watterson, licensed by Andrews McMeel Syndication; Don Farrall/GI; TomasSereda/GI; Anatolii Babii/ASP; Craig Ruttle/Bloomberg /GI; Dovapi/GI; Danita Delimont/GI; Photo 12/ASP; Image Courtesy of The Advertising Archives; PNC/GI; Image Courtesy of The Advertising Archives (x4); Amit Bhargava/Bloomberg/GI; Image Courtesy of The Advertising Archives; Milind Shelte/India Today Group/GI; Image Courtesy of The Advertising Archives; © Jacky Fleming - www.jackyfleming.co.uk; kali9/GI; Image Courtesy of The Advertising Archives; ronstik/GI;